# French Cultural Studies

# French
## Cultural Studies

## An Introduction

Edited by Jill Forbes
and Michael Kelly

OXFORD UNIVERSITY PRESS

*Oxford University Press, Great Clarendon Street, Oxford* OX2 6DP

*Oxford New York*
*Athens Auckland Bangkok Bogota Bombay*
*Buenos Aires Calcutta Cape Town Dar es Salaam*
*Delhi Florence Hong Kong Istanbul Karachi*
*Kuala Lumpur Madras Madrid Melbourne*
*Mexico City Nairobi Paris Singapore*
*Taipei Tokyo Toronto*
*and associated companies in*
*Berlin Ibadan*

*Oxford is a trade mark of Oxford University Press*

*Published in the United States by*
*Oxford University Press Inc., New York*

© *Jill Forbes and Michael Kelly 1995*

*First published 1995*
*Paperback edition reprinted 1996*

*British Library Cataloguing in Publication Data*
*Data available*

*Library of Congress Cataloging in Publication Data*
*French Cultural Studies: an introduction/edited by Jill Forbes and Michael Kelly.*
*Includes bibliographical references and index.*
*1. France—Civilization. 2. France—Cultural policy. 3. Social evolution.*
*4. Politics and culture—France—History—20th century.*
*I. Forbes, Jill. II. Kelly, Michael, 1946-  .*
*DC33.7.F7258 1995*
*944.08—dc20 95-5606*
*ISBN 0-19-871501-3 (Pbk.)*
*ISBN 0-19-871500-5*

10 9 8 7 6 5 4 3 2

*Printed in Great Britain*
*on acid-free paper by*
*Bookcraft Ltd.*
*Midsomer Norton, Avon*

# Preface

THIS is an introduction to French cultural studies. It therefore offers a wide-ranging, but selective, view of French culture from 1870 to the present day, and also seeks to exemplify a range of approaches which draw connections between different aspects of that culture, and between culture and its contexts.

The book is divided into three parts based on the chronological divisions 1870–1944, 1945–67, and 1968–95, paying more detailed attention to the period after the Second World War. Each part is introduced with an outline of the historical and social background, and presupposes little prior knowledge of France or French history. Each chapter contains essays on those aspects of French culture which are of particular interest and significance for the period discussed. At the end of each part are to be found suggestions for further reading which have been selected for ease of access, and with an English-speaking readership in mind. An appendix contains an extensive chronology which juxtaposes social and political events, developments in the world of science and technology as well as those in the arts, leisure, and entertainment. The annotated illustrations, which are distributed through the book, serve to elaborate on questions raised in the section in which they appear, though these are also linked together thematically in various ways. The book concludes with a detailed index of names, works cited, genres, and cultural forms.

The reader may therefore read the book sequentially as an extended analysis of French culture, which explores the themes and issues outlined in the general introduction. Alternatively, the book can be dipped into, or browsed through. With the help of the index and the chronology, it will not be difficult for a reader to focus on a particular period, a particular cultural form, or a particular theme. Throughout, the authors have sought to acquaint the reader with the debates that animate French cultural studies today and to suggest interesting avenues of further exploration.

J. F.
M. K.

*Bristol and Southampton*
*September 1994*

# Acknowledgements

THE writing of this book has been a process of dialogue between the editors and the contributors, which has informed and enriched the work as a whole. Individual contributors were, however, responsible for particular sections of the text, as follows: Margaret Atack, pp. 78–91; Rodney Ball, pp. 263–267; Elizabeth Fallaize, pp. 119–124; Alec Hargreaves, pp. 267–272; Nicholas Hewitt, pp. 61–69; Tony Jones, pp. 152–163; Bill Marshall, pp. 272–276; Gordon Millan, pp. 12–37; Keith Reader, pp. 212–230; Anna Ridehalgh, pp. 135–139 and pp. 276–283; Brian Rigby, pp. 37–53; Michael Scriven, pp. 54–61; Michael Worton, pp. 191–212. All other material, including the illustrations, is the responsibility of the editors, who wish to thank the private individuals and public bodies who kindly gave their permission to use the illustrations, details of which are provided on page x.

The editors wish to thank the British Academy, the Carnegie Trust for the Universities of Scotland, and the Universities of Southampton and Strathclyde for their generous financial support in the preparation of this book. We are also grateful to the many friends and colleagues whose encouragement and erudition have assisted us along the way, and in particular to Bill Brooks, Rosemary Böck, David Edgar, Michael Freeman, and Diana Knight. We have greatly appreciated the care and enthusiasm of Andrew Lockett and Vicki Reeve at O.U.P. We are especially grateful to our respective partners and families for their understanding and support.

# Contents

# List of Illustrations

# Notes on Contributors

**Margaret Atack** is Professor of French at the University of Leeds. She is the author of *Literature and the French Resistance: Cultural Politics and Narrative Forms* (1989), and co-editor of *Contemporary French Fiction by Women: Feminist Perspectives* (1991).

**Rodney Ball** is a Lecturer in French at the University of Southampton. Currently his main research field is the sociology of the French language, with particular reference to recent developments and the conflicting reactions to which they give rise.

**Elizabeth Fallaize** is a Fellow of St John's College, Oxford. Her books on twentieth-century literature include *The Novels of Simone de Beauvoir* (1988) and *French Women's Writing: Recent Fiction* (1994). She is currently working on French literature of the 1980s.

**Jill Forbes** is Ashley Watkins Professor of French at the University of Bristol and author of *INA French for Innovation* (1984), *The Cinema in France After the New Wave* (1992), *Contemporary France: Politics, Economics, Society* with Nick Hewlett and François Nectoux (1994), and the forthcoming study *Les Enfants du paradis*.

**Alec Hargreaves** is Professor of French and Francophone Studies at Loughborough University of Technology and author of *The Colonial Experience in French Fiction* (1981), *Immigration in Postwar France* (1987), *Voices from the North African Community in France: Immigration and Identity in Beur Fiction* (1991), and the forthcoming *Immigration, 'Race' and Ethnicity in Contemporary France*.

**Nicholas Hewitt** is Professor of French at the University of Nottingham. He is the author of *The Golden Age of Louis-Ferdinand Céline* (1987) and *Les Maladies du siècle* (1988), editor of *The Culture of Reconstruction: European Literature, Thought and Film 1945–1950* (1989), and co-editor of *France and the Mass Media* (1991) and *Popular Culture and Mass Communications in Twentieth-Century France* (1992).

**Tony Jones** is Lecturer in French at the University of Southampton. His principal teaching interests are twentieth-century French fiction and theatre, and he has written on Samuel Beckett and Annie Ernaux.

**Michael Kelly** is Professor of French at the University of Southampton. He is the author of *The Ideas and Influence of Emmanuel Mounier* (1979), *Modern French Marxism* (1982), and *Hegel in France* (1992), and co-editor of *French in the 90s* (1992) and *France: Nation and Regions* (1993). He is currently working on French cultural history of the 1930s and 1940s.

**Bill Marshall** is Senior Lecturer in French at the University of Southampton. He is the author of *Victor Serge: The Uses of Dissent* (1993), and of articles on French film and television. He is currently working on a book on narrative and national identity in Quebec cinema.

**Gordon Millan** is Professor of French at the University of Strathclyde, author of *Pierre Louÿs ou le culte de l'amitié* (1979) and of *A Throw of the Dice: The Life of Stéphane Mallarmé* (1994), and editor of Stéphane Mallarmé, *Œuvres complètes* (1983).

**Keith Reader** is Professor of French at the University of Newcastle-upon-Tyne, and author of *Intellectuals and the Left in France since 1968* (1987), *The May 1968 Events in France* (1993), and a forthcoming monograph *Régis Debray*.

**Anna Ridehalgh** lectures in French at the University of Southampton and researches on African literature in French. She is currently working on political themes in Senegalese literature.

**Brian Rigby** is Professor of French at the University of Hull, and managing editor of the journal *French Cultural Studies*. He is the author of *Popular Culture in Modern France* (1991), and has edited *French Literature, Thought and Culture in the Nineteenth Century* (1992) and co-edited *France and the Mass Media* (1991).

**Michael Scriven** is Professor of French Studies at the University of Bath. He is author of *Sartre's Existential Biographies* (1984), *Paul Nizan Communist Novelist* (1988), and *Sartre and the Media* (1993), and co-editor of *European Socialist Realism* (1988) and *War and Society in Twentieth Century France* (1991).

**Michael Worton** is Professor of French at UCL, University of London, author of *Michel Tournier: 'La Goutte d'or'* (1992), translator of René Char, *The Dawnbreakers* (1992), and co-editor of *Intertextuality: Theories and Practices* (1993) and of *Textuality and Sexuality: Reading Theories and Practices* (1993).

# Introduction: French Cultural Identities

THE diversity of French-speaking culture is intrinsically resistant to simple classification and summary. For almost any generalization a dozen exceptions can readily be adduced. And yet there are patterns. Underneath the apparent chaos of voices and images lies a basic question which cultural events and activities are called on to answer, and which acts somewhat like the 'strange attractors' of the new science, giving to the totality a shape and texture which cannot easily be discerned in individual constituents. This basic question is that of identity: who am I? The question also widens to include who was I? who will I be? who are we? who are they? The answers are diverse and often contradictory, sometimes a paradox, sometimes a refusal, sometimes another question. And because of the passion and intelligence with which the quest has been conducted within it, French culture has been taken very seriously, both in the French-speaking world and in a broader international context.

One of culture's primary purposes is to negotiate the insertion of the individual into society, and it does so by exploring a multiplicity of identities, past, present, and potential, which people (whether as producers or consumers) can recognize and relate themselves to. These identities are the carriers of norms and values, embodied in social structures and relationships of power, and represented in high and popular culture, in symbols, stories, myths, rituals, routines, and exemplary figures. The ways in which they are embodied and represented are complex and infinitely varied over time and place. But in French culture over the last century and a quarter, there are three dominant zones of social identity around which cultural exploration has turned, summarized in the Republic's motto, 'Liberté, égalité, fraternité', but also in the Vichy alternative to it, 'Travail, famille, patrie'.

The first is national identity, asking what it is to be French, who is included in the nation, on what criterion of ethnicity, territory, or culture, and what relations are possible within the nation, and with other nations or nationalities. The second is class identity, probing the divisions within and between socio-economic groups, and asking what power, privilege, or disadvantage attaches to groups by virtue of their property or birth, and what might be done to maintain or change their relationship. The third is gender identity, exploring the respective condition of men and women, asking what the basis is in nature, society, or consciousness for the manifest inequality between them in the family and the community, and what relations are possible between them. The three social identities of nation, class, and gender intersect with one another, and with other subordinate identities based on region, language, religion, generation, education, and other divisions. They also intersect with preoccupations of personal identity, exploring the relationship of an individual to his or her body, desires, and memories and to the communities to which he or she belongs.

The foreigner, looking at French culture, is likely to ask first what makes it distinctively French. The same question has been a major preoccupation of that culture, echoing the historical struggles in which France has constructed and maintained its national identity. If a nation is, in Benedict Anderson's expression, an 'imagined community', then it is not surprising that the nation should be present in culture, inscribed in the images and stories in which the community imagines itself most vividly. The noticeable prominence of Frenchness is perhaps one of the distinguishing features of French culture, just as conversely an attachment to culture is a distinctive signal of Frenchness. Paradoxically, national identity is most strongly asserted when it is most sharply challenged, and the internal and external challenges to the French have been substantial in the century and a quarter encompassed by this study.

Underlying modern France is *la guerre franco-française*, the internecine struggle inaugurated by the Revolution of 1789, which overthrew the Catholic monarchy and founded the secular Republic. The Revolution confirmed a fault-line in French society which reappeared in different guises for most of the following two centuries. At several moments in recent history it erupted into virtual civil war: in 1871 with the bloody repression of the Paris Commune; in 1940–4 with the battle for France between *la France combattante* and the collaborationist Vichy regime; in 1958–62 with the attempted army *putsches* from Algeria, and in 1968 with the *événements* of May–June. In each of these crises, the form of the state was in question, and with it, the nature of the French nation. Outside these moments, preparing them or consequent on them, the undeclared civil war has simmered and sputtered, pervading all the images and stories.

Partly but not entirely overlapping the undeclared civil war are the ethnic divisions which make France such a diverse nation. Many versions of the north–south divide continue, sharply focused by the two German occupations of 1870 and 1940, and more recently by French and European regional policies. Important regions have quite different experiences of their place in the nation: the eastern provinces of Alsace and Lorraine were not part of France from the Franco-Prussian War until the end of the Great War, and were again separated during the Occupation years; Brittany and Corsica have at different times produced their own nationalist movements, demanding some degree of autonomy from France. Waves of immigration have left their traces: the earlier part of the period was marked by political refugees from eastern and central Europe, and economic migrants from Mediterranean Europe, while the post-war period saw the growth of immigration from North Africa and from other former colonial territories. In culture perhaps more than any other area, the hegemony of Paris over the rest of the country has generated tensions. Added to these factors is the increasingly acknowledged importance of the international French-speaking community spread through neighbouring countries (especially Belgium and Switzerland), and as far afield as North America, Africa, and Asia. With striking frequency, the expression of Frenchness is inflected by the specific experience of groups who perceive their own place within the nation as distinctly problematic.

Finally, the most emphatic challenge to, and confirmation of, French identity has arisen from its external Others, the palpably non-French nations, partners and enemies, against whom the French assert their distinct existence. Several countries have played important roles in providing France with an external figure on which to project her self-questioning, including Britain, Russia, China, and Japan, but none more than Germany and the United States, who in both cases exercise a major economic influence on contemporary France. For much of the period the primary Other was Germany, France's enemy in three devastating wars, but especially since 1945, the dominant Other has increasingly been the United States, whose economic and cultural presence in Europe has become so pre-eminent. The relationship has been of both repulsion and attraction, in which, at almost every level, France has both vigorously rejected and enthusiastically welcomed the social and cultural models which its German and American partner-enemies have offered.

The second major identity articulated in French culture is that of class. The industrial revolution which gathered momentum throughout the nineteenth century accelerated the division of society between the modernizing industrialists and entrepreneurs on the one hand, and the wage-labourers whom they employed, on the other. It aggravated the growing rift between town and country and the precariousness of the intermediate strata of tradespeople and small farmers. For much of the period, the changes were expressed in two polarized figures: the bourgeois and the worker. Originally applied to town-dwellers of the *bourg*, 'bourgeois' first came to mean the urban middle classes before centring on the wealthy upper strata who controlled industry, commerce, the professions, and the state. From the 1930s, bourgeois became a catch-all moral and political category used by writers of both Left and Right to castigate the decadence and complacency of the ruling classes, and to dismiss the ideas associated with them. Among the intellectual and artistic Left who dominated for thirty years after the Liberation, the bourgeoisie became the archetypal demon, though in these and other circles the bourgeois also exercised the relentless fascination of the rich and powerful.

A similar conflict of attitudes surrounds the figure of the worker. For most of the period, the urban proletariat accounted for a growing proportion of the French population. From the end of the nineteenth century, the trade unions and the communist and socialist parties associated with them became central actors in political life, mainly identified with the struggle, often violent, to defend or improve their living and working conditions. As a result, depiction of workers in culture is typically distributed between three main figures. First, the hero of class struggle is depicted by left-wing writers as the doughty fighter for justice and social progress against the predatory capitalist classes and their agents. Second, the unwashed barbarian is depicted on the Right as a dangerous subversive, probably a paid agent of Moscow, seeking to wreck social order and progress. Third, the long-suffering labourer is depicted from a centrist viewpoint as a downtrodden work-horse, poor but probably honest if rather limited, and a hapless victim of the heartless but inevitable march of progress.

Since the 1950s, the representation of these issues has tended to concentrate less on classes and their individual representatives, and more on the nature and effects of the social structure viewed as a system. The processes of social aliena- tion have been shown through the fragmentation of experience and the internal- ization of conflicts and contradictions within individuals. The effects of modern social development are seen to be distributed throughout the social hierarchy, with the rich perhaps even being the most alienated, prisoners of their possessions and obligations. The dispossessed, in various guises, are often in contrast pre- sented as having kept contact with authentic values and realities which the pace and abstraction of modern life tend to obscure. The moral and political climate of class has also shifted. The polarized representations of the earlier period often carried clear imperatives, ranging from the violent overthrow of the capitalist order to the unmasking and rooting out of disruptive elements. Common to both ends of the spectrum was the acceptance of stern social discipline. More recently, it is social discipline itself which has come under attack, as culture probes strate- gies for personal survival in the social system. Means are explored of evading and disrupting established structures, and salvation is sought in transgression.

The third major identity is that of gender. In some respects, it has always been a key dimension of culture, because personal relations have always been a pre- occupation of images and narratives in any culture. However, the characteristic of French culture has been to probe the nature of these relations with increasing sharpness, and to relate the problems to broader social questions of wealth and power. Undoubtedly the main impetus for this has been the changing place of women in French society, and in the recent period the growing opposition of women to inequalities which they have traditionally endured.

In the late nineteenth century, women's education was accepted and promoted by the state, precipitating the entry of women in growing numbers into employment outside the traditional industries of domestic maintenance. The two world wars accelerated this process, though it was not until 1944 that women were granted the right to vote in parliamentary elections. Women's enhanced economic and political roles as workers and voters were modulated by their role as consumers in the 1950s. Women were identified as the main decision-makers in the purchase not just of domestic appliances but of an increasing range of goods and services on which economic growth depended. Demands for equity in employment and greater individual control over fertility combined to spur the formation of a wide range of independent movements aimed at securing improvements in women's rights and conditions in nearly all sectors of life.

A first effect of the changing position of women was that they were represented culturally in a wider range of roles as time passed. Women's accession to particular roles, especially of power and influence, was frequently hampered either by deliberate male intervention or by entrenched structures which ensured or implied exclusion, and many narratives explore the difficulties and dilemmas to be faced, and possible strategies for overcoming them. A second effect, which emerged particularly in the 1970s, was that women increasingly gained access to the means of cultural production and began to transform not only the representation of women in culture, but also the cultural processes themselves, including the viewpoints and values they convey, the forms of desire they manipulate, and the language in which they are articulated.

The reformulation of women's identity in turn transformed conceptions of relations between women, between women and men, and between men. Along with changing social relations went changing emotional and sexual relations, and changing perceptions of the individual's relationship with his or her own body and reproductive functions. Homosexual relations emerged into the domain of open public representation from the covert or coded forms under which they had previously led a marginal existence. In this as in other gender issues, culture produced discourses and representations capable of successfully embodying the range of identities which gradually became socially available.

Each of the three major identities, nation, class, and gender, is cumulative, recursive, and interactive. They are cumulative in that each identity is built on the patterns and traditions which have preceded it; they are recursive in that each new formulation recasts and reinterprets the earlier ones; and they are interactive in that they intersect with and inflect each other. To take one example, the cumulative national identity builds on the heroes and high moments of French history, but the recursive effect arises as elements of that history are retrospectively selected as an appropriate tradition for present purposes. The national meanings are modulated by class and gender associations. Vichy, for example, defined Frenchness through Jeanne d'Arc, the French Catholic saint who was burnt at the stake by the English, while the Resistance defined it through Valmy, the battle in which the armies of the French Revolution had decisively beaten the royalist aristocrats and

### *Fête de Jeanne d'Arc*

Jeanne was canonized in July 1920, amid a wave of post-war French triumphalism. During the occupation, 1940–4, the Vichy Régime adopted her as a national symbol, emphasizing her energy, piety, and patriotism, which were offered as a model to Vichy youth movements, as this poster suggests. Her peasant background fitted well with the Vichy policy of 'Back to the Land', though her warrior status clashed with its policy of promoting the maternal role of women within the family. Later, Vichy's emphasis shifted to her role in fighting against the English, who were blamed for her death, by burning at the stake, in 1431. The Resistance tried to counter this propaganda, emphasizing that Jeanne had fought for French independence, which Vichy had effectively abandoned, and pointing out that her native province of Lorraine had once more been annexed by the Germans. Since 1945, Jeanne has been the subject of many books, plays, and films, exploring different aspects of the complex range of identities she embodied. Politically, however, she continues to be used as a symbol by the right-wing successors of Vichy, and has recently featured prominently on the banners of Jean-Marie Le Pen's Front national.

the Germans. Jeanne's peasant origins chimed well with Vichy's advocacy of a return to the land, though her sex clashed somewhat with the domestic role it envisaged for women. The citizen armies of Valmy chimed with the Resistance's mobilization of the working class, though their assertive maleness rather narrowed its appeal to women.

In each case, this then sparked popular and learned re-examinations of what the glorious or inglorious precedent was, and what other meanings it might support. Subsequent discussion of either event has necessarily been overlaid by its mythical wartime invocation. Similar processes affect the class and gender identities, when stories of class struggles and social relationships, or episodes and images from the battle of the sexes, are invoked to challenge or support positions on current social issues. In the present day, any historical comparison drawn by public figures in France will rapidly be followed by features examining these issues in newspapers and magazines, radio and television broadcasts, books and exhibitions. Many publications specialize in this, reweaving the identities of the past into role-models and object lessons for the present.

The reciprocal interaction of the past and the present, and of nation, class, and gender with each other, gives cultural identities a slippery dialectical character in which change rather than stability is their dominant mode. In some respects this may appear unsettling and confusing, as even France's past refuses to remain constant. But in other respects it is heartening and invigorating, since French culture thereby becomes an almost inexhaustible inheritance to be drawn on in the present. If, as Lévi-Strauss suggested, a society's culture is the language in which it speaks to itself, then French society obviously speaks to itself in many voices. The richness and multiplicity of its cultural discourses are a guarantee that it will continue to find powerful and vivid ways of articulating new identities. And for this reason French culture is a precious resource not only for France, but also for others who are willing to listen.

# Part
# I

# Industrialization
# and War
# 1870–1944

# Industrialization and its Discontents (1870–1914)

THE years between the foundation of the Third Republic in 1870 and the outbreak of the First World War in 1914 were years when France was clearly transformed into a modern industrialized society. It was a period of rural exodus and the growth of cities, of the establishment of a powerful industrial working class with its own social, professional, and cultural organizations, of the introduction of compulsory military service which took country boys away from their farms and gave them their first taste of travel to more or less exotic places, of the introduction of universal elementary education which gradually eliminated the use of *patois* and local dialects and ensured that the great majority of French people became literate, of the expansion of secondary and higher education and of women's education, of a communications revolution powered by the expansion of the rail, canal, and road system, followed by the telephone, the automobile, and the aeroplane. It was also a period which saw legislation preventing child labour, limiting women's work, and ensuring a day of rest for all employees, of a transformation in domestic life through the gradual extension, at least in towns, of facilities such as running water, gas, and electricity, utilities which also transformed the cities from dangerous criminal haunts to illuminated pleasure domes.

The expansion of public transport in the cities and their surroundings, and the exploitation of new technologies, powered the burgeoning leisure and tourist industries which were a new and characteristic feature of this period. Three stand out as being of particular significance: the launch of mass circulation newspapers, several of which had a readership touching a million on the eve of the First World War; the invention of the gramophone, which put an end to popular extempore musical entertainment and substituted the dissemination of maestro performances to a large public; and the invention of the cinema, which rapidly took over from the theatre as popular entertainment, at least among the working and lower middle classes. These developments were by no means unique to France. Indeed, although France was a world leader in some technologies such as the cinematograph, in others like the petrol engine or the gramophone it ceded that place to America or Germany. But what is unique to France is that such deep and lasting social and cultural changes took place against a backdrop of immense political uncertainty, right up to the turn of the century.

The Third Republic was born in blood with the Prussian invasion and occupation of 1870, the capitulation of the French army, the loss of Alsace and parts of Lorraine, and the short-lived and bloody experiment in socialism of the Paris Commune in the spring of 1871. Thereafter the regime moved from political crisis to political crisis as the republican party, itself by no means homogeneous, put in place the framework which eventually ensured that a secular Republic would endure, and its assorted opponents—monarchists, Orléanists, and Bonapartists on the Right, syndicalists and anarchists on the Left—would all, finally, come together in a 'union sacrée' to fight Germany again in 1914. Yet during this truly remarkable half-century important and lasting developments took place in the fields of painting, sculpture, literature, music, and architecture as a whole host of conventions, beliefs, and traditions were questioned, found wanting, swept away, and replaced by a completely new set of values, techniques, and approaches which can now be recognized as the first tentative manifestations of modern art. And it is this extraordinary coexistence of political and cultural experiment and the different ways in which, over time, these transformations have been analysed and interpreted which are explored in the pages which follow.

## From Symbolism to Modernism

Faced with a bewildering array of what, at times, must have appeared to be totally contradictory tendencies, contemporary observers and critics quite understandably sought to impose order upon this chaos by applying what they took to be easily recognizable and meaningful labels. For the most part, these labels went unchallenged and were willingly adopted by a grateful public, and in some cases by artists and writers themselves, who saw in them a successful form of publicity. This quasi-scientific approach, so clearly in tune with the spirit of an age which sought to rationalize and categorize any and every aspect of human activity (the newspaper *enquête* or popular survey reached epidemic proportions at this time), gave rise to a seemingly endless list of 'schools', 'movements', groups, and 'isms'.

Despite the obvious attraction of handy labels such as Impressionism, Post-Impressionism, Symbolism, and Modernism many of these terms are in fact highly problematical. Some of them were applied retrospectively, when the movement they purported to describe had already lost its momentum. Others, including Impressionism itself, were in reality the outcome of pure chance, the witty creations of journalists forever in search of an eye-catching headline or telling phrase. Others again, such as Symbolism, which was officially launched upon the world by the long since forgotten poet Jean Moréas, were primarily the inventions of opportunists and self-seekers whose obvious aim was to advance their own cause. Finally, many of these expressions, initially intended for and restricted to one particular discipline or medium, were then indiscriminately, and in some cases quite inappropriately, applied to others.

The main objection to categorization of this sort, however, lies in its tendency to distort by over-simplification. It imposes upon loose groups of individuals (whose significance resides precisely in their individuality) a uniformity which, upon closer examination, frequently proves to be more apparent than real. This was certainly true in the case of the so-called Impressionist group of painters, whose backgrounds, interests, political views, and indeed painting practices, as recent studies have shown, actually varied quite considerably. Again, such simplification has always proved inadequate in the case of the great writer and artist, whose life and work by their very complexity, inner contradictions, and inconsistencies can never be contained within such narrow confines. Finally, and most importantly of all, every creative artist's view of the world is inevitably coloured and in part determined by his or her own personality, by his or her particular experience, background, and circumstances. This important point is well made by Stéphane Mallarmé (1842–98), himself one of the key figures of the period, who, when asked by a journalist how it felt to be the acknowledged leader of the Symbolist school of poets, replied: 'J'abomine les écoles et tout ce qui y ressemble: je répugne tout ce qui est professoral appliqué à la littérature qui, elle, au contraire, est tout à fait individuelle' (I absolutely detest literary schools and anything which resembles them. Such academic distinctions seem totally repugnant to me when applied to literature, which, on the contrary, is entirely a matter of individual originality) (reply to Huret's *Enquête sur l'évolution littéraire*, 1891).

More seriously still, facile classifications which delight in setting groups, schools, theories, or even individuals against each other frequently exaggerate polarities and divisions which, with the benefit of hindsight, often turn out to be much less clearly defined. Such an adversarial and dialectical view of culture was of course much favoured by contemporary journalists who, faced with the challenge of producing preferably amusing copy for a largely conservative readership, often simplified, distorted, and exaggerated the situation, depicting the slightest break with tradition or deviance from the norm as an act of anarchy and revolution in order to pander to the anxieties of the reader and thus improve newspaper circulations. As a consequence, by the last quarter of the nineteenth century in France, in the eyes of the predominantly conservative middle classes, innovation in the arts and left-wing subversive politics had, rightly or wrongly, become inexorably linked. This view greatly reinforced the growing and persistent belief that the gulf between the artist and the general public had somehow immeasurably widened during this period. The idea itself of course was not new. It had been steadily gaining ground since the end of the previous century when it had made its appearance as one of the major themes of Jean-Jacques Rousseau's influential and appropriately entitled collection of essays *Les Rêveries d'un promeneur solitaire*. It had received additional impetus thanks to Henri Murger's *Scènes de la vie de Bohème* (1847–9), which glorified and romanticized the image of the artist as a rebel pursing his dreams against the wishes of his family and society. Furthermore, the notion of the solitary outcast, marginalized and rejected by a philistine public, was promoted not only by cynical journalists but by several important artists themselves who clearly felt ill at ease in the predominantly materialistic and capitalist societies of the Second Empire and the Third Republic. In the interview with Jules Huret referred to above, Stéphane Mallarmé goes on to complete his remarks on the fundamental individuality of the writer with the following equally sweeping statement: 'Pour moi, le cas d'un poète, en cette société qui ne lui permet pas de vivre, c'est le cas d'un homme qui s'isole pour sculpter son propre tombeau' (As far as I am concerned, the situation of a poet in a society like this, which does not allow him to exist, is that of a man who withdraws from others so as to spend his time chiselling his own tombstone).

The reality of the situation, as will become apparent from what follows, was much more complex. Whether they chose to acknowledge it or not, indeed whether they were themselves aware of it or not, all of those who were responsible for the new ideas and techniques which were to transform every branch of the creative arts were themselves products of the age in which they lived. It is for this reason, therefore, that before any attempt can be made to assess the nature of the profound changes which overtook the worlds of painting, literature, and music during this period it is essential to start with an overview of the period itself and to examine the special combination of factors which ensured that such a radical and profound revolution should take place at this precise moment in the development of French culture.

Here three key points need to be borne in mind. First, the setting for most of these exciting new developments was Paris. Secondly, despite this important fact, these revolutions were by no means exclusively French in origin and in practice were often the result of fruitful contact not only with France's European neighbours but also with cultures from much further afield. Finally, and perhaps most significantly of all, directly or indirectly, these momentous changes can all be traced to the impact which the industrial revolution and consequently scientific and technological progress were having on everyday life.

## Paris, the Capital of Art

For historical and geographical reasons Paris was an ideal setting for such dramatic change. It was the undisputed art capital of the world and enjoyed a deserved reputation as a thriving cultural centre unrivalled by any other city on the continent of Europe. Its relatively central location made it easily accessible, and the recent and profound transformation which it had undergone at the hands of Baron Haussmann and his architects had made it physically more attractive than ever. One of Haussmann's objectives had been to make the city a technological and leisure metropolis to be displayed to the world at the *Exposition universelle* of 1867. In this he had more than succeeded. With its new sewage system, electric lighting in some of its central streets, its recently created public parks, race-courses, spacious squares, wide boulevards, department stores, cabarets, circuses, theatres, and of course, its cafés with their wide *terrasses*, Paris presented a permanent open-air spectacle to the visitors who flocked there in their hundreds of thousands from all four corners of the world.

The permanent population of the capital had increased dramatically too. From just over half a million in 1801 it had risen to just over a million in 1836. This had doubled to over two million by 1877. Many of these newcomers had come in search of employment. Others, however, were artistic and creative people, ambitious provincials and foreigners drawn to Paris not only by the prospect of work but by the incomparable resources which the city offered with its museums, its art galleries, its libraries, its concert halls, its prestigious educational establishments, its publishing houses, its newspapers, its magazines and reviews. Above all the city offered those who lived there an unprecedented number of opportunities for relaxing, meeting people, and exchanging ideas. Some of these meeting places were the numerous restaurants, theatres, and, above all, cafés which had proliferated since the middle of the century. It is estimated that by the turn of the century there were a staggering 24,000 cafés in the greater Paris area alone. Many of these cafés, such as the Café Guerbois or the Nouvelle Athènes (which quite legitimately could claim to be the birthplace of Impressionist painting), were conveniently situated near painters' studios or the showrooms of art-dealers. Others flourished close by the offices of review and newspaper editors. Some of the most important meeting grounds, however, were much less public. People gathered regularly in the houses of rich patrons or met in one another's homes. Talented newcomers were thus easily and continuously absorbed into a rapidly expanding community made up of a loose network of interlocking groups which tended to gravitate around key individuals. At different times during this period Édouard Manet, Émile Zola, and Stéphane Mallarmé all came to assume such a role. During the 1880s and 1890s, for example, the regular Tuesday evening gatherings in Mallarmé's modest fourth-floor flat in the Batignolles area—'ma petite maison de Socrate' (my little Socratic house), he liked to call it—became the very centre of French cultural life.

Such a positive and dynamic atmosphere, in which painters, composers, writers, and critics met, discussed, and argued over each other's work, contributed greatly to one of the characteristic features of this period—the gradual erosion and blurring of the boundaries which had traditionally existed between the different art forms. More importantly still, it acted as a catalyst, stimulating debate, curiosity, and above all the desire to innovate and experiment, which would prove such a distinctive feature of the intellectual climate of the time.

Another important factor which greatly encouraged a general willingness to consider new ideas and to question old ones was increased contact with other civilizations and cultures. In some cases this contact did not even require the inconvenience of a tiresome journey. Until the 1840s, in Europe as a whole, museums and art galleries had been relatively few in number. After that date they became a feature of modern life as most European capitals began to expand their cultural institutions. In Paris, thanks to the influence and acquisitions of Napoleon and later of Louis-Philippe, the Louvre expanded its collections, particularly those of the Spanish masters such as Velázquez and Goya, which made a much greater impression upon Édouard Manet, for example, than the ten days or so he actually spent in Spain. At the beginning of the twentieth century the rich collections of the Trocadéro with its 'primitif' African masks were to have an equally important impact upon the work of Pablo Picasso.

Another circumstance which greatly contributed to the growing awareness of the cultures of other peoples was the peculiarly nineteenth-century phenomenon of the great international exhibition or world fair designed to provide a means of keeping up with major scientific and technological developments of the day. The first of these, a celebration of the commercial might of British industry, had been held in Hyde Park in London in 1851. Determined not to be outdone, Napoleon III secured Paris as the venue for the following exhibition in 1855. Similar events were repeated in the French capital in 1867, 1878, 1889, and 1900. These spectacular extravaganzas, which ensured that for the second half of the nineteenth century Paris remained the cultural capital of the world, not only attracted visitors in their droves (the *Exposition universelle* of 1867 attracted about eleven million, that of 1878 about ten million), they also allowed the French to show off the treasures of their rapidly expanding colonial empire and provided a unique opportunity to learn of new and exciting art practices from the other side of the world. It was at the *Exposition universelle* of 1889, for example, that the composer Claude Debussy first encountered the Javanese music and dancing which were to have a profound influence on his own work.

Even without these extraordinary international fairs, Paris had always been a remarkably cosmopolitan city and its artistic community had always been aware of what was taking place in other parts of the continent. The two European countries which, from a cultural viewpoint, fascinated the French and had the greatest impact on their culture during this period were undoubtedly England and Germany (or Prussia as it was known until 1870). For centuries there had been regular two-way traffic between Paris and London, but this accelerated during the late nineteenth century. It was in London, to which they had fled to avoid the troubles of the Franco-Prussian War and the Commune, that the painter Pissarro first introduced his compatriot Monet to young art-dealer, Paul Durand-Ruel, who, likewise seeking safety in the English capital, had rented premises in New Bond Street and who, a few years later, was to become in Paris the main dealer for the Impressionists. It was, furthermore, during that same stay in London that, during a visit to the National Gallery, Monet, Pissarro, and Sisley discovered the works of Turner and Constable which made such an impression on them all. Likewise, a few years later Paul Verlaine and Arthur Rimbaud sought refuge in London during a difficult period in their relationship, and many of the spectacular and surreal modern townscapes to be found in Rimbaud's collection of experimental prose poems, *Illuminations* (1886), owe much to the powerful impact which the changing face of industrial London had upon his imagination. Stéphane Mallarmé was quite familiar with the literary circles of the English capital and it was in a London magazine, the *Art Monthly*, that he published one of the first and most important comprehensive accounts of French painting, 'The Impressionists and Mr Manet'. The English art scene itself exerted a strong influence upon the French. The Pre-Raphaelite group of painters scored a notable success at the *Exposition universelle* of 1855 and the English Arts and Craft movement pioneered by William Morris and his friends was likewise to play an important part in the development of art nouveau.

Although equally important for the development of French culture, the relationship between France and Germany was much more ambivalent. France had always been suspicious of the military intentions of its closest neighbour and its fears were more than justified by the Prussian invasion of 1870. The invasion itself and the subsequent annexation of Alsace and part of Lorraine by the rapidly expanding German Empire did little to appease French anxieties. Although married to a German woman and himself interested in German literature, Stéphane Mallarmé, for example, categorically refused to set foot on German soil. But even more than the military might of Germany, it was the musical and theatrical ambitions of the composer Richard Wagner which cast their huge shadow over the artistic aspirations of the French during the latter half of the nineteenth century.

Wagner had come to Paris in 1860 to conduct *Tannhäuser*. The opera was a dismal failure, however, and had to be taken off after only three performances, mainly as a political protest against Napoleon III's pro-Austrian policies and the fact that the patron of the event had been none other than the wife of the Austrian ambassador to the French capital. Widespread hostility to Germany and to Wagner persisted in France for the next few years. So much so in fact that when, in 1869, the enthusiastic young Catulle Mendès, his wife Judith Gautier, and their friend Villiers de l'Isle-Adam travelled to Munich to attend the first performance of *Das Rheingold*, the only way they could subsidize their trip was to agree to report on the latest paintings at the Munich festival as no Parisian newspaper was at that time willing to commission an article on Wagner himself.

Despite these initial set-backs, Wagner's theories of the *Gesamtkunstwerk* or total art work incorporating music, dance, and poetry (for which he himself painstakingly designed the Bayreuth festival theatre, eventually opened in 1876) gradually became known to a small circle of French admirers, first through the articles of Mendès and Villiers de l'Isle-Adam, and later through the writings of the music critic Edmond Schuré, whom Mendès and Villiers had met at Munich in 1869. Schuré's major study, *Le Drame musical*, first published in 1875 (and reprinted many times), heralded Wagner's achievement as the culmination of dramatic art as it had evolved from its first stirrings in Greek times. After Wagner's death in 1883, despite the relative failure of the Bayreuth *Festspiel*, his work began to exert a powerful influence on European culture. In France his theories became much better known through *La Revue wagnérienne*, launched in 1885 by a recent graduate of the Conservatoire, Édouard Dujardin. By the time this review ceased publication some three years later, extracts from Wagner's operas had become a regular feature of the Parisian concert scene, and for the next few years Wagnerian fever was at its height. By this time, dissatisfied with mere extracts, many French people (including the composer Claude Debussy) were now prepared to make the journey to Bayreuth to witness in person full performances of Wagner's tetralogy.

## *Le Japonisme* or the Challenge to Europe

Other external influences on French life and culture during this period came not from Europe, but from much further afield. During the nineteenth century, France's Eurocentric culture was exposed to several new civilizations. On his Egyptian campaign of 1798 Napoleon had been accompanied by scholars and artists who faithfully recorded and documented a culture which, previously regarded as barbaric and second rate, turned out to be a revelation. Similar discoveries followed with regard to so-called primitive and tribal art, as in the latter part of the nineteenth century France, along with its neighbours England and Germany, greatly expanded its colonial conquests in Africa and the South Seas. But without a doubt, the country which had by far the greatest impact upon Europe, and particularly upon France, was Japan.

Until the middle of the nineteenth century Japan had remained virtually cut off from the Western world. When Captain Perry's gunships opened up a trade route in 1854, art objects poured into the West. Japanese prints were first displayed officially in Europe at the London International Exhibition of 1862 and such was the favourable response that a mission from the Japanese government immediately set about planning for the 1867 Paris sequel. By the time that exhibition opened Japanese fever had taken over Paris. The art critic Philippe Burty (1830–90) had by then an extensive library of Japanese albums and prints and with some

### Édouard Manet *Émile Zola, écrivain* (1868)

Manet's portrait of Zola at the age of 28 shows the writer after the publication of his first novel *Thérèse Raquin*. Zola was making a living as a journalist and art critic, roundly supporting Manet and the new painting in a series of essays and pamphlets, one of which is shown here propped up on his desk. In testimony to the orientalist vogue stimulated by the *Exposition universelle* of 1867, the writer is framed by a Japanese screen, while the walls of his study are hung with fashionable images of the period: a Japanese samurai print, a reproduction of Manet's painting *Olympia*, itself a celebration of exoticism in the contrast of white courtesan and black servant, and, in deference to the influence of Spanish painting on Manet, a reproduction of Goya's engraving of Velázquez's *Los Borrachos*. Zola's later career as a successful novelist and radical journalist, and his unsympathetic portrait of the artist Claude Lantier, protagonist of *L'Œuvre* (1886), have tended to obscure his early career as an influential art critic.

friends had founded the exclusive Société du Jing-Lar, whose ten members met dressed in kimonos and drank tea from a specially commissioned tea-set which copied designs from Hokusai's *Manga*. Shops specializing in oriental items, such as La Porte chinoise and L'Empire chinois, had been opened by several art-dealers who had already visited Japan. Another art critic, Théodore Duret (1838–1927), himself visited Japan in 1871, returning with large numbers of Hokusai and Ando Hiroshige prints, and in 1875 his example was followed by the art-dealer Samuel Bing, whose shop henceforth became a mecca for oriental curiosities. By the 1880s fans, bronzes, illustrated books, prints, and all kinds of Japanese artefacts were avidly sought after, and not only by collectors. Such, by then, was the fashion for *le japonisme*, as Burty christened it, that albums and fans were readily available to the mass market through Parisian department stores like Le Bon Marché in the rue de Babylone.

Although it is difficult to assess accurately the effect of all of this, the clarity and simplicity of Japanese prints, their unusual compositional devices, their lack of perspective, and above all their striking use of colour certainly provided much food for thought for a whole generation of French painters and encouraged new ways of looking at and responding to nature and to the everyday world. In one of the earliest studies of the new painting, Théodore Duret had no doubt that the impact had been enormous:

If you stroll along the banks of the Seine, at Asnières for example, your eye can find itself absorbing at a single glance the red roof and shimmering white wall of a chalet, the gentle green of a poplar tree, the yellow of the road and the blue of the river. At noon in the summertime every colour will appear harsh and intense, with no possibility of fine gradation or absorption into some vague half-tone. Though it may seem strange, it is still the case that it took the arrival here of Japanese albums for someone to dare to sit down at the edge of a river and place side by side, on the same canvas, a roof which was decidedly red, a wall which was white, a poplar green, a road yellow, and some blue water. Before we discovered Japan, such a thing was impossible, the painter always lied. (*Les Peintres impressionnistes*, 1878)

## Science, Technology, and the Growth of the Mass Market

The radical reappraisal which took place in all the arts during this period can be seen both as a consequence of and as a reaction to the scientific and industrial revolutions which completely transformed nineteenth-century France. At the beginning of this period, largely thanks to the sustained efforts of writers like Hippolyte Taine and Ernest Renan, whose influence only began to wane with their deaths in 1892 and 1893 respectively, the positivist and deterministic ideas expressed by Auguste Comte in the first half of the century were still immensely popular. Comte believed firmly in the notion of progress and in the ability of the human mind to arrive by observation and analysis at general laws which would explain all known and knowable phenomena without recourse to mystical or metaphysical speculation. Whilst the search for such all-embracing systems was on, science and scientific method continued to enjoy enormous prestige. Furthermore, on a practical level, scientific discoveries had already resulted in processes which had not only transformed daily life but fundamentally altered the way in which people perceived the world in which they lived. This was particularly so in the case of the artist and his or her view of external reality, which was transformed by the development of the railway engine and the invention of the camera. Until the 1830s nobody regularly travelled at more than about 15 miles an hour. The expansion of the railways altered all that. The ability to travel at 50 or 60 miles per hour reinforced the transitory and subjective nature of experience. Notions of time and space were radically transformed as communications improved and places which had hitherto been inaccessible were suddenly found to be within reach. The vogue for direct open-air painting was in fact a direct consequence of a hugely extended railway system which made the countryside immediately surrounding Paris and beyond extremely accessible, and of the invention in about 1840 of collapsible tin tubes in which paint could be easily transported. The invention of the camera, the 'pencil of nature', liberated the artist from the tedious and restricting duty of recording and documenting people and events but also, as Manet, Monet, and Degas among others quickly discovered, it proved to be an extremely useful tool, allowing them to study in detail and at length subtle details of light, surfaces, and movement which they had been unable to see and hence to record before.

The application of the steam engine to other processes had equally dramatic consequences. Its use in printing combined with the invention of the rotary press to provide cheaper books and newspapers and, thanks to an improved education system, led to a mass reading market. Daily papers such as *Le Petit Parisien* achieved huge circulations and specialist magazines of every type and description began to proliferate. In the mid-1880s a literary magazine like *La Vogue*, whose contributors included so-called 'difficult' writers such as Verlaine, Mallarmé, Villiers de l'Isle-Adam, and Laforgue, reached a staggering circulation of 15,000 copies. By the last two decades of the century graphic art flourished, thanks mainly to new developments in cheaper reproduction techniques. In a short working life of about fifteen years Toulouse-Lautrec (1864–1901) produced an amazing 368 prints. Print-sellers published regular catalogues of prints and posters, for which there was by now a large market. The public displays of posters by Lautrec and Jules Chéret (1836–1932), and the proliferation of book illustrations often by experimental artists, gradually led to a breaking down of the old barriers between high and popular art and dissipated much of the hostility to innovation which had characterized the first half of the century.

Social change, itself a direct result of rapid industrialization and urbanization, resulted in increased leisure for the middle and lower middle classes. Whereas 150,000 people attended the Salon or official art exhibition in the 1840s, this figure had risen to 560,000 by the 1880s, and almost one million people visited the Fine Art section of the 1855 *Exposition universelle*. Likewise, a new type of art patron was created, as those who made quick fortunes sought to invest in art. This in turn encouraged the need for art critics and dealers, as most of the people who had money to spend knew little about painting and required guidance and advice.

Clearly, not all of these forces had an impact on all artists, nor, when and if they did respond to such pressures, did artists do so in any standard or uniform way. A remarkable number of these important cross-currents, however, are brought together in the life and work of Stéphane Mallarmé, who on these grounds alone can be seen as representative of the period as a whole.

## Mallarmé: the Total Artist

Although actually born in Paris, Mallarmé left the city when he was still a young child and did not return to it until he was almost 30 years old. Before that, at the age of 19 he had run away to London, where he spent almost a year with a German woman several years his elder who would subsequently become his wife. Through this combination of circumstances he made early contact with the two major cultures, those of England and Germany, which would have an important influence on his own development as a writer. Mallarmé returned to London regularly during the rest of his life, first as a free-lance journalist reporting on its Great Exhibitions, later simply to maintain contact with his growing number of English friends. When in 1875 he co-founded an avant-garde Parisian review, provocatively called *La République des lettres*, it was Mallarmé himself who ensured the collaboration of several English writers, including Algernon Swinburne, who sent a poem for the very first number. For the next twenty years or so Mallarmé did all he could to promote cultural understanding between Paris and London, sending to the *Athenaeum* regular reports on the artistic community of the French capital, and writing for the London-based *Art Monthly* one of the first serious attempts to analyse the painting of Manet and his friends. In 1894, only a few years before his untimely death at the age of 56, he travelled to Oxford and Cambridge to deliver an important lecture, 'La Musique et les lettres', which had as its subject an account of the most recent developments in French literature.

It was not his friends from across the Channel in England, however, but rather someone closer at hand, on the continent of Europe itself, who exerted a strange fascination on Mallarmé. Through his German wife Marie, then later through his friendships with Catulle Mendès, Judith Gautier, and Villiers de l'Isle-Adam, he became aware, with growing disquiet, of the work of Richard Wagner, whose dream of a single polyvalent art form was remarkably close to his own preoccupations.

From the time when he settled definitively in Paris in the summer of 1871 until his death in 1898, Mallarmé's life provides the perfect illustration of just how easy it was for a talented person from the provinces to integrate himself within the artistic community of the capital. Through Catulle Mendès and the latter's publisher Alphonse Lemerre, he met Philippe Burty, who introduced him to his painter friends. Mallarmé thus met Manet, whom he defended vigorously in the French and London press. Through Manet he was introduced to Monet, Renoir, Degas, and Berthe Morisot, all of whom became close friends. From this nucleus of poets and painters, he gradually began to amass a steadily growing number of friends drawn from every sector of artistic activity in the capital. During the last two decades of the century, thanks to his own growing reputation, his modest little flat in the unfashionable Batignolles area of the city and its famous Tuesday evening gatherings, *les mardis* as they were known, became a focus for the leading intellectual and artistic figures of the day.

Through his acquaintanceship with men like Burty and Manet, Mallarmé likewise became fascinated with Japanese art, decorating the study of his summer home in Valvins in the Japanese style and producing, in collaboration with Manet, a luxurious edition of *L'Après-midi d'un faune* for which the foliage motif of some of the illustrations was copied from plants and flowers depicted in Hokusai's *Manga*. When, some ten years later, Mallarmé entertained the idea of having his works illustrated by his painter acquaintances, he thought of giving the collection as a whole the title of *Le Tiroir de laque*, thus reflecting the craze for things Japanese which was so typical of the time.

Mallarmé's delight in Japanese artefacts reflects that part of him which reacted violently to the vulgarity and blatant commercialism of the period. His earliest poems are passionate and highly idealistic. In them he rejects contemptuously his own bourgeois background and the values for which it stood. Its materialism and greed are mercilessly lambasted in the closing stanzas of the poem 'Les Fenêtres' in which an onlooker casts a disgusted eye over the world which can be seen from his window:

> Mais, hélas! Ici-bas est maître: sa hantise
> Vient m'écœurer parfois jusqu'en cet abri sûr,
> Et le vomissement impur de la Bêtise
> Me force à me boucher le nez devant l'azur.

(But, alas! Life is the Master: its haunting obsession | Pursues me and sickens me even in this safe place, | And the foul vomit of crass Stupidity | Forces me to block my nose before the clear blue sky.)

Disgust at the vile commercialism and materialism of his own contemporaries, the exquisitely produced but extremely expensive limited editions of *L'Après-midi d'un faune*, *Le Corbeau* (translated from Edgar Allan Poe's *The Raven*), and the *Poésies*, along with such admittedly demanding poems as his later sonnets which frequently take as their subject the act of writing itself, all these things inevitably contributed to Mallarmé being viewed in his own lifetime, as indeed he is still frequently regarded today, as an élitist and deliberately obscure writer. Indeed,

Mallarmé himself, in some of his later pronouncements, seems to reinforce the myth of the man of genius reviled by the masses, thus apparently perpetuating the divide which is commonly held to exist between 'high' and 'popular' art during this period.

However, such a view, which faithfully reflects some aspects of Mallarmé's poetic output and one side of his personality, is, as recent studies have shown, an inaccurate representation of his work as a whole. In actual fact, during the crucial years which Mallarmé spent in the provinces he made some important discoveries which led him in a diametrically opposed direction. Far from the hustle and bustle of Parisian life with its limitless distractions, he had undergone an extraordinary personal experience. While working on the ambitious projects of *Hérodiade* and *L'Après-midi d'un faune* (which were originally intended for the theatre), Mallarmé made an important discovery concerning the nature of language itself. In his efforts to condense as many layers of meaning as possible into a single line of verse, whilst at the same time attempting to establish as close a link as possible between the sound pattern of his line and the meaning which it conveyed, he had painstakingly subjected every word, syllable, and phrase to the most intense scrutiny. By delving so deeply into the mystery of poetic creation, he came to the inescapable and extremely upsetting conclusion that, in the French language at least, the kind of harmony or correlation which he sought simply did not exist. In other words, he became aware of the fundamental truth which nearly fifty years later the Swiss linguist Ferdinand Saussure would place at the heart of his revolutionary theory of linguistics, namely that language is a code or convention and the relationship between meaning and expression, between *le signifiant* and *le signifié*, is fundamentally arbitrary.

This was a devastating discovery for someone who, as a writer, had placed all his trust in the power of words. Unfortunately at about this same time Mallarmé's own health was extremely poor. Convinced of his own imminent death and alarmed by the deaths of other people whom he held most dear or whom he respected, he began to attribute to existence itself the void which he had discovered at the centre of language. Through this combination of circumstances, long before Albert Camus or Jean-Paul Sartre, Mallarmé became acutely aware of the fundamentally absurd and totally irrational nature of existence, of the extremely fine line separating absence and presence, being and nothingness, life and death. In the light of this discovery, he became aware of how extremely narrow in scope and how exclusively centred upon himself his poetry had so far been. He now saw that the real function of Art and the artist lay in their ability to express universal truths. The role of the poet, as he now defined it, was not to indulge in a subjective account of his own experience but to adopt an objective, impersonal stance, speaking not for himself but rather on behalf of his fellow men. The only legitimate challenge, he now realized, was to find a means of expressing in all its complexity the basic unresolved and unresolvable paradox of the human condition perpetually hovering between absence and presence, what he later referred to as 'la qualité tout d'insaisissable finesse de la vie' (the haunting yet quite untranslatable quality of life itself). Adopting a fundamentally atheistic perspective, he would remain a lyric poet celebrating not himself or the glory of God, but rather the glory of the potential of the human spirit. Furthermore, in order to do justice to this desperate but courageously honest subject, he decided to study the various ways in which, throughout history, mankind had responded to the realization of the totally absurd nature of existence. This ambitious goal, which led Mallarmé to spend years investigating the relationship between language, myth, and ritual, proved an extremely demanding undertaking, with moments of spectacular insight frequently undermined by recurring doubts and anxieties. There were times when, over the next few years, his dogged pursuit of his 'Rêve', as he liked to call it, brought him to the very edge of despair.

Despite such moments of doubt, Mallarmé had by now convinced himself that such an undertaking was not only possible but necessary. The dream of the Great Work or 'Le Livre', as he frequently referred to it, had been born. What was envisaged was something modern which could stand comparison with the masterpieces of the Classical Age and the Renaissance. Western civilization, Mallarmé felt, had produced two major artistic achievements. The first of these, the *Venus de Milo*, was the product of classical or pre-Christian times and expressed an essentially pagan innocence. The second, the *Mona Lisa*, was the product of the Christian era and expressed the loss of innocence. What was required now, he decided, was to produce something which expressed the values of a modern, scientific, and fundamentally post-Christian culture:

Yesterday I finished my first outline of the Work, clearly delineated and totally endurable, if I myself endure. I contemplated it quite calmly and without horror and, closing my eyes, *I saw that it existed*. The *Venus de Milo*—which I like to attribute to Phidias, so generic has the name of that great artist become to me, and the *Mona Lisa*, seem to me to be and *are* the two great shimmerings of Beauty on this earth—and my Work, such as it is imagined, is the third. Absolute and unconscious Beauty, which is unique and inalterable in Phidias's *Venus*; Beauty whose heart, with the arrival of Christianity, received the venomous bite of the Monster, painfully resurrected with a strangely mysterious smile, but a smile of forced mystery which she *senses* to be the condition of her being. Finally, Beauty which, through the knowledge of Man, has rediscovered in the Universe the relative stages of its development . . . remembering the secret horror which forced her to smile—in Leonardo's time, and to smile in a mysterious manner—smiling mysteriously now, but happily and with the eternal inner serenity of the *Venus de Milo* which has been recovered, having understood the mystery of which the *Mona Lisa* could only know the fatal sensation. (Letter to Eugène Lefébure, 1867)

Such an undertaking was hugely ambitious. Within a few years of this breathtaking statement, Mallarmé was temporarily forced to lower his sights. He decided to concentrate not on the Great Work itself but on the preliminary studies which he soon realized were essential if he was eventually to find a way of giving full expression to his complex and paradoxical vision of the world. 'We have all been so far behind as far as Systems of Thought are concerned that I have spent no less that ten years elaborating my own,' he confided somewhat cryptically to Paul Verlaine several years later.

In fact, each of the projects upon which Mallarmé embarked in the remaining years of his life was intended to make some contribution to this overall goal. His expensive edition of *Vathek* and *L'Après-midi d'un faune*, even the little philological study of the English language, *Les Mots anglais*, all provided ways of experimenting with the visual layout of the text and the use of different typefaces which would eventually culminate in the bold visual and typographical experiments of *Un Coup de dés*. In its own way, *Les Mots anglais* allowed Mallarmé to continue his linguistic studies and to examine, in another language and culture, the complex relationship between the sound, the shape, and the meaning of words. *Les Dieux antiques* provided a useful introduction to the various processes at work in the formulation of myths, rituals, and religion which remained at the very heart of the proposed masterwork.

Mallarmé had long since come to the conclusion that an appropriate vehicle for his work was the theatre, primarily because it had the potential of communicating with a mass audience. Only the theatre, along with the concert hall, seemed capable of providing the setting for the collective, quasi-religious experience which was to be the focus of the Great Work:

I believe that literature, rediscovering its origins which are a combination of Art and Science, will provide us with a Theatre of which the performances will be the truly modern religious celebration; a Book which is an explanation of man able to satisfy our greatest dreams. I believe that all of this is written in nature in such a way that only those who are not interested in looking at things cannot see it. This work exists, everyone has attempted it without realising it; there is not a genius or a fool who has not discovered some part of it, albeit unknowingly. To demonstrate this and thus lift a corner of the veil of what just such a poem can be, is, in my isolation, my joy and my torture. (Letter to Vittorio Pica, 1886)

Such remarks were not unrelated to the activities of Richard Wagner. Mallarmé had kept abreast of the Bayreuth festival project and clearly felt it a threat not only to himself but to the entire French nation. Writing about the forthcoming inauguration of the new Paris opera-house in January 1875, Mallarmé greatly regretted that, 'A défaut d'un ouvrage français, exceptionnel et subjuguant l'Europe entière' (For want of an exceptional French work which would overwhelm the entire continent of Europe), a foreign work would have to be used for the opening concert. Indeed from that time onwards Mallarmé began to work feverishly on a theatrical project of his own. Theoretical notes which have survived from that period reveal that what was envisaged was a kind of modern mystery play, a mixed-genre spectacle incorporating music, text, mime, and dance. In practice, however, like Wagner, Mallarmé found it extremely difficult to blend together the scenic, verbal, and musical elements of the work. In the event, Mallarmé's response on behalf of the French nation to Wagner's four-part *Ring Cycle* never materialized, although it is clear from Mallarmé's extant papers that even at the moment of his death he was still desperately searching for something of the sort.

During the remaining years of his life Mallarmé debated with himself the relative merits of the theatre and the book as the ideal vehicle for his Great Work. He also began seriously to question whether the mass public of his day (for whom, as the poignant prose poem 'Conflit' reveals, he felt genuine affection and understanding) was in fact ready for such an experience. In the event, the whole question remained unresolved at the time of his unexpected death in 1898.

By expressing the need for a modern secular work to replace the outmoded myths and rituals of the past and by investigating the nature of language itself, Mallarmé was asking the kind of fundamental questions which were beginning to be asked elsewhere. Not only in literature, but in music and in painting, similar root and branch reappraisals were taking place as the traditions and the conventions of the past came under intense scrutiny. Here a common pattern emerges as an initial enthusiasm for, and general faith in, science and its methodology gives way to a gradual questioning of and, eventually, a total rejection of it, as the rationalist view of the world as a solid identifiable reality is replaced by the notion of a multiplicity of subjective universes. This shift in perspective is expressed by a general tendency to move away from representation in recognizable form (verisimilitude) to various degrees of, but, significantly, not total, abstraction. At the same time, the function of art changes from depicting, in the sense of recording, to interpreting.

## The Heritage of Wagner

This shift was certainly less dramatic in the case of music, where Wagnerian and classical opera continued to dominate the scene for some considerable time. None the less, like all the other arts, music began to be influenced by technical progress, by easier communication which encouraged contact with other worlds and cultures. Here as elsewhere, the boundaries between high and popular culture began to change. The public for music grew and diversified as a direct consequence of rapid industrialization and urbanization; operetta, musical revue, music-hall, *café-concert*, and other forms of popular music flourished alongside classical opera. Claude Debussy (1862–1918) was aware of and sensitive to the music of other cultures and his exposure to foreign influences such as those of Javanese music and American ragtime is manifest in his work. He was one of the first French composers to begin to break away from a strict dependence upon the system of major and minor keys which had been the basis of Western music since the seventeenth century. His *Prélude à 'L'Après-midi d'un faune'* (1894), based on Mallarmé's poem, gently frees itself from a diatonic tonality. Instead of echoing a distinctive theme and developing it, the *Prélude* presents a hesitant arabesque constantly turning back on itself, with numerous excursions from the main theme followed by returns to it. Debussy's *Pelléas et Mélisande* (1902), based on a play by the Belgian writer Maurice Maeterlinck, is full of delicate shifts of mood and elusive undercurrents which deliberately seek to avoid the heavy orchestration and narrative mode of Wagnerian opera. His experimental sketches *La Mer* (1903–5), the first edition of which significantly bore on its cover a Hokusai print *The Wave*, are likewise an attempt to liberate himself from the traditional constraints of the symphony. Compared to the strident tones and insistent primeval rhythms of Igor Stravinsky, whose *Rite of Spring* caused total outrage on its first performance in Paris in 1913, Debussy's quiet revolution, like the harmonic experiments of his compatriot Erik Satie (1866–1925), went largely unnoticed at the time, and would really only be fully appreciated after the Second World War, when its impact was to prove decisive. The same, however, could not be said of the radical transformation which the visual arts underwent during this same period.

## The Birth of Impressionism

In one sense, the fundamental changes which took place in painting during the second half of the nineteenth century and the first quarter of the twentieth century were part of an attempt to loosen the stranglehold which, until then, the French state had exerted on the art world. Founded in 1648, abolished in 1789, but re-established in 1815, the Académie laid down the curriculum for the state art school L'École des beaux-arts, which trained the artists at whose studios most art classes took place. The state was likewise the organizer of the annual exhibition, the Salon, which provided the main public arena for art sales. As such, the Académie enjoyed a monopoly of the art world and was at the same time the main arbiter of taste and the main purchaser of art works. The values which it cherished in art reflected its aristocratic inheritance. There was a strict hierarchy of genres with historical, mythological subjects, and portraiture given precedence over contemporary subjects and landscapes, which were ranked only slightly above still lifes. Drawing and composition were prized over painting, which was frowned upon, as was excessive use of colour, which was seen primarily as a way of filling in the drawing and of little importance in itself. Desperate to avoid any visible sign of manual labour, academic art was obsessed with *le fini*, in which no trace of brushwork could be perceived.

As the nineteenth century wore on, however, the state's monopoly began to be challenged as French society became much less aristocratic and much more bourgeois. By the 1830s and 1840s technological progress and industrialization began to produce a new breed of art patron who sought paintings which could be understood and appreciated without the benefit of a classical education. This middlebrow, or *juste milieu*, art, as it was known, which required competent drawing, clear composition, and lively story-telling based on contemporary and not mytho-logical figures, provided a new and extremely lucrative market. Alongside the official art world of the Salon, alternative venues soon began to appear as dealers and critics grew in number to service the needs of wealthy patrons seeking advice and instruction.

It was one of the most stimulating of these new critics, the poet Charles Baudelaire, who, discussing the Salon of 1846, remarked that the profound and momentous changes taking place in French society, highlighted by Haussmann's transformation of the capital, seemed to have completely escaped the attention of the exhibitors. 'Celui-là sera le peintre, le vrai peintre', he commented, 'qui saura arracher à la vie actuelle son côté épique et nous faire voir et comprendre, avec la couleur ou le dessin, combien nous sommes grands et poétiques dans nos cravates et nos bottes vernies' (The true painter will be he who is able to draw out the epic quality from everyday life and make us see and understand, by means of colour or drawing, how great and poetic we are in our ties and our patent leather boots).

Painters who began to respond to this challenge soon found that their work was not welcomed by officialdom. One of the first of those who found himself in this situation was Édouard Manet (1832–83). The first painting which he submit-ted to the Salon with the appropriately Baudelairian subject of *Le Buveur d'absinthe* (1859) was automatically rejected. Two years later his paintings, of a Spanish dancer and a portrait of his parents, were accepted, but when in 1863 he submit-ted his *Déjeuner sur l'herbe* a scandal ensued. It was not his depiction of a female nude accompanied by two fully dressed men which caused the uproar, since such a compositional device was quite traditional. Furthermore, Manet's nude was much less sensually arousing than other nudes exhibited at the same time, includ-ing Cabanel's *Naissance de Vénus*, which was the success of the Salon that year and was in fact purchased by the Emperor himself. What actually caused the conster-nation was the fact that Manet had taken the traditional theme of *la fête champêtre* and transformed it into a modern idiom, replacing an idyllic and safely mythologi-cal setting with one which depicted picnickers who were clearly recognizable as contemporaries of the spectators. In that context, the nude was disturbing.

Two years later Manet's *Olympia*, an attempt to modernize the hackneyed clas-sical theme of the reclining nude, although accepted by the Salon, again succeeded in scandalizing the public. Manet's original intention in both of these paintings had not been to cause offence. The son of a judge, a man of independent means, and an elegant and witty conversationalist, he never thought of himself as a rebel or a revolutionary. He refused to exhibit alongside other avant-garde painters and until his dying day sought no greater prize than the official recognition that came from having a canvas exhibited at the Salon. Manet's primary aim in these paint-ings was to modernize old subjects whilst retaining whatever lessons he had learned from the masters of earlier ages. His boldness, however, encouraged others to turn their attention to more obviously modern themes and subject-matter. The gardens, parks, cafés, and boulevards of Paris, not to mention the boating parties, leisure, and entertainments associated with the river Seine and the countryside surrounding the city, became the subjects of a whole generation of artists who frequently found their work excluded from the official Salon. Unable to display their paintings to the buying public because of this constant rejection, these artists eventually had no alternative other than to band together to form a co-operative whose first group exhibition, the *Salon des refusés*, took place in April 1874 in the empty studio of a photographer. Manet, who regarded this as a peripheral event, refused to contribute any painting. However, one of the canvases which was exhibited, *Impression, soleil levant* by Claude Monet, was singled out for a scathing attack published in the magazine *Charivari* by the art critic Louis Leroy, who made great play with its title, calling his article 'Exposition des Impressionistes', thus lumping together into a movement which in reality never existed a disparate group of artists whose sole purpose had been to find a means of selling their paintings.

Whilst it would be dangerous to impose a fictitious stylistic unity on a group of very different painters, there were certain things which those who exhibited at that first or the other seven 'Impressionist' exhibitions had in common. Their bold use of colour was in part due to the recent invention of artificial pigments, but it owed just as much to the liberating influence of Japanese prints. Japanese prints again, along with the example of photography, probably explain the framing devices and unusual angles of vision frequently encountered in the paintings of these artists. More significantly still, all of them sought to produce a pictorial equivalent of what they actually saw rather than what conventions dating back to the Renaissance had until then demanded. More than Paris and its environment, time, space, light, and movement constitute common and recurrent obsessions. In this context, the reflective and refractive properties of water constituted a particular challenge and in the paintings of Pierre-Auguste Renoir (1841–1919) the traditional preoccupation with clear line, true perspective, and chiaroscuro shading is abandoned in an attempt to capture light as it is actually perceived by the human eye out in the open air. The series of paintings of *La Gare Saint-Lazare* by Claude Monet (1840–1926) not only provide powerful images of the industrial revolution and the machine age but also attempt to capture on canvas the effects of steam. His fascination with light and colour found its purest expression, however, in the series of paintings of haystacks, poplar trees, and Rouen Cathedral undertaken in the 1890s which tackle the intricate relationship between light, atmosphere, and time. These experiments would eventually lead to the huge paintings of *Les Nymphéas*, inspired by the lilies in his specially designed Japanese garden, upon which he worked incessantly towards the end of his life.

This attempt to express the perpetual metamorphosis of life led Manet, Monet, and others to the apparently careless, 'unfinished' brush strokes and blurred mirage effects of momentary perception. In fact, what they had invented was a

### Georges Seurat *Une Baignade à Asnières* (1884)

Like other Impressionist and post-Impressionist artists such as Renoir, Bazille, and Caillebotte, Seurat frequently painted river scenes. Here Parisians are depicted at play on the banks of the Seine, profiting from the explosion of leisure activities and pleasure haunts made possible by the processes of modernization. The growth of public transport brought expeditions outside the city within the reach of many town dwellers, who are typically depicted drinking and dancing in 'guinguettes' like La Grenouillière, painted by Monet and Renoir, or boating and bathing at Gennevilliers or Asnières. The flat expanses of colour in Seurat's painting recall the frescoes of Puvis de Chavannes, while the boy standing in the water is reminiscent of a baptism scene. But in the background of the painting is a reminder of the economic transformation which underpinned these new leisure activities, the belching chimneys which were all too rapidly to engulf districts like Asnières and to turn them into an indistinguishable part of the Paris conurbation.

refined realism in which they sought neither to idealize nor to represent reality but rather to fragment, analyse, simplify, and reassemble it in the spectator's eye. This was a perceptual revolution which reinstated and legitimized the subjectivity of the artist and allowed him to retrieve his function as an interpreter, not a recorder, of the experience of the world, and it constituted a major breakthrough. The way in which these painters used colour was just as significant. By destroying the traditional notion that colour was merely a descriptive adjunct of form, and by showing that it was something which existed in its own right and could be exploited to express feeling and emotion, they initiated a revolution which would eventually culminate in abstract art.

One artist who took both of these concepts a little further in this direction was Georges Seurat (1859–91). In *Une Baignade à Asnières* (1883–4) he put into practice the theories of contemporary scientists like Eugène Chevreul who had argued that colours could be juxtaposed in such a way that they were mixed in the mind of the spectator rather than in the artist's palette, thus producing the vibratory qualities of light as experienced in real life. Encouraged by his earliest experiments, Seurat proceeded to cover the entire canvas with tiny round dots or points of paint in the place of regular brush strokes, in a technique which became known as *pointillisme*. A similar analytical approach but which, this time, was concerned with shapes and structures rather than with colour was adopted by Paul Cézanne (1839–1906), whose paintings of le Mont Sainte-Victoire outside his native Aix-en-Provence mark an important step towards the mathematical and geometrical kind of analytical art later associated with painters such as Picasso and Braque. In his brief and traumatic life, Vincent Van Gogh (1853–90) also flirted for a while with pointillist techniques, but he was much more interested in exploiting the symbolism of colour and its potential for expressing feeling. His *Café de minuit* (1888) with its crude colours and the clash of greens and reds and the vibrant yellow of the floor echoed in the eerie light of the lamps suggests a hellish vision of the emptiness of café life.

It would be wrong to infer from what has preceded that technique, line, and colour were the only preoccupations of the painters of this time. Manet's paintings, as Mallarmé (but not the jury of the Salon) was one of the first to realize, are frequently quite subversive and disturbing; as well as trying to capture the movement of horses or of the human form as in, for example, the case of ballet dancers, Degas (1834–1917) provides intimate pictures of women at their *toilette* which, like those of Lautrec, have been simultaneously considered sympathetic and moving yet strangely disquieting; these artists, and others such as Gustave Caillebotte (1848–94), whose *Pont de l'Europe* remains a powerful evocation of the total emptiness at the heart of urban society, were all shrewd observers of the period in which they lived and their paintings frequently carry political or moral messages hinting, sometimes not too subtly, as recent studies have shown, at the squalor, greed, and loneliness which frequently existed behind the glamorous façade of modern urban life.

## The Neurosis of the *Fin de siècle*

Anxieties of a similar kind were expressed both in painting and in literature by those who were quite uneasy with such sudden change. An extreme example of this is to be found in the writings of the German scientist Max Nordau, whose book *Die Entartung* (1893) translated as *Dégénérescence* enjoyed a great popular success in France. A rag-bag of pseudo-scientific theory and personal prejudice expressing the fears and anxieties of a reactionary in a rapidly changing world where Symbolists, Feminists, and Socialists were all portrayed as pernicious enemies of the established order, Nordau's apocalyptic vision captures well the neurosis of the age and explains attempts to escape from the harsh threatening forces released (potentially at least) by urban industrialized culture. This in some ways understandable reaction can be seen in the unprecedented interest in alternative philosophies, sciences, and magic of all kinds which was such a feature of the final decade of the century. People turned to alternative philosophies, to Buddhism, to the occult, and even to hypnotism, as is demonstrated by Charcot's voyeuristic and chauvinistic experiments in hysteria at the Salpétrière hospital which allowed him to parade before an exclusively male audience hysterical women in various stages of undress. Painters such as Paul Gauguin (1848–1903) sought to flee the evils of consumer capitalism and to find a source of spiritual renewal, first in what he naïvely took to be the unsullied backwaters of Pont-Aven in Brittany, and later in the apparently just as attractive but finally equally unrewarding setting of Tahiti.

Similar reactions to the sophistication and decadence of urban industrialized culture can be found in the dreams, fantasies, and eroticism of Gustave Moreau (1826–98), whose paintings along with those of Félicien Rops (1830–98) can similarly be seen as a complex expression of the neurosis and frustrations triggered by fears that the established order, namely male bourgeois supremacy, was threatened or about to be obliterated by new and uncontrollable forces represented primarily by women and the mob. For his part, Moreau replaced the uncertainties of the present and the future with a dream world set in the mythical past where woman was fetishized, that is to say once more turned into a tamed object of desire. Rops settled for the world of erotic fantasy where the male is willingly subjugated by a powerful yet strangely desirable dominant female persona. This curious blend of art, religion, sublimated sex, and reactionary forces was all brought together into a most potent, heady, and totally ridiculous cocktail in the person of Joséphin Péladan (1858–1918). As self-appointed master or Sâr, who took his lead from the teachings of a fifteenth-century mystic called Christian Rosenkranz, he founded the Salon de la Rose + Croix catholique (1892–7), which was held annually in the gallery of Durand-Ruel. Defining art as the guardian of traditional values, he banned from his exhibitions anything whose subject-matter was concerned with modern life, war, Judaism, or natural landscapes. His quite unreadable novel *Le dernier Bourbon* (1895) describes his fundamentally Wagnerian dream of an international freemasonry of high culture.

Such reactions, although extreme, were not isolated phenomena. The period had begun with an absolute and uncritical faith in the scientific spirit of the age as exemplified by the novels of Émile Zola (1840–1902), who, inspired by the writings of Darwin and the experimental methods of the biologist Claude Bernard, sought in his Rougon-Macquart novel series to place a naturalist's magnifying glass over various aspects of Second Empire society in order to demonstrate the impact of heredity and environment upon human behaviour. Such a mechanistic view of the world, irrevocably linked to the notion of progress, soon began to be challenged, however, not just by eccentrics like Nordau and Péladan, but by writers, such as Joris-Karl Huysmans (1848–1907), who had initially shared Zola's deterministic outlook. In *A Rebours* (1884) he created a remarkable hero Des Esseintes who is so disgusted by the crass materialism and spiritual emptiness of the modern world that he turns his back on it and retreats into his own private world. In *Le Disciple* (1889) Paul Bourget (1852–1935) seriously began to question the ideals of the scientific approach to life. Positivism was also undermined by the writings of the philosopher Henri Bergson (1859–1941), who, in his *Essai sur les données immédiates de la conscience* (1889), and his public lectures at the Collège de France, stressed the existence of intuitive forces within human beings totally at odds with the mechanistic view of human behaviour as exemplified by determinism. Encouraged by the work of Bergson, by the critique of Western civilization, Christianity, and morality contained in the writings of Friedrich Nietzsche (1844–1900), and by the liberating experience of travelling in North Africa, André Gide (1869–1951) was one of the earliest to propose an alternative to traditional moral values, first with his lyrical, pagan, and profoundly hedonistic *Les Nourritures terrestres* (1897), later with *L'Immoraliste*, and finally in *Les Caves du Vatican* (1914), which, published only a few weeks before the outbreak of the First World War, offered a merciless onslaught not only on the rational thought, positivism, and intellectual systems of the nineteenth century but, from the technical point of view, on the form of the novel itself.

## Cubism and the Impact of 'Primitive' Art

While Gide and Marcel Proust, whose first volume of *A la recherche du temps perdu* appeared in 1913, were busy experimenting with the novel, the fundamental changes brought about in painting during the second half of the century were about to culminate in equally daring experiments. The technical revolution accomplished by the Impressionists had already gone some way towards freeing painting from imitation and representation. Contact with the art of Japan, and more recently with the so-called 'primitive' art and sculpture of Africa and Oceania, had shown that there were viable alternatives to the conventions of perspective and harmony established in Europe at the time of the Renaissance. As a consequence it seemed to painters like Georges Braque (1882–1963) and Pablo Picasso

(1881–1973) that the work of art no longer needed to be illusionistic, that it did not have to be judged on the grounds of its success in accurately depicting reality. In the case of Braque, this led to a fascination with shape, structure, and mathematical form which particularly struck the art critic Louis Vauxcelles, who wrote in *Gil Blas* of 14 November 1908: 'he [Braque] constructs deformed metallic men which are tremendously simplified. He despises form and reduces everything, places, figures, and houses, to geometrical shapes, to cubes. Let us not make fun of him, since he is sincere. Let us wait and see.' The term 'Cubist', although not actually used in this article, had been born.

A year earlier Picasso had completed a massive canvas entitled *Les Demoiselles d'Avignon*. In some respects it is a revolutionary painting which breaks with a whole series of conventions. It does not respect the classical norm for the human figure: human anatomy is here reduced to geometric shapes. Spatial illusionism, traditionally achieved by a single-point perspective, is abandoned. The painting contains a profile of a nose combined simultaneously with a frontal view of the face. In the case of the figure in the lower right-hand corner, a mask-like face, the back, and the breasts are all visible at once. In other respects, however, the painting deliberately refers back to earlier traditions. The subject is a brothel scene which echoes Ingres's famous painting *Le Bain turc*, with its display of nubile female flesh in the exotic setting of a harem. The central figure follows the conventions of the female nude of the nineteenth century as epitomized by yet another of Ingres's paintings, *La Vénus anadyomène*. But the painting is not merely an exercise in style. The mask-like face in which one eye is chillingly empty expresses Picasso's own fascination with and fear of venereal disease, which in his mind is linked to the central theme of prostitution.

Here as elsewhere in his work, Picasso retains a specific relationship with external reality. In some of his later works this link gradually weakens until the painting runs the risk of becoming an object in itself, not just an illusion of the visual world. At this point, where the painting is about to become a total abstraction, Picasso prevents this by introducing into the composition a whole series of visual clues (letters, numbers, newspaper titles, puns) which anchor its subject in the real world.

Picasso's rejection of total abstraction is interesting. Whilst a comparison between, say, *Les Demoiselles d'Avignon* and Manet's *Déjeuner sur l'herbe* or between Gide's *Les Caves du Vatican* and Zola's *Thérèse Raquin* reminds us of the great changes made during this period, both Gide's *sotie* and Picasso's painting are still eminently recognizable. Both are fundamentally works of a period of transition during which we are beginning to move from 'easy' to 'difficult' art, and this is accompanied by a move in which the reader or spectator exchanges a position of passive reception for one of active participation.

During this period the real gulf which has begun to open up is not so much between high and low culture (if anything that divide begins to disappear) but between the artist and his or her public. The profound change which has taken

## Pablo Picasso *Les Demoiselles d'Avignon* (1906–7)

Often called 'the first great cubist canvas', Picasso's seminal painting was slow to gain a reputation. Though finished—or abandoned—in 1907, after some reworking of the two figures on the right, it was purchased by the collector Jacques Doucet in the 1920s, at which point its name was changed from the humorous 'Le Bordel philosophique' to its ironically demure present title. André Breton's magazine *La Revue surréaliste* published a reproduction in 1925 and the canvas was first shown publicly at this period. As well as establishing Picasso as the inventor of cubism, the painting illustrates his debt to the 'primitive' art of Africa and pre-classical Greece, while recent commentators have also underlined and criticized the striking violence and passion with which the figures of the prostitutes are executed.

place during this critical period in French culture is to be found in the relationship between the work of art and the person who listens to it, looks at it, or reads it. Nothing is any longer just given or received. For the work of art to succeed an exchange now has to take place. Through a tacit contract, the reader, listener, or spectator is required to participate, to make a positive contribution. Paradoxical as this may seem, what we have been witnessing is the gradual democratization of art. For a poem of Mallarmé to work the reader has to engage with the text and solve the puzzle. For Monet's painting of a steam train at the Gare Saint-Lazare to work, in his or her head, the spectator has to transform into meaningful shapes what, when viewed from close up, are no more than specks of colour. In short, the art of this period is modernist, rather than modern. Modern art as we now understand it will only come about amid the cataclysmic upheaval caused by two world wars as a result of which people's perceptions of the world and of themselves undergo an even more radical transformation.

## The *Belle Époque*?

In recent years, studies of the culture and society of the French Republic of the late nineteenth and early twentieth centuries have increasingly characterized the period as one of crisis, anxiety, and decadence. Anglo-American cultural historians, in particular, have rejected any rosy notion of a 'belle époque', and scholars have opted for a decidedly chilling view of a *fin de siècle* society in the throes of fragmentation and chaos, subject to severe systems of repression, and undermined by sexual antagonism, class tension, and concerns over moral and political authority in 'mass' society.

The emphasis placed by modern cultural historians on anxiety, chaos, pathology, and degeneracy as the key underlying topoi of the period 1870–1914 is totally at variance with the received notion that the Republicans of late nineteenth-century France—traditionally seen as the great inheritors of the Enlightenment secular faith in reason, education, and progress—were successful in bringing into being a more unified, more civilized, more just, and more affluent society. In the face of such radical revisions of perspective, one needs to be reminded that there are still many historians of the period, particularly many French historians, who maintain that the generation of highly idealistic and austere Republicans of the late nineteenth century were, indeed, responsible for laying the solid foundations of modern France, and that the republican ideals in which they believed actually embodied a moral and cultural spirit which remains the bedrock of French society.

In the course of contemporary French self-questioning on issues of national identity and national culture, positive images and interpretations of the Third Republic still loom especially large. So whereas Anglo-American scholars may be happy to think of the period 1870–1914 in France as having been one of fragmentation, repression, and decadence, many French scholars and intellectuals refuse to take up such an unmitigatedly pessimistic and negative position, obviously feeling that France's contemporary cultural identity depends crucially on a belief in historical continuity and on an enduring faith in the achievements of the French republican tradition.

This debate is pursued in *Les Lieux de mémoire*, a recent and important series of essays devoted to the study of the roots of Republicanism and to the analysis of the continuing place and significance of republican culture in the French collective memory. This leaves one in no doubt that the civic ethos which dominated the culture of the period 1870–1914 has played an exemplary role in French cultural, intellectual, and political life, and that the ideal of civic Republicanism has continued to exercise its power and its attraction, despite all the profound changes undergone by France in the twentieth century. Although a few contributors to *Les Lieux de mémoire* were ready to proclaim the final death of the tradition of civic Republicanism, and one was even prepared to assert that virtually nothing had survived in the French collective memory of those elements of late nineteenth-century republican culture—emblems, symbols, ceremonies, festivals—which had been handed down by the founding fathers of the Republic, the editor of *Les Lieux de mémoire*, Pierre Nora, was not himself willing to accept this pronouncement of death over the body of republican culture. Instead, he gives an appealingly intimate and subtly measured postmodern account of the way in which a citizen of contemporary France simultaneously experiences a sentimental attachment to, as well as a critical detachment from, the French republican tradition, 'a tradition which we still recognize as our own but which we can no longer experience as such'. According to Nora, while diversity, pluralism, and the collapse of ideologies have now made the idea of a unified national republican culture an unattainable— and even undesirable—ambition, there remains a vestigial identification with the symbols of that culture. For Pierre Nora, the desire to commemorate, and even to celebrate, republican culture accompanies the impulse to demystify or to desecrate it; the desire to belong to a unified republican community runs alongside the recognition of contemporary social, cultural, and ethnic diversity; the belief in the possibility of justice, order, and progress survives the evidence of chaos, fragmentation, and decadence. Late nineteenth-century republican culture, therefore, stands not only as nostalgic, utopian memory, but also as the enduring basis of a possible civic ethos in contemporary society.

## The Imposition of the New Moral Order

In the Third Republic, the principal means of creating a common republican culture was through the state's establishment of a universal system of national education, whose principal aim was to make every child in every corner of France into a full and worthy citizen of the new secular, republican nation. It was in the primary schools that religious superstition and traditional folk ways were to be combated, and a new civic morality was to be taught, a morality based on rationality, science, patriotism, industriousness, thrift, and self-denial. In this state project to educate, cultivate, socialize, moralize, and modernize the Nation, it was the primary school teacher—the *instituteur*—who took on the role of missionary and who came to achieve the status of a mythical hero in the collective memory of France.

In his or her unshakeable belief in education and culture as the sole means to achieve progress, and in his or her undying commitment to the ideals of secularism, Republicanism, and patriotism, the *instituteur* embodied the essential spirit of late nineteenth-century republican culture. It fell to the *instituteur* to turn, in Eugen Weber's phrase, 'peasants into Frenchmen', to transform the uneducated and uncouth into the educated and polite, to organize a disorderly rabble into a body of modern citizens. The *instituteur* was not, however, simply a teacher of good manners, for he or she was nothing less than the 'lay priest' of a new secular religion; the classroom was the new temple of knowledge; and the school manuals were the new holy writ, teaching science, history, morality, citizenship, and patriotism. In his study of this generation of schoolteachers, *Nous les Maîtres d'école* (1967), Jacques Ozouf revealed the monastic existence of self-denial that was lived by this new secular clergy. Profoundly committed to their mission, these schoolteachers led solitary lives, isolated from the people they taught by virtue of their very status both as exemplars of civic virtue, and as initiates in the higher knowledge which it was their task to impart to those around them. In this way the schoolteacher was to be admired and respected for his achievement in leading the local, benighted peasants out of their primitive, barbaric existence into the higher form of life of civilization and culture that the French Third Republic believed it had brought into being.

In recent times, cultural historians have, to say the least, been unsympathetic to this attitude. Indeed, they have taken as their principal target of criticism precisely the integrity and the aims of the professional classes of late nineteenth-century France—the teachers, university professors, lawyers, scientists, doctors, psychiatrists, writers, urban planners, politicians, in fact, the whole range of middle-class professionals who, at the time, perceived their task as that of working for the progress and improvement of French society.

It is undeniable that the profound shift in commonly accepted values that has taken place since the late nineteenth century has meant that few historians can whole-heartedly share the attitudes, perspectives, and ambitions of the late nineteenth-century republican state and of its devoted disciples in the professions and in the public services. However, the evidence of modern cultural history more than suggests that historians and critics have gone much too far in single-mindedly highlighting the deficiencies and the wrong-headedness, not to say the corruption and the repressiveness, of late nineteenth-century republican society, as administered by the state and the professional classes. Drawing amply on the work of Michel Foucault, such historians have taken over wholesale his denunciation of the Enlightenment project as a system designed to impose hegemonic control through rationalization, rather than, as it claimed to be, a system designed to produce social progress and democratic freedom through rational and scientific means. They have also gone to extremes in disregarding the degree of economic and social improvement achieved in late nineteenth-century France and in depicting it as a deeply undemocratic, inegalitarian, and intolerant society which stigmatized and mistreated those it considered to be deviant and dissident (prostitutes, criminals, political opponents), which promoted a narrow and repressive bourgeois morality (*l'ordre moral*), which encouraged a militaristic ideology of chauvinism and xenophobia, and which failed to respond to the needs and rights of its many varied constituents and minorities. For such historians, the Third Republic merely applied a thin veneer of civilization, culture, and order over a turbulent ocean of unresolved conflicts and injustices, and the apocalypse of the First World War is, therefore, commonly seen by them as the final judgement on a profoundly corrupt and decadent society.

One of the most dominant views now held by cultural historians is that the works of writers, artists, and intellectuals in the Third Republic embodied attitudes and values which were identical to those of their professional peers in other areas such as science, medicine, psychiatry, law, health and social welfare, urban planning, and education. Their creative works are repeatedly said to contain, and to give form to, the same self-interest, the same prejudices, fantasies, blind spots, desires, fears, and so on, which have been said to characterize the discourses and practices of state servants and members of the professions, who, although they claimed to be engaged in the disinterested task of improving the lot of the people, were, in reality, carrying out a massive exercise of stigmatization, surveillance, and control. The aim of producing an orderly, efficient, and just society has, therefore, been interpreted as a determination to impose a strict order at all costs, depriving the full range of citizens of freedom, individuality, and dignity. In the same way, the ambition to create a civilized and cultured society has been seen as the imposition of one system of cultural values, and cultural forms, which necessarily involved the repression and destruction of alternative systems.

It is, indeed, undeniable that the thoroughgoing attempt by late nineteenth-century Republicans to introduce a new moral order into society was to a crucial degree driven by their fear and suspicion of those they perceived as the uncontrollable masses, whom they considered to be a prey to irrationality and base instincts. In their eyes, any ambition to organize society more efficiently, achieve social progress, and bring about a higher level of civilization and culture inevitably required that the masses be educated in such a way that they would come to be assimilated into the ranks of civilized, cultured, and ordered society. This ambition also required that the masses be managed in such a way that they would not, meanwhile, threaten the possibility of order and progress. Modern cultural historians have tended to interpret this dual strategy of management and education in a highly critical fashion, claiming that the irrational fears felt by the state and by professional élites towards marginal groups and types (working classes, women, ethnic minorities, criminals, drunkards, prostitutes . . .) led not only to misguided and unfounded prejudices, but also to institutionalized forms of control, injustice, and repression. These cultural historians have also claimed that the intellectual, artistic, and scientific work of professional élites, which was alleged to be disinterested, was, in fact, motivated by fear and self-interest and was often based on fallacious systems of thought masquerading as objective, scientific inquiry.

In her study of medical, psychiatric, and legal practices at the end of the nineteenth century, Ruth Harris, for example, shows how the supposedly disinterested and humanitarian activities of these professions were profoundly compromised by the fact that they rested on untenable theoretical assumptions, and served specific social, political, and moral objectives. Given the dominance of the civic ethos in the Third Republic, and given the new religion of science in which the republican state's secularism and anticlericalism were grounded, medicine assumed a role as central as that of education in the fight for social progress and justice. Indeed, according to Harris, it was the scientific authority of medicine which provided the overarching ideological justification of the social and political programme of the regime. The supposedly objective nature of medical knowledge was, therefore, used to legitimize official, institutional, professional, and legislative practices during the Third Republic, practices which, though it was claimed they were serving the interests of the people, were in fact designed to carry out a wide-ranging project of social control.

Harris suggests that 'medical knowledge provided some special defining role in *fin de siècle* society' (p. 11). For Harris, doctors and psychiatrists share the hygienist perspectives which dominated state policy and the attitudes and practices of professional élites in the period. 'Medical men were thus not seen simply as doctors healing the sick, but were rather discussed—favourably and unfavourably—as the embodiment of certain moral and social philosophies, ideals, and aspirations. Physicians were prophets of progress, positivists who espoused a theory of knowledge which rejected metaphysical explanation' (p. 11).

The need to regulate and control the unruly masses, in order to improve them, was universally conceived of in terms of cleansing and sanitizing society. The attempt to impose superior and universally applicable moral and cultural codes was seen as a way of protecting the social body from infection by morbid, pathological, and degenerate elements. Those people who were perceived at the time as dangerous, immoral, debased, and primitive (rioting working classes, hysterical women, Jews, criminals, prostitutes, drunkards . . .) were treated as physiologically abnormal. This abnormality was diagnosed as an excessive susceptibility to irrational, socially deviant, and subversive behaviour. In order to account for such abnormality and deviancy, a whole range of pseudo-scientific theories emerged in late nineteenth-century France, which lacked any verifiable basis and which simply confirmed existing social prejudices. Such theories served to intensify further the pathologization of marginal and repressed groups and types, who by their very biology were deemed incapable of becoming the rational agents which they were required to be, if they were to merit full citizenship of the Third Republic. In Harris's eyes, therefore, medical men were too caught up in the politics of hygienism to be able to perform their tasks professionally and dispassionately. Social policing too often took priority over humane healing.

The perception of marginal groups as irrational and potentially dangerous was above all a fear of crowds. Civilization and social order seemed most fragile when people were massed into what appeared to resemble hordes of primitive barbarians. It was thought that in crowd situations individuals lost their own sense of rational control and moral responsibility, due to irrational mechanisms akin to hypnotism and magnetism, or near-physical processes of infection and contagion. Thus historians have seen the élites' fascinated fear of the crowd as a central feature of all late nineteenth-century culture: crowd psychology—the 'science of mass behaviour'—appeared in France not long after the Franco-Prussian War, thrived in the stormy decade between 1885 and 1895, and captured the imaginations and fears of men working in a variety of fields: fiction, collective animal behaviour, criminal anthropology, and history. The novels of Émile Zola, Gustave Le Bon's celebrated text *La Psychologie des foules* (1895), and Gabriel Tarde's *Les Lois de l'imitation* (1890) all show how the masses were perceived and represented in the writings of late nineteenth-century professional élites.

The fear of the masses is often now described as an irrational fear which provoked an excessive reaction in the authorities and in the professions. The growth of the working-class movement with its strikes and demonstrations, the threat of a Boulanger *coup d'état*, the rise of anarchist terrorism—all these exacerbated the fears of a revival of revolution and of a return of the terrible civil war of the Commune. In the same way, individual and highly rare events, such as the assassination of the President of the Third Republic, Sadi Carnot, by an Italian anarchist in 1894, or the notorious 'defenestration of Decazeville' in 1886 (on which occasion a deputy director of a coal-mine was thrown out of a window by strikers and left to the mercy of the crowd), had been taken as typical and frequent occurrences by crowd theorists and novelists, and had fuelled a generalized terror of the revolutionary and murderous potential of the crowd.

The dangerous potential of the crowd was closely associated with the alleged irrationality and savagery of stigmatized groups. Women, drunkards, criminals, prostitutes were all deemed to be likely to revert to a bestial and primitive state. However, equally alarming was the common idea that *all* individuals were susceptible to the infectious violence of a crowd and were capable in such situations of reverting to barbarism. Underlying the official distaste for mass behaviour, and, indeed, the suspicion of all forms of assembly, was the belief in the need for each individual to be at all times a fully rational moral agent, since only sober and responsible citizens could fulfil the high ideals of the republican community. A novelist such as Zola, with his naturalist pretensions to the objectivity of science and to the precision of medicine, claimed that his dispassionate documentary approach was imbued with a humanitarian and democratic spirit, and he therefore saw himself as the literary equivalent of the humane professional—not only the doctor, but also the lawyer, the teacher, the social planner. Yet in novels such as *L'Assommoir* (1877) and *Germinal* (1885) it has been suggested that he shared the fantasies, prejudices, and fears of his fellow professionals, for, like them, he persistently represented women, striking miners, and drunkards as potentially primitive and savage beings who threatened the rational, civilized order of society. In this way intellectuals and writers can also be seen as defenders of the moral order of the Third Republic.

## The Eroticization of the Public Domain

Zola was, of course, the author of *Nana* (1880), a novel which registers neo-regulationist panic about the dangers of working-class female sexuality. In recent studies of the society and culture of the Third Republic, the subject of prostitution has probably attracted more attention than any other. This is not only because it is seen as absolutely central to the Foucauldian history of regulationism and hygienism, already referred to above, but also because it is considered as particularly germane to the history of the social treatment and the cultural representation of women, which has now become such an essential part of cultural history and cultural studies. One of the most influential studies of the official attitudes to, and treatment of, prostitutes in the latter part of the nineteenth century is Alain Corbin's *Les Filles de noce* (1978). Like many of his fellow historians, Corbin's primary concern is with the way in which the authorities and the professions perceived and 'managed' the mass phenomenon of prostitution. In addition, he stresses the fact that it was men who managed prostitution, who spoke of it in official discourses, and who represented it in cultural forms.

The authorities regulated prostitution, the better to preserve the existing social, moral, and cultural order of the Third Republic. The official project was not, therefore, to ban prostitution, but rather to subject it to rational control, to hive it off from decent society, and thereby prevent it from spreading its infection. According to Corbin, the fear of syphilis underlay the generalized *fin de siècle* anxiety that the nation was being destroyed from within by the contagious influence of the dangerous classes, and it 'thoroughly imbued' the fictional works of a writer such as Huysmans. This fear was fully exploited by conservative nationalists who claimed that, in allowing the health and the vitality of the population to be sapped, France's military power was being irreparably weakened in the face of German competition and aggression. However, attempts to restrict and control prostitution through the system of *maisons de tolérance* (licensed brothels) were shown to be futile. Sexual activity came to permeate all areas of social, cultural, and leisure activity, and it was impossible to contain it within official regulatory channels:

Just as the 1970s saw the proliferation throughout society of erotic images, records, magazines, and gadgets, so the final decades of the nineteenth century, despite all the efforts of legislation and of the innumerable societies for the improvement of morals, saw the spread, at least through the lower-middle and middle classes, of tastes, fantasies, and techniques that had formerly been the preserve of aristocratic eroticism.

It is also clear that this development was bound up with artistic and literary movements that had brought eroticism to the forefront. Prostitution and its world had become essential themes in fiction and painting; symbolist and decadent literature and art testified to a collective neurosis that found expression through a vertiginous attraction for, as well as a morbid fear of, female sexuality. (pp. 125–6)

The authorities liked to think that an obvious line of demarcation could be drawn between licit and illicit sex, between the orderly and disorderly classes, between the private and public domains, but the deeply sexualized leisure and culture of late nineteenth-century French society proved that this was not the case. The middle classes were themselves profoundly implicated in, and fascinated by, prostitution. Indeed, it was to an important degree the middle classes who kept prostitution going. What is more, it came to be realized that the moral order of bourgeois family life was not destroyed by prostitution. On the contrary, when middle-class men sought their sexual satisfaction outside marriage, they did so to maintain the bourgeois moral order, not to destroy it.

Despite the intensification of moralizing evangelical campaigns towards the end of the century, the evident failure of regulationism and neo-regulationism to keep sexual disorder in its place, and to isolate sexual contagion, caused an even greater panic in the authorities and in the professions. As a result, the culture of the *fin de siècle* and of the opening decade of the twentieth century was shot through with the fear of syphilis and of racial degeneracy, characteristic examples of the 'venereal panic' being Charles-Louis Philippe's novel *Bubu de Montparnasse* (1901), Victor Margueritte's novel *Prostituée* (1907), and Picasso's *Les Demoiselles d'Avignon*.

The failure of a policy of enclosure and containment of prostitution, together with the widespread eroticization of the public domain, made it far more difficult to differentiate decent middle-class wives, mothers, and daughters in public places from less decent women and, above all, from prostitutes. The consequent challenge to the sexual identity of middle-class women, and the frightening prospect that they would be opened up to the contagion of sexuality, seems to have particularly aroused panic in the defenders of the moral order. So as to sustain the idea that the middle-class wife/mother was a figure of unimpeachable virtue, untainted by lust and active sexual desires, it was regarded as sacrilege to associate her in any way with the supposedly debased and primitive nature of the lewd, bestial prostitute. Cultural historians have traced this male splitting of women into 'housewife or harlot' to 'the obsessive fear of women's sexual nature epitomized by the prostitute that pervades the male imagination, both novelistic and scientific, throughout the nineteenth century and that reaches a kind of hysterical paroxysm in its last two decades', to such a degree that the history of modernist culture, as it emerged and came to fruition in this period, cannot be understood without putting the male pathologization of women and the female body at the centre of this history (Charles Bernheimer, *Figures of Ill Repute*, 247).

## The Feminist Critique

This point of view has been corroborated and powerfully expressed in the work of feminist historians. Evoking both Manet's *Olympia* and Picasso's *Les Demoiselles d'Avignon*, Griselda Pollock calls on art critics to recognize modernist painting 'not exclusively as the heroic struggle for individual expression or the equally painful discipline of purification and stylistic innovation but as a more fundamental discourse around the paradoxes and anxieties of masculinity which hysterically and obsessionally figures, debases and dismembers the body of woman' (*Vision and Difference*, 159).

This call has been taken up regularly in the wake of Foucault and Corbin. Hollis Clayson, for example, declares that her operative assumption is that 'art was itself compliant in the regulation of sexualities'. Starting from the fact that artists such as Toulouse-Lautrec, Manet, and Degas endlessly and obsessively painted prostitutes, Clayson analyses their paintings and drawings as evidence, not only of the way in which Western modernist culture subjected women to certain forms of artistic representation, but also of the way in which women were actually perceived and treated in society at large. Thus Degas's representation of prostitutes in his more than fifty small monotype prints of brothel interiors revealed him as sharing the dominant male fear of, and fascination with, prostitutes. On the one hand, he criminalized and pathologized them, in the manner of the regulationists, seeing them 'not only as sexual deviants but as threatening *social* deviants'. But he also manifestly displayed his erotic attraction to 'atavistic female sexuality' in, for example, his repeated depiction of their prominent buttocks.

The painters of the later nineteenth century adopted the point of view of the *flâneur*, inaugurated by Charles Baudelaire, namely, that of the leisured male urban stroller and spectator, who made the city and its inhabitants the object of his lustful, aesthetic gaze, and one of whose principal targets was the commodified woman *par excellence*, the whore. Impressionist painting sexualized and commodified a whole range of working women—waitresses, shop assistants, laundresses, flower-sellers, milliners—and turned them simply into the objects of male sexual attention. Indeed, the whole public domain became a male sexualized space in which, simply by being shown as drinking in a café, sitting in a theatre, attending a race meeting, walking in the street, or shopping, a woman was subjected not only to the male erotic gaze, but was also in danger of being perceived as a prostitute. Clayson refuses to accept the traditional view that artists such as Manet and Degas produced ambiguous, elusive, or significantly more liberal representations of women in their art. On the contrary, she judges that 'by singling out sites that

### The Construction of the Eiffel Tower

Designed by the engineer Gustave Eiffel (1832–1923), the Tower to which he gave his name was erected between 1887 and 1889 for the *Exposition universelle* held in Paris in 1889, just as the Palais du Trocadéro, glimpsed through the legs of the Tower, was built for the 1878 *Exposition universelle* on the site of what is now the Palais de Chaillot. As Roland Barthes pointed out in *La Tour Eiffel* (1964), the Tower has become such an integral part of daily life that it is almost a natural phenomenon like stone or the river, and there is scarcely a place in Paris, except the top of the Tower itself, from which it cannot be seen. In this way, for Barthes, it can be limitlessly deciphered, as a symbol of Paris, of modernity, of communications, of scientific progress, or of the nineteenth century, resembling a rocket, the stalk of a plant, a derrick, a phallus, a lightning conductor, or an insect.

were commonly associated with covert prostitution—the boulevard café, the millinery shop, the brasserie, the nightclub—or situations that suggested uncertainty, the avant-garde actually reinforced reductive female stereotypes and exacerbated the commodification of public female identity that prostitution epitomized' (*Painted Love*, 153).

## Leisure, Consumption, and Popular Culture

The massive late nineteenth-century expansion of the world of leisure, consumption, and popular culture, driven by technological change and urbanization, experienced its apotheosis in the *Expositions universelles*. These quintessential state-promoted events of the Third Republic had already been staged in Paris in 1855, 1867, 1878, and 1889, but it was at the *Exposition* of 1900 that it became strikingly apparent that the mission to educate and civilize the people, which had been so characteristic an ambition of late nineteenth-century republican society, had given way to a readiness to entertain and excite the vast public which flocked to it.

Although the Exhibitions had initially set out to demonstrate the technological, scientific, and commercial progress of nations, they gradually became more like bazaars and fairgrounds for the masses, offering all the luxury and pleasures of a futuristic city devoted to the undiscriminating and unbridled pursuit of consumption and hedonism. With their eclectic jumbling together of modern technology and colonial exoticism, scientific displays and circus side-shows, the Exhibitions foreshadowed the postmodern Disneylands of the later twentieth century. The quest for scientific truth, social utility, and moral order was being replaced by a huge project of commercialized seduction in which spectators were lured into an artificial, make-believe world, and in which scientific achievements were served up as amusing curiosities for an uninformed public.

One of the most spectacular ways in which scientific achievement was exploited in the search for novel ways to entertain was the cinema whose early experiments figured prominently in the *Exposition universelle* of 1900 and which, by the outbreak of the First World War, had become the principal entertainment of the mass public. Cinema was launched in France when Louis Lumière held the first public screening in Paris in December 1985. Though Lumière was the son of a photographer, and himself an industrialist who was primarily interested in the technological possibilities of the cinema, his firm produced some of the most celebrated films of the silent period. Initially Lumière's films appeared exotic or frightening to an uninitiated audience. *L'Arrivée d'un train en gare de La Ciotat* (1895), for example, is said to have sent its first audience running screaming from the room as the train appeared to bear down on them from the screen. But there was also room in Lumière's repertoire for films in the comic or domestic genre, such as *L'Arroseur arrosé* (1895) or *Le Déjeuner de bébé* (1895). His supreme achievement, however, was the creation of a specific documentary genre, as the example of one

### The *Cinématographe Lumière*

With his father Antoine and his brother Auguste, Louis Lumière (1864–1948) ran a hugely successful photography business in Lyons, which employed over three hundred people and specialized in manufacturing the emulsion for photographic plates. In 1884 Antoine Lumière bought one of Thomas Edison's kinetoscopes, and by February 1895, inspired by the mechanism of the sewing machine, Louis had patented the 'Cinématographe' designed for filming and projecting moving pictures. He made short films to demonstrate the new machine, which was seen publicly for the first time in March 1895. At the gala presentation at the Salon Indien of the Grand Café in the Boulevard des Capucines in Paris which took place on 28 December 1895, the programme included such classics as *La Sortie des usines Lumière*, Le *Déjeuner de Bébé*, *L'Arrivée d'un train en gare de La Ciotat*, and *L'Arroseur arrosé*, otherwise known as *Le Jardinier*, which is illustrated in this poster advertising the event. Present in December 1895 was Georges Méliès, who attempted, unsuccessfully, to persuade Antoine Lumière to sell him a cinematograph.

of his earliest films *La Sortie des usines Lumière* (1895) demonstrates. In positioning his camera at the factory gates and filming the workers as they streamed out, Lumière invented an image which, even today, in countless television news programmes and documentary films, signifies the labouring masses. His successors, such as the producer Léon Gaumont, were to exploit the invention of the documentary film in the regular production of newsreels, which until the advent of television were a primary source of information about current affairs and world events.

However, cinema also entered the world of popular entertainment via the theatre and, it has been argued, brought together in a single art-form the multiple entertainments of the fairs that used to be a regular feature of Parisian street life until the middle of the nineteenth century. Georges Méliès, the proprietor-illusionist of the Paris Théâtre Robert Houdin, purchased a cinematograph after viewing Lumière's spectacle and produced large numbers of films which he wrote, designed, acted in, directed, and produced. These varied from the filmed conjuring tricks of *Escamotage d'une dame chez Robert Houdin* (1896) to the wildly exotic fantasies *Voyage dans la lune* (1902), with a strong emphasis on exotic orientalism as in *Le Palais des mille et une nuits*.

Méliès's films are the antithesis of those of Lumière in that they obviously create a spectacle and provide entertainment rather than doing so inadvertently. Méliès places his camera in the position of the theatre-goer in front of the proscenium arch, and his actors perform as though to a theatre audience, bowing at the end of tricks, for example, so that one can almost hear the applause. His films are a profusion of special effects, an early inventory of many of the techniques such as fading, irising, superimposition, slow motion, that were to become a standard part of the cinema repertoire.

Yet looking at Méliès's films today is also a fascinating experience for a viewer interested in daily life at the time of the *belle époque*. These short episodes are full of figures of repression—policemen, bailiffs, customs officers, judges, lawyers, prison warders, hangmen—in short just the kind of public servants and middle-class professionals who, as we have seen, were attempting to impose the new morality on the people who made up the larger part of Méliès's audience. The distant origins of such figures are undoubtedly to be found in fairground Punch and Judy shows, but in Méliès's films it is not people who subvert the forces of law and order so much as objects. The paraphernalia of domestic interiors and new technologies, so typical of the period, is mobilized to take on a life of its own. Inanimate objects become animate, disappear and reappear, fly across the room, grow and shrink in size as they do in the contemporaneous *Alice in Wonderland*. Furthermore people themselves, and particularly women, are treated like objects—sawn in half, hurled against walls, ejected from spaceships, and so on. Méliès's treatment of the inanimate world prefigures that of the Surrealists and it is no accident that many Surrealist artists took a particular interest in cinema. But it is also a poignant testimony to the insecurities of *fin de siècle* society, of a social

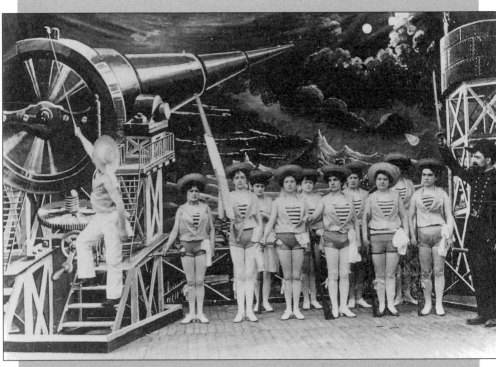

**Georges Méliès *Voyage dans la lune* (1902)**

As this still from his most celebrated film suggests, Méliès combined a fascination with new technology with a keen sense of showmanship. The girls in sailor suits come straight from the vaudeville and music-hall and prefigure the formation dancers in American musicals of the 1930s in which the female body is treated as an abstract figure. Here the dancers add erotic spice by showing off their legs and serve to underscore the oneiric qualities of Méliès's moon shot. The theatrical antecedents of Méliès's cinema are clearly visible in the painted backdrop and the staged disposition of the figures, while the discrepancies of scale owe much to his experiments with film, and the range of compositional incongruities point up the appeal that his films were later to have for the Surrealists.

structure threatened on all sides by apparently uncontrollable forces where certainties of scale and time are profoundly disturbed, and where the unexpected lurks just around the corner.

Predictably, there was entrenched resistance to this new spellbinding form of popular culture from the intellectual moralists who tended to regard cinema as a medium which, at best, pandered to childish illusions, or, at worst, reduced the viewers to a state of passivity, enthralled them in a world of harmful fantasy, and prevented them from becoming full and active citizens. Indeed, the mass consumer culture of shopping, leisure, and entertainment provoked widespread fear and contempt among the intelligentsia and the defenders of the moral order. The new world of consumption was often depicted as destructive of morality and identity. The very act of shopping in the big new department stores of the kind depicted in Zola's novel *Au Bonheur des dames* (1883) brought with it anxieties over the moral well-being of bourgeois ladies who, it was feared, would be seduced into a *louche* existence of kleptomania and prostitution.

This censure of consumerism was matched by the critique of mass culture to be found in the work of Decadent artists whose aestheticism, typified by the character Des Esseintes in Huysmans's novel *A Rebours*, expressed their disgust at the degradation of democratic society but also the 'futility of an isolated effort to escape the mass market, the impossibility of wholly autonomous consumption cut off from the rest of society, the spurious nature of pride in being above the ordinary run of mankind' (Williams, *Dream Worlds*, 151).

Yet whatever the fears of élites, there is little doubt that in the period 1870–1914 large numbers of people experienced not just considerable material gains but also vastly increased opportunities for access to forms of leisure, culture and entertainment not just in the theatre, the music-halls, the *café-concerts*, and the cinemas, but also through the development of holidays and tourism, as well as sporting activities such as cycling and gymnastics. Paris, and especially the district of Montmartre, became the capital of pleasure and entertainment with its dance halls, cabarets, and circuses, such as Le Moulin rouge, Les Folies Bergères, Le Chat noir, and Le Cirque Médrano, and the most celebrated images of the period remain the publicity posters produced by Toulouse-Lautrec and Jules Chéret for these popular entertainments. Leisure and 'idleness' were justified as a 'right' by theorists such as Paul Lafarge in his *Le Droit à la paresse* (1883), although it was not until several decades later under the Popular Front that the right to leisure was embodied in legislation which guaranteed all employees paid holidays.

The massive late nineteenth-century expansion of the world of leisure, consumption, and popular culture has presented modern cultural historians—as it did the nineteenth-century defenders of the moral order—with special problems. One of the most telling ironies in the modern academic critique of late nineteenth-century intellectual, cultural, and political life is that, while highlighting the prejudiced, self-interested, and repressive nature of late nineteenth-century intellectual conceptions and artistic representations, modern scholars have often failed to realize that they themselves are engaged in a project of surveillance and control, that they are themselves policing the culture of the past and the present, in the interests of their own particular political ideology. Just as late nineteenth-century defenders of the moral order wanted the domains of leisure and culture to be governed by a high moral sense, so evidently do modern cultural historians, although the criteria of moral and political correctness have inevitably changed over time. What late nineteenth-century defenders of the moral order share with modern radical historians is a suspicion towards the commercialized world of popular culture, leisure, and entertainment, whose enormous growth was such an important aspect of late nineteenth-century French life. Like their nineteenth-century forebears, modern cultural historians have refused to see culture and leisure as relatively free areas in which individuals express themselves and take their pleasures. Nineteenth-century 'regulationists' saw culture and leisure as occasions for barbarism, immorality, excess, and potential subversiveness. Modern radical historians have tended to see them exclusively as the sites of prejudice, domination, and repression. What underlies both points of view is a shared puritanism, a moral earnestness which is repelled by a society in which matters of moral conscience and social responsibility seem to be flouted in what appears to the moralists as the universal pursuit of material goods and cheap sensations (sexual and cultural).

A more satisfactory approach is to be found in the work of the historian Rosalind Williams. She can find no sympathy for the aesthetic, extreme individualistic, and aristocratic response to mass culture, but she is highly receptive to the solidarist search for a new social and communal morality, as represented in the work of economists like Charles Gide, crowd psychologists like Gabriel Tarde, and sociologists such as Émile Durkheim, attracted by their commitment to elaborating a new social morality, but also their belief in the need to embrace 'a creative, active, shared austerity'. In identifying Stoicism as absolutely central to the ideas of late nineteenth-century French intellectuals, Williams no doubt comes much closer to a real understanding of the period than all those cultural historians who have seen in their stringent and austere idealism veiled forms of social, cultural, and political power:

Of all the ancient philosophies, Stoicism proved the most pertinent to the dilemmas of the modern consumer. In its counsel of detachment from material things, based on a theoretical distinction between the active soul and passive matter, the Stoics directly addressed the question of the proper relationship between a person and his possessions. Furthermore, their distinction between soul and matter led to an ethical code nearly identical with the Christian one which was based on a religious distinction between spirit and flesh. To turn-of-the century French intellectuals who were not Christian believers, Stoicism had great appeal, for it supported traditional Christian virtues, such as poverty, discipline of desire, and scorn for carnal pleasures, without recourse to supernatural sanctions. (*Dream Worlds*, 252–3)

The intellectuals, the politicians, and the professional classes were all deeply imbued with a philosophy of asceticism, and it was austerity and self-denial that they tried to teach the masses, as the way to create morally and socially responsible citizens.

## References

**Bernheimer, Charles**, *Figures of Ill Repute: Representing Prostitution in Nineteenth Century France* (Cambridge, Mass.: Harvard University Press, 1989).

**Clayson, Hollis**, *Painted Love: Prostitution in French Art of the Impressionist Era* (New Haven: Yale University Press, 1991).

**Corbin, Alain**, *Les Filles de noce* (Paris: Aubier Montaigne, 1978); trans. Alan Sheridan as *Women for Hire: Prostitution and Sexuality in France after 1850* (Cambridge, Mass.: Harvard University Press, 1990).

**Harris, Ruth**, *Murders and Madness: Medicine, Law and Society in the Fin de siècle* (Cambridge, Mass.: Harvard University Press, 1989).

**Nora, Pierre** (ed.), *Les Lieux de mémoire*, 7 vols. (Paris: Gallimard, 1984–92), vol. i: *La République*.

**Pollock, Griselda**, *Vision and Difference: Femininity, Feminism and the Histories of Art* (London: Routledge, 1988).

**Williams, Rosalind**, *Dream Worlds: Mass Consumption in Late Nineteenth Century France* (Berkeley and Los Angeles: University of California Press, 1982).

# Wars and Class Wars (1914–1944)

## War and Revolution (1914–1920)

THE thirty years from 1914 to 1944 were some of the most turbulent in France's history. Marked by wars and rumours of war, they stretch from the outbreak of the First World War to the end of the Second. During this time, France's social and political fabric was tested almost to destruction, as it was buffeted by deep-seated contentions both internally and internationally. The efforts of its inhabitants to live with and make sense of this stormy environment are inscribed in the culture of the time. It registers the sense of passion and fragility generated by bitter conflicts, especially between France and its rivals, and between social classes within France. They are conflicts which have continued to haunt France in a variety of forms since that time, investing the images and narratives of these years with a continually renewed life and energy.

The six-year period which opened in August 1914 was characterized above all by the violent clash and intermeshing of national and international politics: by war and revolution. It embraced the Great War, whose bloodiest campaigns were fought on French soil; the Russian Revolution, which echoed throughout the world, and the botched peace which was signed at Versailles. These great struggles were reflected within French society, and were symbolized in the acrimonious division of the French labour movement at its Congress in Tours, in December 1920.

In the initial stages of the war, popular patriotic fervour coalesced around the concept of the 'union sacrée', a broad alliance uniting in a common cause all shades of French public opinion: Republicans, monarchists, socialists, nationalists, Catholics, Jews. Its aim was to preserve national sovereignty and identity from the threat of a warmongering German state. Progressively, however, patriotic fervour dimmed amidst the grisly, murderous reality of trench warfare. The withdrawal of Russian troops from the conflict in the aftermath of the Bolshevik seizure of power, together with the subsequent and decisive American intervention in the war, highlighted the extent to which international politics were increasingly dominating the French national scene.

The end of the war in November 1918 signalled the defeat of Germany and the preservation not only of French territorial integrity but also of the constitutional structures of the Third Republic. But the Versailles settlement underlined at the same time both the conflicting international ambitions of the major powers and the illusions of the majority of the French nation. Most French people sought in escapist fashion to recapture the affluence and well-being of the *belle époque*, rather than confronting the socio-economic realities of the 1920s and 1930s. The split in the socialist movement at the Congrès de Tours in 1920 pitted the revolutionary supporters of Lenin and his Moscow-based Third (Communist) International, on the one hand, against the reformist supporters of Western European social democracy, on the other. It also emphasized the impact of international events on French domestic politics and sowed seeds of class hatred that were to remain for many years to come.

The Great War also fundamentally dislocated traditional patterns of living on the home front. Most dramatically, the terrible carnage wreaked in the trenches left the nation bereft of a generation of young men, compounding the endemic problems of France's low birth-rate that dated back to the mid-nineteenth century. Gender roles were inevitably reversed during the war, women being drawn into the labour market to replace their menfolk at the front, only to be sent back to domesticity once the war was over. These dislocations in patterns of social behaviour occurred at the same time as popular cultural forms were beginning to challenge the hegemony of traditional high art. Alongside poetry, the novel and the theatre, the cinema and the press played an increasingly significant role in cultural production.

The shattering impact of the Great War was reflected to varying degrees and in differing ways in the literature of the time. It has been estimated that over 500 writers died in the conflict, and among them were major figures such as Charles Péguy and Alain-Fournier. A number of prominent literary figures such as André Gide, Marcel Proust, and Paul Valéry kept their distance from hostilities and remained virtually silent. Others, however, such as Paul Bourget and Maurice Barrès, considered that their moral duty as writers was to offer a systematically uplifting and optimistic vision of the war. They promoted a popular patriotism which drew many of its themes from the cult of Jeanne d'Arc, who was eventually canonized in July 1920, nearly 500 years after her death at the hands of the English. Maurice Barrès's *Chronique de la Grande Guerre* offers a particularly striking example of such pro-nationalist sentiment. Equally, a writer such as René Benjamin, whose novel *Gaspard* was awarded the Prix Goncourt in 1915, although less motivated by a sense of nationalistic duty, presented the war as an epic and glorious affair conducted by soldiers whose ideas and emotions were unswervingly patriotic.

In contrast, there were those writers who were simply appalled by the atrocities of the war and who sought to present a realistic account of the life and death struggle of the combatants. Georges Duhamel (*La Vie des martyrs*), Maurice Genevoix (*Ceux de 1914*), Jean Paulhan (*Le Guerrier appliqué*), and Roland Dorgelès (*Les Croix de bois*) fall into this category. Similar portrayals also emerge in the poems of Guillaume Apollinaire, who was himself severely wounded in the fighting and died in 1918. His collection *Calligrammes* combines avant-garde poetic techniques with an intense lyrical evocation of the experience of war.

Finally, there were those few writers who sought not merely to describe the terrifying carnage and brutality of the war, but also to counter the nationalistic warmongering with a message of peace and international solidarity. One of the most notable was the novelist Romain Rolland, who moved to neutral Switzerland and published a series of articles in *Le Journal de Genève*, denouncing the atrocities, brutality, and inhumanity of the war. Undoubtedly, the most effective of the pacifist writers was Henri Barbusse, whose novel *Le Feu* gave perhaps the most striking testimony to the brutality of the Great War, and was awarded the Prix Goncourt in 1916. By 1918 the book was an international best seller with sales in excess of 200,000 copies.

*Le Feu* constitutes a key literary statement not only on the war itself but also on its aftermath. Written in 1915, the novel is a fictional transposition of Barbusse's personal experiences at the front line, focused on the daily activities of a squad of soldiers on the Western Front. By 1915 the confrontation had degenerated into a military stalemate, a process of attrition in which the war of movement had been replaced by an endless struggle in the trenches. What emerges from *Le Feu* is the author's undying respect and sympathy for the front-line soldiers subjected to the bestiality of war:

They are not soldiers: they are men. They are not adventurers, warriors, made for human butchery—butchers or cattle. They are recognizably ploughmen and workmen in their uniforms. They are uprooted civilians. They are ready. They wait for the signal of death and murder . . . but you can see, looking at their faces between the vertical rows of bayonets, that they are simply men. (trans. from Flammarion edn., 201)

Barbusse's opposition to all forms of mystification and exploitation linked to the war also emerges with searing clarity. Whether it be the deceptions and falsehoods of the nationalistic, propagandist reporting of the war (pp. 34–5), or the

## Lookout man at the loophole

There are two enduring images of the First World War: muddy battlefields strewn with corpses, and the trenches. For most of the soldiers, most of the time, the trenches were their daily reality, a deeply ambiguous experience. On the one hand, they were a relatively secure place of shelter from the shells and bullets, and all too often the only way out was to go over the top into the muddy battlefields of no man's land. On the other hand, they were an appalling environment in which men had to live for weeks on end with little protection from the elements, from vermin, or from disease. Even the shelter from military hazards was only relative, as the trenches were vulnerable to gas attacks, and snipers on both sides constantly sought to pick off unwary inhabitants in the trenches opposite. The ambiguities are evoked in this postcard, where the lookout is apparently caught unawares by the camera as he looks out over the battlefield of Verdun. The loophole through which the soldier looks can also provide an opportunity for the enemy sniper to take an accurate or lucky shot. The reader perhaps gains some aesthetic distance from the subject by feeling that it may have been deliberately posed.

deep-rooted social and military injustice that separated those risking their lives at the front line and those 'sheltering' on the home front (pp. 93–108), Barbusse is unequivocal in his condemnation. What remains in the mind, however, are the graphic descriptions of men dying at war, a war transformed not merely by the introduction of new armaments, notably the machine-gun, but also by a military strategy of attrition in which the objective was not primarily to take possession of military targets, but simply and crudely to kill as many enemy soldiers as possible: 'This plain, which then gave me the impression of being all on a level and which, in reality, was on a slope, is an extraordinary charnel house. Bodies are lying everywhere. It is like a cemetery with the top taken off' (p. 219). The graphic description of the death and destruction of modern warfare which then follows is symptomatic of the traumatizing impact of the entire experience on Barbusse the writer. Not only did the proximity of death bring him face to face with his own mortality, but also it pushed him towards the need to record what had happened as a testimony and as a warning, lest the world forget the senseless brutality of it all. The final section of the novel, entitled 'L'Aube', frequently criticized as excessively ideologically motivated, is none the less understandable, given its moment of production in 1915. Barbusse wished to call to account those whom he perceived as the real culprits of the war: 'entire peoples are going to the slaughter, in their herds, so that a caste of gold-braided princes can write their names in the history books' (p. 281). He also wanted to demythologize war itself: 'Heroes, some sort of extraordinary people, idols. Come now! We were butchers. We did an honest job of butchering' (p. 285). These are not only an expression of pacifist and internationalist sentiments, they are at the same time an explanation of the subsequent development of the French labour movement. It is often suggested that the principal reason motivating those who opted in 1920 for the Third International was the disillusionment of a majority of ex-soldiers. They responded to the Bolshevik ideal of Lenin and spurned the tarnished compromises of the social-democratic Second International, which had supported the war.

Barbusse's demystification of the war in Le Feu chimed with the widespread disillusionment expressed in other countries at the same period. It continued to echo throughout later fictional accounts of the Great War, such as may be found in Céline's Voyage au bout de la nuit (1932), Drieu la Rochelle's Comédie de Charleroi (1934), Giono's Le Grand Troupeau (1931), Martin du Gard's L'Été 1914 (1936), Romain's Prélude à Verdun (1937) and Verdun (1938), and many others.

The conditions of war also placed considerable constraints on the freedom of expression available to writers and other cultural producers. Censorship was a crucial issue for cinematic production and press publications between 1914 and 1918. The French film industry was undoubtedly transformed by the outbreak of hostilities in 1914. On the one hand, outlets for French films were severely restricted: the central European market was immediately closed off, and the British market was increasingly abandoned to Hollywood film production. On the other hand, when the major film companies, Gaumont and Pathé, resumed production in 1915 after the threat of a German invasion of Paris had passed, the emphasis was on propaganda. Films such as *Pour la France* and *Sous l'uniforme* were aimed at bolstering the resolve of the French public. Although subsequently there was a return to the successful serial films of the pre-war period, such as *Les Vampires* by Louis Feuillade, the exploitation of the cinema as a means of instruction and entertainment during wartime remained a contentious issue. It needs to be noted, for example, that theatres in Paris were closed in order to ensure that they were not a source of discontent to soldiers on the front line. Cinemas remained open, however, and were extremely popular. They also attracted large numbers of students and young intellectuals such as the later Surrealist leaders Louis Aragon, Philippe Soupault, Paul Éluard, and André Breton. They were an attraction for children, and Jean-Paul Sartre, for example, remembered with nostalgia his childhood visits in the company of his mother to the Parisian cinema at this time, in his autobiography *Les Mots*.

There also emerged around the figure of Louis Delluc an avant-garde film movement centred notably on the work of Léon Poirier, Jacques de Baroncelli, and Abel Gance. Gance was undoubtedly the dominant personality of the French cinema industry towards the end of the war, as was graphically illustrated in the film *J'accuse*, completed in 1919. Although produced in conjunction with official military circles, the film constitutes both an attack on the bestiality and hardship of war itself, and a critical comparison between the suffering of the front-line soldiers and the perceived indifference of those on the home front. Gance described himself as aspiring to be the 'Victor Hugo and Henri Barbusse of the Great War'. He comes close in *J'accuse* to realizing his ambition. In the central scene of the film, the main protagonist, called J'accuse, invokes the dead to rise up and fight against the injustices perpetrated by a nation which had allowed them to die in brutal combat, whilst more privileged social groups were shielded from suffering far from the trenches. Gance's somewhat extravagant cinematic style captures perfectly the sense of rebellion and disenchantment experienced by front-line soldiers towards the end of the war. It also has striking similarities to Jean Renoir's later and better-known evocation of the Great War in his film *La Grande Illusion* (1937).

Although the cinema unquestionably played a significant role in projecting images of the war, it was doubtless the popular daily press with its huge readership which shaped public opinion most substantially. In *Le Feu*, for example, Barbusse describes front-line soldiers eagerly reading newspaper reports of the war despite the fact that they were fully aware that the reports themselves were no more than lies and propaganda (p. 35). In the pre-broadcasting epoch of 1914–18, when information was acquired principally from newsprint sources, circulation figures of several million were not unusual. The circulation, for example, of *Le Petit Parisien* on 12 November 1918, the day on which the signing of the armistice was reported, was in excess of three million copies. Although the printed texts themselves survive purely as historical documents, the extent to which newspapers such as *Le Petit Parisien* influenced public opinion during the war is consequently immeasurable. Equally, given the fact, for example, that throughout the war Jean Dupuy, the owner of *Le Petit Parisien*, worked in close collaboration with the government of the day, on occasions assuming ministerial office, it is hardly surprising that the role of a large section of the press was principally one of propaganda support for the French government and the French state. The ideological tenor of press publications none the less varied enormously. Nationalist sentiments were vigorously proclaimed in *L'Écho de Paris* and *L'Action française*. New publications such as *L'Œuvre* and *Le Canard enchaîné*, in contrast, began towards the end of the war to offer an alternative to such nationalistic brainwashing. Barbusse's *Le Feu*, for example, was published in serialized though censored form in *L'Œuvre* from August 1916.

The end of the war in 1918 and the signing of the Versailles peace settlement in 1919 brought into the open deep-seated cleavages not only between the various members of the international community, but also between divergent social and political factions within France. Victory over Germany appeared at one level a vindication of French nationalism. The obligation placed on a defeated German nation to pay extensive war reparations, together with the imposition of a demilitarized zone, lulled the majority of French people into a false sense of security. Others, however, were less complacent, particularly those who had directly experienced the trauma of the war at the front line and who considered that a reliance on the discredited values of nationalism was now unthinkable. Such views were held not merely by Rolland and Barbusse, but also by potentially more radical intellectuals such as Raymond Lefebvre. Lefebvre angrily articulated his views in the opening paragraph of his pamphlet *La Révolution ou la mort*, published in 1920:

*Revolution or Death*: I am not the one who is shouting it out to you, it is your century, it is your masters, who are fomenting your destruction. *Revolution or Death*: that is the choice you are left with after four years of war, an insane treaty, and an unbridled caste which is now ten times stronger than before, which has lost all interest in your survival, which is terrified by your ability to organise yourself, which looks with hatred on the awakening of your consciousness of the justice of your cause, and which squanders the resources of a dying dictatorship on the work of wrecking what it is still pleased to call *its country*.

Lefebvre was drowned in the Baltic Sea on his way back to France after attending the ten-nation Proletarian Culture conference in Moscow in August 1920. He consequently did not participate in the socialist Congrès de Tours held in December 1920, at which a majority of the French labour movement decided to align itself with Lenin's Third International, thereby creating a fundamental division between socialists (SFIO) and communists (PCF). Although not present at the Congress, Lefebvre, like so many of his intellectual peers on the French Left, scarred by the war, disillusioned by the hollowness and sterility of a self-interested nationalism, yearning for a new beginning, would almost certainly have committed himself to the class struggle of the Third International.

The impact of the Great War on artists and intellectuals should not be underestimated. The carnage, brutality, and destruction of 1914–18 forced an entire generation of French men and women to confront the bitter reality of their individual and social existence. Not only were they brought face to face with the awe-inspiring destructive capability of modern weaponry, which itself engendered a sense of human frailty, but they were also obliged to reassess fundamental beliefs and allegiances to nation and to class. The war was, in short, a deeply traumatic experience which left a far-reaching cultural legacy.

## Les Années folles (1920–1929)

It is a commonplace that France emerged from the First World War massively damaged, physically, economically, and emotionally. A total of 1.3 million active males had been killed in the four years of hostilities, with a further 1.1 million seriously wounded and constituting a heavy economic burden on the state. The population in 1921, at 31,210,000, was critically low and below the figure for 1891, with severe consequences for industrial recovery and national security. The battlegrounds and the occupied territories of the north and east were devastated and required complete rebuilding. In addition to the costs of war damage, and the consequent losses in agricultural and industrial production, France came out of the war hugely indebted, with a deficit of 110,000 million francs in gold. Emotionally, the nation as a whole was forced to come to terms with mass bereavement, with the consequences of four years of uncertainty, deprivation, and suffering, with incompetence and profiteering by those in power, and with deep divisions within the army and industry. At the same time, this battered, impoverished, and apparently disunited country was about to enter a decade of unparalleled industrial expansion and economic growth, in which the French as a whole showed considerable ability in adapting to the new conditions of the post-war world. It was only halted by France's export-led recovery being vulnerable to international trade conditions, and in particular to the international aftermath of the 1929 Wall Street Crash, which reached France in 1931.

In the 1920s, in spite of a failure to reduce both the agricultural sector and the predominance of artisanal production in consumer-goods manufacture, the French were able to expand their steel industry, vastly aided by the return of Alsace and Lorraine, though too heavily reliant on German coking coal. They were able to develop modern automobile manufacture, with the pre-war producers Renault, Panhard, and Peugeot being joined to Citroën to make France the largest motorcar manufacturer in Europe, with 245,610 models produced in 1929. They were also able to create an up-to-date chemical industry. The inevitable inflation resulting from the combination of post-war debt and accelerated expansion was successfully brought under control by Poincaré's stabilization of the franc in 1926.

Not surprisingly, this economic boom of the 1920s, engendered by adaptation to, rather than fear of, the new world, was reflected in French culture at all levels. At the same time, however, the darker effects of the French war experience made themselves felt within that very same culture. The war itself is also a salutary reminder of the independence and imperturbability of cultural evolution in the face of even the most dramatic of historical forces. Alongside the cultural innovation and experimentation of the 1920s can be seen a clear pattern of continuity from the pre-war era: the triumph of Cubism in the 1920s was the consecration of experiments begun in the first years of the century; the post-war avant-garde had its origins in pre-war Futurism; the dominant literary and intellectual journal of the inter-war period, *La Nouvelle Revue française*, was similarly the product of the 1900s.

If the image of French culture in the 1920s as one delighting in experimentation and the modern masks a more complex pattern of continuity, nostalgia, and uncertainty, it also conceals two further crucial divisions: between high and low culture, and between Paris and the regions. The emphasis upon formal experimentation and aesthetic complexity tended to limit still further the accessibility of high culture and to increase the divide between it and a popular culture growing in organization and technical sophistication. Similarly, in the 1920s French high culture remained an essentially Parisian culture, with only sporadic and, largely, assimilated regional manifestations, such as Ramuz and the francophone Swiss modernists, or Pagnol and Marseilles.

In all the arts constituting this Parisian high culture the modern dominated in the 1920s. In the novel it was symbolized by the, mostly posthumous, publication of Proust's *A la recherche du temps perdu* as an annual literary event until the appearance of *Le Temps retrouvé* (1927), and by Gide's modernist classic *Les Faux-monnayeurs* (1926). Less adventurous at a formal level, Colette helped to open up the literary exploration of sexuality, particularly from a female perspective, in her novels *Chéri* (1920) and *La Fin de Chéri* (1926). At the same time, the avant-garde continued both to exploit and to denigrate the cultural élitism implied by modernism. The installation in Paris in 1920 of Tristan Tzara, the founder of the Dada movement in Zurich during the war, brought to France a familiar mixture of the classic ingredients of the pre-war avant-garde: loathing of the bourgeoisie and its institutions, rejection of that bourgeoisie's fossilization of art in a narrow definition of high culture, an ambiguous but real enthusiasm for the mechanical properties of the new century, and, in the light of the European conflagration, a hatred of militarism and war. Tzara was adopted on his arrival in Paris by the editors of the journal *Littérature*, André Breton, Louis Aragon, and Philippe Soupault, who rapidly moved beyond the negativism which was the chief fuel of Dada to a more constructive concept of avant-garde art which was to become Surrealism.

Breton's *Manifeste du surréalisme* (1924) set out the essential Surrealist beliefs in a metaphysics and aesthetics rooted in the unconscious and released by chance associations. The theory relies heavily on a certain reading of Freud, but moves far beyond this to a fascination with all forms of irrationality which unlock the

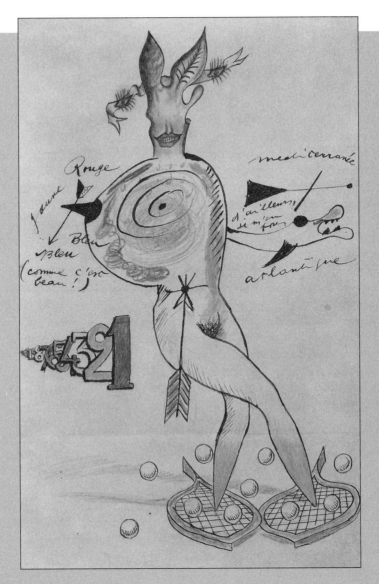

## Exquisite corpse

Surrealism explored all manner of techniques for jolting human awareness out of limited everyday perceptions to open itself up to the realms of super-reality. Many of these tricks, traps, or shocks were aimed at juxtaposing apparently unrelated items so as to evoke hidden layers of experience within which the items could be seen as related. One such device, similar to the party game 'Consequences', required successive participants to add a word or image to previous ones which they had not seen. It was named 'Cadavre exquis' after an early verbal version produced the sentence 'the exquisite corpse will drink the new wine'. The example shown here, from 1927 or 1928, is a composite drawing by leading Surrealist artists Joan Miró, Yves Tanguy, Man Ray, and Max Morise. Like much early Surrealist work, it emphasized the collective nature of the activity rather than an individual author, and it was unconcerned with the commercial value of the product, almost to the point of regarding commercial success as a betrayal. The drawing exemplifies many typical Surrealist preoccupations, including the female body, passion and desire, human links with the animal and vegetable worlds, mutilation, dream, and the relations between image, text, and numbers.

door to a higher reality: the 'sur-real'. Initially, the movement was conceived of as exclusively literary; embodying automatic writing, group composition, and images drawn from dazzlingly improbable juxtapositions, but also celebrating such concepts as 'l'amour fou' or inviting the reader to look anew at hitherto unrecognized features of the Parisian cityscape, as in Aragon's *Le Paysan de Paris* (1926). Almost simultaneously, however, it became a vehicle for the visual arts, with the photography of Man Ray and the painting of figures as disparate as Salvador Dali, Giorgio de Chirico, Max Ernst, and Jean Arp. Visually, the cultivation of automatism was pursued through techniques such as Arp's use of collage, but more generally Surrealist painting based itself upon a carefully constructed transposition of the state of dream or nightmare. Nor were the Surrealists slow to recognize the possibilities offered by new mechanical art-forms: Man Ray's experiments with photography; Dali's use of air-brush technique; and, particularly, Luis Buñuel's exploitation of the possibilities of cinema in *Un chien andalou* (1928), and *L'Âge d'or* (1930). What is significant about Surrealism is that it combines the ability to outrage, as in Marcel Duchamp's early exhibit of a urinal, with a genuinely constructive exploration of the aesthetic properties of the unconscious in a movement which was highly cosmopolitan. It was also surprisingly durable, and the prominence of former Surrealists such as Jacques Prévert, Raymond Queneau, and Marcel Duhamel, the founder of Gallimard's 'Série noire', was a major cultural characteristic of France just after the Second World War.

In painting, as in literature, the 1920s witnessed the triumph of the modern: the lessons of Cézanne had taken root and given rise to two distinct but interrelated lines of development, both rejecting the representational ambitions of Impressionism and experimenting with formal composition in shape and colour: the 'Fauves', Matisse, Derain, and Vlaminck, who, with Georges Rouault and Chagall, retained the notion of the subject; and the Cubists, Picasso, Braque, and Léger, who fully exploited Cézanne's dictum that all nature could be reduced to the sphere, the cone, and the cube. Representational art was now confined to the growing importance of the French photographers, led by Henri Cartier-Bresson.

In fact, the consecration of Cubism, nearly twenty years after its avant-garde inception in Picasso's *Les Demoiselles d'Avignon* in 1907, came, not merely through increased prices at the art-dealers, but in one of the single most significant cultural phenomena of France in the 1920s: the *Exposition des arts décoratifs*, held in Paris in 1925, and the style it enshrined, 'art deco', which brought into the world of design at all levels the formal principles of Cubism. Nor was this restricted to posters, furniture, and household objects: at the 1925 exhibition, the young architect and Cubist painter Le Corbusier revealed his plans for a functionally redesigned Paris, and went on to found the International Style in architecture with the Villa Stein, at Garches, in 1927, built for Gertrude Stein's brother, and the Villa Savoie at Poissy, built between 1929 and 1931.

Musically, the 1920s saw the same pattern as that operating in literature and the visual arts and comprising essentially a rejection of both nineteenth-century tradition and Impressionism, embodied in the work of Maurice Ravel and, especially, in the grouping of younger composers, among them Honegger, Milhaud, and Poulenc, under the title 'Les Six'. In his manifesto for the group, in 1918, Jean Cocteau emphasized the need to break away from the influence of Debussy and to adopt instead the lessons of jazz. This modernizing tendency in French music was amplified by the presence in Paris in the 1920s of exiled composers such as Stravinsky and Prokofiev, who helped make the French capital the most exciting musical centre in the world. At the same time, however, it is worth recalling that French music in the 1920s, experimental as it was, never moved outside the established tradition of Western harmonies, unlike the German composers of the same period, Schoenberg, Webern, and Berg. In the realm of ballet, considerable innovation continued through the work of Diaghilev, permanently exiled in Paris after the 1917 Revolution, which involved collaboration between musicians, writers, such as Cocteau, and painters, such as Picasso. Indeed, Diaghilev's troupe is an important reminder both of the way in which artistic modernism in Paris in the 1920s crossed formal boundaries and of its essentially cosmopolitan nature: Paris, after the war, was, with Berlin, the pre-eminent cultural centre. Montparnasse, with its artists like Picasso, Modigliani and Chagall, and its American writers like Hemingway and Scott Fitzgerald, took over the role of pre-war Montmartre as the capital's cultural centre of gravity, beginning the intellectual and cultural dominance of the Left Bank which was to last into the 1960s.

If the 1920s is an extraordinary decade of productivity and experimentation in all forms of high culture, it is also the scene for an unprecedented organization and expansion of popular culture, often the result of the availability of new technologies. In popular music, the decade saw the transition from the dominance of the street singers and sheet music, epitomized by Benech and Dumont's compositions *Du gris* (1920) and *Nuits de Chine* (1922), to gramophone recordings. It also witnessed the shift from the more intimate *café-concert* to the more spectacular music-hall, and the creation of new stars, such as Mistinguett, Lucienne Boyer, whose 'Parlez-moi d'amour', along with Maurice Chevalier's 'Valentine', was the hit of 1925, and Joséphine Baker. Musically, the 1920s was dominated by the popularity of jazz, imported from the United States at the end of the war and impinging on both high and popular culture, and by the one authentic indigenous dance-form, the Java.

The greatest challenge to sheet music and the street singers was in the form of radio, which began permanent popular music broadcasts in 1926. The first private radio station, Radiola, later to become Radio-Paris, was inaugurated under the direction of Émile Girardeau on 6 November 1922, broadcasting from the Eiffel Tower, and was followed by private regional stations in Lyons, Agen, and Fécamp in 1924 and in Bordeaux, Toulouse, and Montpellier in 1925. In Paris, Radiola was rapidly accompanied by other stations, such as Radio-Vitus and Radio LL. Initially, these stations broadcast news and sports coverage, often in collaboration with powerful daily newspapers, such as *Le Petit Parisien*, which inaugurated its own station in 1924, but they also broadcast concert programmes. By the end of the 1920s, even though there were only 600,000 radio receivers in 1928, radio was poised to become a major media force in the 1930s.

Unquestionably, however, the dominant form of modern popular entertainment was cinema, silent throughout the 1920s but ready to break into sound with René Clair's *Le Million* (1931). Although France had lost its pre-war dominance in popular cinema production to Hollywood, it still continued to make highly successful popular feature films, with directors such as Bernard Deschamps, Raymond Bernard, Diamant-Berger, and Henry Roussel. Popular successes of the period included Henri Fescourt's *Les Misérables* (1925), Léonce Perret's *Koenigsmark* (1924), and his *Madame sans Gêne* (1925), starring Gloria Swanson. It was, however, in the experimental and art cinema that the French excelled in the 1920s. Cinema became an automatic vehicle for the avant-garde and the subversive, with products such as Buñuel's *Un chien andalou* (1928) and Vigo's *A propos de Nice* (1929), but also established itself as a serious major art-form, particularly under the influence of the critic Louis Delluc, who directed a number of major films in the early 1920s, and Abel Gance, who, with films like *J'accuse* (1919), *La Roue* (1922), and especially *Napoléon* (1927), became the single greatest director of the decade. At the same time, the period saw the silent-film production of a number of directors who were to achieve considerable reputations in the sound era: Jacques Feyder, Jean Renoir, whose *Nana* appeared in 1926, and René Clair, whose *Un chapeau de paille d'Italie* (1927) remains a classic of the silent cinema. It is worth bearing in mind that the cosmopolitanism of French cultural life in the 1920s, which was so valuable to literature, music, and the visual arts, also impinged upon French cinema, with the actor-director Ivan Mosjoukine and the director Alexander Volkoff, who produced a version of *Edmund Kean* in 1924.

If French popular culture in the 1920s benefited from enhanced technology and organization in all fields, nowhere was this more visible than in sport. Association football became organized in 1919 into the Fédération française de football association (FFFA), with the establishment of Colombes as the national ground; rugby was similarly organized, with the foundation in 1920 of the Fédération française du rugby (FFR), and encouraged the following year by the recommencement of the Five Nations Tournament involving France, England, Wales, Scotland, and Ireland. Cycling continued its pre-war success as a major participant and, especially, spectator sport, with the expansion in popularity of the Tour de France and establishments such as the 'Vél'd'hiv', the Vélodrome d'hiver in Paris. Internationally, France's reputation rode high: Paris hosted the 1924 Olympic Games; Georges Carpentier won the World Light-Heavyweight Championship in 1919, before being knocked out by Jack Dempsey in 1921; and, in tennis, the 'Mousquetaires' Borotra, Brugnon, Cochet, and Lacoste, whose nickname 'le Crocodile' was to give rise to an advertising icon of another era with his sportswear company, became international stars in the 1926 Davis Cup.

If French culture in the post-war era reflected, at both popular and high-cultural level, the ability of the nation to come to terms with a modern world and modern technologies, its high culture particularly also conveyed an undercurrent of severe disquiet, combining the profound destabilization wrought by the war itself and a certain nostalgia for a past life-style now irretrievably lost—it was in the 1920s, after all, that the term 'belle époque' was coined to describe the 1900s, and, with one 'entre-deux-guerres' already experienced, that between 1871 and 1914, France had the uneasy sensation of entering a similar period in which the 'War to end all wars' was merely the prelude to the next. This unease became rapidly articulated, under the influence of Nietzsche, Spengler, and the Freud of *Civilisation and its Discontents*, as a wide-ranging pessimism regarding the future of Western civilization itself. In 1919, in a series of essays in the *Nouvelle Revue française* entitled 'La Crise de l'esprit', Paul Valéry reflected on the possibility of Europe joining the great civilizations of the past as a mere stage in human development and painted a bleak picture of European culture in a post-war world in a state of Hamlet-like intellectual paralysis. Proust's *A la recherche du temps perdu*, whilst being a triumph of modernist fiction, is also the picture of a 'Heartbreak House of capitalist culture', swept away by the war and leaving the ghostly remnants of *Le Temps retrouvé*. For the younger generation of French writers, the problem of the disappearance of a firm cultural base was compounded by the way in which they found themselves in a position analogous to that of the first generation of Romantics: the 'mal du siècle' which informed and poisoned the perceptions of those born in 1800, who came to maturity just after the fall of Napoleon, was repeated in the 'nouveau mal du siècle', formulated by Marcel Arland in an essay of 1924, in which a similar generation, born at the beginning of the twentieth century, was brought up in the heroic atmosphere of the Great War with a philosophical and moral set of values which was totally inappropriate to peacetime existence. It is in the context of this 'nouveau mal du siècle' that the vocabulary of 1940s existentialism and the concept of the absurd first appear, encapsulated in Malraux's essay of 1926 *La Tentation de l'Occident* and 'D'une jeunesse européenne', of the following year, which combine a vivid depiction of the intellectual paralysis in which his generation finds itself with a broader evocation of the bankruptcy of Western values.

This generational crisis, which forms part of a larger debate on civilization which goes back at least as far as the pre-war avant-garde's discovery of Pacific sculpture, carried within it its own solution: if intellectual reflection is pointless in the face of intellectual paralysis, positive values may still be sought in the non-intellectual and the concrete, in action rather than thought. Once again, in the emphasis on deed as the defining characteristic of human identity, the 1920s anticipates the key element of existentialism. The combination of the themes of action and cultural relativism in the post-war period succeed in producing a powerful fictional subgenre, that of the adventure novel. The 1920s was the period of Joseph Conrad's greatest influence in France: on his death in 1924 the *Nouvelle Revue française* produced a special number in his honour. Conrad's explorations into various hearts of darkness were subsequently taken up by writers as different as Malraux himself, Saint-Exupéry, the Céline of *Voyage au bout de la nuit* (1932), Paul Morand, and, his most perceptive commentator, Pierre Mac Orlan.

Amongst intellectuals, this issue of civilization came to dominate the 1920s. The French Communist Party, the PCF, founded in 1920, represents an attempt to overthrow bourgeois Western culture and replace it with a new civilization. In the 1920s, however, as opposed to the 1930s, the direct cultural impact of the PCF was limited: the party, in the ten years following the Congrès de Tours, was a small, tightly knit, workers' party, with essentially social and political, rather than cultural, aims. Despite the policy of Moscow, from 1927 onwards, to encourage Western communist parties to develop their own proletarian literature, the PCF showed little interest initially in fostering working-class culture within France, and the only French communist outlet of any major cultural significance was the weekly journal *Monde* established in 1928 by the author of *Le Feu*, Henri Barbusse. It was not until the international crises of the 1930s that the PCF established itself as a key cultural element on the Left. Nevertheless, there was one spectacular recruitment: at the end of the decade, some of the Surrealists, particularly Aragon and Éluard, saw enough common ground between the 'révolution surréaliste' and the 'révolution prolétarienne' to join the party. Impelled to political involvement by revulsion against the French colonial war in the North African Rif (1921–6), their alliance with communism was on the face of it as implausible as their annexation of Freud but, especially in the case of Aragon, proved remarkably durable.

Unsurprisingly, the French Right was disturbed both by the growing assault on Western values and by the emergence of the communist party, which, to them, was merely the representative in France of an alien, barbarian power. It is important to bear in mind, however, that in matters cultural, as well as in matters political, the Right was by no means in a minority. Indeed, politically it was the dominance of the Right in government, in spite of electoral parity, which contributed to disaffection in the 1930s. The ascendancy gained by the nationalist *Bloc national* grouping in the elections of 1920 was so overwhelming that the parliament became known as the 'Chambre bleu horizon', a reference to the colour of military dress uniforms. It was interrupted by the election in 1924 of the centre-left *Cartel des gauches*, but rapidly restored in 1926 with the return of Poincaré as Prime Minister. The 1920s was also the period of greatest power of Action française, a movement which, like the PCF on the Left, proved markedly more attractive to right-wing intellectuals than the Republican Right. Action française's claim to constitute the 'Parti de l'intelligence' was not merely an assertion of the royalist cause as the only sensible option for post-war France, but a recognition that the movement carried considerable intellectual weight behind it: not merely was it led by men of some artistic and intellectual ability, including its leader Charles Maurras, the essayist and polemicist Léon Daudet, and the historian Jacques Bainville, but it had attracted, and continued to attract, creative writers as diverse as Georges Bernanos, André Gide, and François Mauriac. What united this intellectual Right was a distaste for Republicanism and parliamentarianism and a passionate belief in the values of the West, epitomized by Henri Massis's essay *Défense de l'Occident* (1927).

As in the case of the PCF on the Left, the cultural impact of French fascist movements in the 1920s—Pierre Taittinger's Jeunesses patriotes and Georges Valois's Le Faisceau—was largely deferred until the 1930s, when Doriot's Parti populaire français (PPF) could attract figures such as Drieu la Rochelle, and when dissidents from Action française, such as Lucien Rebatet and Robert Brasillach, formed the editorial team of the weekly *Je suis partout*. At the same time, it is possible to talk of an essentially right-wing culture, encompassing the attraction for Le Corbusier of a technocratic regime and a more nebulous socialite Right to be found, for example, in the Right Bank night-club Le Bœuf sur le toit, and including figures such as Jean Cocteau and Raymond Radiguet, Paul Morand, François Mauriac, and Drieu la Rochelle.

In fact, there is no figure more representative of French culture in the 1920s than Drieu. He was the disabused ex-combatant of the Great War, who shared the cultural pessimism of his friends Malraux and Marcel Arland; and the intellectual with a keen interest in the avant-garde, in particular the experiments of his friends the Surrealists. He was the future political activist, seeking solutions to the 'nouveau mal du siècle', first on the Left, then on the Right, but never with complete satisfaction; and the writer obsessed with death, and particularly suicide, as in the case of the minor Surrealist and another *habitué* of Le Bœuf sur le toit, Jacques Rigaut. Above all, he was the most accurate chronicler of France's first Jazz Age, its 'années folles', when, beneath the delight in the modern, and frenetic enjoyment of freedom, there lay a growing melancholy and sense of emptiness. If French society successfully negotiated the decade following the war and was able to exploit and enthusiastically embrace the possibilities of the new world, it also stored up problems which would only become apparent in the 1930s. In the same way, the culture of that decade, at all levels, is as dazzling and successful as at any period in French history, but already marked by a sense of its own fragility.

## Crisis and Commitment (1929–1939)

Looking back, it is clear that the 1930s began with the Wall Street Crash of 25 October 1929. At the time this was not generally perceived in France, which was enjoying the illusions of peace and prosperity. In November the Prime Minister, André Tardieu, was announcing new heights of post-war prosperity. But within a year France was following the rest of the developed world into the worst economic depression of modern times, which lasted for most of the decade. By 1938 French economic activity had barely regained the levels of 1913.

The illusion of prosperity was linked to the illusion of peace. In 1930, French troops ended their post-war occupation of the Rhineland and veteran statesman

Aristide Briand proposed a federal European Common Market based on Franco-German co-operation. At the same time, work was started on France's Maginot Line of military defences along the border with Germany, where the National Socialists were becoming the second largest party in the Reichstag. When Adolf Hitler became Chancellor in 1933, there was a dawning suspicion that the post-war had slipped into another pre-war.

Within France, the end of peace and prosperity triggered a polarization of political forces. The far right groupings gained ground. There is some dispute whether paramilitary *ligues* like Colonel de la Rocque's Croix de feu or Charles Maurras's rejuvenated Action française should be considered as fascist. But certainly they looked to Germany and to Mussolini's Italy as models, for values, for policies and strategies, for discipline, organization, and style. On the Left, the small and marginal French Communist Party (PCF) abandoned the more sectarian policies urged on it by the Third International's 'class against class' strategy, and began to make overtures to socialist and centrist groupings it had previously denounced as social-fascist. As a result, the PCF rapidly increased its popular support.

The high point of the *ligues* was 6 February 1934, when they organized a protest against suspected government involvement in the Stavisky Affair. This small-time criminal, who apparently had connections in high places, had died in mysterious circumstances. He was adopted as a symbol of scandal and corruption in government, and as a pretext to challenge the republican constitution. The protest march became a riot and almost a *coup d'état*, in which 15 people were killed and 2,000 injured. The Prime Minister was replaced, but the events triggered a joint response of left-of-centre parties and groups to defend the Republic, which rapidly coalesced into a broad anti-fascist movement. A succession of weak and divided centre-right cabinets provided the opportunity for this alliance to unite in a *Rassemblement populaire* dominated by the communist, socialist, and radical (that is, liberal) parties.

The movement of unity attracted a number of leading writers, artists, and intellectuals, who were energized by its spirit of freedom, social change, and humanitarianism. A key moment of the campaign was the offer of the PCF leader, Maurice Thorez, to join hands with Catholic workers and intellectuals, who had previously been the object of anti-religious attacks. Though Thorez's *main tendue* was only taken up by a small minority of Catholics at the time, it signalled the beginning of a longer-term *rapprochement* which ultimately shifted the centre of gravity of French Catholicism from Right to Left.

This coalition won a slender majority in the 1936 parliamentary elections and, though the communists declined to enter the cabinet, a *Front populaire* government was formed under the socialist leader Léon Blum. On a wave of popular enthusiasm, it introduced a programme of social reform, including the five-day week and paid holidays for workers. In the longer term, these were important steps towards increasing opportunities for most French people to participate in cultural activities during their leisure time. It provided enormous momentum for travel, leisure cycling, walking, climbing, water sports, camping, caravanning, the commercial development of mountain and seaside resorts, and the institution of the 'colonies de vacances', providing summer camps for workers' children. These changes, together with measures aimed to clamp down on paramilitary organizations, and to improve employment, health, and social services, in due course gave the *Front populaire* a mythical status, on the Left as a utopian vision, and on the Right as a nightmare scenario.

In the short term, the '*Front popu*' was soon divided by the intractable long-term problems of the economic crisis, and by its response to the Civil War in neighbouring Spain. The newly elected Spanish *Frente popular* government faced an armed revolt launched by right-wing officers, led by General Franco, and supported by the Catholic Church, Hitler, and Mussolini. Fearing the possibility of similar movements in France, Blum endorsed the British policy of non-intervention, despite widespread left-wing calls to arms against fascist advances.

By the end of Blum's second spell as Prime Minister in the spring of 1938, Hitler had occupied the Rhineland, had annexed Austria, and was claiming part at least of Czechoslovakia. It was the conservative Édouard Daladier who finally liquidated the social reforms and then flew to Munich to join Neville Chamberlain in negotiating the partition of Czechoslovakia in appeasement of Hitler and Mussolini. But talk of 'peace in our time' and the shame-faced relief which accompanied it were short-lived. In France, as in Britain, the remaining pre-war months were dominated by the race to rearm and prepare for a war which was now recognized to be inevitable.

The painful changes in social and political life had a profound impact on the generation of writers and artists born before the Great War, who came to maturity in the 1930s. One of the liveliest debates of the late 1920s was provoked by Julien Benda's polemical work *La Trahison des clercs* (1927), which castigated intellectuals for abandoning the pursuit of reason and turning to the passions of politics. In the 1930s dispassionate reason became a lost cause, which even Benda abandoned, as the imperative shifted to involvement in public affairs: *l'engagement*.

Characteristic of the mood was a group of young thinkers brought together by the Swiss cultural historian Denis de Rougemont, in a special issue of the leading literary and intellectual journal *Nouvelle Revue française* (December 1932). Under the title 'Cahier de revendications', a reference to the lists of grievances presented to the King before the Revolution of 1789, they presented their indictments of contemporary society. Drawn from all points of the political spectrum, these writers shared a perception that France, if not the Western world as a whole, was confronting a crisis in civilization. Their contempt for the bankruptcy of the political establishment was often linked with a strong sympathy for the embattled working and unemployed people. They expressed their deep hostility to the capitalist system and spoke of the need for revolution. But behind the veneer of unanimity lurked divergences which led them to very different solutions, as a glance at some of the contributors reveals.

Thierry Maulnier wrote for several of the 'New Right' magazines, with titles like *Revue française* and *Revue du XXe siècle*. His essay *Demain la France* (1934), written with Robert Francis and Jean-Pierre Maxence, was a manifesto of the young Right. Their anti-capitalism was in part a nostalgia for the monarchy, and the revolution they sought was a return to order and authority. Maulnier eventually joined the staff of the extreme right-wing *Action française*, where he remained throughout the war, before moving to the conservative daily paper *Le Figaro*. A distinguished literary critic, he became a member of the Académie française in 1964.

At the other extreme politically were Henri Lefebvre and Paul Nizan, young philosophers who, like the Surrealists before them, joined the communist party and saw a socialist revolution as a historical necessity. Lefebvre became France's leading Marxist philosopher and sociologist, developing a sophisticated theory of human alienation, inspired by Hegel as much as by Marx. He used it to account for the mystifications and conflicts in modern societies, from the great public affairs of economics and politics through to the spheres of art and of everyday life. Throughout his long and prolific career (he died in 1990) his independent views frequently led him into controversy. Nizan, a friend and class-mate of Jean-Paul Sartre, became an influential journalist and communist intellectual. His novels, of which the best known is *La Conspiration* (1938), explored the interaction of personal and political issues especially for students and young people. He died in the fighting at Dunkirk in 1940, having left the communist party in protest against its opposition to the war.

Between these positions, Rougemont himself and many of his contributors were looking for an alternative to Right and Left, which they thought led to rigid and artificial divisions in society. Best known of them is Emmanuel Mounier, a Catholic intellectual who had just founded the monthly review *Esprit* as a forum for a 'third way' between capitalism and communism. He developed a philosophy of 'personalism' which recognized that the human person has physical, social, and spiritual dimensions all of which need to be developed in balance. In the growing political polarization of the 1930s and 1940s, he leaned as far to the Left as Catholics could without coming into conflict with the Church, though he has been criticized for participating for a time in the youth movements sponsored by the Vichy regime. Despite his early death in 1950, his ideas were highly influential in the Second Vatican Council and the subsequent development of the Catholic Church.

After February 1934, the political and intellectual middle ground was sharply reduced. Many writers and artists were swept into the anti-fascist movement, which came to dominate Left Bank Paris, and therefore the cultural environment of an entire generation. Veteran pacifist writers Henri Barbusse and Romain Rolland had gained support for their Amsterdam–Pleyel peace committee. It was largely subsumed by the more militant Association des écrivains et artistes révolutionnaires, founded in 1932, with an influential monthly journal *Commune*. The secretary of the AEAR, Paul Vaillant-Couturier, used his considerable personal influence to draw in both fellow communists like the former Surrealist Louis Aragon, and fellow-travellers like the novelist André Malraux. Even the notoriously disengaged André Gide participated. His account of a journey in the Congo was one of many attempts by writers to draw attention to the brutal and oppressive nature of France's rule over its colonies in Africa and Asia. He later reasserted his political independence with equally critical accounts of a visit to the Soviet Union.

The shift in cultural attitudes in this period can be measured by contrasting two great exhibitions held in Paris. In May 1931 the *Exposition coloniale* opened at the Bois de Vincennes. Planned since 1914, it sought to present the grandeur and wealth of France's colonial empire, 'la Grande France', and in retrospect marked the high point of imperial aspirations. Dominated by a full-scale replica of the temple of Angkor Wat in Cambodia, it was a belated and certainly self-conscious assertion of France's role in the wider world.

The *Exposition internationale* of 1937, at the Trocadéro, was designed as a showcase for technological advance, and to emphasize France's place among the great powers of Europe. The massive German and Soviet pavilions faced each other across the central fountains, but the artistic focus was the pavilion of the embattled Spanish Republic, which housed several major paintings and sculptures, among them Picasso's huge masterpiece *Guernica*. Inspired by revulsion against the aerial bombing of the Basque town by the German Condor legion, the painting asserted the role of culture in resisting the barbaric assault of fascism. Picasso combined national and political references with religious references, including the Crucifixion and the Massacre of the Innocents, in a powerful statement against the physical and emotional suffering inflicted on innocent people in war. After the exhibition, *Guernica* was shown in several countries as part of the international fund-raising campaign for refugees and other victims of the Spanish Civil War.

The Spanish conflict inspired many responses, though few writers or artists could be found to applaud Franco. Even Georges Bernanos, author of the very Catholic novel *Journal d'un curé de campagne* (1936), and of outspoken right-wing essays, was moved to write a polemical denunciation of the nationalist forces and the role of the Spanish Church in supporting them, in *Les Grands Cimetières sous la lune* (1938). Many intellectuals of the Left joined the International Brigades to fight fascism directly. Most visible of them was André Malraux, who led an air squadron in Spain. In his novel *L'Espoir* (1937), which he subsequently made into a film, Malraux offered exemplars of the man of action who throws himself into a cause. More than his earlier novels such as *Les Conquérants* (1928) and *La Condition humaine* (1933), both set in revolutionary conflicts in China, *L'Espoir* focuses on political and social issues rather than on the individual reasons which drive a person to take part in action.

The earnestness of the 1930s was not all expressed in political commitment. Few people were more earnest than Jean-Paul Sartre, who devoted himself to philosophical explorations, including two years (1932–4) in Berlin and Freiburg studying the German philosophers Husserl and Heidegger. In a series of works, culminating with *L'Être et le néant* (1943), he developed the main ideas of existentialism, which became so influential in the late 1940s. His theories of perception, imagination, emotions, and consciousness lent themselves well to fiction and drama. His novel *La Nausée* (1938) presents the diary of Antoine Roquentin, a historian who is gradually overwhelmed by the breakdown of meaning and coherence in the face of a realization that his existence, and that of the world, is wholly gratuitous. Only in the experience of the war did Sartre adopt the strategy of creating meaning through political commitment.

Other European thinkers were also attracting followers. Hegel appealed to Marxists like Lefebvre, but also to existentialists like Alexandre Kojève, and Jean Hyppolite, who appreciated his subtle philosophy of consciousness. Kierkegaard and Nietzsche attracted Christian and existentialist thinkers like Emmanuel Mounier and Jean Wahl. Freud too was gaining recognition, partly because he had been taken up by the Surrealists, but partly also because he was beginning to influence clinical psychology. It was for all these reasons that the young Jacques Lacan began to develop his challenge to the prevailing interpretations of Freudian psychoanalysis.

Outside the high Parisian culture, and particularly in the provinces, cultural life was largely focused around cheap popular entertainment. In this increasingly commercial market, the presence of American cultural products became particularly noticeable. Comic books and magazines aimed at children are a significant example. The adventures of Mickey Mouse and the rest of the Walt Disney pantheon gained instant access to French children's imaginations, largely supplanting the usually rather staid illustrated stories which were domestically produced, around figures like the country girl Bécassine, the ragamuffins Zig and Puce, or even the anarchic scoundrels of the pre-war *bande des Pieds Nickelés*. But along with Disney came the less morally hygienic adventures of assorted superheroes and crimebusters: Buck Rogers, Dick Tracy, Tarzan, Flash Gordon, Superman, Batman, and others. The lurid excitement and sensuality which thrilled young French readers was a cause of alarm for many of their elders, who saw both moral and political danger in them.

It was an attempt to rival their attraction that provoked a young Belgian scoutmaster in 1929 to devise the adventures of cub reporter Tintin for the Catholic children's weekly *Le Petit Vingtième*. Using the characteristic techniques, then rare in French, of speech-bubbles and narrative through images, Georges Rémi, under his pen-name Hergé, rapidly turned him into the premier character in the French cartoon industry. The resourceful Tintin was depicted outwitting villains successively in the Soviet Union, the Belgian Congo, America, Egypt, the Far East, and other exotic locations, where the superiority of French (or Belgian) intelligence and civilized values were regularly vindicated. The sharp outlines of his *ligne claire* figures became the house style of French-speaking cartoons for a generation.

Heavily sponsored by the Catholic Church, Hergé's output eventually became the mainstay of a small publishing empire, though his main success came after the war.

The Catholics and the political Left also shared wider interests in promoting and shaping popular culture. They were both active in a variety of cultural spheres, such as mounting adult education programmes, promoting the singing and playing of French traditional music, or running the networks of cinema clubs which played an important role in the development of film culture in France. Alongside commercial cinemas, theatres, and concert halls, there was an important role for church halls, municipal halls, and trade union halls as important, often competing, venues in the cultural life of the French people. In the heyday of the Popular Front movement, artists and writers made extensive use of these and other communal spaces to present their performances of revolutionary songs, political theatre, satirical poetry, or socially conscious painting. The poet Jacques Prévert and his brother Pierre brought together a collection of writers and performers from various left-wing backgrounds to form the Groupe Octobre. Between 1932 and 1937 they performed concerts, readings, and dramatized texts around France and abroad, using their talents to raise awareness of social and political issues and raise funds for campaigns related to them. Without doubt their most successful presentation was *La Bataille de Fontenoy* (1932), a knockabout anti-militaristic satire of France's governing élites, which was constantly updated to include references to contemporary events. Pitched at working-class audiences, it raised eyebrows and even indignation among Parisian theatre critics, but its agitprop style of Surrealism, slapstick, caricature, and political comment became something of a model for subsequent political theatre.

Cinema was perhaps the most popular form of culture, both in the large numbers of people who followed it and in its appeal to working-class audiences. During the 1920s, the French film industry gradually merged into two major groups: Pathé-Nathan-Ciné-romans and Gaumont-Aubert-Franco-Films, who competed for control of production facilities and distribution networks with the German Tobis and the American Paramount groups, which also had bases in France. The costs of both production and distribution rose sharply from 1928 with the introduction of sound-track, followed rapidly by fully speaking films. Despite the instant popularity of the new technology with audiences, film-makers were reluctant to adapt to sound, with the leading director René Clair denouncing it as pointless and dangerous, a view shared by many critics. Though they soon bowed to the inevitable, many film-makers of the early 1930s still worked within the conventions of the silent movies, narrating through visual details and conveying emotion through stylized facial expressions and bodily posture. None the less, the talkies gave a vigorous boost to film-making and French output rose from 94 films in 1929 and 1930 to a high point of 143 in 1933, before the economic crisis took its full effect.

René Clair did make a successful transition to sound, however, and with Jean

### Zola avec nous

The Popular Front movement mobilized the resources of French culture past and present to cement a broad common front against fascism and in favour of social progress. Some of its supporters argued the need to reject the bourgeois culture of the past and create a new workers' culture. Most, however, argued that the best of the culture of the past, much of it inevitably bourgeois, should be made available to the people. Zola was a particularly attractive writer from this perspective, both because he had been an almost legendary advocate for the Dreyfus cause, and because he had pioneered the movement in literature and art to depict what life was really like for working people. His novels *Germinal* and *La Terre* were greatly admired for their representation of mining and farming communities respectively, though some left-wing critics followed George Lukács in regretting that he did not go beyond depiction to a more political analysis. Many of these issues are alluded to in this design for a float in the 14 July parade of 1936, made by artists Marcel Gromaire and Jacques Lipchitz.

Vigo, director of *L'Atalante* (1934), established a style of 'poetic realism' which dominated the decade. In his films *Le Million* and *A nous la liberté*, both released in 1931, Clair gives lyrical depictions of people from various social backgrounds, in their ordinary working and living conditions, but engaged in fables marked by extraordinary events bordering on fantasy. He left France in despair after the failure of his film *Le Dernier Milliardaire* (1934), a light-hearted satire of dictatorship which clashed with the new earnestness of French politics after the February riots.

His torch was taken up by Jean Renoir, who had funded his first films in the 1920s by selling paintings left to him by his famous Impressionist father. Renoir's more socially committed realism caught the mood of the times. A series of films, *Toni* (1935), *Le Crime de Monsieur Lange* (1936), and *Les Bas-fonds* (1937), showed working-class characters struggling to make their lives bearable against the oppression of those with money and power. Inspired by its socialist humanism, Renoir became a militant supporter of the *Front populaire*, and made films sponsored by the communist party (*La Vie est à nous*, 1936) and the CGT trade union (*La Marseillaise*, 1938), celebrating the courage and optimism of the working people.

Behind the optimism, however, lurked the growing apprehension of a slide into war. If the optimism of the *Front populaire* temporarily eclipsed this fear, it was nevertheless a constant presence throughout the 1930s. It lurks in the dark grotesqueries of Céline's novel *Voyage au bout de la nuit* (1932), a descent into the heart of darkness. It is at the centre of Aragon's realist novels *Les Cloches de Bâle* (1934) and *Les Beaux Quartiers* (1936), set in 1912, which drew explicit comparisons between the 1930s and the eve of the Great War, holding out little hope that the forces which had precipitated war in 1914 could be prevented from doing so again. The same concern is at the centre of the stage in Jean Giraudoux's play *La Guerre de Troie n'aura pas lieu* (1935), one of many works to draw on classical Greek tragedy to underscore its sense of foreboding. The fear of war also produced what is widely regarded as Renoir's masterpiece, *La Grande Illusion* (1937). Set mainly in a prisoner of war camp during the First World War, the film explores the complex interaction between national loyalties and class solidarities, between French and German soldiers, and between officers and men. It argued strongly for human fraternity against the folly and futility of war.

Renoir could not hope that his call would be heeded and his last film before leaving France for Hollywood, *La Règle du jeu* (1939), was an embittered tale of the decadence and disarray of the French upper classes on the eve of war. Like Marcel Carné's more successful *Le Jour se lève* (1939), it translated the sense of crisis, confusion, and pessimism which pervaded France in the months before the declaration of war. The same mood is captured in Sartre's novel *Le Sursis* (1945), which presents a fictionalized account of the last week of September 1938, from various points of view. The final paragraph offers a description of Prime Minister Daladier's welcome at Le Bourget airport on his return from Munich; he fears that the large crowd there intend to attack him for the shameful agreement he has reached with Hitler to dismember Czechoslovakia:

The plane had taxied to a halt. Daladier emerged painfully from the cabin and stood at the top of the steps; he was pale. An enormous roar went up and people started to run, breaking through the police cordon, sweeping the barriers away . . . they were shouting: 'Long live France! Long live England! Long live Peace!', they were carrying flags and bouquets of flowers. Daladier had stopped on the top step; he was watching them with astonishment. He turned towards Léger and said with gritted teeth:
'Bloody fools!'

The paradox of Daladier's contempt for his supporters is one of many antitheses which characterize the last months of peace. In many respects it was a phoney peace, followed by a phoney war. France mobilized for a war it did not believe in and did not want. Militarily its *État-major* prepared to fight the First World War again, despite the warnings of some junior staff officers, among them Charles de Gaulle, that warfare had entered the era of tank offensives. Politically, the Left were viscerally opposed to a war in which the working people would again be the main victims, while the Right were politically opposed to a war against the countries they most admired. The communists were almost the only ones to oppose Munich and call for vigorous action, but they then reversed their position in August 1939 in the wake of the Molotov–Ribbentrop treaty of mutual non-aggression between Germany and the USSR. Riven by its contradictions and uncertainties, France went half-heartedly into a war for which it was ill prepared both socially and culturally.

### Les Années noires (1940–1944)

Despite the misgivings of those who resented being asked to 'die for Danzig', France joined Britain in declaring war after Hitler launched his invasion of Poland. The general mobilization of the active male population was not followed by any concerted military initiative, beyond refining the basic defensive strategy which had been adopted. What quickly became known as the 'drôle de guerre' (funny or phoney war) was for most French people a period of waiting in a climate of unreality. Reality struck with the lightning offensive of the German army across the Ardennes on 10 May 1940. The French army and supporting British units were outmanœuvred and overwhelmed. Some 340,000 troops, a third of them French, were evacuated from Dunkirk by 4 June, and ten days later the Germans entered Paris. In an extraordinary wave of collective panic, six or seven million people fled into the countryside with whatever belongings they could take. The *exode* (exodus), as it became known, was but the first of the miseries and humiliations which the French people endured during *les années noires* from the Fall of France to the Liberation.

It is difficult now to recapture the extent to which the defeat of France in just six weeks, after nine months of waiting and preparing for war during the 'drôle de guerre', was an absolutely devastating shock. French expectations of the Second

World War had largely been framed by the First World War, 'l'autre guerre', with the trench warfare and long static battles for small territorial advances. They were not prepared for the blitzkrieg. Like all modern wars, the campaign of 1939–40 was accompanied by extensive polemical, literary, and analytical material, in a range of media, devoted to offering elucidation of the meaning of the extraordinary experience being lived through. These amplified not only the sense of waiting, but also then the shock of defeat. Antoine de Saint-Exupéry's novel *Pilote de guerre* (1942) gives a sense of the disorientation and incoherence attendant upon the fragmentation of the nation, as, in addition to losing the war, it lost sovereignty, government, administration. The rump of the Third Republic's last parliament handed over all state powers to the 84-year-old hero of the First World War, Marshal Pétain, who saw no further than the chaos of an army routed, several million French refugees on the move, and German might, and sought an armistice. Hitler, always alert to symbolic gestures, insisted that the armistice be signed in a replica of the railway carriage in the forest of Compiègne where Germany had signed its surrender in 1918. France was divided into two main zones: Paris and the industrial north occupied directly by the German army; the largely rural south unoccupied (until November 1942) and governed directly by Pétain's 'État français' from its capital in the spa town of Vichy. Pétain's was a regime born in a fragmented France, and fragmentation was also its lot.

In their majority, the French people were relieved to have a dignified and respected leader, and a government which was French and might be expected to shelter them from the worst ravages of war. However, the initial popularity of the Vichy regime slowly waned as the extent of its ultra-conservatism emerged, along with a realization that its co-operation with Germany involved a growing subordination to the German war effort. The rounding up and deportation of thousands of Jews, the waves of arrests, often followed by torture and execution, and the conscription of young workers to undertake forced labour in Germany, all made it increasingly difficult to distinguish the official 'collaboration' from the espousal of Nazi values and objectives which was urged by some of its most enthusiastic French supporters.

Of course for many, including Saint-Exupéry, this was but a battle lost, and the war went on. Few French people heard the BBC radio broadcast of 18 June 1940, in which the former Under-Secretary for Defence, General Charles de Gaulle, called on them to join him to carry on the fight. But his reputation spread and the regular broadcasts of the Free French from London reached a growing audience. Within France, sporadic gestures of defiance gradually developed into organized and effective underground movements, painstakingly welded together by de Gaulle's envoy, the legendary Jean Moulin.

As the tide of war turned, the Resistance grew in numbers, sophistication, and effectiveness. Though the communists were very active in it, especially after Hitler's invasion of the Soviet Union, it attracted people of almost all political complexions and from all backgrounds and conditions. Its successes were met with increased

## Handshake at Montoire

During the summer of 1940, following defeat and Armistice, Marshal Pétain elaborated a policy of co-operation between the French State, of which he was the Head, and the German Reich. Through his Prime Minister, Pierre Laval, he requested, and was granted, a meeting with Hitler, which took place in October at Montoire, a small town in the Loire valley. A joint statement of principle was issued setting the direction for future close collaboration between the two states, and was followed over the next six months by discussions leading to detailed agreements. At the meeting, Hitler reportedly greeted Pétain with all courtesy due to his military stature, and they shook hands. Photographs of the handshake were widely published, promoted assiduously by the German Propagandastaffel. Its symbolic significance made a major impact both in France and internationally. It was taken as the material token of a radically new relationship between France and its conquerors, coming as a shock even to some of Pétain's political supporters. Official commentators stressed the respect Hitler had shown him, and the Marshal was obliged to broadcast a public appeal for trust in his policy of state collaboration. By general consensus, it was a defining moment in France's wartime development.

repression, often led by Vichy's paramilitary militia, the Milice, in co-operation with the German SS and Gestapo. They also provoked intensified propaganda, spearheaded by the Paris-based pro-collaboration groups, through the neo-fascist political parties of Jacques Doriot and Marcel Déat, through collaborationist newspapers such as L'Œuvre, Gringoire, and Je suis partout, and through the German-dominated broadcasting of Radio-Paris. There were many last-minute and retrospective conversions to Resistance in the wake of the Allied landings in Normandy, as the Vichy government inexorably collapsed. But right up to the Liberation of Paris at the end of August 1944, France remained a suffering and divided country.

One of the enduring paradoxes about the Occupation was the incongruous coexistence of war and peace in a country subject to military occupation over several years. It was not war, although it was for many, and it was not peace, although many aspects of normal life continued. In his introduction to La Vie culturelle sous Vichy (1990), Jean-Pierre Rioux offers two examples of this strange double life from periods of actual warfare: 'It was reported that in May 1940, a total of 3,000,000 went to the cinema; in June 1944, at the height of the allied landings, Abel Bonnard, the collaborationist Minister of Education, angrily turned on his subordinates to denounce . . . the poor technical arrangements under which the baccalaureate examinations were being held.' Camus's La Peste (1947) also underlined this with its emphasis on the crowded cinemas and theatres. It has been noted that public gatherings could never be allowed in a real plague; none the less, in relation to the Occupation, on which the historical narrative of the novel is based, Camus's depiction is very faithful. Cultural activity under the Occupation was changed by the situation, but it certainly was not halted. Theatres were full, books sold in large quantities, and cinema audiences increased over the four years.

The French film industry was a particular beneficiary from the Occupation, as the rising audiences combined with the virtual absence of imported Hollywood films. German films were readily available, as they had been before the war, but remained a minority taste. The insatiable demand for the moving image led to some 220 films being produced and distributed in France during the four-year period. This was only half the pre-war level, but the relative commercial success was in sharp contrast to the sluggish response of the 1930s, when the two leading French production and distribution companies, Gaumont and Pathé, had both fallen into receivership. While many leading directors and actors went into exile in America, many more aspiring film-makers came forward to take their place. The most senior director, Marcel Carné, took scripts by Jacques Prévert to make two blockbusters, Les Visiteurs du soir (1942) and Les Enfants du paradis (1945), which have remained classics of the French screen. And important young directors like Jean-Jacques Becker and Louis Daquin made their débuts. Undoubtedly the most controversial French-made film was Henri-Georges Clouzot's Le Corbeau (1943), a dark thriller set in provincial France and revolving round a pre-war episode of anonymous threatening letters. Its cinematic effectiveness, reminiscent of Hitchcock, prompted criticisms that it painted too negative a picture of the French people, and Clouzot was briefly blacklisted after the Liberation.

The years of the Occupation saw a proliferation of words and images in all directions, since cultural activities played such a crucial role in projecting the new national and political identities. The depth and breadth of Vichy's cultural project, its determination to remould the self-image of the nation and its values in its own political image, were quite remarkable. Particular care was given to youth programmes, and educational activities. Equally characteristic was its manipulation and control of the public sphere. Vichy was a regime of spectacle and image—something it shared with the other populist movements of the times. The political rallies of Jacques Doriot's Parti populaire français were matched by the grandiose meetings of the Légion des volontaires français, who volunteered to enlist in the German army. This can be placed alongside the powerful use of the figure of Pétain himself. He could be seen being acclaimed by the masses on newsreels, or staring out from countless photographs, cartoons, portraits, posters, textbooks, and children's books. And on the radio, the 'quavering voice' of Pétain calling for an armistice in his broadcast of 17 June 1940 was one of the key symbolic instances of the period.

In addition to theatre and cinema, Paris saw a wide range of journalistic and literary publications supporting collaborationist policies. There were major exhibitions, such as the one famously devoted to Arno Breker, the German artist fêted by the Nazis, which ran in the Orangerie from May 1942, and the anti-Semitic *Le Juif en France* exhibition mounted at the Palais Berlitz in September 1941 by the collaborationist Institut d'étude des questions juives. There was high-profile cultural interaction with Germany, in the form of visits by writers, singers, actors, and other performers. Publishers were signatories to agreements on censorship lists, which particularly banned Jewish, American, and communist authors. It has been suggested, controversially, that the very fact of seeking or agreeing to publish within the constraints of censorship compromised and tarnished the clarity of opposition. Two notable cases are the communist party newspaper *L'Humanité*, which unsuccessfully sought permission to appear in the occupied zone, the party having been banned by the French government since September 1939; and Emmanuel Mounier's intellectual journal *Esprit*, which appeared between November 1940 and August 1941 in the southern zone, before being banned.

The Resistance also took its message into the public domain through clandestine channels, publishing and distributing *sous le manteau*, first with roneotyped tracts, then with secretly printed material, growing to a great clandestine production of newspapers. Underground publishing houses in northern and southern zones put out short stories and collections of poetry. Poems proved a particularly subtle and effective way of spreading the call to resist, and Resistance writers like Aragon, Éluard, Emmanuel, Tardieu, and Guillevic produced some of the most popular and moving poetic writing of the century. The most sustained output came from Vercors's Éditions de minuit. Contraband publishing, through committed journals such as *Poésie* or *Confluences*, or articles in the press relocated in the south, such as *Le Figaro*, provided another conduit for anti-government and anti-German expression. But here too the debate continues as to how dull-witted the censors really were, and whether more sophisticated games of toleration and 'normalization' were being played.

The censoring of all cultural programmes and initiatives introduced a sharp line between that which was officially approved and public, and that which was illegally produced. However, the existence of 'contraband' writings, that is to say, approved by the censor but seeking to smuggle past the censor's control a resistance message, blurred the possibility of a similarly sharp line between legal and illegally expressed views of the situation. *La Pensée libre*, an early Resistance newspaper, might polemically proclaim, 'legal literature means literature of betrayal', but this cannot be sustained as a statement of fact. It is one extremely important view within a diverse and voluminous cultural production, where cultural comment and analysis was an integral and constitutive part. In such a charged political and military context, all cultural expression appeared inescapably partisan, particularly perhaps from a Resistance point of view. Clear lines were perceived between the values and political opinions expressed, and the official permission to publish. Uncontroversial writing which did not directly address the actual situation was none the less often criticized for furthering German or collaborationist objectives by making it appear possible for life to go on as normal under the Occupation: it was therefore denounced as complicity and acquiescence.

As a result, the Occupation was one of the key defining moments of the mission of the intellectual in twentieth-century French history, to the extent that the massive philosophical manifesto which came out of it, Sartre's *Qu'est-ce que la littérature?*, all but buries the memory of previous debates of the necessary relation between culture and politics. From the Dreyfus Affair onwards, the social role of the intellectual has been forged through the defence of political and moral values, and denunciation of the abuse of power, however defined. The Dreyfus Affair is also archetypal in the sense that the definition of the nation and its true values are at the heart of the controversy. Under the Occupation too, the nation was both the battleground and the prize for the victors.

This has wider implications for the importance of the Occupation to French cultural history. Discourses on and about the nation and nationhood play a vital role in the dynamics of subjectivity and identity, and their relation to social and cultural processes. A sense of nationality results from very complex sets of identifications, beliefs, knowledge, and history. Times of war both concentrate and recharge collective national consciousness, since by definition they involve extreme persuasive efforts to mobilize action in defence of the nation. War is one example among many of the social role played by culture and literature. No one goes to war without preconceptions and assumptions about the nature of war and the behaviour which will be expected of them, however outmoded and inappropriate those expectations prove to be. The intensity of the experience of war, and its power over imaginary identifications and projections onto a collective identity, have a long-lasting effect, and in this the images and narratives of literature and culture play a central role. What is important about the Occupation is that the context for this voluminous cultural production was a country in a state of virtual, some would say actual, civil war. The 'German occupation' is also frequently referred to as an episode in the 'Franco-French War' or even as the 'Franco-German occupation'. No facet of life remained untouched by this situation.

If there was one leitmotif recurrent in the discourses of all parties and factions, it was the desire for change. Building a new France was a cliché of the times, although the content altered radically across the spectrum of views. 'From the Resistance to the Revolution' was the masthead of the clandestine newspaper *Combat* and, allowing for a fairly generous interpretation of what the word revolution signified, was not untypical of the Resistance. The pro-Nazi collaborators' crusade to rid France and Europe of communists and Jews was also to sweep away the old and bring in the new. Vichy inaugurated its own revolution, 'La Révolution nationale', which offers the most pertinent example of the cultural and political importance of the processes of subjectivity, especially nation, class, and gender. At the heart of the 'Révolution nationale' were three key terms of the *État français*: 'Travail, famille, patrie', which it actually substituted for the Republican motto of 'Liberté, égalité, fraternité'. For Vichy, and in a sense for France, nation, class, and gender have a special resonance, for they lie at the intersection of the state and its cultural revolution.

The geographical and political fragmentation of the nation was mirrored in the context of cultural activities and practices. There were bitter divisions over what should be the truly patriotic response to the situation, what position should be adopted on behalf of the real France, and who its true representatives should be. One way of making sense of this now is to agree with Robert Brasillach and say that there were several 'Frances' under the Occupation. Together with Pierre Drieu la Rochelle, Brasillach was one of the most prominent intellectuals committed to collaboration. His novel *Six heures à perdre*, which was serialized in the review *La Révolution nationale* in 1944, stresses the uncertainties and confusions attendant upon the state of the nation, and concludes: 'France today is neither simple, nor clear, nor precise.' Drieu la Rochelle's *Les Chiens de paille* (written 1943) is another example of an overview of the inter-French struggle for France. Others in this cultural war over the meaning of France were more concerned to assert the validity of their claims to represent the nation to which all true French men and women would owe allegiance. It is not in the nature of Resistance discourse, or Vichy discourse, or Gaullist pronouncements, to take an overview of competing values and stress the confusion of the individual placed before them. Both Drieu and Brasillach fully identified with support for the German Nazi programme in rebuilding a new Europe in its image. By the end of 1943, it was appearing increasingly clear that the collaborationist cause was not going to triumph, which may be what prompted these writers to reflect on their choices within the overall situation, while the battle was still raging around them. But they also display a common literary technique which, by showing all values to be relative and contingent, and by denying any validity to the notion of universal values, allows particular universalist claims to be undermined. Only cynicism or scepticism emerge as knowledgeable positions in such a context. Céline's pamphlet *Les Beaux Draps* (1941) is another example. It piles up its denunciations in a paroxysm of disgust, including Jews and the decadent nation among its targets. It pleased some, but also managed to offend many, among them the Vichy authorities, who banned it. By a different route *Les Beaux Draps* arrives at the same result: there is no transcendent truth or value to aspire to or to validate one's actions and choices. Much post-war literature later adopted the same approach, in a less absolute way, and with the more or less explicit intention of specifically undermining the moral authority of the Resistance.

Céline's anti-Semitism and denunciations of decadence were perfectly in tune with many collaborationist themes. The title of *Les Décombres*, by Lucien Rebatet, the best seller of 1942, summarizes very well the widely held view in collaborationist circles of the need for a completely new departure for the ruinously decadent French nation. Redefining the nation could well have been their watchword, as indeed it could for Vichy, which drew on the same metaphor. One famous cartoon of *La Révolution nationale* has, on the one side, a crumbling ruin of a house lurching to one side, under a star of David, filled with jumbled, broken words such as *égoïsme, radicalisme, parlement, juiver, specul, demo, craties, avarice, capitali, pastis, franc-maçonnerie*, and standing on foundations of *paresse, démagogie, internationalisme*; on the other, the smart, clean lines of a sturdy house, France, on the pillars of *école, artisanat, paysannerie, légion*, supported in turn by double foundations: *discipline, ordre, épargne, courage*; and on the base, *Travail, Famille, Patrie*. The voluntarist nature of Vichy's project to remould the French nation has often been commented on. It is a most singular feature of the regime that it was determined to effect political change by decree. All areas of French social and political life were to be reordered in line with the new values which would eliminate social conflict and build a new society on the basis of the 'natural' groupings, as Pétain never ceased to stress in his broadcasts, of the family, the *cité* (not, it should be noted, *la ville*), and the professions.

Vichy's populism meant that class in the widest sense, of a politics of society and social identity, was a prominent ideological and cultural feature. Since Yves Durand's small but invaluable *Vichy 1940–1944* (1972), arguments have continued over the extent to which Vichy should be seen as a break with or a continuation of the past. It certainly sought to break with the class heritage of the Popular Front, by stressing technocratic management and a cultivated apolitical approach in economic affairs. Its corporatist vision, placing the emphasis on social alliances centred on professional activity, was another plank in its policy of reorganization of labour and the economic infrastructure. In the complex network of relationships constituted by economic realities, literary and cultural representations, and the political imaginary, Vichy's attempt to forge a new national image of social groupings and national history placed the image of the peasant and rural folklore at the centre of its web of propaganda. Forms of popular culture were very significant in this process, folk customs, dress, music, dance, and songs were enthusiastically promoted, with the long-term result that, because of these wartime associations, post-war France has never experienced a significant folk revival. The land of France, the French people, and particularly the inheritance of the French countryfolk replaced the imagery of class, industry, and urban proletariat. Jeanne d'Arc, the peasant girl who fought the English, was adopted as an icon. Youth and culture were key themes of the Popular Front era, but now were harnessed by Vichy into a new context which evacuated labour and industry from major components of the national figuration.

Like the ultra-collaborationists, Vichy did not have a good word to say for the Republic. Across Resistance writings, however, particularly towards the end of the Occupation, republican values underpinned both a sense of tradition and the hope for renewal of the nation and of French society. The defence of France was seen as rooted in the French land, a source of key patriotic values faced with the foreign invader. The Resistance also had its regionalism: the authors' pseudonyms for the clandestine Éditions de minuit were symbolically chosen from the regions of France. They included Vercors (Jean Bruller) himself, who kept the name after the war, but also Cévennes (Jean Guéhenno), Argonne (Jacques Debû-Bridel), Minervois (Claude Aveline), and Forez (François Mauriac), among others. It asserted the universalist claims of the rights of the individual, enshrined in the Republic, and the central unifying value of France itself, seen as playing a unique spiritual role in European civilization. Nationalism was placed on a continuum with the universal, as embodying transcendent, absolute, and necessary values. Failure to recognize this and act accordingly was viewed as pure betrayal.

Reforging the nation, in Vichy discourse, involved realigning a certain definition of France with a reworked vision of French society and classes. In Resistance writings the foreign enemy, the Nazi oppressor, was frequently identified as a class enemy, laying the foundations for the view that liberation from military occupation should at one and the same time be a liberation from oppressive social structures. The worker-hero, son of the people, aware of the history of class warfare, occurs in a range of writings. In 'FTP', one of the short stories by Édith Thomas, a group of Resistance fighters derail a train and shoot its German occupants. The personal history and political motivation of each one is enumerated as they move forward to the ambush.

Drôle de jeu (1945), the prize-winning novel by Roger Vailland, also has its 'workerist' side, in its espousal of the communist party view that the working class is the most clear-sighted and militant of all. The corollary of this is that Vichy and indeed the Occupation itself are presented as serving the interests of the bourgeoisie, who are therefore portrayed as unpatriotic and morally decadent,

## The National Revolution

In its early months, Vichy attempted to define a new ideology for the nation, based on the theme of a national revolution. Sharp conflicts arose between different intellectual currents who sought to shape its content, and eventually the most extreme groupings prevailed, with results indistinguishable from German-style fascism. This well-known cartoon, published in Avignon, shows a crumbling house under a star of David, perched on jumbled words lumping together greed, corruption, speculation, drunkenness, parliament, democracy, Jews, capitalism, and Free-masonry. It stands on idleness, demagogy, and internationalism. Its opposite is a smart sturdy house, standing on the pillars of school, the trades, the peasantry, and the Légion française (a Vichy support movement); its foundations are discipline, order, thrift, courage, and the Vichy motto of Work, Family, Country. The metaphor of France as a house was widely used in debates over what brought about the defeat of 1940 and which aspects of pre-war France should now be built on. Among the many connotations of house is that of a (family) firm, emphasizing Vichy's appeal to property-owners, the middle classes, and rural communities, rather than to apartment-dwelling townspeople and the working classes. Its defensive parochialism is implicitly also aimed against Paris, where Pétain's writ did not run.

incapable of placing other interests above their own. One of the most eloquent exponents of this view is Vercors, whose Resistance stories often contrast the need for a true patriotism with the self-serving interests of the 'rulers', as in the section 'Le Règne des avares' in his short novel *La Marche à l'étoile* (1943). André Chamson's *Le Puits des miracles* (1945) is another example, depicting the morally and physically grotesque rulers thriving at the expense of the poor, and welcoming the Germans as they invade the southern zone. *Alexis Slavsky* (1945) by Elsa Triolet offers a very negative portrayal of the social and economic gulf between the painter Alexis and the wealthy milieu of the patron who takes him in.

This is one area, among several, where clear similarities are found between Vichy and Resistance perspectives. In both, there is a drive to transcend difference in the name of the nation. *Le peuple* and *la classe ouvrière* are invested with a vital energy and sense of mission for the nation as a whole. In both, recognition of division is at the heart of the drive for unity, to which rhetoric and propaganda are subordinated. A unified Resistance representing the whole nation demands alliances between traditional antagonists. 'The nationalist bourgeoisie is holding out its hand to us,' comments the hero of Simone de Beauvoir's *Le Sang des autres* (1945), and Aragon urged the unity of 'he who believed in heaven, he who did not believe in it'. One should not forget, however, that the implementation of Vichy's policies, particularly in relation to anti-Semitism, anti-communism, and finally its fight against its fellow countrymen and women in the Resistance, is a far cry from its rhetoric, and perhaps proves the point that exclusion is the other side of the coin of essentialist views of the nation.

The prominence accorded to 'Famille' in Vichy ideology indicates the extent to which the reforging of social and political identities in France passed through feminine identity. The invocation of 'natural' units of social existence on which to found a new social order enabled the family to be placed as one of the cornerstones of the edifice, defining individuals in relation to natural rather than social relationships. The traditional values of the past therefore included motherhood as the primary definition of femininity. Official speeches, government legislation, and propaganda, such as that for 'la relève' (seeking skilled workers for the German economy), follow the same dynamic of valorizing motherhood. It is striking that there is no hint that this might be problematic or controversial, whereas in other spheres, such as class for example, the existence of social divisions and antagonisms, and alternative political views, is at least acknowledged, even if only to deplore them, to consign them to the unenlightened past, or to ascribe them to an invasion of alien ideas. But in relation to wives and mothers, the picture is quite homogeneous, and is paralleled by the use of family and gender in the rhetoric of nation and state by Pétain and his hagiographers. In an introduction to a 1941 collection of his speeches, he is described as both the father of the nation and its husband, in an analogy recalling Christian imagery of the Church as bride of Christ. He proclaims the 'unity of the mother country and the empire', he is the father of the 'orphaned nation', 'father of the fatherland', the 'son' and 'saviour' of the French. He fuses characteristics of the paternal, the maternal, the patriarchal, and the filial in his exceptional person. More importantly, in the positive endorsement of the patriarchal state, the discourse of Vichy moves between the language of family and paternalism and the language of power ('a strong State', 'a strong leader'). The rhetoric of the family offers a means of transcending social dissension and difference by subsuming it under the naturalized relations of gender.

In the cultural politics of text and representation, other examples of the mediating role of gender and sexual difference can be noted. If Pétain and France are the two individual figures symbolizing the spiritual marriage giving birth to the new France, the device is not specific to Vichy. Vercors's short novel *Le Silence de la mer* (1942) presents perhaps the best-known example of the theme of national confrontation being enacted through the interpersonal tension of the two figures of the text: the German officer, von Ebrennac, and the girl of the house in which he is billeted, *la nièce*. The question of the attraction of collaboration, which is the underlying issue of the narrative, generates a remarkable sexualization of relations and elements throughout it. Von Ebrennac's game leg and pronounced limp suggests at one and the same time male power and male impotence, if one were to read it in classic Freudian terms. The story of Beauty and the Beast which he uses as a parable of their situation, albeit reversing the conventional views of who is gaoling whom under the Occupation, relies upon the transformation of the attractive man into sheer bestiality (which is also feminized in French as *la bête*), both powerful and victim. Von Ebrennac's desire for the marriage of the two nations, France and Germany, finds its obvious parallel in the powerful emotional attraction each of these two young protagonists has for the other, endowing each with a noble aura of personal sacrifice in the choices they are making. Meanwhile, the traditional brutality associated with Germany in French culture is projected onto the one negative female figure of the text, von Ebrennac's repudiated German fiancée.

Two women novelists of the Resistance offer strikingly different pictures of the situation of women at the time. Elsa Triolet's short story 'Les Amants d'Avignon' (1943) depicts her central character, Juliette Noël, rising to the challenge of a totally different life in her dangerous work for the Resistance, drawing on strengths and qualities she never guessed she possessed. The stories of *Les Contes d'Auxois* (1943) by Édith Thomas offer a range of female characters who, while not themselves being engaged on clandestine activities, have a vital role to play in encouraging or giving a lead to their various partners in the elaboration of Resistance values and carrying out dangerous work. In general, the difference between Vichy and Resistance narratives of womanhood offers one of the most distinctive contrasts between the two.

What is not distinctive to either is the gendering of political rhetoric. If, for Vichy, true manhood lies in fatherhood and the assumption of the patriarchal role, the Resistance also ties together masculinity and nationality, most obviously in its depiction of collaboration and deviance. Collaboration is consistently portrayed and denounced as a 'feminine' option; the decadence of the collaborator and his attraction towards, or desire for, his victor and master is embodied in a discourse of homosexual desire. Collaborators are depicted as weak men, masochists, and decadent. They are not true Frenchmen; they are not true men. In the sexual politics of representation, discourses of nationality and gender mutually reinforce their central, normalizing messages.

The polarizations and conflicts of the years 1940–4, with all their complexities and ambiguities, have haunted French consciousness throughout the post-war period. Films, essays, novels, articles, memoirs, and histories bear witness to the extraordinary nature of the experience and the powerful mark it made, both upon individuals and upon their collective response to the recent history of their nation. During the late 1940s and early 1950s, cultural and political battles were waged over the politically dominant Resistance and the authenticity of its claims to moral superiority, and over the judgement and eventual pardon of former collaborators. During the 1950s and 1960s, the dramas of the Occupation were not written out of French history, but it became widely accepted that the prevailing image of the nation at war was mythical, rather than objectively historical in nature. The official story or received opinion did not deny the fact of collaboration, but saw it as an isolated phenomenon, atypical of the national response, and whose few famous names were quickly dealt with as traitors. From the perspective of 1950, it was often the Cold War and the fearfulness unleashed by atomic and nuclear weapons which dominated thinking about the war and its aftermath. A film such as *Hiroshima mon amour* (1959) was prophetic of later works in its complex handling of the themes of war, memory, and transgression. So too in many ways was Semprun's novel *Le Grand Voyage* (1963). But it was only in the late 1960s that the questions which have become obsessively familiar over the last thirty years began to be aired: the political and personal divisions of the French; the broad consensus of support for Vichy and particularly for Pétain; the active pursuit of collaborationist and anti-Semitic policies by Vichy; the metaphysical, philosophical, and experiential consequences of the Holocaust; and the demolition of the powerful Gaullist and communist 'myths' of a nation united in its resistance to Occupation and a handful of traitors. By general consent the catalyst for this process was Marcel Ophuls's film *Le Chagrin et la pitié* (1971).

The continuing debate and controversy must in part be explained by the painful, difficult nature of the experience itself. For many years much was said about it, but much was also left unsaid. The articulation of speech and silence haunts the telling of this past, both at the time and now. In a recent number of the *Magazine littéraire*, Jorge Semprun talks of his long silence, lasting nearly two decades, about his experiences at Buchenwald, a silence finally broken by the writing of *Le Grand Voyage*. The same number also makes the point that Céline's pamphlets are still considered unpublishable today. The role and participation of women in the

Resistance, and indeed the centrality of women's experience to understanding the Occupation, have only been considered seriously in the past few years. The experience of the camps problematized the very existence of art, literature, and humanist culture; from Jean Cayrol's novels to Claude Lanzmann's film *Shoah* (1985), the question of how to talk about the Holocaust has been bitterly insistent, and never divorced from the equally bitter question of French responsibility. The tearing apart of a nation also partakes of language and silence, brilliantly encapsulated in Patrick Modiano's first novel, *La Place de l'étoile* (1968), where the fabric of national ideology and culture is the setting for a voyage into the madness of self-destructive incompatible identities, symbolic of the fate of the nation which turns to consider the inheritance of a period that placed the mark of exclusion at the heart of its own self-definition. It is not surprising that the processes of memory and commemoration in national consciousness have become an increasingly important dimension of contemporary reflection on the Occupation years.

# Suggestions for Further Reading

### The historical background (1870–1945)

There are several good studies in English of French social and political history of the period. There is a good succinct account in Roger Price, *A Concise History of France* (Cambridge: Cambridge University Press, 1993). James F. McMillan, *Twentieth Century France: Politics and Society 1898–1991* (London: Edward Arnold, 1992) is an accessible and up-to-date survey of most of the period which contains an excellent bibliography. Maurice Larkin, *France since the Popular Front 1936–1986* (Oxford: Clarendon Press, 1988) is an excellent standard history of the later period, with a very helpful select bibliography. Jean-Charles Asselain, *Histoire économique de la France*, 2 vols. (Paris: Seuil, 1984) is an invaluable economic history from the eighteenth century to the 1970s, while Tom Kemp, *The French Economy 1913–1939: The History of a Decline* (London: Longman, 1972) focuses on one quarter of a century.

Theodore Zeldin's now classic *France 1848–1945*, 2 vols. (Oxford: Clarendon Press, 1973–7) contains a wealth of fascinating detail and stimulating speculation on life-styles and beliefs, presented in cheaper and less academic form in *The French* (London: Collins, 1983). Donald Charlton (ed.), *France: A Companion to French Studies* (2nd edn. London: Methuen, 1979) contains useful historical and cultural surveys.

In French, the relevant volumes of the 'Nouvelle Histoire de la France contemporaine', published by Éditions du Seuil 1975–6, cannot be beaten as short introductions with useful bibliographies and chronologies. They are J.-M. Mayeur, *Les Débuts de la Troisième République 1871–1898*; Madeleine Rebérioux, *La République radicale? 1898–1914*; J.-J. Becker and S. Berstein, *Victoire et frustrations 1914–1929*; Dominique Borne and Henri Dubief, *La Crise des années 30 1929–1938*; and Jean-Pierre Azéma, *De Munich à la Libération 1938–1944*. J.-P. Azéma and M. Winock, *La Troisième République 1870–1940* (Paris: Calmann-Lévy, 1970) is still very useful.

### The early Third Republic

Eugen Weber remains the leading English-language authority on the period up to 1914. His studies of the modernization of rural France, *Peasants into Frenchmen* (London: Chatto & Windus, 1979), and of right-wing movements, *Action française* (Stanford, Calif.: Stanford University Press, 1962), will not be superseded for a long time. René Rémond's classic *Les Droites en France* (Paris: Aubier Montaigne, 1982) makes sense of much of the political ferment of the early Third Republic, while Raoul Girardet's anthology *Le Nationalisme français* (Paris: Seuil, 1982) contains useful extracts from key texts and his *L'Idée coloniale en France de 1871–1902* (Paris: Table Ronde, 1972) places discussions of nationalism in the perspective of colonial acquisition.

### Republicanism and the rise of the intellectual

Maurice Agulhon, *Marianne au pouvoir: l'imagerie et la symbolique républicaines de 1880 à 1914* (Paris: Flammarion, 1989) studies republican iconography. Katharine Auspitz, *The Radical Bourgeoisie, la Ligue de l'Enseignement and the Origins of the Third Republic 1866–1885* (Cambridge: Cambridge University Press, 1982) looks at the significance of the reform of education. Christophe Charle, *La Crise littéraire à l'époque du naturalisme* (Paris: Presses de l'École normale supérieure, 1979) is a sociological study of writers and intellectuals by a member of Bourdieu's school. The Dreyfus Affair is discussed in N. Kleeblatt (ed.), *The Dreyfus Affair: Art, Truth and Justice* (Berkeley and Los Angeles: University of California Press, 1987) while Claude Nicolet, *L'Idée républicaine en France* (Paris: Gallimard, 1982) looks at the spread of Republicanism.

### Literary and artistic movements up to 1914

Malcolm Bradbury and James McFarlane, *Modernism: A Guide to European Literature* (London: Penguin Books, 1991) is a good starting-point for an appreciation of artistic movements in late nineteenth-century France, while Mikulas Teich and Roy Porter, *The Fin de siècle and its Legacy* (Cambridge: Cambridge University Press, 1990) and Shearer West, *Fin de siècle: Art and Society in an Age of Uncertainty* (London: Bloomsbury, 1993) concentrate on art in French society. Gordon Millan, *Mallarmé: A Throw of the Dice* (London: Secker & Warburg, 1994) shows why this poet was exemplary and contains much additional information about contemporary literary movements, while Paul Griffiths, *Modern Music* (London: Thames & Hudson, 1992) places Wagnerism in context.

There is a wealth of material on French painting 1870–1914. Useful starting-points are Bernard Denvir, *Encyclopaedia of Impressionism* (London: Thames & Hudson, 1990), *Post-Impressionism* (London: Thames & Hudson, 1992), and Edward F. Fry, *Cubism* (London: Thames & Hudson, 1978). David Britt (ed.), *Modern Art: Impressionism to Postmodernism* (London: Thames & Hudson, 1992) is a stimulating collection of essays, many of which relate to this period. Timothy J. Clark, *The Painting of Modern Life: Paris in the Art of Manet and his Followers* (London: Thames & Hudson, 1990) and Robert L. Herbert, *Impressionism: Art, Leisure and Parisian Society* (Cambridge, Mass.: Yale University Press, 1988) both offer new interpretations of late nineteenth-century French art in its social context, while Debora Silverman, *Art nouveau in Fin de siècle France* (Cambridge, Mass.: Harvard University Press, 1986) concentrates on questions of design in social context and Phillip Dennis Cate (ed.), *The Graphic Arts and French Society 1987–1914* (London: Rutgers University Press, 1988) discusses the impact of mass circulation newspapers and the rise of consumer culture on the arts.

### Culture and leisure before 1914

Eugen Weber, *France fin de siècle* (Cambridge, Mass.: Harvard University Press, 1986) is a witty and entertaining essay on cultural and leisure activities, discussing matters which range from corsets and bicycles to electricity and how often French people took a bath.

Similar questions are studied in Rachel Bowlby, *Just Looking: Consumer Culture in Dreiser, Gissing and Zola* (London: Methuen, 1985), Louis Chevalier, *Montmartre du plaisir et du crime* (Paris: Éditions Robert Laffont, 1980), Richard Holt, *Sport and Society in Modern France* (London: Macmillan, 1981), Michael Marrus, *The Emergence of Leisure in Industrial Society* (New York: Harper & Row, 1974), Kirk Varnedoe and Adam Gopnik, *High and Low: Modern Art and Popular Culture* (New York: Museum of Modern Art, 1991), and Rosalind H. Williams, *Dream Worlds: Mass Consumption in Late Nineteenth Century France* (Berkeley and Los Angeles: University of California Press, 1982). The best book on the origins of the French cinema is Richard Abel, *French Cinema: The First Wave* (Princeton: Princeton University Press, 1984) which may be complemented by Pierre Jenn, *Georges Méliès cinéaste* (Paris: Albatros, 1984) and Madeleine Malthête-Méliès (ed.), *Méliès et la naissance du spectacle cinématographique* (Paris: Klincksieck, 1984).

### Sexuality and gender before 1914

These issues are a fashionable and fertile area of contemporary investigation and a number of recent studies have contributed to reinterpretations of the first part of the Third Republic. James F. Mcmillan, *Housewife or Harlot: The Place of Women in French Society 1870–1940* (Brighton: Croom Helm, 1981) is a historian's consideration of 'the woman question' in France. Some of the same material is covered in volume 5 of the more recent Georges Duby and Michelle Perrot (eds.), *Histoire des femmes en Occident*, 5 vols. (Paris: Plon, 1991–2), although the scope of the book is much broader. Antony Copley, *Sexual Moralities in France 1780–1980* (London: Routledge, 1989) is a polemical essay on the institution of sexual difference; Griselda Pollock, *Vision and Difference: Femininity, Feminism and the Histories of Art* (London: Routledge, 1988) and Richard Kendall and Griselda Pollock (eds.), *Dealing with Degas: Representations of Women and the Politics of Vision* (London: Pandora, 1992) look at how images of women were constructed in this period, as does Bram Dijkstra, *Idols of Perversity: Fantasies of Feminine Evil in Fin-de-siècle Culture* (New York: Oxford University Press, 1986).

### The First World War

The war is well covered in standard histories already mentioned. In addition Jean-Jacques Becker, *The Great War and the French People* (Leamington Spa: Berg, 1985) is a good social history of the period. There are useful essays in Michael Scriven and Peter Wagstaff (eds.), *War and Society in Twentieth-Century France* (London: Berg, 1991). M. Tison-Braun, *La Crise de l'humanisme*, vol. ii (Paris: Nizet, 1967) deals with some of the intellectual implications, while the literary aspects are dealt with in a number of works, including F. Field, *Three French Writers and the Great War* (Cambridge: Cambridge University Press, 1975), John Flower, *Literature and the Left in France* (London: Macmillan, 1983), Denis Hollier (ed.), *A New History of French Literature* (Cambridge, Mass.: Harvard University Press, 1989), and John Cruickshank (ed.), *French Literature and its Background*, vol. vi (Oxford: Oxford University Press, 1970). The role of the press in general is discussed in P. Albert and F. Tarrou, 'La Presse en France dans la Grande Guerre', in *Histoire de la presse* (Paris: Presses universitaires de France, 1988), and a particular case is discussed in M. Dupuy, *Le Petit Parisien* (Paris: Plon, 1989). Cinema is succinctly covered in Georges Sadoul, *Le Cinéma français* (Paris: Flammarion, 1962).

### The 1920s and 1930s

The inter-war period is amply described in the general histories mentioned, though useful particular studies are offered by N. Greene, *From Versailles to Vichy: The Third French Republic* (New York: Cromwell, 1970), C. Fohlen, *La France de l'entre-deux-guerres, 1917–1939* (Paris: Casterman, 1972), J. Jackson, *The Popular Front in France* (London, 1988), and René Remond, *Les Catholiques, le communisme et les crises 1929–1939* (Paris: Armand Colin, 1960). The reportage of the *Manchester Guardian's* correspondent Alexander Werth is still good reading, especially *France in Ferment 1933–1935* (London: Jarrolds, 1935), and *France and Munich, before and after the Surrender* (London: Hamish Hamilton, 1939).

David Caute, *Communism and the French Intellectuals 1914–1960* (London: Macmillan, 1964) is still highly informative. Adrien Dansette, *Destin du catholicisme français 1926–1956* (Paris: Flammarion, 1957) is still the standard work on religious developments. Technological advance is described in Anne and André Lejard (eds.), *50 années de découvertes: bilan 1900–1950* (Paris: Seuil, 1950). Olivier Barrot and Pascal Ory (eds.), *Entre deux guerres: la création française 1919–1939* (Paris: François Bourin, 1990) gives some excellent essays on a wide range of cultural objects and events, as does Guillaume Guilleminault (ed.), *Les Années folles* (Paris: Denoël, 1958). Michèle Cointet, *Histoire culturelle de la France 1918–1958* (Paris: SEDES, 1988) is a useful overview. Pontus Hulten (ed.), *Paris–Paris 1937–1957* (Paris: Centre Georges Pompidou, 1981) is the very rich catalogue of a major exhibition covering the whole cultural field, while Douglas and Madeleine Johnson, *The Age of Illusion: Art and Politics in France 1918–1940* (London: Thames & Hudson, 1987) is an excellent evocation of the period through commented contemporary images.

Pascal Ory and Jean-François Sirinelli, *Les Intellectuels en France, de l'affaire Dreyfus à nos jours* (Paris: Armand Colin, 1986) gives an excellent intellectual history. Cinema has been well documented, most recently in Colin Crisp, *The Classic French Cinema 1930–1960* (Bloomington, Ind.: Indiana University Press, 1993), while Keith Reader and Ginette Vincendeau (eds.), *La Vie est à nous: French Cinema of the Popular Front* (London, National Film Theatre, 1986) contains much useful material. Among the innumerable works on Surrealism, Alexandrian Sarabem, *Surrealist Art* (London: Thames & Hudson, 1978) and Maurice Nadeau, *Histoire du surréalisme* (Paris: Seuil, 1964) are particularly accessible.

Literature of the period is most often studied by author, but wider syntheses can be found in Nicholas Hewitt, *Les Maladies du siècle* (Hull: Hull University Press, 1988) and Max Adereth, *Commitment in Modern French Literature* (London: Gollancz, 1967). On popular culture, useful works are Henri Filippini, *Dictionnaire de la bande dessinée* (Paris: Bordas, 1989), Jean-Claude Klein, *Florilège de la chanson française* (Paris: Bordas, 1990), and Georges Petiot, *Le Robert des sports: dictionnaire de la langue des sports* (Paris: Robert, 1982).

### The Second World War

The Fall of France, the Occupation, the confrontation between Vichy and the Resistance, and the Free French have been the subject of voluminous commentary, which continues unabated. The best short introduction in English is H. R. Kedward, *Occupied France: Collaboration and Resistance 1940–1944* (Oxford: Blackwell, 1985). On Vichy, Robert G. Paxton, *Vichy France: Old Guard and New Order 1940–1944* (New York: Barrie & Jenkins, 1972) is still a classic, while in French Yves Durand, *Vichy 1940–1944* (Paris: Bordas, 1972) and Jean-Pierre Azéma and François Bédarida (eds.), *Le Régime de Vichy et les Français* (Paris: Fayard, 1992) are very approachable. Among the major works on the Resistance Henri Noguères,

*Histoire de la Résistance en France de 1940–1945* (Paris: Laffont, 1967–81) is the standard, and on life in occupied France Henri Amouroux, *La Grande Histoire des Français sous l'occupation* (Paris: Fayard, 1976–89) is almost inexhaustible; Jean-Louis Crémieux-Brilhac, *Les Français de l'an 40* (Paris: Gallimard, 1990) is also useful. French attitudes are well documented in Pierre Laborie, *L'Opinion française sous Vichy* (Paris: Seuil, 1990) and Claude Lévy, *Les Nouveaux Temps et l'idéologie de la collaboration* (Paris: Armand Colin & Presses de la Fondation nationale des sciences, 1974).

The culture of occupied France has attracted much interest, and there are useful essays in Gerhardt Hirschfeld and Patrick Marsh (eds.), *Collaboration in France: Politics and Culture during the Nazi Occupation 1940–1944* (Oxford: Berg, 1989) and H. R. Kedward and Roger Austin (eds.), *Vichy France and the Resistance: Culture and Ideology* (London: Croom Helm, 1985). Excellent French accounts can be found in Christian Faure, *Le Projet culturel de Vichy* (Lyon: Presses universitaires de Lyon & CNRS, 1989) and Jean-Pierre Rioux (ed.), *La Vie culturelle sous Vichy* (Paris: Éditions complexe, 1990). Recent special numbers of journals dealing with these issues in English include 'The Invasion and Occupation of France 1940–1944: Intellectual and Cultural Responses', *Journal of European Studies* (Mar.–June 1993) and 'The Occupation in French Literature and Film 1940–1992', *Esprit créateur* (Spring 1993).

Margaret Atack, *Literature and the French Resistance: Cultural Politics and Narrative Forms 1940–1950* (Manchester: Manchester University Press, 1989) gives a detailed analysis of literary representations of the period, as do James Steel, *Littératures de l'ombre* (Paris: Presses de la Fondation nationale des sciences politiques, 1991) and the collective work *La Littérature française sous l'occupation: actes du colloque de Reims 30 septembre–1/2 octobre 1981* (Reims: Presses universitaires de Reims, 1989). The most accessible work on the poetry of the period is Ian Higgins (ed.), *Anthology of Second World War Poetry* (London: Methuen, 1982), and also useful is Pierre Seghers, *La Résistance et ses poètes* (Paris: Seghers, 1974). In addition to more general histories of French cinema, an excellent focused study is offered by Jean-Pierre Bertin-Maghit, *Le Cinéma français sous Vichy: les films français de 1940 à 1944* (Paris: Revue du cinéma & Éditions Albatros, 1980).

The classic study of the post-war controversies surrounding the period is Henry Rousso, *Le Syndrome de Vichy de 1944 à nos jours* (2nd edn. Paris: Seuil, 1990), echoed in 'Que faire de Vichy?', *Esprit* (May 1992).

# Part II

# Reconstruction
and its Ideologies
1945–1967

# Crises of Modernization (1945–1967)

## Reconstructions of the French Nation

FOR most French people, the end of the Occupation is symbol-ized by the liberation of Paris at the end of August 1944. The weeks following the Normandy landings of 6 June 1944 saw some of the most destructive battles of the war in Europe, leaving towns and villages razed to the ground, and tens of thousands of civilians dead or wounded to add to the high toll of military casualties. The fighting continued throughout the autumn and winter, with Strasbourg, on the German border, liberated on 23 November, and the eventual capture of Ger-man-held strategic pockets in France, mainly coastal ports, stretching until the general surrender of 8 May 1945. The pro-visional government led by General Charles de Gaulle asser-tively installed its administration as territories were freed, though the Allies led by the United States withheld their for-mal recognition until 23 October 1944.

De Gaulle's priority, shared by the Resistance and by the majority of French people in the summer of 1944, was national reconstruction. What this meant is usually described in terms of a political reconstruction, which was probably the most urgent, and an economic reconstruction, which was probably the most important. But it also included a cultural reconstruc-tion, both in the sense that culture played a significant role in political and economic recovery, and in the sense that French culture was reconstructed as a national institution and as a vibrant profusion of ideas, images, and narratives.

By general consent, the most urgent task was political: to reunite the country, rebuilding the sense of nationhood; and to restore France's position in the world. The experience of the Occupation had profoundly divided the nation, and in some respects the Liberation was a civil war. The Allies, including the Resistance and the Free French, fought against French enemies not only in the security forces of Vichy, including the notorious paramilitary Milice, but also in the German army, which included French volunteers even in the SS, and pressed men from the annexed French provinces of Alsace and Lorraine. The urgent task of constructing national unity involved a tightrope walk between punishment and forgiveness: punishing the most conspicuous of those who could be designated as traitors; and forgiving those who might be thought to have made mistakes or misjudgements.

The 'Épuration', as it was called, was an amalgam of official and unofficial reprisals against collaborators, heavily dependent on symbolic gestures. Wild exaggerations have circulated about its extent, and it is clear that it was markedly less severe in France than in other German-occupied countries. There were some 9,000 summary executions of suspected collaborators in 1944, with or without perfunctory hearings, but perhaps the most striking episode was the wave of shearings in the wake of the Allied advance. In dozens of towns and villages, women accused of consorting with German soldiers ('la collaboration horizontale') or of informing against their neighbours, fugitives, or resisters ('la délation') were taken unofficially and had their hair cropped or shaven, usually in public, and sometimes with other physical humiliations such as beating, ducking, or daubing with swastikas. Typically the 'tondues' were paraded around the streets on foot or in trucks, to the shouts and jeers of the townspeople, in a carnivalesque atmosphere of mock ceremony. While the hundreds of shearings have usually been regarded as a spontaneous popular letting off of steam, they clearly point to the deep social and even sexual frustrations accumulated during the Occupation. They also raise questions about why women were targeted as scapegoats, ignoring men who were similarly suspected; and about whether the evident misogyny is intrinsic to all forms of carnival, as some critics now suggest. It is noticeable that these incidents have since been shrouded in silence on the part of both the sheared and the shearers.

The official purges were pursued for several years through the courts, with 767 executions, some 40,000 prison sentences, and 50,000 sentences of national degradation. The leaders and most prominent supporters of Vichy were put on trial amid intense media attention, though for the most part the expected court-room dramas did not materialize. Pétain was sentenced to death, though this was commuted to life imprisonment since French law forbade the execution of people over 80. Pierre Laval, identified as the demon-king of collaboration, was found guilty of treason and executed in October 1945.

## Sheared women

As the Allied troops advanced across France, an apparently spontaneous wave of shearings took place. The victims were women accused of having collaborated with the Germans, either by sleeping with German soldiers, jocularly referred to as 'horizontal collaboration', or by informing against their neighbours. The shearings were officially disapproved by the Resistance movements, Allied forces, and French provisional government. However, photographs often show uniformed participants, and in many cases the authorities turned a blind eye in the hope that this method of letting off steam would forestall more generalized blood-letting. The shearings typically have all the elements of carnival, combining ritual and spectacle with cruelty and misogyny. Hair has powerful symbolic importance in all societies, and the forcible shaving of women's heads was often felt as a public act of rape. The humiliations of the wartime years caused a particular rancour among the male population, and the shearings clearly signal a reassertion of male power over women, anticipating the ethos of the early post-war years. Images such as this one have frequently been used to represent the wider movement of 'épuration' (purge) in which suspected collaborators were punished whether by law or by unofficial actions. French opinion remains deeply divided about this part of its recent history.

Writers and journalists, who had been the most visible face of collaboration, attracted particular opprobrium. Some, like Céline, fled into exile, but many were tried. The case of Robert Brasillach focused many of the issues. As administrator of a pro-Nazi bookshop and anti-Semitic editor of the pro-Nazi paper *Je suis partout*, he was a high-profile collaborator, though by general consent a talented writer. At his trial in January 1945 he was attacked for his writings, but sentenced to death for treason. The Catholic novelist François Mauriac, himself a resister, campaigned for a pardon, persuading several leading writers to sign his petition, including Albert Camus, who despised Brasillach but opposed capital punishment. De Gaulle, however, declined to grant clemency. Many intellectuals expressed their views on the case, disagreeing over how far a writer should be held responsible for the deeds of those who translated his or her words into actions. Brasillach's execution became a symbol for the writer's responsibility, though no further collaborationist writers were forced to pay the supreme penalty.

For a few months after the Liberation, writers and artists of the Right who had supported Vichy prudently kept their heads down. Those who had prospered from the exclusion of Jews and Resistance sympathizers from publishing, the media, the cinema, the theatre, and other performing or visual arts now found the tables turned on them. Apart from the limited official bans and purges, they also had to contend with organized exclusion by their peers. Official purge committees were established in many professions. The most active and most highly publicized was in the field of letters, where the Comité national des écrivains (CNE) brought together former Resistance figures across the ideological spectrum, from the communist poet and novelist Louis Aragon to the Catholic philosopher and dramatist Gabriel Marcel. It included Vercors, Paul Éluard, Jean-Paul Sartre, Raymond Queneau, Jean Paulhan, and many others. The most serious cases were referred to the courts, but a much larger number of suspected collaborators and Vichy sympathizers was identified as meriting moral and political ostracism. When the names were published in the CNE's journal *Les Lettres françaises*, they became the basis of an informal boycott, by publishers who would not accept their work, and by fellow writers who would not agree to appear alongside them: in effect a blacklist. Despite complaints about the unfairness of some inclusions and omissions, the sanctions were a powerful affirmation of the importance of writers within French society, and of the moral and political responsibilities which that entailed. The influence of the CNE waned following well-publicized disagreements among its members, culminating in the resignation of Paulhan, an influential literary impresario, and of some of the more conservative members of the committee in early 1947. By that time the purges, like the literary and intellectual debates, had settled into becoming just another issue in the emerging political confrontations of the Cold War. As the months passed, the courts became more leisurely and more lenient. Public interest slowly waned, and amnesties were eventually declared in the early 1950s, effectively winding up the legal aftermath of the collaboration until the 1980s, when a series of high-profile cases (Barbie, Touvier, Bousquet) brought the events before French courts again.

The purges served to construct the nation by identifying one of its Others, in the form of those who by reason of their treason or cowardice had set themselves outside the nation. There were also external Others, primarily Britain and the United States, who served a similar purpose, as France sought to reassert its place among the nations of the world. The first priority was to establish the right to French self-government, somewhat reluctantly conceded by the Allies in October 1944. A second priority was to assert France's right to participate in shaping the future of the world. Denied a seat at the Yalta and Potsdam conferences of the 'Big Three', de Gaulle succeeded in having a French representative at the German surrender, and in obtaining a permanent seat on the Security Council of the nascent United Nations Organization.

More problematic was the task of constructing the nation by identifying its Self. As head of the provisional government, de Gaulle aimed at the widest possible inclusion. But the wider the net was cast, the greater the disagreements might be between its members: he strenuously, though unsuccessfully, counselled against the formation (or re-formation) of political parties so as to avoid damaging divisions re-emerging. Moreover, too explicit an inclusion of even moderate former Vichy supporters would risk giving retrospective legitimacy to the Vichy state, which could be internally and externally damaging. De Gaulle's preferred solution was a government of national unity, with himself as the head and symbol, embodying the nation. This conception of incarnation drew implicitly on Christian doctrine, and his vision of France's mission combined secular and religious imagery in a way that was typical of the period. Speaking at the Hôtel de Ville in Cherbourg on 20 August 1944, he declared: 'We are well aware that the Calvary (calvaire) we are climbing is the greatest and hardest ordeal in our history. But we are also aware of the abyss from which we are emerging and of the heights to which we are rising.' The *calvaire* to which he was specifically referring was the destruction wrought in the battle of Normandy, and by extension that which could be expected in the continuing battle to liberate France. However, the image of France climbing her own Calvary suggests not only that the worst part of the ordeal is yet to come, but also that it must be undertaken as an expiation. The ascension from the abyss to the heights can only be achieved at the cost of suffering freely accepted. France must take her own sins upon herself and atone through death for the ignominy of the *années noires*.

De Gaulle was not alone in recognizing the value of symbols in surmounting, or perhaps concealing, conflicts and ambiguities. Wall-posters were a potent vehicle for such symbols. One of the most striking images of the period is the poster 'Libération' designed by Paul Colin, dated 17 August 1944, which was pasted on walls in Paris during the fighting for its Liberation. It depicts Marianne, symbol of the Republic in her Phrygian bonnet, standing in front of what might be an execution post and shielding her eyes as she looks into the distance. She may be shielding her eyes from the heat of a blazing building or from the rays of the sunrise. Printed in colours suggesting the French tricolour, she wears a tunic patterned in a way that suggests the shells of ruined buildings, and her hands are scarred in a way that recalls the stigmata of Christ crucified. The symbolism is simple and immediate, but also rich and complex.

It is an inspiring image to mobilize the population to rise up against the occupying forces, and no doubt was not read or intended in any other way. However, it conceals further implications which emerge on closer reading. The conjunction of Marianne and Christ is unusual, not least because of the traditional enmity between the Roman Catholic Church and the secular Republic. However, these were heady days of reconciliation and Colin's poster conceivably helped to encourage the process. The implicit transgression of gender distinctions is not wholly unprecedented, and Jeanne d'Arc is an obvious association, though she would be too strongly connected with Vichy to appear explicitly.

Calling up the connotations of Christ after his physical death and resurrection, passing on to a higher plane, the poster may also suggest that the new France would be significantly different from the old, a point which would resonate with the ethos of the internal Resistance movements more than with de Gaulle's Free French. The ruined buildings, which appear on the tunic like an image on a shroud, also carry the suppressed point that a large part of the destruction was actually carried out by France's allies, and it is worth noting that here as in most French images of the period there is a remarkable lack of clearly identified enemies or allies.

Colin's poster is in one sense highly specific to its moment, the beginning of the week in which Paris was liberated. Appropriately, Marianne has just emerged from the tomb and is looking around, perhaps a little bewildered at the confused action which awaits her, and of which she is a symbol. But in another sense, the poster is a model for the entire period. The symbols of the state and of religion are presented as giving meaning and purpose to destruction and death. What emerges from the ruins is hope, which is directed towards a newly reconstructed France rooted in universality and transcendence.

Colin's patchwork symbolization of France finds echoes in the communist nationalism of Louis Aragon, whose poems of *La Diane française* (1944) helped set the tone of the period. Rooted in the Resistance, Aragon's poems draw eclectically on every myth or legend that can help to mobilize the French people against the oppressor: the famous victories of the French Revolution rub shoulders with Celtic folk-tales of Merlin in the forest of Brocéliande; and martyred Resistance heroes like Gabriel Péri appear alongside Christ crucified and resurrected. Any sectarian prejudices are swept away by the overriding need to save the French nation. The spirit of generous reconciliation, though short-lived, was characteristic of the post-Liberation months and doubtless served to carry France through a perilous moment of political reconstruction.

The most difficult of the reconstructions was economic. In the autumn of 1944, a million families were homeless. Road and rail networks were devastated along with large numbers of vehicles and rolling stock: not one bridge was standing between Paris and the north coast. Energy supplies, especially petrol and coal, were severely depleted: people were burning furniture for fuel during the exceptionally harsh winters of the mid 1940s. Industry was almost at a standstill: production in 1945 was down to 29 per cent of the 1929 level. Food was scarce and expensive, even on the flourishing black market, so that *le ravitaillement* became a daily obsession: bad harvests pushed the daily bread ration down from 350 grammes per head in 1944 to 200 grammes (7 ounces) in 1947–8. And unemployment was rampant among the depleted and poorly paid working population.

The most imaginative element of de Gaulle's response was the Commissariat général du plan, conceived by Pierre Mendès-France and presided over by Jean Monnet. By setting positive targets for industry and offering government incentives for compliance, it became an effective and envied planning mechanism. It was helped by the Marshall Aid arrangements of 1947, which made large amounts of American investment available, and enabled France to recover to 1938 production levels by 1952. Succeeding governments followed the Plan in giving priority to rebuilding infrastructures and heavy industry. Even the communist Minister of Labour, Maurice Thorez, exhorted workers to accept sacrifices in the name of national reconstruction. But as the months passed the mood of national consensus waned, and from 1947 demoralized workers began to launch bitter strikes, which continued until the benefits of economic reconstruction began to trickle belatedly down to the working population in the early 1950s.

The hardship of these years looms large in its culture. It is summed up in a painting by Francis Gruber, exhibited at the Salon de la Libération in October 1944. Entitled *Job*, it depicts a naked man sitting in a contemplative posture on a stool in a back yard beside a broken fence. The darkened face and hands suggest a worker, but the allegorical force is underlined by a sheet of paper at his feet, which carries the scrawled inscription, 'Maintenant encore, ma plainte est une révolte, et pourtant ma main comprime mes sanglots' ('Even today is my complaint bitter: my stroke is heavier than my groaning' in the Authorised Version of the Bible). This takes up a verse from the Book of Job (23: 2), where Job attempts to choke back his rebellious complaint against God. It evokes the long suffering of the people, who have laboured under all manner of deprivation but remain staunch in their faith. The persecution of the Jewish people is also an obvious connotation. No doubt, behind the religious metaphor, it is the French state in the difficult winter of 1944 which is the implied object. The people's revolt, sparked by unbearable conditions, is stifled to protect a provisional state on which their future depends but from which they currently derive little tangible benefit.

A similar sense of *dépouillement* echoes in the elongated sculptures of Giacometti, whose emaciated figures suggest both physical and metaphysical anguish. It surfaces in the endless plates of food which form much of Picasso's ceramic output

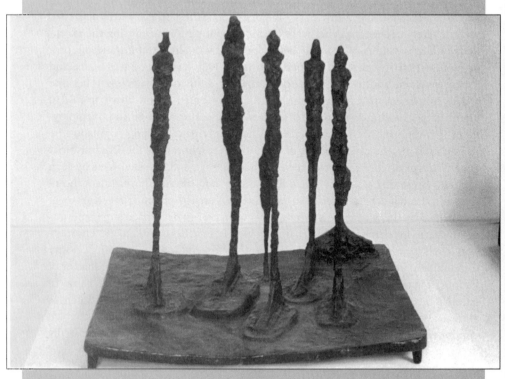

## Giacometti's people

The aftermath of the war left a sense that the human individual had been challenged to the limit. This feeling was expressed in all branches of culture. Many of the philosophers and writers of the period, among them Sartre, Leiris, Genet, and Ponge, looked to the sculptures of Alberto Giacometti as the materialization of what they all felt. His long, emaciated figures suggested the reduction of humanity to a bare affirmation of existence. They seemed to confirm the isolated nature of selfhood, and the brooding awareness that the human individual must constantly confront the reality of its own death. This work of 1950 exemplifies the elongation of the human figure in characteristically stiff poses. Grouped together they are none the less each alone, with no visible communication between them. Entitled 'The Forest', the sculpture evokes the physical and metaphysical resemblance between human life and the inanimate world. It also suggests the widely repeated theme of the 'lonely crowd', which pointed to the alienated, fragmented experience of life in the modern city.

at this time. It overwhelms Boris Vian's Surrealistic novel *L'Écume des jours* (1947), in which an adolescent fantasy of carefree abundance shrinks and dies from contact with adult responsibilities. It forms the meticulously detailed setting for Marcel Carné's film *Les Portes de la nuit* (1946), set in Paris during the hard winter of 1944–5. And it is a recurrent theme of Jacques Prévert's *Paroles* (1946), the poetry collection which was the best seller of the period. Prévert's witty and iconoclastic poems celebrate the joys of love, of innocence, and of freedom. But they mercilessly attack the evils of war, superstition, and exploitation. One of the shortest of the poems is ironically entitled 'La Belle Saison':

> A jeun perdue glacée
> Toute seule sans un sou
> Une fille de seize ans
> Immobile debout
> Place de la Concorde
> A midi le Quinze Août.

(Hungry lost frozen | All alone without a penny | A girl of 16 | Motionless standing | In the place de la Concorde | At noon on the fifteenth of August.)

With deceptive simplicity, Prévert condenses the sense of deprivation into an intense word-painting, contrasting the starving waif with the bustling Paris scene on an August bank holiday. His vision here and in other poems offers a poignant contrast with the optimistic images being circulated by the governing parties, of robust and determined workers rolling up their sleeves to pursue the task of reconstruction.

The fragility of the political and economic fabric of France was matched by the fragility of its cultural fabric. An unmistakable symptom of this fragility was the nostalgia which pervaded popular culture. It was evident in the popular songs of the period. Édith Piaf sang of escaping into the arms of a masterful lover, where she sees 'la vie en rose', a rose-tinted life:

> Des nuits d'amour à en mourir,
> Un grand bonheur qui prend sa place,
> Les ennuis, les chagrins s'effacent.
> Heureux, heureux pour mon plaisir.

(Nights of love you'd die for, | A great happiness which takes its place, | Troubles and sufferings disappear | Happy, happy for my pleasure.)

Performed in the persona of a tiny Parisian street-girl whose voice conveys the suffering she has known, the song is more a plea than a celebration: a beautiful but fragile dream. A more confident nostalgia surged from the urbane and expansive tones of Charles Trenet, whose rendering of 'La Mer' was a hit after the war, though it had been first performed in 1941. He evoked a pastoral idyll:

> Voyez
> Ces oiseaux blancs

Et ces maisons rouillées.
La mer
Les a bercés
Le long des golfes clairs
Et d'une chanson d'amour,
La mer
A bercé mon cœur pour la vie.

(See | These white birds | And these rusting houses. | The sea | Has cradled them | Along clear bays | And with a love song | The sea | Has cradled my heart for life.)

The tranquillity of the sea and the beaches belong to an imaginary world far away, and it has often been remarked that the emotional power of the song derives in large measure from the resemblance between *la mer* and *la mère*, creating an unconscious link between the sea and the mother, which both cradle and sing tender songs. An equally metaphoric approach is at the core of the bitter-sweet song 'Les Feuilles mortes', written by Prévert for Marcel Carné's film *Les Portes de la nuit* (1946) (and sung later by Yves Montand). It opens with the evocation of a past when things were better:

Oh! je voudrais tant que tu te souviennes
Des jours heureux où nous étions amis,
En ce temps-là la vie était plus belle
Et le soleil plus brûlant qu'aujourd'hui.

(Oh! I would so like you to remember | The happy days when we were friends, | In those days life was more beautiful | And the sun burned hotter than today.)

and ends with a recognition that it is irrecoverable:

Mais la vie sépare ceux qui s'aiment
tout doucement sans faire de bruit
Et la mer efface sur le sable
les pas des amants désunis.

(But life separates those who love each other | Very gently without making a sound | And the sea washes away on the sand | The footprints of lovers who drift apart.)

The song has been performed and recorded many times, and the English version, 'Autumn Leaves', is an established 'standard'. While it powerfully articulates the melancholy of a past love affair, and more generally of the gradual ending of things, it is sharply evocative of the nostalgic mood of the Liberation period, looking back to a past when everything now seems to have been good, and reluctantly recognizing that it is no longer available, if indeed it ever was.

In all these songs, the nostalgia was painfully ambiguous in that there was no easily identifiable moment in the recent collective past to which it could refer. All nostalgia is a movement towards an imagined or constructed past, but this past was constructed from relatively sparse elements, and was therefore a double expression of loss, a nostalgia for the good times that had never been. And they often bear the marks of self-awareness which warn the listener not to miss the subtle ambiguities.

Among the losses sharply felt at the Liberation were whole sets of ideas and values which had been substantially discredited. The liberal democracy and secular Republicanism which had dominated the Third Republic had suffered mortal blows in the ignominious defeat of 1940. And its main rival, fundamentalist Catholic nationalism ('l'intégrisme'), was under moral and political ostracism for its role in Vichy. Culture, like nature, abhors a vacuum, and the potential void was quickly filled by a rapidly assembled collage of general moral perspectives which crystallized into humanism. Within weeks of the Liberation of Paris, humanism and *l'homme* were on everyone's lips. Constructed from elements of social democracy and Christian democracy, it affirmed the importance of Man as foundation of morality, and human rights as the foundation of politics. Partly an expression of widely shared revulsion against the inhumanities perpetrated during the war, and partly an echo of the aspirations to a new Renaissance in France and elsewhere, it was also a lowest common denominator shared by all the competing currents of opinion within the provisional government. Based on the socialists and Christian democrats, humanism also enabled the communists on the Left, the Gaullists on the Right, and the centrist Republicans to share the same rhetoric. It thus served as an ideological glue which held the disparate components of the nation together, at least during the first post-Liberation years.

Humanism became a new orthodoxy, albeit a somewhat vague one, and even Jean-Paul Sartre entitled a famous lecture 'L'Existentialisme est un humanisme', despite his earlier attacks on the confused sentimentality of humanists in his prewar novel *La Nausée* (1938). Certainly there were bitter disagreements over what constituted a true humanism, but it was only some twenty years later that respectable figures began to question its usefulness. In the mean time, humanism became the dominant ideological framework in France, and it was generally taken to be self-evidently true that what human beings had in common (a common humanity) should be the guiding principle of human endeavour, and in particular of the state. The loftiness of the ideal was matched by the difficulty of articulating it in terms of specific policies or actions. It therefore served well as a rhetorical discourse within which almost any action could be defended. In due course, its exemplary vagueness enabled it to serve as the house-style of many international organizations, most notably the United Nations. Being so short on specifics, however, humanism presupposes a plurality of contending movements which it can hold loosely together. It was therefore an ideal cocoon within which the exceptional intellectual dynamism of post-war France could develop.

## The French Ideologies

In the reconstruction of France, probably the highest growth industry was the production of ideas. In 1945, two new generations of intellectuals took Paris by storm, and from there exercised an extraordinary influence on the post-war culture of Europe and on the Western world as a whole. The elder generation were men and women born just after the turn of the century, who had for the most part begun to find their feet in the struggles of the 1930s, often outside the mainstream. Their juniors were born after the Great War and came to maturity during the Occupation, mostly through activities in the Resistance. This new cultural élite, unselfconsciously referred to at the time as the new men, were largely able to displace the jaded or discredited establishment, and eager to assume the roles of intellectual and cultural leadership in which the previous generations had conspicuously failed. Broadly speaking, the new intellectuals fell into three linked groupings, roughly corresponding to the political 'tripartisme' of the coalition governments from 1944 to 1947, which brought together communists, Christian democrats, and socialists. In philosophical terms they were Marxists, Catholic personalists, and existentialists, and, though it is the latter who are best remembered, all three had important constituencies, stretching well beyond the Left Bank.

Marxism acquired extraordinary influence from three main factors. First was the major role of the Soviet Union in defeating Hitler. Secondly, the energetic participation of communists in the Resistance was undeniable: the PCF was proud to call itself 'le parti des fusillés', a reference to the tens of thousands of communists who were killed, many executed by firing squad. A third factor was the widespread desire for a revolutionary transformation of society to eliminate war and exploitation, summed up as 'les lendemains qui chantent', a bright new tomorrow. With a quarter of the electorate voting communist, Marxism exercised a strong attraction for intellectuals who wanted to have an impact on historical events. In 1945 the French Marxist tradition was very limited, not least because of the Occupation, when it had been banned and some of its leading theorists killed. Its most experienced and prolific thinker was Henri Lefebvre, whose *Matérialisme dialectique* (1939) had been banned throughout the war, but became a post-war best seller, as later did his *Le Marxisme* (1948). Lefebvre worked to promulgate a conception of Marxism which emphasized the inheritance of Hegel, from whom Marx had adapted the theory of alienation and the dialectical method of thought. Alienation, he argued, is the tendency in society for the products of human activity to be turned against those who produce them. A key example is the experience of workers, whose work produces all wealth but who see that their effort and energy is spent to enrich their employers. Dialectics, he argued, is a method of understanding problems by analysing the contradictory elements within the processes concerned. Continuing the example of workers, a dialectical view understands that, while labour and capital are both necessary for economic production, they are both locked in struggle with each other for control of the process and of its products. Hence he suggested that dialectics offered a guide to action for overcoming alienation, and thus achieving human completeness: 'l'Homme total', Total Man. Lefebvre also traced the ravages of alienation outside the workplace and at

## Dove of Peace

From the mid-1940s the political confrontation between the Soviet Union and the United States divided Europe and much of the rest of the world into two hostile camps, commonly referred to as East and West. A constant threat of this Cold War was that it might degenerate into a military conflict involving the use of nuclear weapons, with devastating results, especially for Europe. There were many movements of protest against this prospect, usually left-wing in orientation, which attributed prime responsibility for belligerence to the American military-industrial complex. Writers and artists were active in the peace movements, contributing their skills to appeal to the mass of public opinion. The Dove was a widely adopted symbol of peace, taken from the biblical account, where a dove returning to Noah's Ark with an olive branch signalled the end of the Flood. The example here is one of several by Pablo Picasso, who during this period was a member of the French Communist Party, and a frequent speaker at conferences of the communist-leaning World Peace Council.

individual level, in what he termed 'everyday life', a concept which later became influential as a measure of human liberation. Lefebvre's humanist Marxism was enthusiastically taken up by young communist intellectuals like the sociologist Edgar Morin. It also attracted leading non-Marxists like the personalist Emmanuel Mounier and the existentialist Jean-Paul Sartre. But as the Cold War began to confine Marxism to a narrowly dogmatic Stalinism, Lefebvre found himself increasingly marginal among communists and ostracized by their opponents.

The leading exponent of Stalinist Marxism in France was the young philosopher Roger Garaudy. In the early period of national consensus, he eagerly portrayed Marx as a great French republican thinker, an heir of Descartes, of the 'lumières' of the eighteenth-century Enlightenment, and of the French Revolution. However, as international relations began to chill, Stalin's lieutenant Andrei Zhdanov issued instructions requiring communist intellectuals to profess obedience to orthodoxy as expressed in Stalin's *Short Course* (1938), a manual of Soviet theory and practice. Garaudy was one of the many to write a self-criticism ('autocritique') and toe the Moscow line. In return he became PCF spokesman on all philosophical matters for almost two decades, eventually having the ironic duty of composing the official repudiation of Stalin's ideas.

But Marxism was not just a body of ideas. Under the PCF's sponsorship, it became a programme of social and cultural transformation, even though the party recognized that the Yalta agreement placed France firmly in the American sphere of influence, and that while they might have seats in government they would only be accepted as a minor partner. Among Marxists' more ambitious enterprises were an encyclopaedia combining all human knowledge in a single synthesis for this new French renaissance; and a plan for a new education system, devised by two leading scientists, psychologist Henri Wallon and physicist Paul Langevin. Neither enterprise came to fruition, but they did help to feed a stream of practical ideas into communist-led local authorities and trade unions. They were also relayed to a wider audience through the network of cultural activities in which Marxists were active. These included newspapers, especially the dailies *L'Humanité* and *Ce soir*; monthly journals such as *La Pensée, Europe*, and *La Nouvelle Critique*; and voluntary associations such as the extremely active women's organization Union des femmes françaises, the student movement, the peace movement, war veterans' organizations, international solidarity and friendship societies, and professional groupings such as the Comité national des écrivains.

In art and letters, the PCF's prestige drew several major figures into its orbit. They included the painter Fernand Léger, whose firm geometrical compositions often evoked strong working-class figures at work or at leisure. The indefatigable Picasso produced drawings of doves for the pro-communist peace movement to use in posters and publications, and even a mildly irreverent sketched portrait of Stalin (1953). Among his major works, in the tradition of *Guernica*, were a number of political paintings on themes of war and peace, most notably *Massacre en Corée* (1951), which implicated US actions in the Korean War. The poet Paul Éluard rejoined the PCF during the Occupation, and modulated his Surrealistic verse to support the party's social and political aspirations. Roger Vailland, whose prize-winning novel *Drôle de jeu* (1945) explored ironies in the work of the Resistance, eventually joined the party in 1952. The worlds of film and theatre also provided prominent members and fellow-travellers at this period, among whom were the director Louis Daquin, the critic Georges Sadoul, and actors such as Gérard Philippe, Yves Montand, and Simone Signoret.

The freedom with which these major figures pursued their artistic vision was, however, something of a contrast to many of their less well-established comrades. Zhdanov's programme included the renewed imposition of socialist realism as the ethos and programme of literature and art, and a good deal of political and peer pressure was exerted on French writers and artists to follow this line. Though difficult to define in specific terms, it was simplified in the slogan of socialism in content and realism in form. It therefore advocated realistic and even documentary styles of presentation, which would be readily understood by ordinary people; and it called for a clear political message supporting socialist (or more precisely communist) policies. Socialist realism was vigorously promoted by the powerful figure of Louis Aragon, whose own earlier novels, culminating in *Aurélien* (1945), were cited as exemplars, despite their preoccupation with the upper echelons of society. He was supported by his wife Elsa Triolet, whose novels and short stories took a strong stance on the political issues of the day. More typical examples are the images and narratives, often evocative and moving, of workers and their families suffering but determined to carry on their struggles, which appear in the paintings of André Fougeron and Boris Taslitzky, and in the novels of André Stil and Pierre Courtade.

The second major cultural movement of the post-war years was Catholic personalism. It sprang from attempts in the 1930s to find a Catholic reconciliation with the modern world in the form of the Third Republic. Gaining some foothold in an otherwise conservative constituency, its supporters were publicly active in the early stages of the Occupation, especially in the official youth movements, before joining the Resistance. At the Liberation they were propelled to the fore as the acceptable face of a Catholicism whose more senior representatives had for the most part been heavily compromised under Vichy. Encouraged by the Christian democratic party, the Mouvement républicain populaire (MRP), the personalists provided intellectual leadership to a large and divided Catholic community.

Undoubtedly the leading personalist was Emmanuel Mounier, director of the influential review *Esprit* since 1932, and author of a substantial *Traité du caractère* (1946), and of *Le Personnalisme* (1949), a widely read popularization in the then recently founded 'Que sais-je?' paperback series. For Mounier, the touchstone of ethics and politics was the human person, considered not as an object but as a point of intersection between three realms: the natural, social, and spiritual. The natural realm is dominated by biology, in which the person is incarnated and embodied, but which the human person is called on to transcend. The social realm is composed of the various groups to which a person belongs, and which they are called on to be consciously engaged in, humanizing or personalizing the communities in which they are involved. The third realm is that of private thoughts and feelings, from which inner strength, conviction, and spirituality flow. Mounier argued that the three domains are mutually supportive and need to be held in balance in order to realize the full potential of the human person.

Personalism provided an inclusive, even eclectic framework, in which St Augustine and Pope Leo XIII rubbed shoulders with Proudhon, Bergson, and Péguy, and which opened links with important Catholic contemporaries. These included Jacques Maritain, who applied St Thomas Aquinas to political philosophy; Pierre Teilhard de Chardin, the Jesuit palaeontologist who applied scientific theories to elucidating the roles of Man and God in the evolving universe; and theologians like Henri de Lubac, Yves Congar, Marie-Dominique Chenu, and Jean Daniélou, who were influential in shaping Catholicism in the second half of the century, especially through the Second Vatican Council. Personalism also provided an intellectual bridge with existentialism and Marxism. Accepting the risks of dialogue, personalism extracted the most powerful insights from these dynamic movements, both of which were considered pernicious by more conservative catholic commentators.

Though *Esprit* established its own correspondents and local groups around the country, its real power lay in the network of Catholic social and cultural organizations which amplified its ideas within France and internationally. The discourse of personalism was adopted in Catholic seminaries, where future priests and missionaries responded to its social concern. It flourished in Catholic schools and university institutes, where new generations of students saw its political extroversion as a viable left-wing alternative to communism. It found a ready welcome in the Catholic trade union movement, the Confédération française des travailleurs chrétiens. And it became common currency in the many Catholic newspapers, magazines, *ciné clubs*, youth clubs, adult education classes, and the like, which brought its language to a wide lay audience.

Personalism fiercely denounced any attempts to regiment culture to suit ideological purposes, but it had a very tangible presence in post-war culture. Its spirit animated the group of young men who had been associated with the short-lived École des cadres at Uriage in the early years of Vichy. They included Hubert Beuve-Méry, who at the Liberation founded and edited France's premier daily newspaper *Le Monde*; Jean Lacroix, the philosophy columnist of the paper for many years, and himself an influential exponent of personalism; and Paul Flamand, whose publishing house Éditions du seuil, founded in 1938, became one of the most powerful in post-war France. Personalist ideas suffused the work of poets like Loys Masson, Pierre Emmanuel, Jean Tardieu, and Bertrand d'Astorg, most of whom looked for a revolution that would be spiritual as well as political. It inspired the literary critic Claude-Edmonde Magny, whose *Sandales d'Empédocle* (1945) wove a spiritual awareness into acute analyses of contemporary writing, and whose *L'Art du roman américain* (1948) offered both an innovative approach to techniques of narration and a more sympathetic view of America than generally prevailed on the Left Bank. Jean Cayrol is now best known for his spoken narrative in Alain Resnais's *Nuit et brouillard* (1956), showing the horror of the concentration camps, of which Cayrol had been an inmate. But his trilogy of novels *Je vivrai l'amour des autres* (1947–50) conveyed the same spiritualist humanism in depicting the struggles of the human spirit in the face of social deprivation and oppression. In a similar though more sentimental vein, Gilbert Cesbron popularized the mission of worker-priests to the working-class suburbs in his novel *Les Saints vont en enfer* (1952), and the activities of foreign missionaries in his play *Il est minuit, Dr Schweitzer* (1952).

By far the most talked about of the post-war cultural movements was existentialism. Much of the talk was focused on the lives and writings of Jean-Paul Sartre and Simone de Beauvoir, who along with Albert Camus and Maurice Merleau-Ponty featured as the stars in popular perception. But the impact of existentialism came from a much wider movement of people and events, all articulating the contradictory mood which was so widespread: torn between hope and despair, between illusion and cynicism, between romanticism and rationalism. It was often described as a new Stoicism, in reference to the classical philosophers who taught mastery of the emotions and submission to the laws of nature. This certainly chimed with the experience of people who had seen the horror and heroism of the war followed by the euphoria and disillusion of its aftermath. But its main focus was on action and the anguish of individuals obliged to exercise their freedom when confronted with difficult but unavoidable choices.

Philosophically, existentialism sprang from the pre-war writings of German thinkers Edmund Husserl and Martin Heidegger. Taking up the long-standing debate between idealists and materialists as to whether the world really exists as we perceive it, they proposed to sidestep the question by concentrating on what we perceive: appearances, or phenomena, rather than realities, or substances, which may or may not underlie them, whence the name phenomenology which they adopted. Sartre was introduced to phenomenology as a student in the early 1930s by his friend Raymond Aron, who was excited at discovering in Berlin a philosophy which allowed people to talk about everyday things.

Sartre explored the implications of these ideas in a series of works, of which the most widely read was a novel, *La Nausée* (1938), in which the main character painfully discovers that the world and his existence in it are contingent rather than necessary: he is therefore strictly superfluous. The same themes were developed in his weighty philosophical treatise *L'Être et le néant* (1943), where he outlines the distinction between three kinds of being. The starting-point is the world, or rather the mass of objects which appears to us as undifferentiated sense perceptions: it simply exists as being *in itself* (*être-en-soi*). Human beings perceive the world, and are aware that they do so, but their consciousness is distinct from the world of objects; as self-consciousness, it is being *for itself* (*être-pour-soi*). Consciousness cannot itself be perceived by the senses, but is a kind of nothingness (*néant*) which inhabits the being of the world (*être*) and gives it form, meaning, and purpose. Not being an object for perception also means that consciousness is radically free and cannot be determined or constrained by anything. However, a person's particular set of physical or social circumstances, their *situation*, is always constrained, and provides them with a context in which, while the options may be limited, the choice is always free. The sharpest restriction on an individual's choices is the existence of other people, who are free to see and behave towards him or her as they choose. Recognizing that we exist for others (*être-pour-autrui*) we are forced into a clash of freedoms: we either attempt to subjugate the other to our view, or try to accept their view and implicitly deny our own freedom. Neither approach can ultimately succeed, since each involves self-deception (*mauvaise foi*). Sartre sets a high value on the authenticity which comes from lucidly recognizing one's situation, however painful, and making conscious choices. He adopted the notion of commitment (*engagement*) to describe the ideal path in which people consciously organize their life around a consistent set of moral and political choices, rather than drifting with the tide.

Sartre's ideas provided a powerful conceptual framework which people could readily apply to their own circumstances, whether to their self-image, to their personal relations, or to their political activities. Many of the issues were dramatized in Sartre's own works, in plays like *Les Mouches* (1943), *Huis clos* (1944), or *Les Mains sales* (1948); in screenplays like *Les Jeux sont faits* (1947) and *L'Engrenage* (1948); and in his trilogy of novels, *L'Âge de raison* (1945), *Le Sursis* (1945), and *La Mort dans l'âme* (1949). In their different ways, each of these works teases out the steps by which people try, and usually fail, to work out their salvation personally and politically. The same themes run through Sartre's prolific journalism, literary criticism, art criticism, public lectures, broadcasts, and interviews: there were few written or spoken media in which he did not intervene. In some respects his most provocative work was *Réflexions sur la question juive* (1946). He drew a portrait of the typical anti-Semite as someone who regards himself or herself as driven by overmastering passions, attempting in this way to avoid having to recognize his or her real freedom to choose. The Jew is seized upon as an ideal scapegoat for all the frustrations and dissatisfactions which beset ordinary middle-class people. Sartre declares that if the Jew did not exist, the anti-Semite would invent him. Jews for their part have to take lucid account of the situation in which others' perceptions place them. They cannot avoid their Jewish identity without falling into inauthenticity, though they are free to assert it in whatever way they choose. However, the responsibility for dealing with anti-Semitism falls on all French people, especially on non-Jews, who are in Sartre's view the cause of the problem. The work has been criticized on many grounds, not least because it perpetuates received stereotypes of Jewishness and casts them in the role of passive victims. But it has two important strengths. First, it openly discussed the situation of French Jews at a time when it was not fashionable or easy to do so. The official anti-Semitism of the Vichy regime was a recent and embarrassing memory. It had secured a good deal of public complicity in the deportation and killing of 100,000 French Jews, and had been highly effective in shaping public attitudes. It was only in the mid-1970s that these issues were publicly confronted. Second, Sartre's essay provided a readily transferable framework for understanding and analysing prejudice, especially racial and sexual prejudice, which is found in any society. Simone de Beauvoir drew on a similar approach in her remarkable book *Le Deuxième Sexe* (1949), which is discussed later. And Frantz Fanon used the same ideas in his *Peau noire, masques blancs* (1952), to analyse the racial prejudice of lighter-skinned people over darker-skinned, especially in a colonized country.

For nearly a decade after the Liberation, Sartre was at the centre of virtually all the major political and cultural debates, giving his forthright views on everything from France's colonial adventures, which he opposed as politically oppressive, to the launching of the 'Livre de poche' paperback series, which he opposed as culturally debasing. Together with Simone de Beauvoir and Maurice Merleau-Ponty, he launched and directed a monthly literary and philosophical review, *Les Temps modernes*, named after the celebrated Charlie Chaplin film *Modern Times*. Merleau-Ponty provided much of the practical political guidance for the review, though he was above all a philosopher, and later became Professor of Philosophy at the prestigious Collège de France. His *Phénoménologie de la perception* (1945) gave particular attention to the role of the human body as both a subject and object of perception, and his later writings questioned the conceptual foundations of political and social theory. With its powerful editorial group, *Les Temps modernes* rapidly became the pace-setter for cultural debate in post-war France. Along with Mounier's *Esprit*, it supplanted the *Nouvelle Revue française*, which never recovered its pre-war influence, even after its relaunching in 1953.

Albert Camus shared many of the existentialists' concerns. Best known for his novel *L'Étranger* (1942) and for the related philosophical essay *Le Mythe de Sisyphe* (1942), Camus developed a philosophy of the absurd. He began from the observation that the world has no inherent meaning or purpose, despite people's ardent wish that it did, and was primarily concerned with how to respond to this basic absurdity, other than by committing suicide. The characters in his novels, stories, and plays explore various strategies for resisting or embracing absurdity: which include seeking the greatest intensity of experience, acting with determined capriciousness, rebelling politically or philosophically, and stoically accepting their lot. As editor of the daily newspaper *Combat* (1944–7) he developed liberal and humane positions on the major issues of the day, earning a reputation as a lucid and compassionate commentator: *un juste*. His heroic Resistance record and good looks (often compared to Humphrey Bogart) also contributed to make Camus an intellectual star. The close personal friendship between Camus, Sartre, and Beauvoir is fictionalized in the latter's novel *Les Mandarins* (1954), and clearly contributed to their reputations being linked. However, their paths gradually diverged as Sartre's political commitment took him towards a revolutionary and pro-communist position while Camus's ethical humanism took him into more moderate and spiritual directions.

Philosophically, existentialism had a good deal in common with the movement led by Jean Hyppolite and Alexandre Kojève to re-examine the German philosopher Hegel. Kojève in his *Introduction à la lecture de Hegel* (1947) popularized Hegel's analysis of the Master–Slave relationship, a metaphor for human consciousness. In it, the Master braves death to secure domination over the Slave, who chooses submission as the price of life; gradually the roles are reversed as the Master becomes dependent on the Slave's service while the Slave learns independence through hard work and coping with tyranny. Like Sartre's *être-pour-autrui*, it was a model that could easily be applied to the complexities of personal relations and to the sharpening political conflicts both national and international.

Though writers and philosophers were the cultural pinnacle of existentialism, they served most potently as the spokespersons or symbols of a much wider movement. In an easily identifiable sense they were identified with the life-style of the Left Bank, and especially the district of Saint-Germain-des-Prés. This was the area where many reviews and publishers had their offices, including of course *Les Temps modernes, Esprit*, Éditions Gallimard, and Éditions du seuil. The leading cultural figures frequented cafés and restaurants in the area, and there are many photographs and accounts of Sartre and Beauvoir writing or entertaining in the Café de Flore or Les Deux Magots. Night-clubs, such as Le Tabou and Le Club Saint-Germain-des-Prés, were opened in cramped and dingy cellars, and soon became a privileged venue for the newly fashionable jazz scene, greatly influenced by black American jazz and bebop artists, like Charlie Parker, Coleman Hawkins, and Kenny Clark, who were regular visitors, as were American writers like James Baldwin, Chester Himes, and Richard Wright. The *habitués* of these places, popularly labelled *troglodytes*, or cave-dwellers, were students, young bourgeois (*les zazous*), and bohemians, who excited a mixture of scandal and envy with their often uninhibited behaviour. They might expect to come across 'germanopratins' like the novelist Boris Vian, an enthusiastic jazz trumpeter and chronicler of Saint-Germain; or the singer Juliette Gréco, female icon of existentialism; or young writers of Sartre's circle such as Jacques-Laurent Bost or Jean Cau.

The Left Bank of the late 1940s was not the exclusive property of existentialism, even combined with the personalist and Marxist movements which were close to it. But the subsequent work of myth and tourism has marked this as the moment of existentialism. The movement had many critics and detractors, who at the time denounced it as depraved, subversive, or even blasphemous. Ironically, they helped to strengthen the myth, giving existentialism the attraction of the forbidden fruit. In a commercial and diluted form, the ideas, images, and sounds spread through the proliferating media which accompanied the eventual economic recovery. Existentialism's political influence was negligible: it had a clandestine presence in the communist party, a more substantial impact on the socialist party, in competition with personalism and Marxism, and some following in the fragmented

Trotskyist and anarchist groupings. Its real importance was in the wider but less tangible underlying beliefs and values which responded to and shaped the mood and climate of post-war France. At this level, the bleak euphoria of liberated France resonated responsively to the message of existentialism.

## Existentialism and *The Second Sex*

'I had begun to look at women with a fresh eye and surprise followed surprise. It is strange and it is stimulating to discover suddenly at forty years of age, an aspect of the world which has been staring you in the face and which you were not seeing' (*La Force de choses*, i. 258). So Simone de Beauvoir described her discovery of the subject for which she is primarily remembered. She had published three novels and a number of philosophical essays when, in 1946, she began thinking of writing something more directly related to her own life. She describes her starting-point in her autobiography: 'I realized that the first question to be posed was: what had it meant for me to be a woman?' (*La Force des choses*, i. 135). Attempting to answer this crucial question soon became such an absorbing project that Beauvoir dropped her original plan and began work on a study which was to become an onslaught on contemporary ideas about women and a founding text of the women's movement in the second half of the twentieth century. Many of the ideas which she developed have become so much a part of received thinking that it can be hard to empathize with Beauvoir's initial astonishment at her own discoveries. Yet the furore that the publication of her book *Le Deuxième Sexe* (1949) caused demonstrates the extent to which it radically questioned the social and moral values of the era in which it was produced. Why was Beauvoir able to engage in such a radical rethink?

The time was right in the sense that women as a group had emerged with new confidence from the war and Occupation. The right to vote, which women in England had had since 1918 for women over 30 and since 1928 for those over 21, was abruptly conceded to French women in August 1944, immediately after the Liberation. Women had played their part in the Resistance and were needed in the workplace in the post-war effort to rebuild. Beauvoir, however, had not waited for the war to build an unusually independent life for herself. Earning her own living and occupying a series of cheap hotel rooms she had no obligations towards a husband or children and no household to maintain. Her lack of domestic and family responsibilities particularly set her apart from the majority of her contemporaries since, despite the encouragement for women to work outside the home, state pro-natalist policies simultaneously encouraged women into having as many children as possible. Beauvoir had also benefited in an exceptional way from the expansion of opportunities for women in education, succeeding in becoming the youngest person (and one of a handful of women) to pass the prestigious *agrégation de philosophie*, a qualification permitting her to teach philosophy in the *lycées*.

Looking back on her position thirty years later she freely admitted that she had been one of the 'femmes-alibis' (token women) that later generations of feminists were to identify as helping to shore up patriarchy. Ironically, and perhaps inevitably, it was thus the very conditions of privilege enabling her to write *Le Deuxième Sexe* which would later become the focus of criticisms of her.

One of the most serious of these criticisms was her adherence to the existentialism of Jean-Paul Sartre, and her apparently complete intellectual and emotional dependency on him. There is certainly some truth in the idea of this dependency, yet, in the same way as being childless gave her the time and energy to collect the materials for her book, her partnership with Sartre seems to have spurred her on in her natural intellectual audacity. Sartre encouraged her project and supported her findings, even if this appears to have made little noticeable impact on his actual behaviour. Existentialism itself also proved a double-edged sword. On the one hand it provided her with the framework of her argument and the ethical impulse behind it: since, in the existentialist perspective, the individual can only construct him- or herself meaningfully through a series of free choices, independent of any pre-existing moral or social imperatives, it follows that any woman who chooses to live a secondary existence automatically cuts herself off from any authentic existence. Such a woman, argues Beauvoir, finds herself cast in the role of object to the man's subject; she chooses to hide from her freedom and is thus guilty of conniving at her own subjugation. This gave the book a very positive dimension since it implies that women can and should take control of their own destinies. On the other hand, the existentialist approach stresses individual responsibility and is unable to take into account the way in which patriarchy functions as an institution. Fortunately, *Le Deuxième Sexe* steps well outside existentialist guidelines and examines in detail the roles which women have historically been allotted and those which biology and contemporary society beguile them into playing.

Beauvoir's argument begins with a series of attacks on the notion that there is a fixed destiny for women. Turn by turn she investigates what biology, psychoanalysis, and Marxism (more particularly Engels) appear to prescribe about women's lot. Her argument is that women are not inevitably doomed to oppression by their physiology, their psychoanalytic situation, or their economic role. The section on biology has proved particularly controversial, since despite concluding that female physiology offers no justification for the hierarchy of the sexes, Beauvoir's portrait of the female body is a dismal one. Women's bodies emerge as something of a disaster area, and the female genitals are described with undisguised revulsion and compared unfavourably to the male's. Many aspects of the female reproductive cycle may well indeed have been burdensome in an age which had relatively inefficient means of dealing with menstruation and in which contraception was a constant problem. However, the impact of Beauvoir's Catholic upper middle-class upbringing is also clearly visible here (as a child she was taught to dress and undress in such a way that she never glimpsed her own body), together perhaps with an unconscious adoption of Sartre's anxieties about the female body.

Another major section is devoted to a wide-ranging survey of women's historical role from Ancient Greece and Rome up to the 1940s. It describes women as fundamentally handicapped by maternity from the earliest times and stresses women's role as a medium of exchange from the time of the appearance of the earliest economic structures. Already here a strongly materialist note thus intrudes into the ontological analysis. The roles of Christianity, of the feudal system, of the Napoleonic code, and of many other systems are analysed to show how women have been kept on the margins of history. Beauvoir seems to have little doubt that this is where women have always been, though later feminist historians do not necessarily agree. The following section focuses on the myths of femininity which Beauvoir argues have been invented to reinforce the concrete powers which men have always held. This is a rich and interesting analysis which ranges from a discussion of the images of Eve and Mary in Christianity to the myth of the feminine mystique. It ends on a discussion of five male writers, showing how literature has served as a vehicle for the creation and circulation of myths about women. This analysis later became the inspiration for the work of Kate Millett and the whole branch of feminist criticism which reads male-authored texts with a deconstructive eye.

The rest of the essay is largely devoted to a series of demonstrations of Beauvoir's fundamental thesis that women are not born but made: 'On ne naît pas femme: on le devient' (*Le Deuxième Sexe*, 285). Tracing the girl's development through childhood, Beauvoir stresses the mother's role in socializing her daughter into an acceptable model of femininity. Up to puberty, Beauvoir nevertheless credits the young girl with a strong sense of her own autonomy; it is at the moment when puberty installs itself in her body that, according to Beauvoir, the inescapable traits of female sexuality finally convince the girl of her secondary role in life. A section considering female sexual response and case-histories of women's first experiences of sexuality follows. Drawing on the recently published Kinsey Report, and on other studies of sexuality, Beauvoir gives frank and detailed consideration to female sexual pleasure, including a discussion of the infamous distinction between the vaginal and clitoral orgasm. Orthodoxy on these questions has naturally considerably evolved since the 1940s; what is striking to a modern reader is the enormous stress laid on the pain and difficulty of sexual intercourse for women, and the very modest expectations of it which Beauvoir, an experienced woman in the throes of a happy affair with American writer Nelson Algren at the time of writing the book, appears to have. Some emphasis is put on the discrepancy between romantic courtship and the brute reality of a sexual encounter: both here, and in discussing the details of the female orgasm, Beauvoir is engaged in the kind of demystifying task which is at the heart of her endeavour. Somewhat naïvely, perhaps, she decided to publish this section in *Les Temps modernes* ahead of the publication of the book. Despite the fact that the publication of the Kinsey

Report had made possible serious public discussion of sexual matters, Beauvoir's chapter caused a storm, and François Mauriac, the Catholic novelist, led a campaign to have it banned as pornography. It was rapidly placed on the Vatican's Index of Prohibited Books. Several accounts of the work by women who read it at the time of publication remark on the fact that it was their first written introduction to the details of female sexuality. The difficulties of heterosexual sex lead Beauvoir to conclude that most women have a tendency towards homoeroticism. A chapter on lesbianism, which also receives mixed reaction today, was nevertheless progressive in treating lesbianism as a positive choice for women.

Almost as shocking as the discussion of sexuality was Beauvoir's analysis of the roles of wife and mother. Love is in itself a dangerous condition for women, Beauvoir concludes, because it tends to encourage their dependency on men and discourage them from pursuing their own goals. Marriage she describes as based on an 'obscene' principle, because it makes a duty of what should be a freely given exchange. It is also closely linked to the role of women as maintainer of the home—a thankless task, according to Beauvoir, because of the ephemeral nature of tasks such as cooking or cleaning which have to be endlessly repeated. Motherhood, another concomitant of marriage, is equally viewed by Beauvoir as highly problematic. Pregnancy seems to her to be a positive incitement to women to sink passively into a fixed destiny; after the birth, the mother–child relationship is described as a battlefield yielding few positive results for either party. She sees the future for child care as being organized within a collective framework.

Other sections deal with the importance of dress, of social rituals, of prostitution, and of the significance of old age for women. Throughout them all Beauvoir urges her reader to accept that femininity is a social product. If we can accept this, she argues, then we can change society to change the possibilities open to women. The book ends by pleading for men and women to work together towards this, and on the expression of hope that socialism will eventually create a society in which everyone will be free.

This rather unsatisfactory ending is indicative of the academic rather than campaigning spirit in which Beauvoir wrote the book; it was not until over twenty years later that she declared herself publicly a feminist, in the sense of actively pursuing the women's struggle independently of any broader political movement. *Le Deuxième Sexe* thus met the fate on publication both of causing outrage and of falling into something of a vacuum as far as an immediate political effect is concerned. When its impact gradually came to be felt, it was largely through the English translation which an American zoologist, H. M. Parshley, carried out in a truncated form and published in 1953. A generation of American and English women including Kate Millett, Betty Friedan, Germaine Greer, and Ann Oakley read it during the 1950s and 1960s and carried on its work.

The American dimension of the work's impact was peculiarly appropriate in the sense that Beauvoir's frequent visits to the United States in the late 1940s clearly fuelled her thesis that femininity takes on different forms in different societies. Her letters to Sartre written during her first visit and her account of it given in *L'Amérique au jour le jour* (1948) record her observations on American women. These observations in turn find their way into *Le Deuxième Sexe*, which, despite its scholarly tone, in fact draws so heavily on Beauvoir's own experience and that of her immediate circle of friends that we are reminded of her original intention to write an autobiography. This is not necessarily a devaluation of Beauvoir's arguments; as Judith Okeley has remarked, the study may resemble an anthropological village study, in which the village is Montparnasse, but the hidden use of herself and her friends as case-studies may be one reason why women readers have responded to it.

Beauvoir's autobiographical impulse later found expression in first a strongly autobiographical novel, *Les Mandarins* (1954), which won the Goncourt Prize, and then a series of autobiographical volumes beginning with *Mémoires d'une jeune fille rangée* (1958) and continuing through *La Force de l'âge* (1960), *La Force des choses* (1963), and *Tout Compte fait* (1972). *Une Mort très douce* (1964) recounts the death of her mother and *La Cérémonie des adieux* (1981) focuses on the last ten years of Sartre's life. Each of these volumes has its own interest, but the first, *Mémoires d'une jeune fille rangée*, covering the years from her birth in 1908 to her meeting with Sartre and her departure from the family home in her early twenties, is particularly interesting from the point of view of revealing how Beauvoir viewed her formative years from the vantage point of the late 1950s, with the discoveries of *Le Deuxième Sexe* already ten years behind her. The title of the volume, with its ironic, distancing ring, itself proclaims her basic thesis that the two forces with which she had most to contend in these years were her social class and her gender. The issue of class and Beauvoir's belief that by her early twenties she had managed to liberate herself from the clutches of the bourgeoisie is certainly foregrounded. The fate of her cousin Jacques, a man who represented a romantic hero to Beauvoir in adolescence and whose decision to marry a wealthy bourgeoise and run the family business, against what Beauvoir sees as his real inclinations, ends in bankruptcy, alcoholism, and premature death, is used in effect as a lesson of the dangers she congratulates herself on having avoided. A second and more tragic lesson is derived from the death in her early twenties of her schoolfriend Elisabeth Mabille, who equally becomes a victim of family pressures; the volume ends on Beauvoir's dark confession that 'for a long time I thought that I had paid for my freedom with her death'.

Commentators sometimes express their disappointment at how little the volume explicitly considers gender as an issue, but it is clear that Elisabeth functions not just as an example of submission to class pressures but also as a model of femininity which Beauvoir would reject. Thus, despite being as intellectually able as Beauvoir, Elisabeth cooks, sews, plays the piano well, and plans to have a large family. Beauvoir's own lifelong insistence that she would never become a mother and would never occupy her life with washing-up is recorded as being already firmly in place in these years. The volume also shows Beauvoir negotiating her femininity and describes, albeit discreetly, her earliest intimations of sexual pleasure, her first menstruation, and the torments of puberty and adolescence. The deep impression left on her by fictional heroines such as Jo in Louisa Alcott's *Little Women* and Maggie in *The Mill on the Floss* is underlined. Her meeting with Sartre is also allotted a crucial role in the narrative of her personal liberation; in the succeeding volumes of her autobiography the account of the couple she forms with Sartre becomes a dominant theme. Indeed, the public face of their couple which Beauvoir constructed made them into one of the most famous couples of their time. Beauvoir described in *La Force de l'âge* the pact which they made: each would be free to pursue whatever relationships he or she wished, but they would tell each other everything and each would remain secure in the confidence that their relationship was 'essential' whereas others would only be 'contingent'. The principle of individual freedom which lay at the heart of existentialism and which Beauvoir had applied to women in *Le Deuxième Sexe* thus became incorporated into their personal life. With the publication in the 1980s and 1990s of their correspondence, the fixity of their image as a couple in dialogue seems immutable. However, as the autobiographies occasionally admit, their arrangement often caused Beauvoir a great deal of pain and probably suited Sartre much more than it did herself. Part of the motivation for the volume of her memoirs seems to have been the drive to convince others that she and Sartre were inseparable.

Few women's lives have been chronicled to the extent which Beauvoir's has. Part of her inspiration to women world-wide has derived from her life-style as much as from her work, though *Le Deuxième Sexe* seems likely to be considered by future historians to be one of the most influential texts of the twentieth century, affecting the lives of millions of women who have never heard the name of Simone de Beauvoir.


## Politics and Culture from the Cold War to Decolonization

Within two years of the Liberation, France's repaired political fabric proved sufficiently robust to weather two crises: first, the departure of Charles de Gaulle, who resigned his presidency in January 1946 to become a focus for opposition, and second, the rejection of the first draft constitution by referendum in the following May. Thenceforth, the temporary consensus rapidly broke down, as a series of fault-lines opened up to reveal divisions as bitter as any in the long-running *guerre franco-française* (Franco-French War). Economic divisions between the winners and losers of the post-war miracle intersected with divisions on a range of key political issues, of which the three most important were the balance of democracy and authority, the question of communism, and the future of the Empire.

The question of democracy and authority was already central to the two early crises referred to, and concerned the form in which state power should be wielded. De Gaulle pressed strongly but vainly for a powerful executive leading a government of national unanimity from which party political sectarianism was absent. The opposition to his *césarisme* (Caesarism) was the main point on which the communist, socialist, and Christian democratic parties were united. Their disagreements turned on whether there should be a single sovereign National Assembly, or whether a second chamber with a panoply of checks and balances should supplement it, preventing any one party from wielding undue power in a single chamber. The two-chamber model, which was finally adopted in a second referendum, largely reproduced the structures of the Third Republic, and like its predecessor proved strong on blocking mechanisms and weak on stable and decisive administrations. Governments fell with depressing regularity, and the premiership changed hands twenty-three times in the space of twelve years, after which most French people were willing to trade in some checks and balances for a measure of strong leadership.

In contrast to the lethargy of the regime, the critics of the Fourth Republic provided much of the energy in political debate, both on the Left with the communist party and its supporters, and on the Right with the Gaullists and a conservative spectrum beyond them. De Gaulle continued to agitate on behalf of his conception of strong national leadership, and in April 1947 founded a movement, the Rassemblement du peuple français, which like all subsequent Gaullist movements avoided appearing as a party, and resembled above all a support group for its leader. This coincided with a generalized *rentrée* into public life of the political Right, after two or three years of keeping a discreetly low profile. Much of its activity was channelled into the RPF, which also began to attract the conservative wing of the Christian democratic MRP, and rapidly took over one-third of the electorate.

The RPF's cultural support was organized under the title of *Liberté de l'esprit*, comprising a book collection directed by Raymond Aron and a review edited by Claude Mauriac, son of the novelist. Both published serious studies by moderate right-wing intellectuals as well as translations of their British and American counterparts. The senior cultural spokesman of Gaullism was André Malraux, whose last novel, *Les Noyers de l'Altenburg* (1948), suggested a path from the struggle against absurdity to the creation of an organic national community as deeply rooted as the walnut-trees of his title. The obverse of Malraux's exaltation was the wave of cynicism directed against the Republic's pettiness and corruption. Its most corrosive exponent was Marcel Aymé, who poured derision on *le résistentialisme* and the high-minded posturing of the government parties. His novels *Le Chemin des écoliers* (1946) and *Uranus* (1948), adapted as a film by Claude Berri in 1990, and his short stories of *Le Vin de Paris* (1947) take a comic view of the pettiness and self-seeking of the 'new men'. Clothing themselves in heroic rhetoric, the former members of the Resistance prove, if anything, more cowardly, dangerous, and corrupt than the former collaborators they so mercilessly harry.

A more dynamic right-wing vision was expressed by a new generation of writers, who looked to the values of leadership and authority in ways that recalled

Drieu la Rochelle and Antoine de Saint-Exupéry. They adopted the label 'les Hussards' (Hussars), following the success of Roger Nimier's novel *Le Hussard bleu* (1950). Nimier, together with Jacques Laurent, Antoine Blondin, Michel Déon, Kléber Haedens, and Stephen Hecquet, constructed a vigorous young right-wing culture. With their roots in the Parisian collaboration circles and the pre-war extreme Right, they developed a network of weekly and monthly reviews such as *Opéra, Arts, La Parisienne*, and the violent *Rivarol*. Anti-parliamentary, anti-republican, and anti-Semitic in tendency, they combined elements of Malraux's heroic vision with Aymé's cynicism, challenging the seriousness and morality of the dominant culture, and valorizing frivolity and insolence as its antidote. The prevailing humanism was a particular target, and *Le Hussard bleu* ends with its hero declaring, 'All that is human is foreign to me,' parodying Terence's classical humanist dictum *Homo sum; humani nil a me alienum puto* (I am a man, and reckon nothing human alien to me).

The combination of Gaullist authoritarianism and a resurgent Right raised the ghosts of an all-too-recent past, and in December 1947 a special number of *Esprit* warned that 'the interlude in fascist movements has ended'. Though, with hindsight, this may appear an exaggerated reaction, it accurately reflects the fear, which continued to lurk beneath French political conflict, of the return of fascism and the destruction of the democratic Republic. It was a fear which has continued to inject unusual passion into relations between Right and Left, especially in the moments of major crisis. For five or six years Gaullist nationalism posed an implicit challenge to the regime, until its leader abandoned hope of achieving anything with the RPF, and withdrew to write his memoirs. Malraux reportedly commented wryly that 'General de Gaulle led us to the Rubicon, but it turned out to be a fishing trip', a reference to the General's unwillingness to turn his strong popular support into a bid for state power.

By the mid-1950s, the dynamism of the extra-parliamentary Right was articulated by the populist movement of Pierre Poujade. In the image of this *petit-commerçant* strong-man, Poujadism made a powerful appeal to traditional nationalism, with blunt slogans and simple solutions. The surge of popular support it received served to keep the fear of fascism alive in the mid-1950s, until Poujade too was superseded by the hard-nosed supporters of Algérie française, and notoriously the Organisation de l'armée secrète, whose fascism was of a much more tangible order.

The question of communism became a major issue as the international climate degenerated into the Cold War. From March 1946, when Churchill, speaking at Fulton, announced the drawing of an Iron Curtain across Europe, the process of international polarization gathered pace, separating East from West. The same process was replicated in France, as in most Western European countries, by the political isolation of the communists and their supporters. Communist ministers were dismissed from the tripartite coalition government by Premier Paul Ramadier in May 1947 after divisions over economic and colonial policy, marking a decisive shift into the new climate. For the next quarter-century, the communist party, with up to a quarter of the electorate, became the excluded internal Other. The gravitation of Eastern Europe into the Soviet bloc culminated in the communist seizure of power in Czechoslovakia in 1948. This fuelled fears of communism's predatory nature, which were reinforced by succeeding events, notably the show trials of the late 1940s, and the crises in East Germany (1953) and Hungary (1956). The parties of the Cominform, the PCF among them, were whipped into a tightly disciplined ideological conformity by Stalin's lieutenant Zhdanov from 1948, lending credence to perceptions that they were in effect the agents of Soviet interests.

Communist influence in France was deeply rooted, not only by virtue of the wartime record of the PCF and the Soviet Union. Communists were widely accepted as representing the interests of working people, the larger part of the trade union movement, and the liberation movements in developing countries. They were strongly organized in a wide range of associations and pressure groups, and they articulated a powerful claim to possess the conceptual key to understanding the world (Marxism) and the political means to transform it (revolution). For intellectuals in France the dilemma was felt as a painful one. If they rejected communism they condoned the supremacy of capital and the oppression of working people in France and elsewhere. But if they accepted communism they condoned intellectual dogmatism and the oppressive practices of the Soviet regime and its satellites. Forced to choose between freedom and solidarity, between the individual and collectivity, between capital and labour, between the USA and the USSR, they chose often in anguish and always under pressure. Many wished or even attempted to have the best of both worlds, or to occupy a space between them. But two signal characteristics of the Cold War, especially in its early years, were that both camps regarded no man's land as an advanced post of the enemy, and that rational discussion was largely replaced by polemical invective. An attempt to construct a middle way for the non-communist Left was launched by Sartre, Mounier, and their circles in February 1948. But within a year their organization, the Rassemblement démocratique révolutionnaire, foundered in the face of attacks from both sides, compounded by the political inexperience of its members.

Consequently many intellectuals supported or sought dialogue with the communists during the twenty years prior to 1968. Broadly they may be grouped under three headings: the loyalists, the repudiators, and the fellow-travellers. The first group were writers, artists, and intellectuals who stayed loyal to the party through thick and thin, concealing whatever reservations they felt on particular issues. The loyalists included Picasso, Aragon, Elsa Triolet, Georges Cogniot, Frédéric Joliot-Curie, Jean Kanapa, André Fougeron, Paul Langevin, Fernand Léger, and Georges Sadoul. The second group were those who joined but eventually left or were expelled from the party in disagreement over some event or policy which crystallized their reservations, and often became bitter critics of communism. This road was travelled among others by Marguerite Duras, Edgar Morin, Annie Kriegel, Roger Vailland, Marcel Prenant, Georges Friedmann, Henri Lefebvre, and even by arch-Stalinist Roger Garaudy. The third group did not join the party but gave their qualified support to some extent and for some period. These fellow-travellers ranged from people close to the PCF through to those who only sought to maintain dialogue with it. They were frequently courted by the party, and at different times included Jean-Paul Sartre, Simone de Beauvoir, Vercors, Maurice Merleau-Ponty, Emmanuel Mounier, Albert Camus, Jean Cassou, Paul Ricœur, Julien Benda, and Claude Bourdet.

Controversy has abounded over the position of these intellectuals. There were many voices warning against giving any heed or succour to the communists, from the veteran socialist Premier Léon Blum to the Jesuit Resistance activist and Hegelian philosopher Gaston Fessard. A papal decree of 1949 forbade Catholics to co-operate in any way with communists, under pain of excommunication. Raymond Aron's *L'Opium des intellectuels* (1955) is perhaps the classic treatise, suggesting by his title that if, to take Marx's phrase, religion was the opium of the people, then intellectuals might be said to use communism as their particular opium. Aron argued that intellectuals practised a voluntary blindness to the evils of communism, largely to allay their sense of guilt at their own social privilege and to compensate for their political impotence. Some recent commentators have been equally categorical: most trenchantly Tony Judt, whose *Past Imperfect* (1992) depicts the fantasies and errors of the intellectuals as the result of overweening arrogance coupled with a radical lack of political morality.

These anti-communist positions share with their adversaries the Manichaean assumption of a world which is divided into two camps: one right, the other wrong. This assumption structured the intellectual field throughout the Cold War. It reflected a global political environment which divided the world into East and West: two superpower blocs eventually capable of mutually assured destruction, exploring coexistence through protracted negotiations and summit meetings. Every move, intellectual and cultural as well as political, was measured somewhere for its contribution to the balance of power between the two camps. Among French intellectuals, both sides were acutely aware of the wider context, and invoked it in the frequent attacks they launched against each other in writing, in other cultural forms, and even at times in the courts. Both sides used arguments selectively, applied double standards, lost their moral and intellectual balance, and seized gleefully on the excesses and inconsistencies of the other.

The resulting tumult and controversy provided some passionate debates, and moving cultural experiences, which attracted world-wide attention. Usually, it was the communist sympathizers who provided the focus, either through the forcefulness of their presentation, as with Sartre's advocacy of communist claims to represent the forces for peace, or through the scandal which their positions occasioned, as with the Catholic *progressistes'* use of a symbol showing the Soviet hammer and sickle superimposed over the Christian cross. But sometimes it was the anti-communists who seized the initiative, as with the *émigré* Viktor Kravchenko's denunciation of the Soviet Union in 1947, and the libel suit which he pursued against his communist critics. The polarizations of the period vested their cultural expression with an uncommon passion and excitement. But there was a price: along with pressure on reason and morality, there were professional and personal strains. Communists or their sympathizers found that state channels of patronage and preferment were firmly closed to them, and in several cases were even dismissed from their posts: Lefebvre and Joliot-Curie were prominent examples. Communist publications were often refused by distribution agencies or retailers, and, conversely, their authors might be disciplined by the party for publishing their work in the 'bourgeois press', as Morin discovered. Sartre's work was placed on the Catholic Index of forbidden books in 1949.

The corrosive effects of polarization of personal relations are evident in the public disagreements between Sartre and three of his closest and most respected friends: Aron, Camus, and Merleau-Ponty. Each in turn diverged from him politically and intellectually as Sartre became more firmly convinced of the historical need to support communism. The most celebrated quarrel was with Camus. Their divergences erupted following the publication of Camus's *L'Homme révolté* (1951), which attacked revolutions, especially communist ones, for leading to systematic dehumanization and oppression. Stung by Francis Jeanson's pointedly critical review in *Les Temps modernes*, Camus took the journal (and implicitly Sartre) to task in a long and polemical 'Letter to the Director of Les Temps modernes', reprinted in his *Actuelles II* (1953). In particular he criticized the armchair revolutionaries who justified terror and repression by appealing to historical necessity, without any concept of what History might be. Sartre responded in an even longer and more polemical 'Reply to Albert Camus', reprinted in his *Situations IV* (1964). He particularly chided Camus's aloof stance which buttressed the status quo by passing a harsh judgement on any determined action the oppressed might take in support of their own advancement. Neither side conceded, and they remained unreconciled up to Camus's death in a road accident in 1960. However, each writer's later works bear the scars of the encounter and a degree of rethinking. Camus's novel *La Chute* (1956) invites the reader to share the guilt of a judge whose self-satisfaction has been punctured, while Sartre's essay *Questions de méthode* (1957) and his longer treatise *Critique de la raison dialectique* (1960) attempt to develop an existentialist conception of history within a broadly Marxist framework. The flavour of these exchanges is vividly caught in Simone de Beauvoir's novel *Les Mandarins* (1954), which colours in the personal tensions that were also part of the context.

Towards the end of the 1950s, the communist question began to lose some of its bitter edge. International tensions were easing, though the Cold War still had plenty of turns to take. Within France, the threat from the extreme Right began to draw the PCF back into an anti-fascist democratic alliance. And intellectually, Marxist theories were gradually gaining currency in circles well beyond the PCF.

The legitimization of Marxism and its dissociation from communism were well advanced though not completed by 1968. The number of ex-communist intellectuals with enduring Marxist beliefs grew progressively. The dialogue between Marxists, existentialists, and personalists accelerated, with much of the Marxist theory of historical materialism passing into the cultural inheritance of intellectuals of any complexion. It was hardly contentious to refer to the struggle between labour and capital, to the role of economics and class in shaping the state and the legal system, or to the importance of social structures in generating ideas and culture. Alienation, and its virtual synonym reification, became *une tarte à la crème*, a catch-all notion to describe any personal or social dissatisfactions, especially with its overtones of Brecht, who had begun to influence the theatrical avant-garde, and Lukács, who was influencing literary theory. One of the latter's admirers, Lucien Goldmann, was among the first to introduce Marxist theory into French academic discourse. In his thesis on the classical seventeenth-century writers Racine and Pascal, *Le Dieu caché* (1955), he argued contentiously that their Jansenist view of relations between Man and God reproduced the historical relations between the French monarchy and the court aristocracy of their time, the *noblesse de robe*.

The assimilation of Marxism into French culture rested initially on the reassertion of a consensual humanism, which Roger Garaudy was urging the PCF to accept as its post-Stalinist orthodoxy, in emulation of its Italian counterpart. His *Perspectives de l'homme* (1959) were an ambitious attempt to open dialogue with all major traditions within a humanist framework, incorporating comments by Gabriel Marcel, Jean Lacroix, Jean-Paul Sartre, and Henri Wallon, among others. And he was a frequent speaker at public meetings with similarly ecumenical platforms. However, there were new movements tending in the opposite direction and bidding to disrupt the returning consensus. Their leading theorist was Louis Althusser, a communist and also an influential tutor at the élite École normale supérieure.

Althusser dismissed humanism as a mystification and an obstacle to knowledge. In two key works, *Pour Marx* (1965) and *Lire 'Le Capital'* (1965), he argued that a rigorous reading of Marx showed the kernel of his work to be a scientific theory of social formations rather than a philosophy of Man, and that the two are flatly incompatible. Social formations are composed of practices: processes in which raw materials are transformed into products by a particular means. The principal practices are economic, political, ideological, and theoretical, and they are combined in a structure where each practice is over-determined, that is, governed by the state of relations existing between all practices in the social formation. This structural conception of Marxism appealed to many young intellectuals who saw it as a more satisfying and sophisticated account than the humanist alternative. It chimed well with the structuralist ideas of Lévi-Strauss, Lacan, and Foucault, and it had resemblances to the thought of Mao Tse-tung, which began to attract more radically minded students in the early 1960s. Challenged by Garaudy and others, Althusser qualified the apparent supremacy accorded to theoretical practice, and therefore to intellectuals. But his adventurous formulations and academic prestige propelled Marxism to the centre of intellectual debate for a decade, helped rather than hindered by the somewhat dissident position he occupied within the PCF.

The future of the Empire was the political question which came to dominate French politics of the first two post-war decades in a way that distinguished it from other European countries. While the process of decolonization was comparable to what confronted Great Britain, in France it became the crucial focus of the *guerre franco-française*, and brought the country to the brink of civil war. The recovery of its Empire was an integral part of France's return to international prestige. During the war some colonies had been occupied by other belligerents, notably Japan in South-East Asia, while the rest, or at least their governing élites, had taken various positions with regard to Vichy and the Free French. With an eye to the resulting sensitivities, the constitution of October 1946 brought all former colonies together with metropolitan France into an ambiguous *Union française*, where France would lead all nations and peoples towards democratic self-government, with equal citizenship. Not all colonial peoples were enthusiastic, and serious rioting on VE Day by Algerian nationalists at Sétif was brutally punished, laying the foundations for later conflict. And in Madagascar, an attempted insurrection two years later was suppressed with a ferocity that left 90,000 Africans dead.

But France's first prolonged post-war colonial war arose in Indo-China, recently liberated from Japan by Britain and China. The leaders of the pre-war anti-colonial struggle, under the direction of the communist Ho Chi Minh, were eager for independence. Instead they were offered a fatal mixture of half-hearted negotiations and military reoccupation by Leclerc's 2$^e$ *Division blindée*, fresh from liberating Europe. Ho's national liberation movement, the Viet Minh, organized its forces under General Giap to begin a lengthy guerrilla war. They succeeded in driving the French out of Indo-China in May 1954, with the fall of the last French base at Dien Bien Phu, though the increasing American involvement meant that this was far from marking the end of conflict in Vietnam. The early stages of the Indo-Chinese conflict were followed at some distance in France, though, as the fighting and costs intensified, it became an increasing factor in domestic politics. The case of Henri Martin, a young sailor imprisoned for protesting against the war, became a *cause célèbre* of the early 1950s in which many left-wing intellectuals became involved. While the Left agitated against 'la sale guerre' (dirty war) which was killing thousands of Vietnamese peasants and destroying their homes and crops, the Right defended the military operations as a necessary bulwark against the spread of communism. In 1954, for the first but not the last time, a government fell because of its colonial failure.

Dien Bien Phu triggered intensified nationalist activities in North Africa. Within two years, Morocco and Tunisia were granted a negotiated independence, though not before causing the downfall of Pierre Mendès-France's widely admired administration. Algeria, however, presented a more intractable problem which proved the undoing of the remaining five administrations and of the Fourth Republic itself. Algeria was France's oldest colony, and its three departments had constitutionally the same status as those of the *métropole*. With its relative economic strength, its newly discovered oilfields, and its large European minority of *colons*, amounting to a tenth of the population, there was a strong official commitment to retaining *l'Algérie française*, constantly reaffirmed from 1954. As the nationalist FLN stepped up its activities, the French government refused negotiations until order was restored, and both sides entered a deadly spiral of attacks and reprisals, atrocities and counter-atrocities, which mobilized and polarized first the population of Algeria, and then that of metropolitan France.

The unauthorized formation of a committee of public safety in Algiers with army support triggered a crisis in May 1958 which threatened a military coup and civil war. It was only resolved by the return of General de Gaulle, with a free hand to write a new constitution. Buttressed by referendums, the presidential structure of his Fifth Republic gave him scope to settle the Algerian war, at the expense of disappointing his erstwhile supporters who expected him to secure permanent French sovereignty over Algeria. In the process he had to survive repeated assassination attempts and an abortive military *putsch* of April 1961 led by disaffected colonels and retired generals. The popular support for disengagement from the war extended to the hundreds of thousands of conscripts who, unlike their officers, had no stake in it and no taste for it. The Évian agreements of March 1962 led to full Algerian independence, despite the last-ditch campaign of terror launched by the OAS. In all some 18,000 French soldiers died, almost a third of them in 'accidents', and 250,000 Muslims were killed, more than a third of them by the FLN.

In the eight years of the war, the mass media played an often crucial role both in France and in Algeria. The widespread availability of transistor radios provided the French government with a powerful means of shaping opinion. In the two coup attempts it enabled the government to appeal directly to the people, bypassing the insurgents. This proved a particularly decisive point in April 1961, when de Gaulle's radio and television broadcast stiffened the reluctance of conscripts to follow officers who would have joined the *putsch*. An appeal by Prime Minister Michel Debré two days later had the residents of Paris blocking the roads with their vehicles to forestall any parachute invasion of the capital by the rebels, among whom the paratroops were reputedly the most fearsome and determined.

The role of the press was also important in forming opinion, but in this case the government could not exercise the same close tutelage as with broadcasting. As a result it implemented a regime of censorship which enabled it to seize and destroy the entire issue of a newspaper or magazine which contained unwelcome information or comment. Most of the left-wing press fell victim to seizure at some stage. It was not uncommon for the police to exercise this power at their own initiative, and even conservative newspapers were at times seized to prevent their distribution in Algeria. For the most part, censorship was aimed at creating what

Pierre Vidal-Naquet called 'the eiderdown of indifference' in the general population, and resignation on the part of the half-million young men conscripted into the army. It particularly targeted material which would present the French army in an unfavourable light, and was in some cases followed up by prosecutions. The progressive Catholic intellectual André Mandouze was one of the first to be convicted of demoralizing the army, in November 1956. His imprisonment sparked a vigorous press campaign for his release.

The publishing houses Seuil and Minuit were active in producing books which might lift the veil of silence, the most striking of which was Henri Alleg's *La Question*, published by Minuit in February 1958. Alleg, a communist journalist, recounted the story of his arrest in Algiers several months earlier by General Massu's paratroops, graphically narrating the appalling tortures to which he was subjected during interrogation. The most shocking revelations were not so much the brutality as the extent to which torture had been organized as a routine operation, similar to a factory system, and capable of high levels of productivity. The book sold 65,000 copies in five weeks before it was banned and seized by the government.

Some intellectuals went further than verbal protest. Francis Jeanson, a leading member of the *Temps modernes* team, was one of many who engaged in serious political activism. Using methods reminiscent of the wartime Resistance movement, he animated a network of volunteer workers to give support to the Algerian Front de libération nationale. The *réseau Jeanson* was uncovered by the police, and its members arrested and tried for their illegal activities. Just as the trial was beginning in September 1960, a text circulated declaring support for *le droit à l'insoumission*, the right of soldiers to absent themselves without leave rather than serve in the unjust Algerian war. Immediately banned from publication, it became known as the *Manifeste des 121*, after the number of prominent intellectuals who signed it, including Beauvoir, Blanchot, Boulez, Breton, Duras, Glissant, Lefebvre, Leiris, Lindon, Maspéro, Robbe-Grillet, Rochefort, Sarraute, Sartre, Simon, and Vercors. The trial itself was skilfully turned by top defence lawyers Roland Dumas and Jacques Vergès into an indictment of French actions in Algeria, and many gestures of support were made on behalf of the defendants, who were none the less found guilty and imprisoned. Many of the 121 intellectuals were prosecuted, especially those in state employment. But President de Gaulle declined to prosecute Sartre and the more prominent intellectuals, remarking that he would not arrest Voltaire. The presidential pardon naturally caused indignation among its beneficiaries, though it marked both a secular canonization for Sartre and an official recognition of the privileged status that intellectuals held in French society. Not all of Sartre's opponents were as forgiving, however, and his apartment was twice bombed with plastic explosive, in 1961 and 1962, as part of the OAS's widespread campaign of terror aimed at preventing Algerian independence.

The end of the Algerian crisis signalled a sharp fall in political activity in France. To a large extent this was encouraged by de Gaulle, for whom a general depoliticization was both a short-term means of recovering from the near civil war, and a longer-term means of achieving a national consensus outside the political party system. The constitution of the Fifth Republic was presidential rather than parliamentary, and de Gaulle adopted a populist approach to power, preferring to develop policy through televised press conferences or through referendums, rather than in the corridors of the National Assembly. His personalizing of the state recalled Louis XIV's much-quoted assertion that 'I am the State' (*l'État, c'est moi*), and the satirical journal *Le Canard enchaîné* was not alone in depicting him as a latter-day Sun King, attended by sycophantic courtiers. There was a good deal of affection in criticisms of this type, encouraged by the renewed economic boom of the 1960s, which promoted an indisputable feeling of underlying well-being.

The flavour of the mid-1960s is well captured in the popular *bande dessinée* of the magazine *Pilote*, founded in 1959 by René Goscinny with the assistance of Albert Uderzo and Jean-Michel Charlier. Aimed at an older audience than the established children's comics, it was independent of the two major comic publishing networks: the Belgian-based Catholic grouping with its flagship character Tintin, and the Paris-based communist grouping led by Pif the dog. The hero of the new *bande dessinée* was Astérix the Gaul, produced by Goscinny and Uderzo, whose adventures were the centre-piece for *Pilote* from its inception. Republished in albums such as *Astérix le gaulois* (1961) and *Astérix chez les bretons* (1966), they exemplify the extension of comics into an adult market while keeping their appeal to children. In a continuing series of adventures, Astérix and his burly partner Obélix are depicted fighting with Romans around different areas of France, around neighbouring European countries, and in more distant lands, presenting national and regional stereotypes with gentle humour. The wisecracking warriors triumph through a mixture of luck, reckless courage, and a magic potion prepared by the druid.

The many allusions to contemporary people, events, and issues make Astérix a conscious self-representation of the French nation in the early years of the Fifth Republic. The Roman army is as corrupt and stupid as any disillusioned French conscript might believe his own to be, but its Emperor Julius Caesar is a figure of power and respect, with a complicit twinkle in his eye. There is the hint there of an accommodation between the unruly French political parties and the aloof *césariste* President. At the end of each adventure their home village celebrates its rediscovered sense of community, or at least its male members do, having first silenced the bard, who looks uncannily like the singer Johnny Hallyday. Passions roused are soon calmed, and with a little encouragement the shared humanity of people provides a sound basis for getting on with business as usual, in what is still a man's world. The tales of Astérix convey a comfortable and complacent vision of *la France profonde*, which soon became a national institution as well as an international publishing industry. In many senses, they are emblematic of the new France of the 1960s which took them to its heart.

## African Literature and Film in French

The inclusion of African culture in French cultural studies is somewhat problematic, for two principal reasons. First, there are questions as to whether African culture expressed in French should be considered part of French culture. Second, it is questionable how far a generalized *African* experience exists, as opposed to the experiences of a multiplicity of different ethnic or social groupings, and of different nations, classes, and genders. Neither the idea of a francophone sphere of influence, nor that of Africa as a monolithic entity, should be taken unproblematically, but what follows will be based on two premises. The first is that through the experience of colonization by France, and the particular cultural endeavours of French colonialism, the ex-French colonies do at some levels share a unique cultural relationship. The second is that, despite its great cultural, ethnic, and political diversity, Africa's geographical unity and shared historical experience is sufficient to justify its being taken as a whole for some purposes.

The cultural history of the former French colonies has been deeply marked by the theory of *assimilation* which dominated French colonial thinking. According to assimilationist theory, the ultimate aim of colonization should be to raise the inhabitants of the colonies to the cultural level of the French, eventually assimilating them into the French nation. For a number of reasons, the theory was never fully put into practice, and after 1903 it was abandoned in favour of a policy of *association*. In the education system, association was translated into the provision of a syllabus which was thought to give more recognition to the cultures and local conditions of the colonized peoples. However, a few individuals continued to receive a French education, and the metropolitan school syllabus was extended to a minority of schools in French West Africa from 1927. In reality, assimilation thus remained an important ideal and sustained the twin ideas that French civilization was superior to any other and that other, presumably inferior, peoples could be raised to a sufficient level to participate in it. These ideas were immensely influential throughout the colonial period, and have left their legacy.

The result has been an intertwining of the former colonies and the metropolis far closer than exists in the British sphere of influence. The significance of this for the educated élite should not, however, obscure the realities of education provision under colonization. In Senegal, the country with the highest school attendance in French West Africa, less than 1 per cent of children of school-going age were in school by 1938. Nor should the ideological hegemony exercised by France obscure the fact that French colonization was nowhere accepted without resistance, frequently involving armed confrontation. The costs to Africans of what was called pacification were often extreme. Among the French-educated élite, the policy of assimilation produced its own dialectic of acceptance and resistance; the resistance being based upon an assertion of the value of the African personality and the wealth of African culture, against French cultural hegemony.

Africa has a rich tradition of orature, the oral equivalent of literature, largely in the form of tales and songs and, particularly in West Africa, of history and legend handed down by the *griots*, the hereditary custodians of oral history, genealogy, and epic poetry, whose caste also includes musicians and jesters. West Africa also has a tradition of literacy linked to the long-standing presence of Islam. It is thus misleading to talk of the recent rise of African literature, although written African literature in French has only really developed in this century. Phanuel Egejuru suggests that modern African literature in French can usefully be divided into three phases: the period of Négritude, that of analysis of colonialism, and that of examination of post-independence society. The first two stretch from the 1930s to the 1960s.

The pre-eminent figure in the first generation was Léopold Sédar Senghor of Senegal. He exemplifies the dialectic of French assimilation policy. Thanks to a loophole in French regulations, he escaped the effects of the new association policy and received a standard French secondary education, going on to achieve French citizenship and success in the *agrégation* examination. From 1963 to 1980 he was President of Senegal, and in 1983 he was made a member of the Académie française. He is known chiefly for his poetry and for the collections of speeches and theoretical essays published under the titles of *Liberté 1: négritude et humanisme* (1964), *Liberté 2: nation et voie africaine du socialisme* (1971), and *Liberté 3* (1977).

In France in the 1920s and 1930s, first as a student and then teaching classics in a *lycée* in Tours, Senghor collaborated with other African and Caribbean students to found the Négritude movement. The movement drew its strength from a paradox: although it was a reaffirmation of the worth of black civilization, it owed its existence to the fact that black students from different parts of the world had reached the highest levels of the French education system in France. Its medium of expression was necessarily the French language, since few of its representatives were able to write in any other language. And because of the education they had received, their work was heavily imprinted with French culture.

Senghor's contribution to the development of an African literary voice in French is immense. The lyricism of his poetry, and his capacity to draw on African rhythms and vocabulary, produced a distinctive style which made possible the idea that African literature in French could be, in formalistic as well as thematic terms, truly an expression of African preoccupations and values, and thus far more than simply a branch of French literature. His work is often linked with that of Aimé Césaire, the Caribbean poet and dramatist whom he met and worked with in pre-war Paris. Césaire's collection of verse and prose poems resulting from this encounter, *Cahier d'un retour au pays natal* (1947), was published after the war. He drew on the exuberantly rediscovered African tradition and linked it with the dazzling and unsettling techniques of Surrealism. Like Senghor, he also expressed his opposition to colonial abuse in political terms, and served for many years in the French National Assembly as a left-wing *député* for Martinique.

Another dominant figure of the first generation of African writers in French was Camara Laye, from Guinea. His *L'Enfant noir* (1953) is an autobiographical account of childhood in Upper Guinea and of the process by which, as an adolescent, the narrator left his home to study first in Conakry and later in Paris. It is thus at once a celebration of African culture and a record of loss, both personal and communal. Personal because, having left his people at an early age, the narrator is acutely aware that much of their culture remains a mystery to him; and communal, because it celebrates a way of life which was already disappearing during the narrator's childhood.

Négritude, which gave the first major impulse to the development of African literature in French, was both the result of and a challenge to the centralization of cultural life on the metropolis. This literature grew up largely in relation to the French gaze, and the affirmation of cultural worth embodied in Négritude exemplifies this. In an influential essay 'Orphée noir', published as an introduction to Senghor's *Anthologie de la nouvelle poésie nègre et malgache de langue française* (1948), Jean-Paul Sartre describes the turning back of the gaze. Whereas, for centuries, the French have objectified Africans, he argues, it is now their turn to see themselves as others see them, and the experience may not be a pleasant one.

First-generation writers such as Senghor and Laye frequently seemed more concerned to express African cultural values without apparent reference to the French. In fact, the French gaze is always implicit and shapes the very form of the literature. Both Senghor's early poetry and Laye's *L'Enfant noir* focus on the theme of childhood, resulting in an apparently unproblematized depiction of a static African past. Arguably this can be attributed both to a nostalgia for what colonization has destroyed, and to the need for a positive vision in contrast to the image of barbarism portrayed by nineteenth-century French propagandists of the civilizing mission.

The problem of Négritude was subsequently analysed by Frantz Fanon. In *Peau noire, masques blancs* (1952) he argues that if Négritude is seen, as Sartre sees it, simply as a minor term in the dialectic of white–black relationships, then the importance of being black is reduced to relativism. The affirmation of black pride becomes no more than a reaction to white racism, a tactical position which can later be abandoned in the progress towards a common humanity. Fanon protests also against a reasoning which, by identifying the black personality as simply the product of a stage in human development, seems once more to conduct the dialectic on terms dictated by the whites. In *Les Damnés de la terre* (1961), he demonstrates how the initial impulse of Négritude is for blacks to identify themselves in opposition to the definition imposed on them by the colonizers: in other words, in the same terms. Whereas the whites considered all blacks to be uncivilized, Négritude affirms the common civilization of black people everywhere. Only later do blacks escape from the racial definition imposed by whites, and recognize their national differences. Further, a national culture develops not out of the description of a fetishized past way of life, but out of involvement in the people's ongoing struggle for independence.

In both of these discussions, Fanon pinpoints the central problem of Senghorean

Négritude. Senghor's essentialist description of the black soul as being rhythmic and emotional, by contrast to the logic of the white soul, is encapsulated in his famous formulation: 'emotion is black, just as reason is hellenic' (in *Liberté 3*, 24). This goes beyond the description of cultures and arguably verges on a new racism. And yet, to dismiss black essentialism as simply a temporary rallying cry is to negate its very power to rally. Fanon here succeeds in discussing black and white culture in terms which escape from the charge of racism, without falling into what he sees as the other danger in criticizing Négritude: that of completely assimilating black experience to that of other oppressed groups such as classes.

In contrast to writers such as Senghor and Laye, the second generation of African writers in French express a more clear-cut opposition to colonialism, which they tend to see as a class system as well as a racial one. Two of the most prominent members of this generation come, significantly, from French Equatorial Africa rather than from Négritude's home ground of French West Africa. Ferdinand Oyono and Mongo Beti, both Cameroonians, began publishing in the mid-1950s. Oyono's novels *Une vie de boy* and *Le Vieux Nègre et la médaille* both appeared in 1956. Both in their different ways satirize the colonial administration and the role of the missionaries, and show a protagonist progressing from acceptance of white superiority to an awareness of the way in which the colonized are being simultaneously duped and robbed. Significantly, the protagonists in both works are simple people without education: worlds apart from the assimilated élite. Both novels show how the stereotyping gaze of the colonizers can be turned against them. Oyono satirizes the French not only through an exposure of their moral hypocrisy, but also through their physical appearance: in both novels the French characters are likened to animals, and the protagonist of *Le Vieux Nègre et la médaille* has difficulty in telling the whites apart, since they all look alike to him.

Mongo Beti's *Le Pauvre Christ de Bomba* (1956) also turns on the implication of the missionaries in the colonial exploit. The missionaries are not only brutal, repressive, and culturally insensitive in the service of their religion: they also, whether they like it or not, are enmeshed in the coercive business of road-building, and are simultaneously being exploited by corrupt Africans prepared to use the mission for their own profit. In the colonial context, the disinterested preaching of the Word is impossible. Beti's novel *Mission terminée* (1957) deals with the traumas of the educated African caught between two cultures, both of which he finally respects but in neither of which he feels fully confident or at home. As in *Le Pauvre Christ de Bomba*, Beti's target is a class as well as a racial one: he shows the corruption of Africans prepared to collaborate with the colonizers at the expense of their own people.

The Senegalese author and film-director Ousmane Sembène, whose later work will be dealt with in a subsequent chapter, also began producing fiction in the mid-1950s. Sembène is in many ways the antithesis of his compatriot Senghor: self-educated and a Marxist, his preoccupations are with the ordinary people of Senegal rather than the assimilated élite. His first novels deal with colonial themes:

*Le Docker noir* (1956) with African workers in France; *O pays mon beau peuple* (1957) with the efforts of a Senegalese worker returning from France to break the monopoly of colonial traders by setting up a peasants' co-operative; *Les Bouts de bois de Dieu* (1960) with the Dakar–Niger railway strike of 1947; and *L'Harmattan* (1964) with a campaign for a 'no' vote in de Gaulle's 1958 referendum on the French Union. It was with *Les Bouts de bois de Dieu* that Sembène really found his feet as a writer, developing a style of realism capable of expressing the lives of a whole community—or, in this case, three communities living at different points along the railway—and making the community rather than any one individual the main protagonist of the book. Sembène's fiction has increasingly portrayed the internal contradictions and dynamics of Senegalese society as well as its surface. In the 1960s he turned more and more to short stories (*Voltaïque*, 1962) and novellas (*Le Mandat* and *Vehi Ciosane*, 1965), and to film.

Even before independence, cinema was popular in African cities. Distribution was however controlled by French trusts which flooded the market with imported films, thus creating both a public taste and a commercial situation in which it was very difficult for African films to be made or shown. Cinema production in the French colonies, as in the British, began with the training of a few Africans to produce short-length educational and news films, generally concerned with colonial enterprises. In the 1950s the Groupe africain de cinéma, consisting of four directors from Senegal and Dahomey, began to break the mould. In 1965 Ousmane Sembène produced the first African feature-length film: *La Noire de . . . .* Sembène had already produced two short films: *Borom Sarret* (1965) and *Niaye* (1964). Perhaps partly helped by the fact that he had been unable to obtain training in the West and had therefore studied film-making in Moscow, Sembène developed a style which was at the same time Marxist and distinctively African. Using the symbolism of objects such as the mask in *La Noire de . . .* and the intimacy achieved by post-recorded voice-over in *La Noire de . . .* and *Borom Sarret*, he began to explore and interpret the material and cultural alienation of the poor of Dakar.

To some extent, the old centralization of culture on Paris still continues: the concentration of economic resources in France means that much African cultural production is still controlled from outside Africa, and this neo-colonial reality is one against which African artists must constantly battle. However, the development of literature and film to 1968 shows that psychological and economic control being progressively resisted and subverted.

# Modernization and Avant-gardes (1945–1967)

## Modernization and Popular Culture

MODERNIZATION was a central preoccupation of France in the 1950s, as it had been in the 1920s and would again become in the 1980s. Post-war humanism was greatly concerned with the 'modern world' and the role of 'modern man' within it. While it recognized the urgent need for modern scientific and industrial development in rebuilding France, it also had anxieties about the consequences. It was not only Marxists who identified modern society with the oppressions and alienations inherent in capitalist economics, and it was not only Catholics who were concerned about the effect of modern conceptions on the spiritual and cultural traditions of the French nation. In many respects, the two fears were combined in the figure of America, with the potent but repugnant Taylorism and Fordism of its industrial mass production, lampooned in Chaplin's *Modern Times*, and the seductive but corrosive cultural values which accompanied it.

Modernity *à l'américaine* became a focus for the opposition of many groups on the Left and Right who wished to defend France's traditional identities. It resulted in a degree of cultural protectionism, clearly visible in the widespread hostility to the 1946 Blum–Byrnes Agreement, in which the price of US economic aid included increased access of American films to French

## The New Look

After the war, Paris was determined to regain its position as the leading centre of fashion world-wide, and to counter the growing competition from Britain and the United States. Some couturiers, notably the *grande dame* Coco Chanel, had been compromised by their relations with the occupying German forces, and the post-war trends were set by a new group of mostly male designers, including Balenciaga, Balmain, Dior, Givenchy, and Jacques Fath. They introduced a 'new look', typified by this well-known example by Christian Dior from 1948. Contrasting sharply with the 'utility' appearance and limited range of fabrics of wartime fashions, the new look sought to be both beautiful and impractical, despite the continuing rationing and shortages. Recalling the 1860s, it highlighted a wasp-like waist which could normally be achieved only by tight corsetry. Womanly curves were further emphasized by full, swinging skirts, darted and shaped bodices, high-heeled shoes, broad hats, and in some cases padded busts and hips. The new look also played its part in encouraging women to return to a more traditional feminine role of ornament rather than participant in public affairs.

cinemas. A powerful coalition of interests, led by Catholics and communists, secured a measure of renegotiation. A similar coalition also secured legislation applying strict guidelines to publications aimed at children, the *loi du 16 juillet 1949*.
Alongside the moral fervour which had already made brothels illegal in 1946, with
the *loi Marthe Richard*, there was a scarcely concealed determination to reduce the
imports of American children's comics and protect the Franco-Belgian *bande dessinée*
industry which, like the film industry, had flourished in the hothouse conditions
of the Occupation. The fervour of anti-Americanism in some quarters was in
direct proportion to the enthusiasm which all things American elicited in other
quarters. Audiences flocked to watch *Gone with the Wind*, *Casablanca*, and many
other Hollywood productions; children were entranced once again by Mickey
Mouse and Donald Duck; and the intelligentsia became jazz buffs, quarrelling
bitterly over the challenge of bebop to traditional swing. The attraction was not
only a glimpse of prosperity, it was also an image of freedom. Boris Vian's racy
pastiches of American crime fiction, such as *J'irai cracher sur vos tombes* (1946),
published under the pseudonym Vernon Sullivan, were libertarian gestures, aimed
at scandalizing the moralistic conservatism of *bien-pensants* of all complexions.
Then, as since, an imagined America functioned as both dystopia and utopia.

The anti-modernism of nationalists and protectionists was deeply ambivalent.
Most of its supporters were simultaneously proud of the home-grown modernity
of their own industry and culture, certainly as compared to that which they regarded as backward and pre-modern: that is the people of the African, Asian, and
Oceanic territories of the Empire. Modernity *à la française* was treasured as a key
element in France's civilizing mission, *la mission civilisatrice*, which justified its
colonial empire by claiming to confer the benefits of modern civilization on the
colonized peoples. This argument was particularly pertinent at a time when France
was embarking on the reconquest of territories lost in the war and attempting to
consolidate its position in others where the war had weakened its hold.

The modernization of industry was a major priority of the French state, articulated by Jean Monnet's Commissariat du Plan and shared even by the communists. As American funding became available under the Marshall Plan, it was
pumped into public sector developments in electricity generation (22 per cent),
coal-mining (14 per cent), house-building and reconstruction (13 per cent), and
railways (5.5 per cent). The private sector also benefited from strategic investment
and from loans to commercial, industrial, and agricultural enterprises, where they
could demonstrate their adherence to the planning targets for modernization. By
1951, industrial production finally exceeded the output of 1929, the best pre-war
year, and was set fair for the miracle of sustained economic growth which was
later called 'the thirty glorious years' (*les trente glorieuses*). Unemployment was
virtually eliminated and, faced with serious labour shortages, the state and private
employers began aggressively recruiting large numbers of workers who were
persuaded to emigrate from North Africa. The social and cultural repercussions of
this policy only began to be generally recognized twenty years later. Agriculture

was slower to modernize than industry, having been less damaged by war, but mechanization grew strongly in the larger and more export-oriented farms and vineyards. The resistance to such change among small *paysans* added a further dimension of conflict as the question of modernity divided rural communities and accentuated the divisions between town and country. The divisions were echoed in Marcel Pagnol's nostalgic film *Manon des sources* (1952) and his novel developed from it, *L'Eau des collines* (1962), which were the basis for Claude Berri's more recent 'heritage' films *Jean de Florette* (1985) and *Manon des sources* (1986). These works explore the mixture of purity and malice in the rural community and the mutual incomprehension between them and the outsiders who bring science and technology, for good or ill. A much commented court-case in late 1954 focused many of the same issues, when an elderly peasant farmer, Gaston Dominici, was prosecuted and found guilty of a gruesome multiple murder, amid considerable uncertainty about the material evidence and the possible motives.

The human costs of modernization were considerable. Long hours, stagnant wages, and inflation took their toll on industrial workers. Mechanization drove many agricultural workers off the land. Construction work fell significantly short of urgent housing needs. Food production lagged, staying below pre-war levels well after rationing was ended in 1949. And consumer goods such as shoes, clothing, soap, and crockery were well down the priority list. For the majority, it was an unpromising environment for the 'baby-boom' of sharply rising birth-rates which took place in France as it did in the other belligerent countries.

The economic boom of the 1950s, however, was a remarkable achievement. It was not quite as dramatic in France as in neighbouring Germany, but markedly outperformed Great Britain. Production grew by 41 per cent between 1950 and 1958, fulfilling the targets of the Second Plan a year ahead of schedule. France entered the consumer age of detergents, plastics, private cars, washing machines, gramophones, air travel, and television. The *Salon des arts ménagers* launched in Paris in 1953 became the annual show-case for the latest domestic appliances. The 'jeune cadre dynamique', the thrusting young executive, was becoming a familiar figure, with a commitment to business success, modern (American) managerial attitudes, and a life-style of personal development and conspicuous consumption: in Kristin Ross's phrase: fast cars, clean bodies. The lower white-collar professions aspired to the same ideal, vividly depicted in Georges Perec's novel *Les Choses* (1965). His characters, Jérôme and Sylvie, negotiate their scant qualifications into a marketing career while they single-mindedly pursue the dream of an executive life-style. But their desires always outstrip their purchasing power, and their personal lives are atomized in the obsessive hunt for commodities.

As the 1950s progressed, the tangible signs of prosperity began to trickle down to the population at large from the fortunate minority. They brought a mixture of delight and guilt, expressed in two of the most pervasive commonplaces of the 1950s: happiness and hygiene. Both of these were central concerns in the popular media and in advertising, typically emphasizing the duty of women to provide a clean and happy environment for their husband and children, and proposing a dizzying range of products which purported to guarantee success. At the same time, happiness and hygiene became the staple points of reference in moral and political discourse. Politicians promised to clean up crime, prostitution, terrorism, or industrial unrest, just as they had earlier purged France of traitors. Sometimes they were obliged to dirty their hands or regretfully wage *une sale guerre* in pursuit of their ends, though this had its own machismo of the secular saints whose actions were the price paid so that ordinary French people could rest easy in their homes. The end (*le bonheur, l'hygiène*) implicitly justified the unsavoury means.

The logic of his economic growth strategy led Jean Monnet to propose the co-ordination of industrial development at a European level, resulting in 1952 in a coal and steel community. The partnership which grew from this led over five years to the negotiation of the European Economic Community, for which the founding Treaty of Rome was signed by six countries in 1957. Though its long-term aim was political as well as economic stability, the immediate effect of the EEC was to give a further spur to the French economic miracle, through increased access to neighbouring markets for its industrial and agricultural products. These benefits depended on an accelerated modernization, rationalizing and concentrating potentially competitive sectors, while abandoning others to decline. They also depended on a rapid expansion of public education to provide a skilled and flexible work-force, and to meet the swelling demand for white-collar technical and managerial staff, especially in the rapidly growing tertiary sector of service industries. Sociologists like Serge Mallet, Alain Touraine, and Michel Crozier noted the developments, and debated whether they were creating a new working class which might supplant the traditional proletariat of industrially based manual workers; whether they were creating a new power élite based in management and control rather than ownership; or whether they were even ushering in a new post-industrial social and economic order.

An important effect of prosperity on culture was to accentuate the challenge which popular culture offered to high culture. In the publishing industry, the traditionally fixed boundaries between high and low culture were partially undermined by the launch in 1953 of the Livre de poche collection. Supported by a consortium of leading publishers, it was the first of many cheap paperback collections in which the classics of French literature jostled with contemporary popular fiction for a place on railway station bookstalls. Many intellectuals, Sartre among them, feared that culture would thereby be debased, while others hoped it would rather be democratized. These issues fuelled much of the debate around popular women novelists like Françoise Sagan and Christiane Rochefort. Sagan's *Bonjour Tristesse* (1954) was the first of a series of best-selling novels exploring the personal dissatisfactions of young people who took the comforts and distractions of the modern world for granted. Rochefort's *Les Petits Enfants du siècle* (1961) is one of several mildly licentious narratives examining the survival strategies of young people, especially young women, in the modern urban jungle. Critics were uncomfortably divided between assigning them a place within contemporary realist literature and airily dismissing them as pulp fiction. Similar issues arose in art publishing, where the mass production of posters and prints made it as easy to purchase a good-quality reproduction of Van Gogh's *Sunflowers* as it was to buy a copy of Bernard Buffet's spikily sentimental figures of clowns or nude women.

Increasing access to the audio-visual media was an important vehicle for popular culture. Radio broadcasting was well established as the main mass medium before and during the war, and its pre-eminence lasted for more than a decade after it, by which time the number of radio sets was reaching ten million. The state monopoly of Radiodiffusion-télévision française (RTF, later ORTF), created in 1945, ensured that it set aside at least a weekly hour for literary or philosophical culture, though its current affairs and light entertainment programmes attracted much greater audiences. Its power was demonstrated in February 1946 when a daringly realistic programme, *Alerte à l'atome*, simulated an atomic attack and provoked panic around the country. The incident also served to underline the widespread fear of nuclear weapons, then held only by the USA and representing the threatening face of modern technology: the prospect of a modern apocalypse, as many commentators put it. On the air waves there was growing competition from the more unbuttoned French-language stations transmitting from just outside French borders, in Luxembourg, the Sarre, Monte Carlo, and Andorra. American-style popular music and youth culture were a growing proportion of the schedules especially as, in the early 1960s, the battery-operated transistor radio supplemented the mains-powered wireless set.

Radio was a privileged vehicle for popular music, though it also became the site of an unequal struggle between the French musical genres and 'international' rock and pop. In the mould of veterans like Maurice Chevalier, Charles Trenet, and Édith Piaf, who still dominated in the 1950s, younger singers emerged like Charles Aznavour, Gilbert Bécaud, and Barbara. They continued the same melodic and romantic tradition, but added a flavour of transatlantic big-band singers in the style of Ella Fitzgerald and Frank Sinatra, who were popular visitors to France during the 1940s and 1950s. A more distinctive group of singer-songwriters also emerged in the 1950s with their roots in the radical and iconoclastic tradition of the *chansonniers*. Among them Léo Ferré and Georges Brassens proved the most enduring. Often relying on no more than a guitar accompaniment, they sang complex and poetic lyrics to understated melodies which gave scope for expressive vocal interpretation. Their audiences delighted in the morally unconventional and politically anti-establishment sentiments, which frequently led to brushes with authority. Brassens's 'Le Gorille', with its characteristic mix of sexual frankness and social criticism, was one of several songs banned from French radio. Somewhere between the two traditions lay the Belgian-born Jacques Brel, who combined the playful anarchism of the *chansonnier* with the complex and powerful orchestration of the big-band singer. In the late 1950s, the sudden rise of rock-and-roll music transformed the tastes and leisure activities of young people. The children of the baby-boom fed the juke-boxes and jived to the sound of American artists like Chuck Berry and Elvis Presley before shaking to British bands like the Beatles and Rolling Stones after 1964. By the early 1960s a new generation emerged of French rock-and-roll singers, often with Anglo-Saxon names, among whom Johnny Hallyday, Eddy Mitchell, and Sylvie Vartan were the most successful. They were the stars of the top radio programme *Salut les copains* on Europe numéro 1, where the loud, aggressive, and rebellious rock-and-roll movement was soon modulated into the more melodious and socially presentable *musique yé-yé*, named after the Lennon and McCartney lyrics 'She loves you, yeah, yeah, yeah', which had many emulators. In 1962 the programme's producers launched the first teenage pop music magazine, also under the name *Salut les copains*, promoting the radio station, but also sales of records, concert tickets, fashions, and accessories, which featured more prominently as youth culture grew to a major consumer industry.

For the most part, singers began their careers in the small night-clubs, cabarets, and *café-concerts* of Paris and the large provincial centres, graduating to concert tours of which the pinnacle was an appearance at one of the two big Parisian concert halls, Bobino in Left Bank Montparnasse and l'Olympia on the Right Bank boulevard des Capucines. Radio presented them to a much larger audience, especially as from the mid-1950s broadcasting began its symbiotic relationship with the domestic record-player and *chaîne hi-fi*, devoting longer hours to the newly launched single (45 r.p.m.) and long-playing (33 r.p.m.) records which rapidly replaced the old 78 *tours*.

Television was a slow starter in France. Experimental transmissions dated from 1937, and German troops in Paris had been able to enjoy fourteen hours of programmes per day when the transmitter was not disabled by sabotage. After the Liberation, some drama and light entertainment was available, along with special events like Christmas mass in Notre-Dame or the finish of the Tour de France at the Parc des Princes. In 1947 a total of 3,000 sets were able to receive twelve hours of programmes per week, on weekdays only, broadcast from the transmitter on top of the Eiffel Tower. The first regular scheduled programmes were broadcast in the Paris region in April 1950. The twenty hours per week, apart from closures for holidays, included a daily news programme, *Le Journal télévisé*, which provided the main impetus to attracting viewers. By 1960 there were almost two million sets around the country, rising to around nine million in 1967 when colour transmissions began on the second channel. Moral and political censorship was a direct constraint on broadcasting: control of programmes was from 1953 vested directly in the government Ministry of Information, which paid careful attention to the composition and presentation of news, and exercised the right to schedule official announcements. Advertising was not permitted before 1968, though public information broadcasts on matters like health and safety used similar techniques of persuasion on behalf of the public good, as the Ministry understood it. A second channel was opened in 1964 but, with tight controls and comparatively short viewing periods, French television offered a limited output, dominated by news and sport, and interspersed with home-produced adventure series and dubbed American comedy and detective series. Its most lavish productions tended to be historical documentaries and adaptations of classical theatre, generally conveying a sense of the depth and continuity of French national identity.

A striking development of the 1950s was the emergence of mass circulation weekly magazines, as the plethora of newspapers and magazines founded at the Liberation was winnowed out by economic hardship, paper shortages, printing strikes, and fierce competition in an overcrowded market. The most successful survivor of this period was *Elle*, founded in 1945 by Françoise Giroud and Hélène Lazareff. It rapidly became the leading glossy women's magazine, combining fashion, beauty, romantic fiction, household and family concerns. Like others in the same genre, *Marie-France*, *Marie-Claire*, *Femmes d'aujourd'hui*, it offered a mixture of fantasy and practical advice to working women and housewives, carefully calibrating its moral and political stance to be slightly more adventurous than the generally conservative attitudes of its readers. A dominant presence of the 1950s was *Paris-Match*, founded in 1949, whose sales reached 1.5 million per week in 1961. Politically conservative, its feature reports covered a wide range of topics, with a particular preference for the life-style of French and international celebrities, especially royal families. Its special attraction was its high-quality photographic journalism, though this later rendered it vulnerable to the visual competition of television. To the left of centre, *L'Express*, founded in 1953, established itself as an influential commentator on political issues as well as on the burgeoning consumer products industries. Frankly copying the format and layout of the American magazine *Time*, it was a form of import-substitution: a conscious attempt to meet the challenge of US cultural dominance by appropriating American methods.

The weekly and monthly press expanded through the 1950s and 1960s, fuelling and fuelled by the boom in consumption. The reading public was increasingly targeted in niche markets, identified by detailed market research in ever finer categories according to age, sex, occupation, residence, income, politics, religion, life-style, sports, hobbies, or taste in music. As specialized magazines came to challenge the broad-spectrum press, the latter responded by spawning supplements and spin-offs, so that, for example, both *Le Monde* and its right-of-centre competitor *Le Figaro* developed a portfolio of special interest publications, while the top-selling regional daily *Ouest-France* printed up to forty different local supplements.

Culturally, the prophet of this modern age was Roland Barthes, whose *Mythologies* (1957) inaugurated the serious analysis of popular culture in France. Originally a teacher of literature, Barthes adapted the ideas of the Swiss linguist Ferdinand de Saussure on how meaning is produced by language. He used them to suggest that meanings are produced by all forms of social activity and influence people's beliefs and attitudes without their being aware of it. For Saussure, in ordinary language, a spoken or written word (signifier) denotes a mental image or idea (signified), and their combination forms a meaningful communication (sign). Barthes suggested that the same process occurs with images, objects, and events, but goes on to argue that this first level of meaning, the linguistic sign, is overlaid by a second level in which a wider range of associations and connotations is superimposed to produce a mythological sign. So, while 'rose' denotes a particular flower, it also has connotations of love, among other things. The two levels of meaning create ambiguity and duplicity, and the uninitiated may easily fail to notice that in accepting an apparently innocent meaning, at the first level, they are also agreeing to a set of more tendentious meanings at the second.

In the essays of *Mythologies*, Barthes critically examines more than fifty examples of contemporary myths, many drawn from the pages of *Elle, Paris-Match*, and the popular press. A cover photograph showing a fresh-faced West African army cadet provides an implicit justification for France's colonial empire. Spectacular all-in wrestling bouts appear as dramas in the cosmic struggle between Good and Evil. Soap powder advertising attaches images of purity, depth, and moral value to cleansing products. Suspected murderer Dominici is condemned not on firm evidence, but because he looks the part, and speaks like a character in a Jean Giono novel. The newly launched Citroën *DS* ('déesse', meaning goddess) car is the embodiment of spiritual power and magic. The weekly horoscope throws an aura of the occult around vague advice on harmonious relations in the home and workplace. Children's toys carry with them a whole world of social roles and hierarchies. Election posters present images which will package candidates appealingly, regardless of their policies. *Elle's* recipes for elaborate dishes are intended for the imagination, rather than the table of the secretaries and shop assistants who read them.

Barthes combines astute and acerbic commentary with the theoretical framework of semiology, the science of signs. The result is a provocative study which has appealed both to demythologizing cultural critics and to media image-makers and spin-doctors. Much of his analysis became common currency, as the media industries grew from the relatively humble level at which he found them in the early 1950s.

Part of Barthes's enduring attractiveness is undoubtedly the veiled sense of delight in the myths which, like most of his fellow intellectuals, he regarded politically with disapproval. Most intellectuals managed to suppress their sneaking admiration for modern consumerism and the popular culture that went with it. Among the most categorical in this was Elsa Triolet, whose novel *Roses à crédit* (1959) began a trilogy, subtitled 'l'âge du nylon', in reference to the growing popularity of synthetic fabrics. It depicts a young woman who sacrifices love and happiness in her pursuit of domestic appliances and the accoutrements of beautiful living. A latter-day Madame Bovary, she is seduced by easy credit, ruined by debt, and dies in squalor, eaten by rats. Roger Vailland was scarcely less hostile to the economic miracle. In his novel *325 000 francs* (1955) the central character attempts to earn enough to buy a café by working extra shifts in a plastic-moulding plant. He falls short of his goal, crippling himself in an industrial accident as a

## Face decoration

The structuralist movement proposed to delve below the surface of human activity and identify its underlying logic, expressed in terms of the structures or systems which make it meaningful. The anthropologist Claude Lévi-Strauss was one of the pioneers of this movement, exploring the way in which apparently bizarre features of life in primitive tribes could be seen as part of a system of communication. The autobiographical account of his researches among the indigenous peoples of Brazil, in *Tristes tropiques* (1955), analyses, among other things, the practice of body painting to which many tribespeople give great importance. This transcription of typical patterns of face painting shows geometrical shapes focusing on spiral motifs applied to the upper lip. Although the practice has become largely ornamental, its origins are as a mark of the essential difference between humans and animals, between culture and nature. Lévi-Strauss gently points out that these exotic practices have parallels in modern industrial societies, where the human body is also the object of cosmetic alteration, whose meaning might also repay analysis.

result of fatigue. The human price of industrial development is also a theme in Claire Etcherelli's *Élise ou la vraie vie* (1967), where its impact on the North African immigrant community is a major theme.

One of the most characteristic aspects of modernization is that, in marginalizing all of the social and cultural elements which do not correspond to its modernizing project, it constructs an image of those elements as its Other. While this Other may be despised and excluded, it may also become a focus for the loss and mourning which accompany any process of change, and for any opposition to the direction of change. Invested with the nostalgia of lost innocence or the power of a radical alternative, the primitive and the exotic are the atavistic shadow of the modern. Much of this tension is displayed in the work of Claude Lévi-Strauss, the leading ethnologist of post-war France, and founding figure of the structuralist movement. His autobiographical *Tristes Tropiques* (1955) is a moving lament for disappearing worlds. Studying the culture of primitive tribes in the Brazilian jungles, he cherishes the opportunity to step outside the teeming beehive existence of modern civilization and rediscover more fundamental dimensions of human identity.

In many respects, the most damaging cultural effect of modernization in the 1950s and 1960s was to sharpen the contradictions which already existed between the producers of culture and the society in which they lived. For the most successful writers and artists, Sartre or Sagan, Picasso or Buffet, the commercial success of their work provided unprecedented wealth and celebrity; and even at a less exalted level, there were good livings to be made. But *noblesse oblige*, and the consumer, as mediated through publishers, producers, and agents, pressed writers and artists increasingly in the direction of a more professional approach to their work. This favoured repetition over risk, sensitivity to market segment, and an awareness of culture as an industry in which each participant has a particular specialized role. Hence, the privileged status which had previously been accorded to writers and artists was constrained and threatened: a personal alienation which helped to fuel their observation of fragmentation and depersonalization in the world around them, and reflect it in their work. In a series of lectures delivered first in Japan in 1965, Sartre attempted to stem this tide, making an urgent plea for intellectuals to reassert themselves as defenders of universal values. But by the time they were published in book form as *Plaidoyer pour les intellectuels* (1972), they had a distinctly retrospective flavour. With hindsight they may be seen as the first of a long series of interrogations of the imminent demise of the committed intellectual as a historical phenomenon.

As the economic importance of culture grew, it slowly gravitated more into the ambit of the French state. In the immediate post-war period, some limited state intervention took place, building on the different types of action which had been developed by the Popular Front and by Vichy. The Ministry of Education had responsibility for such state involvement as there was, largely focused on Paris but also beginning to extend to the provinces with initiatives on libraries and theatres.

For example, the *bibliobus* project in 1945 set up a series of central lending libraries round the country, with specially equipped buses to take books into remote areas. More adventurous was the initiative of the Direction des spectacles et de la musique, headed by Jeanne Laurent, to establish regional theatrical centres, which laid the basis for the later network of *maisons de la culture*.

A major shift occurred when, on his return to power, General de Gaulle established a new Ministry of Cultural Affairs in 1959. It was run successfully by the novelist and critic André Malraux, who during his ten-year occupancy established it as an international model of arts administration. The foundation of the Ministry sprang partly from the General's wish to give a senior government post to this very prominent intellectual who had been a key political supporter since the Occupation. But more generally, it sprang from de Gaulle's determination to restore his country's international prestige, and his perception of the role which culture could play in achieving that aim. He recognized both that culture was a crucial component of French national identity, and that it was an important asset in establishing France as a country of world rank.

The Ministry was set up by transferring units from Education (notably museums and galleries, music and drama, architecture, national archives) and Industry (the National Centre for Cinematography): a relatively narrow scope in comparison to its resounding mission:

The Ministry responsible for Cultural Affairs has as its objective to make available the major works of humanity, and particularly of France, to the greatest possible number of French people; to ensure the widest possible audience for our cultural heritage, and to promote the creation of works of art and of the mind which can enrich it. (*décret du 24 juillet 1959*)

In the text, the humanist universalism links seamlessly with advancing the national heritage, while increased access to culture sits easily with support for creative work. The reality was less simple since each element had to compete with the others for its position in an order of priority; and the means at Malraux's disposal were distinctly modest. For some, he will always be the man who cleaned up Paris, launching a lengthy programme of sandblasting the grimy façades of major monuments, and refurbishing Versailles. But in cultural circles, his major achievement was the *maisons de la culture*. Building on Jeanne Laurent's decentralized theatre groups, and in some cases on major art galleries, he established eight *maisons* round France, beginning with Le Havre in June 1961 and including eastern Paris, Bourges, Caen, Thonon-les-Bains, Amiens, Firminy, and Grenoble. Malraux's declared intention was to establish one in every *département* as multipurpose centres of cultural excellence. They were to include theatre, music, visual and audio-visual arts, as well as spaces for lectures and exhibitions, and were to be funded in equal parts by the government, by the municipality, and by box-office receipts.

Malraux's vision was greater than his implementation, for the *maisons* were not long in encountering difficulties over funding (they proved unexpectedly expensive to run), artistic policy (in most cases they were dominated by theatre), cultural policy (they emphasized high culture, excluding both popular entertainment and amateur productions), and politics (local councils chafed against central control). Added to this, the most dynamic producers, artists, and performers preferred artistically and politically exciting creations which tended to attract the disapproval of local notables and of government agencies. Sociologically, the *maisons* made little impact in extending access beyond the normal theatre-going public of students, 'cadres', and the liberal professions. All these factors came to a head in 1968 to fuel the deep cultural crisis of modernization which then erupted.

## The New Theatre

The theatre, like any other form of cultural expression, stands in a complex relationship with the moment of its genesis. It bears the imprint of currently prevailing attitudes and perceptions, values and beliefs, whose presence is sometimes overt, sometimes covert, and which a play may seek to confirm or contest, or an ambivalent mixture of the two. This much no doubt can be said of any text, but since theatre involves performance, it is also implicated in other networks of relationships, which make the theatre a special and particularly rich area of investigation. Live theatre always reaches its audience in a mediated form: it has already been interpreted by a director, a cast of performers, and a crew of technicians, who at the least must put flesh on the bare bones of a script. Individual directors have their own views on how exactly plays should be staged. Some will minimize the exploitation of the scenic and technical resources available to them, adopting a bare style which privileges the dialogue, and hence the written text. Others will regard the spoken word as merely one strand, and not necessarily the most important, in a multi-channelled communicative system, wherein every audio-visual element has its own stream of coded messages to deliver. Acting styles evolve, as does the relationship between director and performer, and the relative status of each. The evolution of production methods and values therefore reveals much about the role of theatre in its social context.

The large number of personnel involved in live theatre production makes the putting on of plays an expensive business, and for the survival of any theatrical enterprise audiences must be attracted, and kept. Account must be taken of the tastes, sensibilities, and expectations of the theatre-going public, or, more precisely, of the different theatre-going publics, and how these are shaped and determined. These issues are given an added edge in the case of theatre which is subsidized, whether at national or local level. Sponsors too must not be offended, and prevailing orthodoxies certainly play a part in determining which plays make it onto the stage, and which do not.

Theatre takes place in a public space. The space itself is an active factor which influences the apprehension and experience of theatre: audience response will vary according to the nature of the venue, whether it be the familiar Italianate theatre with picture-frame stage, a café, or a disused warehouse. Equally significant as a shaping factor is the internal organization of this space. Seating-plans may be drawn up on the democratic principle of the single fixed-price ticket, or may be carved up into distinct zones, stratified according to cost. To take the performers out of their enclosed box and to locate them in the centre of the audience, or to have them surround or infiltrate it, is to alter not only the spatial but also the psycho-dynamic relationship between performer and spectator. That theatre-going is an essentially public activity opens up further issues, of collective psychology, or of the role of 'an evening at the theatre' as a kind of public statement, around which various codified social practices can accrete (modes of dress, eating and drinking, for example).

To examine the theatre of post-war France therefore involves more than a study of dramatists and their texts. Live theatre is a point of intersection, a convergence of stage theory and practice, of socio-cultural determinants, of ideologies, economics, and politics. It is for this reason that in recent decades theatre criticism has harnessed the insights of other disciplines (sociology, psychology, linguistics, semiotics) to explore this fertile terrain. They contribute to an understanding of the inventiveness and diversity of the theatre in France in the twenty or so years following the war.

Shortly after the end of the Second World War the Parisian newspaper *Combat* polled its readers on the question of who were the greatest living French writers. The names which emerged at the top of the list (in order: Gide, Camus, Sartre, Malraux) come as no great surprise. But the names of the dramatists who had dominated the stages of the flourishing popular theatres of Paris for twenty years and more (Marcel Pagnol, Sacha Guitry, Henry Bernstein, Steve Passeur) appear nowhere at all. No doubt the readership of *Combat*, largely left-wing intellectuals, was not a wholly representative sector of public opinion, and the criteria for greatness were ill defined. But even so, the absence of popular dramatists in the *Combat* roll of honour is symptomatic of a consistent process of marginalization whereby what is known in France (faintly dismissively) as *le théâtre de boulevard* or (rather more dismissively) *le théâtre de consommation* is perceived as necessarily second rate. It is for this reason that the practitioners of *boulevard* theatre, however prolific and successful, rarely loom large in the manuals of literary history, or consequently in the curricula of educational establishments.

It is instructive to look briefly at the reasons for this cultural downgrading, for it is in contradistinction to the (relatively speaking) perennial constant of *boulevard* theatre that other kinds of theatre have sought to define and locate themselves. One fundamental criticism is that this is an unadventurous theatre. While it is certainly capable of adapting devices perfected in other media (the use of the flashback borrowed from the cinema, for example), by and large it remains on safe ground by dextrously manipulating a set of proven techniques: strong plot construction; carefully engineered dramatic confrontations; a dialogue judiciously studded with double entendres and snappy epigrams. And its concerns revolve primarily around the sempiternal 'human' problems of the family, the couple, love, and sex. More pointedly, it is argued that this is a theatre which delivers what its public wants: entertainment and reassurance. It therefore studiously seeks not to challenge, offend, bewilder, or undermine. It projects back at its spectators a comforting image of a social milieu with which they are familiar, articulates sentiments and beliefs to which they can all subscribe, and by systematically simplifying every issue sends them home with the satisfying impression of having understood the point or message of the play. A theatre in short which, by constantly recycling a repertory of stock themes and techniques, tends always to maintain the status quo. In its most hostile formulation, the verdict on *boulevard* theatre is that it provides its audience with a cosy collective celebration of its own values and attitudes or, more virulently put, of its own myths and prejudices, and a complacent confirmation of their essential rightness. In contrast to this undemanding theatrical mode stands what critical opinion has termed *le théâtre de création*, or more tellingly *le théâtre de contestation*. Theatre here is envisaged as being more than mere diversion: it has an active and constructive role to play in society, challenging accepted wisdom and seeking to promote new awareness, of whatever type.

It is generally agreed that under the German Occupation of Paris the theatre acquired a new lease of life, and this despite the difficulties of movement around the city, Nazi censorship, and the absence of heating in public buildings. In part, no doubt, audiences enjoyed the escape from everyday deprivations into the worlds of fairy-tale whimsy, or colourful historical drama, as furnished by Cocteau and Montherlant respectively. In part too there was pleasure to be derived from detecting the coded messages which had slipped past the censors in Vichy and Paris, such as the calls for resistance against authority arguably embodied in Sartre's *Les Mouches* (1943) and Anouilh's *Antigone* (1944). But perhaps no less important, albeit more diffuse, was the sense of solidarity inherent in the shared experience of collective audience response; the theatre became associated in the public consciousness with the affirmation of a cultural identity, which was ultimately a national identity.

This impetus persisted beyond the Liberation, and there emerged a theatre which concerned itself predominantly with issues of a philosophical and metaphysical nature. Although individual dramatists had their own preoccupations and responses, and adopted different positions and dramatic techniques, the Parisian theatre of the post-war years was informed and shaped by a single underlying vision: a perspective on human existence which convenient shorthand terms 'the Absurd'. The basic premises are simple enough: in a godless universe our world and all it contains (humankind included) exists for no preordained reason or purpose. There is no divine master-plan in which, however dimly, we might see ourselves as having a part to play. There are no eternal God-given values or codes of conduct against which we can measure, regulate, or judge our standards or our actions. Existence is gratuitous and meaningless, and seems to be made a final nonsense of by death. This vision is not entirely original, since it can be traced back to the Greeks, and the term 'absurd' was already being used in the 1920s, with roughly similar connotations, by André Malraux and Armand Salacrou among others. But the disorientating trauma of war and occupation created a climate of uncertainty and mistrust in which such a perspective seemed particularly appropriate.

Despair is the first reaction generated by an awakening to the absurdity of existence. As Camus argued in his essay *Le Mythe de Sisyphe* (1942), the human being has a natural drive to seek for reason and order, a sense of direction and purpose, though it may be questioned whether this drive is truly innate and universal, or whether it is in fact a construct of a Western civilization. Once the props and signposts we habitually use to impose shape and intelligibility on our lives are uprooted, and discredited as fictions of our own concocting, our experience is of loss, separation, and alienation. Indeed the significance of the term 'absurd' derives from its etymological sense of 'discordant': the individual is no longer in harmony with the world.

In the years following the war, the theatre assimilated and projected this vision in a variety of ways. At one end of the scale Jean Anouilh seems to weave it into an agreeably fashionable pessimism, presenting life as irretrievably associated with lost ideals, compromise, and hypocrisy. Those heroes and heroines who take a stubborn stand against such degradation, as Antigone had done, and as do Jeanne d'Arc in *L'Alouette* (1953) and Thomas à Becket in *Becket* (1959), do so in the name of a personal code of values which is, at root, aesthetic. What they refuse to accept is life's ugliness; but their stand is presented as a hopeless one which leads only to isolation and death. Even Anouilh's apparently more light-hearted plays such as *L'Invitation au château* (1947), where all seems to end well, have denouements which are so blatantly contrived and artificial that no one is fooled: happy endings can only occur in the make-believe world of theatre.

It is often suggested that Anouilh's theatre is close to that of the *boulevard*, and certainly many recurring elements in his plays (the clash of generations, embittered marriages, adultery) are reminiscent of the stock themes of *boulevard* theatre. It is also true that what impresses first and foremost in Anouilh is the dazzling surface of his virtuoso dramatic technique. His is an elegant and sophisticated theatre which borrows adroitly from all kinds of dramatic modes (tragedy, farce, melodrama), and which can catapult an audience in seconds from the moving to the grotesque, from cynicism to sentimentality, from laughter to compassion. Yet there is at the heart of his theatre a sombre vision which distinguishes him from the *théâtre de boulevard*. Through his characters' use of meta-theatrical references (*rôle, comédie, dénouement*), or his overt exploitation of theatre within theatre, he suggests that, just as a performer is assigned a given part to enact, so our identity as individuals is determined by the social role we are expected to play. To refuse that role is not to forge a new identity for oneself in a creative affirmation of individuality. It is merely to say 'no', a sterile rejection which is tantamount to self-annihilation. For Anouilh, we are the mask, or we are nothing. Such a vision has the potential to unsettle, as it does in the hands of Jean Genet. But Anouilh's stylish packaging holds centre stage, transmuting the sombre into a palatably bitter-sweet disenchantment, and in the public perception he is primarily a peerless craftsman and entertainer. Which is precisely (or so he claimed) how he envisaged himself and the function of theatre: audiences do not attend the theatre in order to confront harsh realities, but to escape them.

Quite the opposite view was held by Sartre and Camus. For them the theatre should address the anxieties and preoccupations of the time, and mobilize audiences into a collective response to their shared problems. Both spoke of the need to invent a modern form of tragedy to articulate the predicament of the post-war years. It may be doubted whether either of them achieved that goal, but both saw the theatre as a medium capable, ideally at least, of reaching a larger section of society than printed literature could. And both used the theatre as a means of disseminating their responses to issues confronted in their theoretical writings, of which not the least pressing was how life could be conducted in a world without values.

In *Caligula*, written in 1938, but not staged until 1945, Camus portrayed a man wrestling with a sudden recognition of the absurd, and seeking a way of living with that awareness. Caligula's chosen course of action is to spread his new-found awareness by embodying in his own behaviour the inhuman logic of the absurd. It leads to a devastating nihilism, and is at the end of the play condemned by Caligula himself as wrong-headed. It is not altogether clear whether Camus intended his audiences to envisage their own alternative strategies for living, avoiding Caligula's mistakes, or whether the moderation voiced by the character Cherea is intended to serve as a model for all. Cherea's arguments are based rather nebulously on an aesthetic scale of values ('I think that some deeds are more beautiful than others'), and are insufficiently developed to carry much weight. This ambivalence can perhaps be ascribed to the fact that at this stage Camus himself was still working towards a satisfactory answer to a difficult ethical question. Certainly his later play *Les Justes* (1949) presents more cogently the case for collective human revolt against the absurd, together with the need for a relative morality to limit and regulate human behaviour.

A more sustained inquiry into human conduct was carried out by Sartre in a string of plays which appeared regularly throughout the 1940s and 1950s. In what he termed 'a theatre of situations' he sought to impress on his spectators the inescapable fact of human liberty, together with its consequences: the perpetual obligation of making choices in all situations, and the necessity of assuming fully the responsibility for choices made and deeds committed. One of Sartre's principal strategies to demonstrate this austere existentialist ethic is by way of negative examples: his plays are peopled by characters who live inauthentically by endeavouring to deny their own liberty and hence to shed their burden of responsibility; an existence characterized by self-deception, or *mauvaise foi*. There is perhaps good reason for this, beyond the desire to denounce the human being's ingenuity in evading the truth. Sartre's insistence that we each create and define ourselves as individuals through our acts, freely chosen in accordance with our own lights, and without slavish subservience to any external authority, means that the presentation on stage of an exemplary role-model in action could appear undesirably prescriptive: our task is constantly to invent ourselves anew, not to emulate. Even the rare Sartrean protagonists who apparently manage a full recognition and assumption of their liberty, such as Oreste in *Les Mouches* or, more convincingly, Goetz in *Le Diable et le bon Dieu* (1951), reach this moment of self-realization in the closing moments of the stage action.

A charge frequently levelled against both Sartre and Camus is that their theatre, however determinedly it addressed contemporary concerns, remained wholly unoriginal in terms of dramatic technique. At first sight it might seem odd that writers who considered themselves practitioners of a 'new' theatre, and who moreover had proved themselves capable of stylistic innovation in their prose fiction, should be content to espouse a set of dramatic conventions which are, in essence, precisely those which underpin the much decried *boulevard* theatre. Arguably, however, this was more of a strategy than a shortcoming. Both writers were versed in the practical realities of theatre production, and were in a position to gauge the nature and the expectations of the audiences who patronized the large commercial theatres where their plays were staged: the well-heeled middle classes whose cultural experience had familiarized them with the format of *la pièce bien faite*, the well-made play. For a theatre which set itself an instructive goal in engaging with ethical issues there would have been a counter-productive risk of diverting public attention by introducing arresting new techniques.

The theatre of Sartre and Camus is unquestionably founded on an optimism: values and meaning can be created by the exercise of reason; despair can be transcended; the theatre can fulfil a useful role by offering its public guidance in navigating the trackless wasteland which the absurdist perspective opens up. For other dramatists, however, the prime focus of attention was the wasteland itself, and the individual's experience of isolation, alienation, and incomprehension. In the English-speaking world, it has been common practice to group these dramatists together under the banner of the 'Theatre of the Absurd', in the wake of Martin Esslin's influential study of the same title, which appeared in 1962. The label has its disadvantages in that it draws attention to similarities rather than differences, and tends to imply a concerted theatrical 'movement', which was far from the case. The French expression *le nouveau théâtre*, new theatre, is less misleading, and serves both to recall the pervasive concern with the new, and to indicate a parallelism with the contemporaneous emergence of *le nouveau roman*, the new novel. The radical developments in both genres were animated by common concerns, in particular to challenge the concept of unitary meaning.

The major exponents of the new theatre deployed a variety of strategies. In plays like *Les Bonnes* (1947), *Le Balcon* (1956), and *Les Nègres* (1959), Jean Genet takes the practices and paraphernalia of stage representation (ceremony, ritual, and role-play; masks, costumes, and make-up) and uses them progressively to blur any convenient distinction between reality and illusion, until both are emptied of meaning, leaving only a disquieting receding perspective of reflections, and reflections of reflections. Samuel Beckett in *En attendant Godot* (1952) and *Fin de partie* (1957) places his isolated characters in situations they can neither escape nor explain, and where, as often as not, one dimly senses the presence of some presiding power of unknown (but probably malevolent) nature and intentions. Eugène Ionesco's plays from *La Cantatrice chauve* (1950) onwards create a world which is at once zany and illogical, and stiflingly cluttered, where words and objects proliferate out of control. Both Arthur Adamov, in his early plays, and Fernando Arrabal portray hallucinatory worlds where realities and identities are unstable, undergoing transformations which follow the horrid logic of the nightmare, and where human relationships are characterized by oppression, cruelty, and (in Arrabal's case) sado-masochistic eroticism.

It is a theatre founded on impotence, incomprehension, violence, terror, suffering, and death, where the individual is invariably portrayed, in some way or other, as a helpless victim. For some commentators it is merely bleak, sterile, and nihilistic. Others stress the crucial role of comedy, arguing that the laughter these plays generate denotes human resilience and the capacity to defy despair. However, given the problematical nature of black humour, and the elusiveness of a unified and convincing theory of laughter to explain it, such a position remains debatable. Others still see it, in some measure at least, as a realization of the theories of Antonin Artaud, who more than a decade earlier had called for the creation of an irresistibly powerful metaphysical theatre which would bring its audience into a forceful and cathartic confrontation with the mystery and the precariousness of their position in the universe. As he wrote in *Le Théâtre et son double* (1938), 'We are not free. And the sky could yet fall on our heads. And the theatre is meant to teach us that above all.' Such words seem chillingly prophetic for a theatre which can be seen not only as a dramatization of the experience of the absurd, but also as a metaphorical articulation of the unease and disquiet of the Cold War years, lived out under the ever-growing menace of atomic weapons.

Quite apart from the interpretative possibilities it offers, the new theatre occupies a particularly interesting place in the evolution of the theatre in France. Its roots reach back in various directions to areas of inquiry which had all, in their own way, posed a challenge to the comfortable rationalistic vision of the human being and the world as stable, coherent, and knowable entities. Its illogicality evokes the anti-science of 'pataphysics devised by Alfred Jarry at the turn of the century, which holds that every phenomenon is unique, and that our so-called eternal laws and principles are based solely, and erroneously, on strings of observed coincidences. Its oneiric or dream-like qualities, and its externalization of

## Waiting for Godot

The new theatre developed the existentialist preoccupation with the breakdown of meaning and the problematic nature of the human self. Samuel Beckett's plays explore these issues in a way which comes close to abstract art. His first play, *En attendant Godot*, stripped away most of the historical and cultural settings which usually support interpretation, and almost eliminated action. The critic Harold Hobson famously remarked that it is a play in which nothing happens: twice. This photograph is taken from the first production, by Roger Blin at the Théâtre de Babylone in 1953. The two tramps, Didi and Gogo, centre stage, devise various partially successful strategies for keeping themselves occupied while time passes, and demonstrate their incomprehension of the enigmatic events they witness. Here, they watch the Master–Servant duo, Pozzo and Lucky, preparing to move off. Lucky has just delivered a long and incoherent speech filled with intellectual debris which leaves no one any wiser. They will return in the second part in a more dilapidated state. The very bare set designed by Sergio Gerstein has only a tree on it, providing an anchor in space, a measure of time passing, since it acquires a leaf, and an opportunity for a burlesque suicide attempt.

unconscious drives, draw openly from psychoanalysis. Its audacious and arresting stage images owe much to Surrealism.

The very first productions of these plays were staged in the tiny studio theatres in the Latin Quarter, where lower financial overheads meant that adventurous directors could afford, to an extent, to take risks which the big commercial theatres would never contemplate. And in the main its audiences, as might be expected, were drawn from the young and the educated. Yet even in this relatively open and liberal-minded milieu these early productions met with a mixed reception, with enthusiasm offset by bewilderment and downright indignation. Which is conceivably how things might have stayed. But the instant *succès de scandale* in January 1953 of Roger Blin's production of Beckett's *En attendant Godot*, soon to be followed by international success in America and Britain, focused the eyes of the world on Paris as the seed-bed of avant-gardism, and the birthplace of what was being hailed as a theatrical renaissance. The theatre establishment responded adroitly by annexing the new theatre, and by the early 1960s the plays of Beckett, Genet, and Ionesco were being staged, and even premièred, in the capital's state theatres: the Odéon, the Théâtre national populaire, and even ultimately the prestigious Comédie-Française. With extraordinary rapidity the fringe became mainstream, and the iconoclasts modern classics.

What the new theatre succeeded in doing was to loosen the stranglehold of the tenets of the well-made play, which had for a century shaped French dramatic practice and audience expectations alike. It had now to be accepted that linear intrigue could collapse into structures of circularity and repetition. 'Trompe-l'œil' naturalistic setting could be replaced by bold visual metaphor and startling scenic effects, exploiting what Artaud had termed 'the language of the stage'. Psychological consistency could be subverted by unexpected switches in behavioural patterns. The pre-eminence accorded to dialogue, and its meaningful and limpid articulation, could be overturned by a dramatic language characterized by hesitancy, misunderstanding, incoherence, even nonsense. More than anything, perhaps, the new theatre weakened the grip of a concept which was deeply ingrained in the French cultural consciousness: that of *tenue*, or unity of tone and register. To a sensibility reared on Shakespeare, the juxtaposition of high tragedy and broad comedy may be a familiar strategy. To the French it always seemed at best alien, and at worst a deplorable breach of dramaturgical propriety. It is arguably not coincidental that the major exponents of the new theatre were expatriates who had not undergone a regular French cultural training, and who perhaps found it correspondingly easier to breach this particular taboo and dissolve away hitherto watertight boundaries, creating disquieting new hybrids such as, for example, Ionesco's 'farce tragique'.

The success of the new theatre in displacing a dominant cultural form heralded a new wave of experimentation in dramatic styles and practices which was to gather momentum throughout the 1960s and 1970s. In Paris the phenomenon of *café-théâtre* began to appear: youthful, satirical, and irreverent. Directors such as Jean-Marie Serreau and Victor Garcia, and troupes such as Ariane Mnouchkine's Le Théâtre du soleil and Jérôme Savary's Le Grand Théâtre panique (later renamed Le Grand Magic Circus), were to break with tradition in a number of ways. They dispensed with the Italianate theatre with its invisible barrier separating stage and auditorium, using instead multiple stages and simultaneous action. They moved out of central Paris into the suburbs and the provinces, exploiting the possibilities of wholly new theatrical spaces (the disused warehouse, factory, wrestling hall, ice rink, railway station). In some cases the autocratic positions of author and director were replaced by the collaborative processes of *la création collective*, where every member of the troupe would participate in every necessary task, from stage-sweeping to the devising of the spectacle itself. Freed from the constraints of *tenue*, an energetic and exuberant new kind of theatre was born, drawing happily on music and dance, circus and cabaret, improvisation, acrobatics, and mime.

But if in one sense these new theatre forms were the natural successors to the new theatre, in another sense they were a reaction against it. From the beginning of the century the evolution of 'mainstream' theatre had provoked the charge that the theatre in France was dominated by Paris, and that it catered almost exclusively for a minority which was both culturally and economically privileged. The dominant theatre of the 1940s and 1950s did nothing to allay such criticisms. The philosophical and metaphysical nature of the plays that were performed (perceived as intellectually challenging, and hence off-putting), and the topography of the venues where they were staged (plush interiors whose seating arrangements, graded according to cost, were all too obviously hierarchized), made the theatre a place where only the educated and the well-off could feel at ease. What was needed was a theatre with mass appeal, shorn of any élitist mystique: a theatre for the people.

Explicit calls for the creation of a *théâtre populaire* had come, intermittently, from eminent figures: Romain Rolland at the turn of the century; Charles Dullin under the Popular Front government in the 1930s; Jacques Copeau in the early 1940s. The French government had even voted through the establishment of a permanent Théâtre national populaire (TNP), which opened in 1920 under the directorship of Firmin Gémier. But its ideal of transcending class divisions by bringing together audiences, at reasonable prices, in a collective celebration of national ideals and aspirations met with only limited success. This was due in part to insufficient government funding, but in part also to an unwise choice of venue: the Palais du Trocadéro, now the Palais de Chaillot, in the west of Paris. It was not readily accessible from the working-class suburbs to the north and east of the city, and moreover was located in the intimidating terrain of the ultra-fashionable and affluent sixteenth *arrondissement*. Under the directorship of Jean Vilar (1951–63), and with increased financial backing from the government, the TNP sought to overcome this handicap by organizing free transport to the theatre, and by taking touring productions out to the suburbs.

In fact the real progress in broadening the appeal of the theatre lay less in the establishment of a subsidized theatre in the capital, than in the policies of decentralization actively pursued after the war. Between 1946 and 1955 seven *centres dramatiques nationaux* were set up in the provinces, supported by a mixture of central and local funding. The process was continued after 1958 by André Malraux, whose programme of cultural expansion included the creation of government-funded provincial theatre groups known as *troupes permanentes*, and the founding of the *maisons de la culture*. By the mid-1960s there were nine *troupes permanentes* and six *maisons de la culture*, with a further six near to completion. To a large extent it was the success of these ventures in the provinces, which many had thought idealistic and unrealizable, that encouraged the new troupes of the 1960s to turn their back on the theatre-land of Paris, and to move out to the suburbs and the provinces in search of new 'popular' audiences.

While the official decentralization of the theatre was undoubtedly a positive move, it was not without its drawbacks. Commercial theatre owners were, predictably, vociferously opposed to the allocation of government subsidies. In the provinces, theatre directors found that their artistic autonomy did not always square with the desires and interests of the municipality which held the purse-strings. And in the *maisons de la culture* there was a lurking suspicion that the theatre was being used to serve the aggrandizing purposes of the Fifth Republic, and to promote an official state culture.

But the fiercest polemic revolved around the concept itself of a *théâtre populaire*, or people's theatre. To begin with there was disagreement over whether the 'people' should be understood as designating the entire spectrum of society, or whether it should specifically denote the working classes. From that initial debate further questions naturally emerged: what kind of plays should constitute the repertory of a people's theatre, and what role should they seek to fulfil? For some, the aim of a people's theatre was to make accessible to as wide an audience as possible the timeless and universal qualities of the great classics. It was precisely in such a spirit that Vilar's first season at the TNP opened with a production of Corneille's *Le Cid*, though staged here in a compellingly energetic and lively manner far removed from the remote, statuesque, and declamatory style which had long been the French norm. For others, however, appeals to the perennial relevance of the classics were mealy-mouthed, representing no more than a condescending way of admitting the working classes into the realms of bourgeois culture. For such as these, what was required was a completely new, as yet unwritten repertory: a theatre which directly addressed the experience, concerns, and needs of the working classes.

The debate hinged, evidently, on the question of whether the theatre should or should not be politicized. The polarization of views was sharpened from the mid-

1950s onwards, as France began to discover the plays of Bertolt Brecht, and his theories of Epic theatre, which sought to place the spectator not in the position of mesmerized consumer, but in that of an actively reflective and critical observer. Brecht's ideas, and the unfamiliar acting and staging practices they entailed, had a profound influence on directors such as Roger Planchon, dramatists such as Adamov, and theoreticians such as Roland Barthes. A measure of his impact can be gauged from a 1972 survey which examined the most frequently performed playwrights in the decentralized theatres: Brecht came in third place behind Molière and Shakespeare. In one way, the discovery of Brecht was opportune. The radical experimentation of new theatre bequeathed the intimidating challenge to those who came after, of how to 'follow that'. Brechtian theory provided new sets of styles and techniques, and a new set of objectives which could be and were applied to all manner of productions. But at the same time it intensified the rift between those who championed the theatre as a humanizing and harmonizing force, and those who saw it as a means of raising political consciousness and an instrument of social change. The original ideal of the people's theatre as a classless space for the collective celebration of shared values was decried by the Brechtians as promoting a phoney myth of unity and integration. Since the reality of French society was one of division and struggle, they argued, it was on these realities that a truly popular theatre should focus.

Such a confrontation could place directors, particularly those of subsidized theatres, in a difficult position. Vilar, for example, found himself criticized from the Left for failing to stage a proletarian repertory, or to attract a truly proletarian audience, and simultaneously from the Right for putting on plays which were perceived as critical of the regime, or, worse still, of de Gaulle himself. Jean-Louis Barrault, as director of the Odéon, was to experience the divide in harsher terms. When the protesting students of May 1968 occupied his theatre, which they regarded as the cultural flagship of a regressive and authoritarian establishment, he engaged them in sympathetic dialogue. And for his pains was promptly removed from his post by the Ministry of Culture.

Debate over the social role of theatre, quickened by the events of 1968, remains alive, with Artaud and Brecht, metaphysics and militancy, as poles of reference to be set in opposition or to be forged into new syntheses. Questions still hang over the concept of a people's theatre. Is it a utopian ideal? Can the theatre ever be anything more than a minority interest? In a 1987 Ministry of Culture survey, only 7 per cent of those polled had set foot in a theatre in the preceding twelve months. Is the irrepressible *théâtre de boulevard*, with the drawing power of stars made famous through television, the only 'popular' theatre conceivable? Nevertheless, successful strategies for attracting what has become known as *le non-public* into the theatres of France continue to be sought. Which is no doubt appropriate: conflict is the essence of drama, and it is also the mechanism through which the theatre continues to renew itself.

## The New Novel and the New Criticism

The 1950s were not only 'modern', they were assertively 'new'. Modernity was characterized by the constant search for novelty, as the consumer-driven boom imposed the values of change and innovation first in industry and then increasingly in everyday life. The momentum achieved in production reached the point at which the wartime devastations had been repaired and the material shortages of food, clothing, and shelter had been eliminated. The maintenance of prosperity required people now to replace the old with the new, and to experience increased demand for new products. Concepts such as built-in obsolescence and conspicuous consumption expressed this imperative. At the same time, the traumas of Occupation and Liberation began to wane and the convalescent nation felt strong enough to attempt to close that painful chapter and turn its attentions elsewhere. The *rapprochement* with Germany and the first steps towards European integration provided a strong incentive to embrace new political priorities.

In the cultural field, the consensus humanism had provided an ideological splint, well suited to binding fractured mentalities, but it also proved an encumbrance to intellectual adventure. Increasingly it showed itself to be a conservative and backward-looking framework, which became the butt of criticism and the paradigm of an obsolete cultural model, which needed to be superseded by something new. Its first critics were those who had been excluded, the right-wing writers who castigated the hypocrisy of humanist moralizing. But they were soon joined by others who had been pressed into service as humanists against their own serious reservations, prominent among whom were the existentialists and the Marxists. Politically, the combination of Marx, Céline, and Sartre was an unlikely and even unholy alliance. But it provided a starting-point for movements in literature and criticism which were rapidly designated new, and baptized *le nouveau roman* (new novel) and *la nouvelle critique* (new criticism).

Like many other cultural movements, the new novel is difficult to define in such a way as to embrace all the writers usually associated with it, without simultaneously including a host of others from whom they are typically distinguished. In practice, the movement was defined socially by two institutions. The first is the publishing industry, for whom it was an important marketing advantage to be able to identify a group of writers whose books and journals are sufficiently similar to be targeted at a specific audience. The creation of the new novel may in large measure be attributed to Jérôme Lindon, who took over from Vercors as director of Éditions de minuit, and to Alain Robbe-Grillet, literary adviser to Minuit and himself an experimental writer. Together they commissioned and published the work of the writers concerned and successfully promoted them as a new and innovative group. The second defining institution is university departments, especially in English-speaking countries. For them, there are clear advantages in constructing courses and research activities around a coherent body of material with an identifiable place in the cultural canon. The intense academic interest in the new novel coincided with the period of rapid expansion of universities in the 1960s and 1970s, which itself created new marketing opportunities for both publishers and critics.

The new novel is most readily understood as the work of a small group of novelists, of whom Alain Robbe-Grillet, Michel Butor, Nathalie Sarraute, and Claude Simon are the leading members. It is sometimes also extended to include the novels of Samuel Beckett and Marguerite Duras, which were published by Minuit and share many of the same concerns. At a theoretical level, the novelists differed considerably in their analysis of what they were doing and why. For the most part they were insistent that they were writers of fiction rather than literary theorists. This was the explicit view of Robbe-Grillet in his collection of essays *Pour un nouveau roman* (1956), which has none the less been widely regarded as a theoretical manifesto for the movement. These essays notoriously contain contradictory statements on subjectivity, objectivity, humanism, realism, and other concepts. And many points of disagreement can readily be found between Robbe-Grillet's views and those expressed in Sarraute's essays of *L'Ère du soupçon* (1956), or Butor's *Essais sur le roman* (1969).

There was general agreement that Balzac was the classic exemplar of what needed to be revolutionized: a narrative approach which conveys the illusion of reproducing reality, a set of coherent and well-defined characters, a series of actions forming a clear and logical plot, and a moral or political message. Among the 'several outdated ideas' which were to be rejected, Robbe-Grillet listed: character, story, commitment, and the distinction between form and content. Polemically, he argued that 'the only possible commitment, for the writer, is literature'. He and his colleagues had often strongly held views on the political issues of the day; for example, most of them signed the *Manifeste des 121* in 1960 protesting against French actions in Algeria. But they were careful to separate their politics from their professional activity as writers. The same separation lies behind the rejection of the form–content distinction, since 'content' was generally accepted as a code word for moral or political message. Catholic commentators were eager to ensure a healthy moral content, while the communist theory of socialist realism identified socialism as the desired content. In both cases, it was implicit that the content was subject to the judgement of a higher authority than the writer. The new novelists rejected such tutelage and argued for writers' autonomy, at the risk of appearing to endorse an amoral and socially irresponsible Art for Art's sake.

In practice, the new novel distinguished itself primarily by its focus on its own processes, drawing attention to the way in which language is deployed in a written text to produce responses in a reader. The new novelists were particularly concerned to dispel the illusion that the images conjured up by words could be regarded as mystical recreations or reproductions of reality. Their works therefore aimed to disrupt the traditional expectations of the French realist novel. This realist model was thought to correspond broadly to the humanist view that there exists an essential human nature, which is expressed in a number of different personality types, which determines the course of human affairs, and which gives life its objective meaning. Against this, the new novelists followed Sartre's phenomenological view that meaning is created subjectively by the perceptions and choices which each individual makes. They considered that the chief business of writing is not to continue weaving elaborate illusions but to explore and expose the ways in which writing constructs or subverts meanings. Their aim was, as the new critic Jean Ricardou put it, 'non pas l'écriture d'une aventure, mais l'aventure d'une écriture' (not the writing of adventure, but the adventure of writing). The new direction was an invitation to formal experiment, explicitly raising and questioning the conventions of writing in the text itself.

The traditional plot was challenged, along with its assumptions of logic, order, sequence, cause and effect, suspense, climax, denouement, beginning and end. An initial step was to reassert the distinction between a story and its narration, emphasizing that the order in which events are presented in narration may be quite different from the order in which they are supposed to have occurred. Considerable attention was given to the familiar genre of detective stories, which typically reverse the action and its narration, beginning with a crime and gradually unravelling the sequence of events which ostensibly led to it. Robbe-Grillet's first novel *Les Gommes* (1953) playfully invokes this genre, though the title also refers to textual 'erasures' which disrupt the reader's attempts to fathom out a single intelligible plot. The use of flashbacks, borrowed from cinematic narration, also highlights the non-linear nature of narration. Michel Butor's complex novel *La Modification* (1957) narrates a businessman's perceptions on a train journey from Paris to Rome, cutting between what he sees in the train or from its windows, memories of episodes in his past life, visions of his future, dreams, and reflections. Each different layer is readily identifiable, but gives texture and richness to the others within the present consciousness of the traveller, and within the reader's experience of the book. More radically, other novels give the reader few easy clues about where or when the narration is situated in any given passage. Claude Simon uses this approach in *La Route des Flandres* (1960) to produce a sense of confusion and bewilderment wholly in keeping with its historical setting in the *exode* of panic-stricken French people before the German onslaught in May 1940. Robbe-Grillet's novel *Dans le labyrinthe* (1959) describes the surface appearance of people, objects, and events with apparent impassivity and in equal detail, challenging the reader to construct an intelligible plot. It suggests that the text, and even language itself, is a labyrinth within which the reader can expect to wander lost, though the much-used metaphor of the labyrinth also implies a hidden coherence, and an invitation to puzzle-solving which critics and academics have enthusiastically taken up. A similar point is made by Alain Resnais's film *L'Année dernière à Marienbad* (1961), for which Robbe-Grillet wrote the script. A succession of similar scenes from ostensibly different moments in time defies the viewer to reconstruct a logical order or story, and leaves him or her with the uncomfortable conclusion that the 'reality' of the film is the experience of sitting watching it for an hour and a half rather than the problematic relationship between the two main figures who have been depicted.

The attack on character, like the attack on plot, was also an attempt to shift attention from some 'real' situation being narrated to the texture of the narration itself. The novels of Beckett's trilogy *Molloy* (1951), *Malone meurt* (1951), and *L'Innommable* (1953) give increasingly fleeting glimpses of characters which the narrator might have met or might at one time have been. But the fragments of story are progressively discarded as diversions from the unbearable emptiness of the narrator's self, longing for silence but constrained to speak. Sarraute's *Martereau* (1954) depicts the gradual disintegration of its male bourgeois narrator and the emergence of a problematic and uncertain consciousness behind the masks and façades. Duras's *Moderato cantabile* (1958) invests the passion of a bourgeois woman's frustrations into the silences and uncertainties of her conversations with a man in a café, re-enacting in narration the stages of a *crime passionnel*. Robbe-Grillet's *La Jalousie* (1957), whose title refers both to jealousy and to a kind of shuttered blind, presents fragments of what the narrator sees, remembers, or imagines of his house, his banana plantation, his wife, and a male neighbour, pointing the reader to the perceptions and emotions of the narrator rather than the events which are narrated. In these novels, characters appear as inviting illusions which tempt the reader to see them as reflections of a more substantial reality. But ultimately they reveal themselves as figments of imagination, conjured up to distract us from understanding the workings of our consciousness or the process of narration, which in many respects are one and the same thing.

It has frequently been questioned whether the new novel was really new. Some of its major figures had already begun writing before the 1950s. Nathalie Sarraute's first novel *Tropismes* appeared in 1939, and her *Portrait d'un inconnu* (1947) had appeared with an important preface by Sartre himself. Duras and Beckett had also published novels in the 1940s. More significantly, critics have pointed out that many of its innovations can be found at least in embryonic form in earlier French modernist novels, especially those of Marcel Proust and André Gide, or more recently Céline and Sartre. Many of the formal and thematic innovations can also be identified in the modernist novels of other cultures, in such novelists as Joyce, Kafka, Faulkner, or Woolf. In some respects they can be identified in much earlier novels, even in those of Balzac, whose novels can be read in more complex ways than the realist stereotype would suggest. This is undoubtedly true, and it may be more accurate to see the new novel as continuing a path of literary experiment whose direction was already established. Newness, however, is a relative rather than an absolute concept: to describe something as new is to point out a contrast with something else considered old. The new novel was promoted and perceived as new in the 1950s by contrast with the moral and aesthetic conservatism of the 1940s, and by its affirmation of modernist rather than realist literary approaches. It certainly marked a new wave of experimentation in writing, and in the process triggered new re-readings of classical writing, generating as it were a new literary tradition of its own precursors.

By the early 1960s, the new novel was well established and began to intersect with new critical approaches which were being developed. Critics such as Roland Barthes, Jean Starobinski, Jean-Pierre Richard, Jean Ricardou, Serge Doubrovski, and Gérard Genette sought to replace the traditional humanist approaches to literature with new ones drawing on the theoretical resources of the human and social sciences. Just as the new novelists had rejected Balzac, the new critics rejected Émile Faguet and Gustave Lanson, who dominated literary studies in French universities in the early part of the twentieth century. The stereotype they represented was the literary history based on *l'homme et l'œuvre* (the man and his work). Typically, this sees the author's life as the key to his or (more rarely) her literary work, and sees the critic's task as one of elucidating the mind of the great writer by means of biographical research and textual exegesis. The role of the reader, or student, is then to attempt to appreciate and understand the depth, richness, and meaning of the work with which he or she is presented.

The new criticism reversed these priorities, placing the emphasis on reading rather than writing. It suggested that the reader has a creative or productive role, as the maker of meanings. This point emerged from phenomenology, which emphasizes the free choice of the conscious subject to give meaning to what he or she perceives, and also from semiology, which situates meaning in the sign, conceived as the combination of a material signifier with a mental image signified. In this perspective, the printed text appears as a material signifier which provides the reader with an opportunity to weave meanings. Any meanings will be multiple, and since each reader's perceptions will be different, there can be no right or definitive reading of any text. The role of the critic is therefore not to narrow down the possible meanings, but rather to multiply them, discovering further possibilities, and to analyse the textual structures which make meanings possible. The author is then no longer the authoritative source and arbiter of meaning, but rather a producer of text, not so much an author as a writer, one of a number of agents involved in making the text available.

Looking at literature from this point of view produced many new and imaginative readings of well-known texts. It largely dispensed with the intimidating quantities of historical material which stand between the reader and the text in traditional literary historical approaches, symbolized by the Sorbonne doctoral thesis, a life's work which could only be devoted to authors who were already dead. The new approach also provided a means of access to new writing which was often considered difficult. It was in particular ideally suited to the preoccupations of the new novel. However, it very rapidly became clear that the new criticism was not just a new way of viewing literature. Linking together with other theoretical movements of the 1960s, it offered a much more radical reconfiguration of the intellectual landscape. In the first instance, the distinction between author and critic begins to blur, since both are producers of text, or writers. The distinction then begins to blur between literature and other forms of writing, since the possibilities for making meaning exist in all texts to a greater or lesser extent. In his essays of *Le Degré zéro de l'écriture* (1953), Roland Barthes proposed the term *écriture* (writing), rather than literature, to indicate the work of producing text, as distinct from the social institutions of prestige and authority which decree what shall be considered as Literature.

A further development was proposed by Jacques Derrida, in his *L'Écriture et la différence* (1967) and *De la grammatologie* (1967). He suggested that the way writing works can offer a pattern which may be used to understand all other texts. In this more general sense, texts can be any structured traces of meaning and communication. There are obvious ways in which theatre, film, television, art, or architecture can be regarded as texts to be read. But from there it is not a long step to extending the notion of text to any meaningful human situation. Barthes looked extensively at sport, photography, advertising, and fashion. The generalization of the audio-visual media and the rapid growth in information and communications of all kinds made language or discourse the central preoccupation of the social and human sciences. Prominent among the pioneers in this were the ethnologist Claude Lévi-Strauss, the psychoanalyst Jacques Lacan, and the historian of science Michel Foucault.

Lévi-Strauss adapted some of the ideas of Saussure's structural linguistics to address apparently intractable problems in anthropology. His most striking early success was in the debate over the nature of the link between a clan or tribe and its totem, usually an animal figure associated with it. Lévi-Strauss proposed that totemic practices should be analysed as communications, intended to tell the group and its neighbours about itself. In a series of books, of which the best-known was *Anthropologie structurale* (1958), he went on to examine the whole range of social and cultural practices of primitive societies from a similar perspective, analysing kinship relations, dwellings, costume, food, folk-tales, art, and magic. In each case he argued that cultural practices formed a language which enabled people to communicate with each other about their identity, norms, and values. He developed techniques for drawing out the underlying structures of this language, pointing out that the meaning of a ritual or of a myth such as the Oedipus story is not to be found in its surface narrative, but in the way it presents various combinations of the underlying oppositions, for example between undervaluing and overvaluing family bonds. In *La Pensée sauvage* (1962) he argued that many of these oppositions, and the ways of exploring them, were ultimately common to all human societies, including modern ones. In many respects, he suggested, the language of images and metaphors manipulated by the psychoanalyst or the marketing executive is not inherently more sophisticated than that of the Panamanian Cuna Indian sorcerer, and has the same social function.

Jacques Lacan used many attributes of the sorcerer in developing a subtle and enigmatic interpretation of Freudian psychoanalysis. In his *Écrits* (1966) he drew connections between behaviour and the underlying drives in the unconscious, which he suggested was structured like a language. He adapted Saussure's theory of the sign to explore the problematic relations between on the one hand people's often incoherent and apparently capricious words and actions, the material signifiers, and on the other hand the churning desires, neuroses, and complexes of the unconscious signified. The difficulty in achieving meaningful links to the unconscious, in discerning its structure, and in devising therapeutic effects were, in his view, what made Freud's 'talking cure' an art as much as a science.

Michel Foucault adopted a similar concern with underlying structures in his 'archaeological' exploration of the history of the sciences, especially the medical sciences. In his early book *Folie et déraison: Histoire de la folie à l'âge classique* (1961) he showed how attitudes to madness had changed abruptly in the seventeenth century, when mad people were suddenly locked away, and again in the early nineteenth century, when they began to be observed and treated medically. Generalizing the pattern in *Les Mots et les choses* (1966), he argued ambitiously that beneath the discourse of three typical sciences, biology, economics, and linguistics, it was possible to discern an underlying order of thought, which he termed an *épistemè*. From the seventeenth to the nineteenth century, the *épistemè* had been based on classification, identifying resemblances between things. This had then been replaced by the modern *épistemè* based on history, observing developments within things. In due course this would in turn be superseded, making it impossible to sustain the characteristically humanist and historicist preoccupations of modernity. Foucault subsequently refined his analysis and extended it to the penal system and sexual mores.

Theorists in many domains of the social and human sciences re-examined their disciplines in the light of structural linguistics, giving rise to the perception that a concerted movement was taking place, to which the label 'structuralism' was applied. Almost invariably, the initial linguistic turn was the signal for a process of reworking and questioning established concepts and methods, which was frequently accompanied by controversy and conflict. Bitter debates between traditionalists and structuralists were common in the 1960s, spreading internationally through the 1970s and beyond. From the early stages, exponents of the new ideas were cuttingly dismissive of the tradition they sought to replace, and attracted fiercely polemical responses in return. An early skirmish occurred over Barthes's innovative reading of classical French drama in *Sur Racine* (1963), which drew on structuralist and psychoanalytical approaches. This was felt to be the last straw by classical scholar Raymond Picard. In his *Nouvelle Critique ou nouvelle imposture* (1965) he attacked the cavalier way in which the texts were solicited to support sweeping generalizations with no basis in the text or historical circumstances of Racine's life. Picard was swimming against the tide, however, and by the end of the 1960s the new criticism became the new orthodoxy. Its success was largely built on the convergence of intellectuals working in many different disciplines, who turned to the science of language to find methods of understanding the complexities of the modern world. At the same time, the linguistic sign and its attendant concepts were also subjected to intense critical scrutiny by those who adopted them: structuralism gave rise to post-structuralism without it being easy to pin either label satisfactorily on any of the leading participants in the debates. The debates between different tendencies within the new thinking came rapidly to overshadow the dialogue of the deaf between them and their traditionalist opponents, setting the intellectual agenda for the 1970s and in the process confirming the vivacity of French intellectual culture.

## The Cinema from Occupation to New Wave

The German occupation of France, so damaging in many ways to French industry, was a golden age for the French cinema, a period when, despite rationing and wartime shortages, the film industry emerged from the parlous state to which it had been reduced by American competition in the 1930s into new dynamism and inventiveness. Whilst some well-known directors like Jean Renoir, Jacques Feyder, and René Clair went into exile in Hollywood soon after the outbreak of the war, there was no shortage of talented individuals to take their place. New imports of American films were banned and both the occupying power and the Vichy government took a closer interest in supporting the cinema than any pre-war French government had done. The result was that both the German-owned Continental Films operating in Paris, and the producers, like André Paulvé, who worked in the Nice studios in the unoccupied zone, financed large numbers of new French films. In the year 1941 alone, nine films began production at the Victorine Studios in Nice, compared with only thirty made at the same studios during the entire preceding decade. For the first time, France made an attempt to rival Hollywood in the scope and scale of its productions and the cinema became, during the war, an important vehicle for the articulation of French cultural specificity as Carné's *Les Visiteurs du soir* (1942) and, even more, *Les Enfants du paradis* (1945) testify. The wartime situation was summed up by the director Marcel L'Herbier in the memoirs he published in 1979: 'Nous, les auteurs de films, nous avions travaillé pour la plupart, depuis 1930, dans un climat d'esclavage cinématographique, et pourtant alors la France était libre. Désormais, elle ne l'était plus. Et voilà que les choses se contredisent sous la férule allemande: la liberté de création reprenait pour nous tous ses droits' (For the most part we film directors had been working in an atmosphere of artistic slavery since 1930, even though France was then free. Now that it no longer was, and the Germans had the whip hand, the situation was completely reversed and we regained the right to complete artistic freedom).

All this was threatened by the peace since film was one of the export commodities included in the Blum–Byrnes Agreements on American aid for French reconstruction. But fortified by the wartime experience the French government was persuaded to legislate for some protection against foreign competition and to support the domestic film industry with a series of subsidies which gradually moved towards a system of selective support for 'films d'art et essai'. In 1953 financial assistance became available for the production of short films and was instrumental in helping directors like Chris Marker, Alain Resnais, and Agnès Varda. Many of the masterpieces made at this time, including Resnais's *Nuit et brouillard* (1956), Marker's *Dimanche à Pékin* (1955) and *Lettre de Sibérie* (1958), and Varda's *Ô Saisons ô châteaux* (1956) and *Opéra mouffe* (1958), owe their existence to this benevolent regime. To this was added, in 1959, a system of *avances sur recettes* (advances against earnings) enabling producers to part-finance feature films by borrowing from a *fonds de soutien* (support fund) against their eventual profits. Provided the film assisted was not too expensive, the *avance sur recettes* could be, and was, a determining factor in whether it could be made, and most of the *nouvelle vague* directors benefited from it for their early films. The survival of the French film industry benefited enormously from the slow spread of television in France but the structure of subsidy also assisted it in its battle against Hollywood domination since it was possible to continue to produce relatively low-budget art films which could make a profit from domestic screenings alone. In this the post-war French industry differed not only from its Western European counterparts which, one by one, collapsed in the face of American competition, but also from the industry pre-war which had attempted, and failed, to beat Hollywood in the popular market.

The American 'threat' has remained a theme of French cultural policy since 1945 and the cinema, and more recently television, have been seen as the means by which America attempts to impose its cultural will on France, despite all the statistical evidence demonstrating that French films remain more popular than American films in the French market. However, film-makers themselves betray a much more ambivalent attitude towards America. For them Hollywood cinema is infinitely seductive because of what the director Jean-Luc Godard called its 'classicism'. Godard provocatively compared Hollywood cinema to French literature of the eighteenth century because of its 'aisance', the total appropriateness of its means to its ends, its cultural centrality. It was this sense of cultural significance, the knowledge that cinema was the means of artistic expression most suited to the articulation of national concerns, that French cinema had briefly enjoyed during the war and that post-war film-makers sought to recapture even though they knew the project was doomed to failure.

It is perhaps not surprising, therefore, that the definitive analysis and codification of American cinema, and the critical terms in which it is still most frequently discussed, originated in France in the period 1945–60. In André Bazin's essays on the western and on Orson Welles, in Raymond Borde and Étienne Chaumeton's *Panorama du film noir américain* (1955), in Claude Chabrol and François Truffaut's interviews with Alfred Hitchcock we find French critics offering the most sophisticated analyses of American film available. They were, of course, helped in this by the unparalleled facilities available for viewing films in Paris in the 1950s, thanks to the collections Henri Langlois had built up in the Cinémathèque française as well as the adventurous programming policies of cinemas like the MacMahon just off the Champs-Élysées, which devoted its screen to American films. In the same way the journals *Cahiers du cinéma* and *Positif*, both of which were founded in the early 1950s, offered an outlet for critical writing and encouraged an atmosphere of discovery and feverish competition recalled with affectionate amusement in Luc Moullet's film *Les Sièges de l'Alcazar* (1989).

Many of the films of the 1950s enact the fear of and fascination with America. In Jacques Becker's *Touchez pas au grisbi* (1954), for example, the actor Jean Gabin, whose persona in pre-war French cinema had contrived to embody the sensibility of the nation, plays a disillusioned and ageing gangster attempting one last heist before he retires. He is shown as subscribing to a strict code of honour, as appreciative of traditional French cuisine, of formal clothes and manners. His younger gangland rival, on the other hand, wears American-style clothes, drinks whisky, and generally behaves in a boorish fashion. There is no doubt that of the two Gabin is both the more attractive and the more successful, yet the film is permeated with nostalgia for a waning society, a way of doing things that cannot last, and the refrain constantly articulated by Gabin's character is his longing to retire. By contrast, the Americans are youthful, energetic, and extraordinarily attractive. Thus Eddie Constantine in Bernard Borderie's *La Môme vert-de-gris* (1954) is an FBI agent sent to North Africa to solve a mystery that the native (i.e. French) police are apparently incapable of solving and he proves so seductive that even the gangster's moll is persuaded to betray her lover and join the American side. The film is in many ways absurd, yet Constantine's performance was a revelation in France, introducing a new style which depended for its expressiveness on the way the actor relates to his environment. Constantine's ease of manner and his command of space entirely compensated for his gauche and sometimes incomprehensible pronunciation of the French language. Indeed, so persuasive was it that this film, though minor, is often viewed as the first step towards freeing the French cinema from the over-dependence on script and dialogue which was characteristic of many of the films of the early 1950s.

The French fascination with American cinema was typical of the general interest in all aspects of American culture, from abstract painting and jazz to American thrillers, many of which were translated for the 'Série noire' launched by Marcel Duhamel in 1945. However, it was American B pictures, and especially westerns and thrillers, that appealed most strongly because their central topos, the relationship between man and the environment, was perceived as quintessentially modern. In a country in which a rapid rural exodus and equally rapid urbanization were destroying fixed points of reference, in a world of existential doubt, the American cinema proposed a *mise en scène* of domination and control in which the typical protagonists were lawgivers who, through recourse to an inner strength, dictated the course of events rather than submitting to circumstances. In this way the westerns of Anthony Mann and the thrillers of Fritz Lang spoke to the condition of viewers in France more poignantly than anything French was able to do.

Up to the 1970s, therefore, America is a generally positive reference in French films. It can take a variety of forms: in Godard's *A Bout de souffle* (1959) the hero models himself on the Humphrey Bogart he has seen in the movies and dates an American student in Paris; in the same director's futuristic comedy *Alphaville* (1965) an American visitor awakens a French zombie with a kiss; in François Truffaut's *Tirez sur le pianiste* (1960) American cinema is seen as the only possible source of creative activity while the European artist is condemned to failure and repetition, while in the same director's *Baisers volés* (1968) the protagonist Antoine Doinel imagines himself a character in a Hitchcock film. But whatever form it takes, it is interesting that the references to American models in these films are positive and that the critique of mass culture which is particularly strongly pursued in some of Godard's works does not take America as its target. Whatever French public policy towards the American cinema, therefore, French film-makers were in no doubt of its beneficent influence.

Indeed, it was arguably the close study of American cinema which led to the renaissance in French cinema in the late 1950s which was known as the *nouvelle vague* (new wave). Long study of Hollywood films had led many post-war French critics to look for ways to understand and explain how works so clearly produced in a 'factory' could achieve such extraordinary individuality. In the pages of *Cahiers du cinéma* Eric Rohmer, Jacques Rivette, François Truffaut, Jean-Luc Godard, and Claude Chabrol, all of whom subsequently became film-makers, developed what came to be known as the *politique des auteurs*. This was an approach to reading American cinema which was entirely serendipitous and which, in its reliance on the *trouvaille*, the exquisite object which strikes the viewer with its unexpected beauty, is obviously related to Surrealism. In practice, however (and this is parodied in *Les Sièges de l'Alcazar*), it meant a total lack of respect for existing canons of appreciation based on noble subjects and art films, and a preference for popular genres such as the western and the thriller. Thanks to the *politique des auteurs* the *Cahiers* critics were able to attribute a personal style to individual directors which they held to be manifest despite the often banal or unconvincing subject-matter of their films; indeed, they were able to discount subject-matter almost entirely in their appreciation of a director's œuvre, focusing instead on *mise-en-scène*. So successful has this approach been that it seems inconceivable today that Hitchcock's work, for example, should not be viewed as an artistic totality. Yet at the time, the idea that a director should be interviewed at length about the relationship between each of his films, which is what Truffaut and Chabrol did, was completely revolutionary.

The *politique des auteurs*, however, did not just help in making sense of the American cinema, it also became a rallying cry for a revolution in French cinema. In a celebrated article published in *Cahiers du cinéma* in January 1954 which he called 'Une certaine tendance du cinéma français', François Truffaut attacked, among other things, the way in which French film-making was dominated by script-writers rather than directors and called for a cinema in which a film would be an expression of the 'personal' preoccupations of the director. This became the manifesto for the New Wave, a new cinema in which a film is viewed as an expressive totality deriving from *mise en scène* which the director determines, and which is outside the control of the studios and the industry.

At the end of the 1950s many of the *Cahiers* critics began to make films, a move initially made possible by adapting newsreel techniques to feature film-making. The two principal *nouvelle vague* cameramen were Raoul Coutard and Henry Decaë; the former had been a news reporter and maker of documentaries, the latter had been employed in the army film unit and had experience in filming in the difficult circumstances of Indo-China. Their experience of exterior locations, lighter cameras, and faster film, all of which had become available, allowed feature films to abandon studio sets. Films such as *A Bout de souffle* (1959), *Les 400 coups* (1959), and *Les Bonnes Femmes* (1960) all have an extraordinary freshness and immediacy which partly derives from their resemblance to news reporting and partly from the fact that they are shot in recognizable locations (often in Paris) with actors who look and behave like ordinary people rather than dramatic characters. Moving out of the film studio, abandoning the large film crews and heavy camera movements, also made films cheaper—within the financial grasp, in fact, of young men like Godard, Truffaut, and Chabrol, all of whom either came from or married into wealthy families and who financed their first films not with the *avance sur recettes* which helped them subsequently, but with family money. Once again, the disregard for the conventional rules of film-making and film editing, and the way their early films combine daring effects with an amateurish disregard for polish, or *le fini*, are clearly related to the financial freedom within which these privileged individuals operated, what the sociologist Pierre Bourdieu would call their 'aristocratic disdain' for the rules.

Many of these films look like family albums or private diaries: the directors appear in one another's films, cast their wives and girlfriends in leading roles, use their own apartments as sets, show characters entering their favourite cinemas, cafés, and bookshops, listening to their favourite music on the record-player, pinning their favourite posters on the walls. For example, Jean-Claude Brialy and Anna Karina play one entire scene in *Une Femme est une femme* (1961) by taking favourite books off the shelf and using words taken from their titles to insult each other. Godard is particularly adept in using chance elements in the urban environment to convey messages, but Truffaut also succeeds in evoking favourite authors such as Balzac in most of his films while Chabrol frequently pays tribute to the American comic strips he loves. There is thus a thoroughgoing—and over-determined—intimacy in New Wave films which is an essential part of their appeal, since it gives the viewer the feeling that he or she is offered a privileged insight into other people's daily lives.

In keeping with Truffaut's call for a personal cinema, many of the New Wave films are, or appear to be, autobiographical. This is certainly the case with his own work. After his first feature *Les 400 coups* won the Grand Prix at the 1959 Cannes Film Festival Truffaut went on to cast the same actor, Jean-Pierre Léaud, in a series of films about the same character Antoine Doinel, *Antoine et Colette* (1962), *Baisers volés* (1968), *Domicile conjugal* (1970), *L'Amour en fuite* (1979), in which we see him grow up, marry, get divorced, embark on an affair, and so on. Truffaut even published the scripts of the Doinel films with a preface in which he claimed that Doinel was a combination of himself and the actor Jean-Pierre Léaud. What is undoubtedly true, although not always recognized, is that despite its documentary look *Les 400 coups* is very much a fiction, a small boy's subjective account of his relationship with his mother (and recent psychoanalytic approaches to Truffaut's work have emphasized the continuity of this theme across all his films), and that Truffaut, no doubt in pursuit of the personal in the cinema, was keen to give the impression that this is autobiography. In fact his œuvre contains another, alternative autobiography apparent in the films like *L'Enfant sauvage* (1969), *La Nuit américaine* (1973) and *La Chambre verte* (1978), where he cast himself as an actor in his own films.

In increasingly, and perhaps misleadingly, emphasizing the autobiographical dimension of his films, Truffaut disguised the true import of the personal focus of the New Wave corpus, which is that the preoccupations of the characters in them match those of the audience of the films. If much of the French cinema of the 1950s was devoted to literary adaptation and stylized low-life thrillers, the New Wave introduced the idea, explored by Claude Chabrol in an article published in *Cahiers du cinéma* in October 1959 entitled 'Grands Sujets, petits sujets', that the greatness of a film was not dependent on the exceptional nature of its subject-matter. The heroism, or perhaps the anti-heroism, of ordinary life is what animates New Wave films and their moral dimension derives, as Godard said, from *mise-en-scène*. In fact, their typical subject-matter is relationships between young men and women. Unlike the films of the 1950s which typically centred around a middle-aged male protagonist, the heterosexual couple is the focus of New Wave cinema and, with very few exceptions, it is the subjectivity of the young male which structures the films. This can be confirmed from the stream of consciousness voice-over of Jean-Paul Belmondo as Michel in *A Bout de souffle*, in Antoine's 'confession' to the psychiatrist in *Les 400 coups*, and in the indulgence with which the rapist is treated in the highly misogynistic *Les Bonnes Femmes*; and it is also to be seen in the developing fetishization of the young female body in all French films of the period, but particularly in those such as *Et Dieu créa la femme* (1957) or *Babette s'en va-t'en guerre* (1959) starring Brigitte Bardot. Of all the New Wave directors Godard is the most conscious of the fetishistic visual regime within which this cinema operates, and a short sequence in *A Bout de souffle* shows the heroine Patricia briefly adopt the 'male' point of view as she gazes through an improvised lens at Michel in the pose of a sex-object. But such reversals are rare before 1968 and, although there is considerable uncertainty in New Wave films about the role of women, together with a degree of homophobia which is particularly apparent in Truffaut's films, the sex lives of a young couple remain their dominant material.

Although few critics agree on the precise definition and extent of the French New Wave, few would deny its revolutionary impact not just on French cinema but on cinema in general. As far as French cinema was concerned, it ensured the survival of the industry by appealing to the young audience which the cinema retained after the spread of television. In this sense, consciously or not, the New Wave was a form of niche marketing comparable to the many other forms of entertainment and leisure goods—pop music, motor-bikes and scooters, clothes—developed for young people in the newly affluent 1950s and 1960s. But the New Wave also rewrote the grammar of cinema. It broke out of the conventions of Hollywood realism which posited the body as the source of speech, represented dialogue in a system of shot/reverse shot, and based editing on eyeline matches. Instead the New Wave adopted a much more allusive and elliptical style of film-making, freed films from their dependence on storyboards and scripts, and ultimately permitted a much freer and more poetic approach to the cinema which has been almost universally adopted.

## References

Bazin, André, *Qu'est-ce que le cinéma?* (Paris: Éditions du cerf, 1975).

Borde, Raymond, and Chaumeton, Étienne, *Panorama du film noir américain* (Paris: Éditions de minuit, 1955).

Godard, Jean-Luc, *Jean-Luc Godard par Jean-Luc Godard* (Paris: Cahiers du cinéma, 1985).

Truffaut, François, *Les Aventures d'Antoine Doinel* (Paris: Mercure de France, 1970).

—— 'Une certaine tendance du cinéma français' (1954), repr. in *Le Plaisir des yeux* (Paris: Cahiers du cinéma, 1987).

—— and Chabrol, Claude, *Hitchcock* (Paris: Ramsay, 1983).

# Suggestions for Further Reading

### The historical background (1945–1967)

There are many good studies in English of French social and political history of the period. There is a good succinct account in Roger Price, *A Concise History of France* (Cambridge: Cambridge University Press, 1993). James F. McMillan, *Twentieth Century France: Politics and Society 1898–1991* (London: Edward Arnold, 1992) is an accessible and up-to-date survey of the period which contains an excellent bibliography. Maurice Larkin, *France since the Popular Front 1936–1986* (Oxford: Clarendon Press, 1988) is an excellent standard history, with a very helpful select bibliography. In economic history, Jean-Charles Asselain, *Histoire économique de la France*, vol. ii (Paris: Seuil, 1984) is invaluable from 1919 to the 1970s; also useful are John Gaffney (ed.), *France and Modernisation* (Aldershot: Avebury, 1988) and Carlo M. Cipolla (ed.), *The Fontana Economic History of Europe*, vol. vi (London: Fontana, 1976).

Theodore Zeldin's *The French* (London: Collins, 1983) is a witty and stimulating study of French customs and manners, while Donald Charlton (ed.), *France: A Companion to French Studies* (2nd edn. London: Methuen, 1979) contains useful historical and cultural surveys. Emmanuel Todd, *The Making of Modern France: Politics, Ideology and Culture* (Oxford: Blackwell, 1991) sheds light on the values of the period. In French, the relevant volumes of the 'Nouvelle Histoire de la France contemporaine', published by Éditions du Seuil 1975–6, cannot be beaten as short introductions with useful bibliographies and chronologies. They are Jean-Pierre Rioux, *La France de la Quatrième République*, 2 vols., translated as *The Fourth Republic 1944–1958*, vol. vii, The Cambridge History of Modern France (Cambridge: Cambridge University Press, 1987), and Jacques Julliard, *La Cinquième République*.

Useful French narratives of the politics of the Fourth Republic can be found in Georgette Elgey, *La République des illusions 1945–1951 ou la vie secrète de la IVe République* (Paris: Fayard, 1965), Jacques Fauvet, *La IVe République* (Paris: Fayard, 1959), and Pierre Durand, *Vingt ans: chronique 1945–1965* (Paris: Éditions sociales, 1965). In English, two recent works are very useful: Hilary P. Winchester, *Contemporary France* (London: Longman, 1993), and Jill Forbes and Nick Hewlett (eds.), *Contemporary France* (London and New York: Longman, 1994), the former geographical, the latter social and political in focus. D. L. Hanley, A. P. Kerr, and N. H. Waites, *Contemporary France* (London: Routledge & Kegan Paul, 1979) is a standard work, and Philip Williams, *Politics in Post-war France* (2nd edn. London: Longman, 1958) is still useful. Andrew Shennan, *Rethinking France: Plans for Renewal 1940–1946* (Oxford: Clarendon Press, 1989) is an excellent account of early planning approaches, while the colonial issue is well discussed by Anthony Clayton, *The Wars of French Decolonization* (London: Longman, 1994).

## Post-war reconstruction

The political aftermath of the Liberation, the Épuration, has always been controversial, but the authoritative account is still Peter Novick, *The Resistance versus Vichy* (London: Chatto & Windus, 1968). A lively and detailed account is given in Herbert R. Lottmann, *The People's Anger: Justice and Revenge in Post-Liberation France* (London: Hutchinson, 1986), and a more lurid anti-Resistance version in Robert Aron and Yvette Garnier-Rizet, *Histoire de l'épuration* (Paris: Fayard, 1967–75). The cases of intellectuals are detailed in Pierre Assouline, *L'Épuration des intellectuels: 1944–1945* (Brussels: Éditions complexe, 1985). And the only serious study of the sheared women is Alain Brossat, *Les Tondues: un carneval moche* (Paris: Manya, 1993).

General discussions of the period are found in Fred Kupferman, *Les Premiers Beaux Jours: 1944–1946* (Paris: Calmann-Lévy, 1985) and Valérie-Anne Montassier, *Les Années d'après-guerre 1944–1949* (Paris: Fayard, 1980). Attractive visual presentations are given by Anne Bony, *Les Années 40* (Éditions du regard, 1985) and Charles-Louis Foulon, *La France libérée 1944–1945* (Paris: Hatier, 1984).

## French post-war ideologies

There has been an upsurge of interest in intellectuals, well detailed in John Flower, 'Wherefore the Intellectuals', *French Cultural Studies* (Oct. 1991), 275–90, and Jeremy Jennings (ed.), *Intellectuals in Twentieth-Century France* (London: Macmillan, 1993). Debate has been enlivened by the polemical study by Tony Judt, *Past Imperfect: French Intellectuals, 1944–1956* (Berkeley and Los Angeles: University of California Press, 1992). Informative studies include Howard Davies, *Sartre and 'Les Temps modernes'* (Cambridge: Cambridge University Press, 1987), Herbert R. Lottman, *The Left Bank* (New York: Wallace & Sheil, 1981), Pascal Ory and Jean-François Sirinelli, *Les Intellectuels en France: de l'affaire Dreyfus à nos jours* (Paris: Armand Colin, 1986), and Ariane Chebel d'Appolonia, *Histoire politique des intellectuels en France, 1944–1954* (Paris: Éditions complexe, 1991).

Each of the main intellectual movements has been surrounded by much comment. On Catholic thought, Michel Winock, *Histoire politique de la revue 'Esprit', 1930–1950* (Paris: Seuil, 1975) is an excellent sympathetic survey, while John Hellman, *Emmanuel Mounier and the New Catholic Left, 1930–1950* (Toronto: University of Toronto Press, 1981) takes a more critical view. Adrien Dansette, *Destin du catholicisme français 1926–1956* (Paris: Flammarion, 1957) is still the standard work on the broader Catholic context, and Michèle Cointet, *Histoire culturelle de la France 1918–1958* (Paris: SEDES, 1988) offers a useful survey.

Relations between intellectuals and communism are detailed in David Caute, *Communism and the French Intellectuals 1914–1960* (London: Macmillan, 1964) and more rigorously analysed in Janine Verdès-Leroux, *Au Service du parti: le parti communiste, les intellectuels et la culture (1944–1956)* (Paris: Fayard/Minuit, 1983). Among the many studies of Marxism, useful ones in English include Michael Kelly, *Modern French Marxism* (Oxford: Blackwell, 1982), Tony Judt, *Marxism and the French Left* (Oxford: Clarendon Press, 1986), Mark Poster, *Existential Marxism in Postwar France: From Sartre to Althusser* (Princeton: Princeton University Press, 1975), and George Lichtheim, *Marxism in Modern France* (New York: Columbia University Press, 1966).

A useful overview of the existentialists' activities is given in Michel-Antoine Burnier, *Les Existentialistes et la politique* (Paris: Gallimard, 1966). The individual existentialist writers have been widely studied, particularly Sartre and Beauvoir. Michel Contat and Michel Rybalka, *Les Écrits de Sartre* (Paris: Gallimard, 1970) gives a full listing of his works with details of their immediate context. Christina Howells, *Cambridge Companion to Sartre* (Cambridge: Cambridge University Press, 1992) is a valuable guide to the canonical Sartre. Ronald Aronson, *Jean-Paul Sartre: Philosophy in the World* (London: New Left Books, 1980) is a good political and philosophical discussion. Good recent reappraisals of Beauvoir are Elizabeth Fallaize, *The Novels of Simone de Beauvoir* (London: Routledge, 1988), Kate and Edward Fullbrook, *Simone de Beauvoir and Jean-Paul Sartre: The Remaking of a Twentieth Century Legend* (London: Harvester Wheatsheaf, 1993), and Toril Moi, *Simone de Beauvoir: The Making of an Intellectual Woman* (Oxford: Blackwell, 1994). Roger Grenier, *Albert Camus: soleil et ombre: une biographie intellectuelle* (Paris: Gallimard, 1987) is very comprehensive, and there are useful essays in Jean-Yves Guérin (ed.), *Camus et la politique* (Paris: L'Harmattan, 1986). Douglas Beck Low, *The Existential Dialectic of Marx and Merleau-Ponty* (New York: Peter Lang, 1987) is useful, if rather technical. Michael S. Roth, *Knowing and History* (Ithaca, NY: Cornell University Press, 1988) is an excellent study of the Hegelians, especially Jean Hyppolite, Alexandre Kojève, and Eric Weil.

### Post-war cultural context

Several of the issues discussed in this part have been the subject of articles in the journal *French Cultural Studies*, which will repay regular perusal. An excellent evocation of the cultural and intellectual context is given in two catalogues: that of a recent exhibition in London, Frances Morris (ed.), *Paris Post-war: Art and Existentialism 1945–1955* (London, Tate Gallery, 1993), and that of an earlier one in Paris, Pontus Hulten (ed.), *Paris–Paris 1937–1957* (Paris: Centre Georges Pompidou, 1981). Malcolm Cook (ed.), *French Culture since 1945* (London: Longman, 1993) has very useful essays on a variety of cultural areas, as do Brian Rigby and Nicholas Hewitt (eds.), *France and the Mass Media* (London: Macmillan, 1991), and Nicholas Hewitt (ed.), *The Culture of Reconstruction: European Literature, Thought and Film, 1945–1950* (London: Macmillan, 1989), where the French experience is set in a European context. Pascal Ory, *L'Aventure culturelle française 1945–1989* (Paris: Flammarion, 1989) gives a broad thematic analysis. Anne Simonin and Hélène Clastres (eds.), *Les Idées en France 1945–1988: une chronologie* (Folio, Paris: Gallimard, 1989) is also very useful, especially for focusing on a particular moment. Without doubt the most impressive and thought-provoking analysis of the culture of the period 1954–64 is Kristin Ross, *Fast Cars, Clean Bodies* (Cambridge, Mass.: MIT Press, 1995).

### Literary and intellectual development

The novel, theatre, and criticism have been very extensively studied, and only a small selection of works can be mentioned here. Ann Jefferson, *The Nouveau Roman and the Poetics of Ficton* (Cambridge: Cambridge University Press, 1980) is an excellent study of the new novel, as is the earlier work Stephen Heath, *The Nouveau Roman: A Study in the Practice of Writing* (London: Elek, 1972). In French, Jean Ricardou, *Problèmes du nouveau roman* (Paris: Seuil, 1967) is the classic study. The most useful work in English on the theatre of the period is David Bradby, *Modern French Drama 1940–1990* (Cambridge: Cambridge University Press, 1991), though the pioneering study, Martin Esslin, *The Theatre of the Absurd* (rev. edn. Harmondsworth: Penguin, 1968) has stood the test of time well. In French Michel Corvin (ed.), *Dictionnaire encyclopédique du théâtre* (Paris: Bordas, 1991) is highly informative, and there is a useful survey in Christophe Deshouillères, *Le Théâtre au XXe siècle* (Paris: Bordas, 1989). The best general introduction to critical theory is still Jonathan Culler, *Structuralist Poetics: Structuralism, Linguistics and the Study of Literature* (London: Routledge & Kegan Paul, 1975), and there are good discussions in Malcolm Bowie, *Freud, Proust and Lacan: Theory as Fiction* (Cambridge: Cambridge University Press, 1987), Rosalind Coward and John Ellis, *Language and Materialism: Developments in Semiology and the Theory of the Subject* (London: Routledge & Kegan Paul, 1977), and Joseph Harari (ed.), *Textual Strategies: Perspectives in Post-structuralist Criticism* (London: Methuen, 1979).

Of the abundant writing on structuralism, the following are useful general surveys: Eve Tavor Bannet, *Structuralism and the Logic of Dissent: Barthes, Derrida, Foucault, Lacan* (London: Macmillan, 1989), Richard T. and Fernande M. de George, *The Structuralists: From Marx to Lévi-Strauss* (New York: Anchor Books, 1972), Edith Kurzweil, *The Age of Structuralism: Lévi-Strauss to Foucault* (New York: Columbia University Press, 1980), and John Sturrock (ed.), *Structuralism and since* (Oxford: Oxford University Press, 1979).

### African literature and film

On the language question, the most useful sources are J.-P. Lapierre, *Le Pouvoir politique et les langues* (Paris: PUF, 1988) and *Research in African Literatures* (Spring 1992), which is a special issue of the journal, devoted to the language question. The computer programme *PC Globe 5.0* (Novato, Calif.: Broderbond Software, 1992) is also helpful. Literary studies include the standard work, Dorothy Blair, *African Literature in French* (Cambridge: Cambridge University Press, 1976), P. Egejuru, *Towards African Literary Independence* (Westport, Conn.: Greenwood Press, 1980), B. Mouralis, *Littérature et développement* (Paris: Silex/ACCT, 1984), I. Okpewho, *African Oral Literature* (Bloomington, Ind.: Indiana University Press, 1992), and H. M. Zell, C. Bundy, and V. Coulon, *A New Readers Guide to African Literature* (London: Heinemann, 1983). The most useful sources on African film are *After Empire: The New African Cinema* (London: MOMI, 1991), M. Diawara, *African Cinema: Politics and Culture* (Bloomington, Ind.: Indiana University Press, 1992), and P. S. Vieyra, *Le Cinéma africain des origines à 1973* (Paris: Présence africaine, 1975). On Sembène, there is F. Pfaff, *The Cinema of Ousmane Sembène: A Pioneer of African Cinema* (Westport, Conn.: Greenwood Press, 1984).

### Cinema (1940–1967)

The most comprehensive study of French cinema under the German Occupation is Jean Pierre Bertin-Maghit, *Le Cinéma français sous l'Occupation* (Paris: Olivier Orban, 1989). There is a much shorter version in the 'Que sais-je?' series (Paris: Presses universitaires de France, 1994) as well as a stimulating essay by François Garçon, 'Ce curieux âge d'or des cinéastes français', in Jean-Pierre Rioux (ed.), *La Vie culturelle sous Vichy* (Paris: Éditions complexe, 1990), 293–313. The most useful history of post-war French cinema is René Prédal, *Le Cinéma français depuis 1945* (Paris: Nathan, 1991), which is written with university students in mind and contains helpful suggestions for further reading. Jean-Pierre Jeancolas, *Le Cinéma des Français* (Paris: Stock, 1979) covers part of the period from a 'film and society' approach, while Susan Hayward, *French National Cinema* (London: Routledge, 1994) is the most stimulating work available in English. The many works on the New Wave tend to be very dated, although James Monaco, *The New Wave* (New York: Oxford University

Press, 1980) has weathered fairly successfully. There is no good monograph on Godard but Anne Gillain, *François Truffaut: le secret perdu* (Paris: Hatier, 1991) is an accessible and persuasive psychoanalytical approach to a film-maker who has had more than his fair share of ill-informed commentators. Both Godard and Truffaut, of course, were themselves film critics and much can be learned from their articles. Truffaut's criticism can be read in two volumes *Les Films de ma vie* (Paris: Flammarion, 1975) and *Le Plaisir des yeux* (Paris: Cahiers du cinéma, 1987), while Godard's often provocative writings are collected in *Jean-Luc Godard par Jean-Luc Godard* (Paris: Cahiers du cinéma, 1985). Essays on individual New Wave films are to be found in Susan Hayward and Ginette Vincendeau (eds.), *French Film: Texts and Contexts* (London: Routledge, 1990) and in the erudite, stimulating, but sometimes difficult T. Jefferson Kline, *Screening the Text: Intertextuality in New Wave French Cinema* (Baltimore: Johns Hopkins University Press, 1992).

### Popular culture

There is no convenient overview in English of the French radio, television, and press, though useful sections appear in John Flower (ed.), *France Today* (6th edn. London: Methuen, 1993), Malcolm Cook (ed.), *French Culture since 1945* (London: Longman, 1993), and Brian Rigby and Nicholas Hewitt (eds.), *France and the Mass Media* (London: Macmillan, 1991). There are several useful works in French, including four in PUF's popular 'Que sais-je?' series: P. Albert, *La Presse* (1988), P. Albert and A. J. Tudesq, *Histoire de la radio-télévision* (1981), P. Albert and F. Terrou, *Histoire de la presse* (1970), and F. Balle and G. Eymery, *Les Nouveaux Médias* (1987). J. M. Charon, *La Presse en France de 1945 à nos jours* (Paris: Seuil, 1991) is lively and informative.

There is no book in English on French comic strips, but the following recent French books are informative: Marjorie Alessandrini (ed.), *Encyclopédie des bandes dessinées* (2nd edn. Paris: Alban Michel, 1986), Henri Filippini, *Dictionnaire de la bande dessinée* (Paris: Bordas, 1989), Jacques Sadoul, *93 ans de BD* (Paris: J'ai lu, 1989). Popular song is likewise little studied in English, but in French L. J. Calvet's *Chanson et société* (Paris: Payot, 1981) is highly recommended. Other useful French sources include Lucienne Cantaloube-Ferrieu, *Chanson et poésie des années 30 aux années 60: Trenet, Brassens, Ferré . . . ou les enfants naturels du surréalisme* (Paris: Nizet, 1981), Jean-Claude Klein, *Florilège de la chanson française* (Paris: Bordas, 1990), and Pierre Saka (ed.), *La Chanson française: des origines à nos jours*, vol. iii (Paris: Nathan, 1980). On sport, Richard Holt, *Sport and Society in Modern France* (London: Macmillan, 1981) is an excellent study. Also useful is Georges Petiot, *Le Robert des sports: dictionnaire de la langue des sports* (Paris: Robert, 1982).

# Part III

## Revolution and Postmodernity
1968–1995

# Revolution and Postmodernity: May 1968 and After

IN February 1968 students at the university campus at Nanterre in the western suburbs of Paris began a sit-in. By the month of May their protest movement had spread not just to other university campuses but to many sectors of commerce and industry. Widespread strikes and demonstrations took place throughout May, disrupting public transport, closing banks, decimating industrial production, and bringing the country to a virtual standstill. Many expected, and some hoped, that de Gaulle and his government would be brought down by a political revolution. Instead, industrial peace was restored, workers received massive pay increases, and the student protest movement dissipated with the arrival of the university vacation and the promise of institutional reform. The general elections the following year saw a backlash in favour of the parties of the Right, which were returned to the National Assembly with a large majority. De Gaulle resigned in 1969 but he was succeeded by Georges Pompidou, who had been his Prime Minister. Life returned to 'normal'.

But a cultural revolution had taken place. For a visitor to France before and after May 1968 the change was almost tangible. It could be discerned everywhere, in the conduct of social relations, in the sudden lack of formality in dress and speech, in the often mocking disregard for authority, and in the politicization of almost every aspect of daily life. It was also apparent in new social and political concerns, in the emergence of new social actors such as women, peasants, ecologists, and minority groups of all kinds, and in the widespread desire to question the process of modernization on which France had been engaged since the Second World War. It was to be seen in the alternative comedy revues mounted in *café-théâtres* such as the ironically named Le Splendide or Le Vrai Chic parisien, in comic strips such as Claire Bretécher's *Les Frustrés*, in satirical magazines like *Charlie-Hebdo*, in films like Jacques Doillon's *L'An 01* (1973). In the minds of those who took part and, even more, in their memories of the events, 'rien ne serait plus jamais comme avant' (nothing would ever be the same again). And although May 1968 was as much the product of what went before as the precursor of what was to come, it was and remains a symbolic moment, a break in the history of contemporary France, a point from which we can trace many of the social and cultural configurations of the last twenty-five years.

In the aftermath of 1968 France entered a period of febrile political activity, ideological reversals, and extensive social reform, against a backdrop of economic recession. The two oil crises of 1973 and 1979 brought about the first pause in what had seemed the unstoppable rise in living standards since the Second World War. At the same time, the presidency of Valéry Giscard d'Estaing, from 1974 to 1981, saw a programme of social reforms in direct or indirect response to the aspirations of May 1968, which included lowering the age of majority to 18, new divorce laws, the legalization of abortion, giving women equal rights with men within the family, and equal pay legislation.

The French communist party emerged from May 1968 with its reputation tarnished among many people of left-wing political views and in the early 1970s all kinds of extra-parliamentary *gauchiste* groups of varying political persuasions and allegiances, Trotskyist, Maoist, Leninist, and so on, engaged in fierce ideological and occasionally physical combat. Strikes, demonstrations, and 'direct action' were widespread—just how widespread is illustrated by the panic reactions on the part of the French employers' organizations to films such as Marin Karmitz's *Coup pour coup* (1972) or Jean-Luc Godard and Jean-Pierre Gorin's ironically titled *Tout va bien* (1972), both of which depict strikes in which the workers lock up their bosses. The police were conspicuously present on the streets of large cities and television continued to be tightly censored.

Within the spectrum of parliamentary political parties, however, radical re-structuring took place. In 1971 François Mitterrand became First Secretary of the socialist party which in 1972 signed a *Programme commun de gouvernement* (joint programme for government) with the communist party, an electoral alliance which paved the way for Mitterrand's presidential victory in 1981. After he narrowly defeated Mitterrand in the presidential election of 1974 Giscard d'Estaing called for a period of 'décrispation' (lowering of tension) and announced that France wished to be 'governed from the centre'. The years since 1968 have, indeed, seen French governments of whatever political persuasion adopt increasingly centrist policies, but they have also seen the mantle of extremism move from the Left to the Right. Thus electoral support for the communists has declined and *gauchiste* groups have ceased to have real political significance, but the extreme right-wing Front national has become a force to be reckoned with, both inside and outside parliament.

May 1968 also brought into sharp focus France's changed place in the world.

**PAS DE RECTANGLE BLANC POUR UN PEUPLE ADULTE:**

**INDÉPENDANCE et AUTONOMIE de l'O.R.T.F.**

### Pas de rectangle blanc pour un peuple adulte

This is one of the many posters, often produced by students at the École des beaux-arts, which appeared on the walls of Paris and other French cities during the May 1968 events. Bearing all the marks of rapid execution and non-professional reproduction, such images were often based on fluid, strongly drawn lines accompanied by a topical, witty caption. Many touch on conditions in industry, on heavy-handed styles of industrial management, on overcrowding in the universities, or on government control of the media, which were seen as a kind of 'thought police' '[qui] vous parle tous les soirs à 20 heures' ('speaking to you every evening at eight o'clock'—that is, on the main television news). This image of Marianne drawn like a character from a Disney cartoon recalls how strongly American influence on the French media was resented, as well as suggesting the way in which state-run television attempts to infantilize its audience. A white rectangle was normally shown in the corner of the screen to indicate programmes unsuitable for younger viewers. The poster is also an example of 'street art', and the notion of the street as the defining locus of political and artistic action shows the debt of the May 1968 movement to the Situationists and the Surrealists and was an important legacy of May 1968 to the cultural movements of the 1970s.

After de Gaulle and Pompidou had died (the latter in 1974) it became possible to acknowledge openly that France had entered the post-colonial era, that it was a medium-sized economy rather than a world power. The Gaullist dream of acting alone as a 'third force' between two superpower blocks could now be abandoned (though it remained an aspiration or fantasy which resurfaced from time to time). France had to rethink its geopolitical relationships in 'north–south' as well as in 'east–west' terms. It did this by forging new cultural and economic alliances with its former colonies through the creation of a language-based association 'la Francophonie', and by becoming more overtly conciliatory towards the United States (especially after the end of the Vietnam War). Indeed, by 1994 France was planning to reintegrate NATO, from which de Gaulle had withdrawn French forces thirty years earlier. At the same time, particularly under President Mitterrand, European union was strongly promoted, a move which, in its gesture towards the 'common European home', has an obvious and necessary cultural dimension as well as providing another potential means of creating a third force.

The events of May challenged the traditional Marxist concept of revolution by suggesting that it need not necessarily be led by the proletariat. This opened up the possibility that, despite what Marx had written, the revolution could begin within the superstructure, that intellectuals rather than workers could be its van-guard, and that ideological and cultural production could be as important as, or more important than, the production of tractors or automobiles. Questioning the Marxian cosmology of base and superstructure (or, in some versions, economics and ideology) aroused great interest in other politico-cultural revolutions—in Russia, China, and France itself—with China exercising a particular fascination because Mao's Cultural Revolution briefly appeared to offer a more attractive version of socialism than that of the Soviet Union.

The end of the rising affluence of the Gaullist years and the long period of industrial restructuring in the 1970s and 1980s brought about deep social changes which also necessitated a redefinition of the proletariat. The most noticeable change, which is common to many developed economies besides France, is the disappear-ance of jobs for men in heavy industry and, with them, a particular class structure and notion of culture. For as long as the traditional working class existed it was possible to see the people as actors of history and the 'popular' as a relatively unproblematical cultural category. The popular education movements of the 1950s, within the communist party, the Catholic Church, and elsewhere, had concen-trated on integrating the working class into the cultural community. Official Gaullist cultural policy, as we have seen, was also directed to this end. But when white-collar jobs in service industries came to outnumber manual and craft jobs in heavy industry, it was no longer possible to envisage the people in the same way or to view culture in quite the same collective and co-operative manner, as a force for community integration. Industrial and technological change and the growth of the culture industries had subtly turned 'the people' into an undifferentiated and undiscriminating 'mass', and, instead of 'le bon peuple', the working class that remained consisted of 'problem' categories of all kinds—immigrants, the 'new poor', *les exclus* (outcasts). We find, therefore, that, while mass culture was seen as a fascinating object of study in the 1960s (symptomatically, the journal *Communications* was launched in 1961), in the 1970s, and perhaps even more in the 1980s, acute anxiety verging on moral panic about the influence of mass culture gathered increasing momentum.

It is perhaps not surprising, therefore, that cultural politics in France is often considered, by parties of the Left and of the Right, as the pursuit of war by other means. As we have seen, de Gaulle and his minister André Malraux sought to use culture to enhance France's *grandeur* and to promote French influence internationally. But in 1981 another important ideological shift took place. After twenty-five years of political opposition and counter-cultural activity a socialist President and a socialist government were elected to office and the 'hommes de 68', the generation which had led the May events, found themselves in a position to make their dreams come true. Outside France, the Gaullist discourse continued to be applied to cultural policy with the Minister of Culture Jack Lang, in a famous speech delivered in Mexico City in 1982, suggesting that 'mass culture'—and by implication American culture—amounted to interference in the internal affairs of states, claiming the right to 'cultural self-determination', and positioning France as the world leader of the 'culturally non-aligned' countries. Within France, the years of socialist government following 1981 saw a huge rise in government spending on cultural programmes which President Mitterrand emphasized, at a 'States General of World Culture' convened in Paris in 1983, amounted to investing in the economy, but also an attempt to position the socialist regime as the true inheritors of the early Third Republic in which culture and education functioned as a form of social integration or incorporation. In contrast to those of de Gaulle, Pompidou, and Giscard d'Estaing, who had favoured the Champs-Élysées and the tomb of the unknown soldier under the Arc de Triomphe, Mitterrand's inauguration ceremony, stage managed by Jack Lang, took place in the Latin Quarter of Paris and at the Panthéon, a move which signalled the importance of education and which involved honouring the socialist and Resistance heroes Jean Jaurès and Jean Moulin. Similarly, the bicentenary of the 1789 Revolution, which was staged on the Champs-Élysées in 1989, had as its centre-piece an extravaganza designed by Jean-Paul Goude called *La Marseillaise*, which commemorated the moment under the Third Republic when the anthem came to signify the republican unity of the nation and thus the continuity of the republican and socialist heritage from 1789 to 1870 to the Popular Front of 1936 and so to 1981. These two *kermesses* or popular festivals exemplify the rediscovery, *mise en scène*, and exploitation of culture as a form of political and economic activity which was typical of the years in which François Mitterrand was President. Thus the decades since 1968 are years of profound cultural uncertainty, a time when the old cultural and ideological models have been discredited, when France has come to terms with modernization and accepted many of its manifestations, especially the rise of pop culture and mass entertainment, but when, at the same time, concerns about cultural specificity and cultural integrity have become so pressing that they have dominated intellectual debate in the 1980s and 1990s.

The pages which follow will therefore look at writing in the post-1968 period, paying particular attention to the way in which poets and novelists have attempted to engage with the debate over the role of the writer and the reader and of literature in a post-colonial context. They will consider how the theme of otherness has been worked through in the extraordinarily rich intellectual debates and philosophical writing of the period, and they will discuss some of the questions raised by the impact of the mass media and culture technologies on art and on the idea of the nation. They will also look at aspects of cultural diversity both within metropolitan France and in francophone areas outside France and will consider how the defence and promotion of the French language forms a central part of cultural policy and thinking about culture today.

# 5

# The Author, the Reader, and the Text after 1968

## The Revolution in Writing

FOLLOWING the lead given by Sartre in *Qu'est-ce que la littérature?* (1948), many writers and theorists throughout the 1950s and 1960s speculated on the relationship between literature and political ideologies and on the role that literature could play in shaping contemporary society. Their main focus (one might even say their main target) was the novel. This choice is understandable, given the fact that since the nineteenth century the novel, and especially the realist novel, has been the most popular literary genre. However, the seismic social changes brought about by the war and, later, the contestation of authority throughout Europe marked in France by the events of May 1968 led writers to scrutinize urgently and anxiously the nature and the effectiveness of their own writing.

The illusion that the writer could speak to and for all men and women had been shattered once and for all, and writers became increasingly aware that their readership was both changing and diminishing. On the other hand, the French continue to pay lip service to the importance of writers: in 1981, for instance, a survey commissioned by the magazine *Lire* showed that four of the ten most influential intellectuals in France were writers (Beauvoir, Yourcenar, Tournier, Michaux). Furthermore, politicians feel obliged to proclaim a commitment to the arts and especially to literature and often quote from the great writers in an attempt to win votes. Perhaps inevitably, they frequently make mistakes: when he was Prime Minister, Raymond Barre appeared on television's *Apostrophes* to talk about his favourite reading, and promptly badly misquoted the first line of Paul Valéry's *Le Cimetière marin*, and François Léotard, when Minister of Culture, claimed on another edition of the programme that his regular bedside reading was Flaubert's *Journal*—which does not exist. These gaffes may make us smile, but they do reveal that in France literature is still a central element in the ongoing process of the establishment of national identity.

The very real loss of authority for the contemporary writer is thus a particularly thorny problem, because he or she is still expected to fulfil an oracular function, whilst also being now regarded with suspicion as marginal and potentially subversive. This constricting double-bind is, however, transformed by many writers into a freedom from the role of social and moral arbiter, into a liberation which permits and enables them not only to experiment with form but also to push back the frontiers of what is generally accepted as suitable subject-matter.

One of the major features of post-1968 literature is the importance of critical theory. Long the domain of established or would-be creative writers, in the 1950s and 1960s literary criticism was modified into a 'science of literature' and became the preserve of academic theorists who, as we have seen, shifted public attention from discussions for or against 'le nouveau roman' or 'le nouveau théâtre' to debates about 'la nouvelle critique'. May 1968 led, surprisingly perhaps, to an increase in the influence of the universities, and many of the complex considerations of theorists were swiftly disseminated through the (often excellent) dilutions of commentators in the press and on radio and television. Thus, while the radical political positions and the dense formulations of the *Tel Quel* group did not all appeal to a wide public, it was soon generally accepted that they were right in their claim that all writing is political, since it always articulates an ideological position (of which the writer may or may not be consciously aware). This acceptance necessarily changed the relationship between reader and writer, so crucial questions about authorship and authority were now repeatedly posed.

The most famous statement about this was perhaps made by Roland Barthes, who ends his seminal essay 'La Mort de l'auteur' (the death of the author) (1968) with the defiantly provocative claim: 'la naissance du lecteur doit se payer de la mort de l'Auteur' (the birth of the reader entails necessarily the death of the Author). Barthes is not hailing here the death or the reduction to unimportance of the writer; rather, his target is the Author—by which he means the figure of the author who is assigned authority for the meaning of the text. Similarly, Michel Foucault's equally important response to Barthes's crucial essay, his 1969 lecture 'Qu'est-ce qu'un auteur?' (what is an author?), examined the institutional mechanisms by which a society authorizes a discourse. However, it should be stressed that, after 1969, writers felt that they had lost what had previously been seen as their 'natural' authority over their work and that authorship was no longer considered to be a transcendental source and guarantee of meaning, but just one legal, historical, and political category amongst many others. The loss of authority was part of a general movement towards a re-evaluation of the reader, who was now seen as co-creator, as an active participator in the creation of a literary work. It also had the effect of liberating writers from the obligation (and often the compulsion) to be new—which can be a terrible tyranny in that it tends to privilege violent transgression, whereas many writers precisely want to establish their own voices by echoing and conserving what is good in previous works.

Writing, *écriture*, has become both a theory and a practice of textuality in which meaning is constantly—and creatively—mobile. Indeed, perhaps the most important feature of the past twenty-five years is the shift—on the part of both writers and readers—from concerns with the text as a fixed and finite entity to an awareness of textuality. We now recognize that the text is less a structure than a structuration, a process which produces and transforms meaning rather than simply communicating an already existent, authoritative meaning. The author has been destabilized, the reader has been empowered, and new exchanges have been made possible.

It would clearly be impossible to discuss, or even to list, all the forms of literary experimentation that mark the post-1968 period, so we shall focus on certain areas which seem representative of the period, taking as focal examples writers who are constantly playing with and against traditional writing techniques.

## Literature as Rewriting

Every writer rewrites in one way or another the work of his predecessors, and the very act of literary creation involves a certain melancholy at having come too late—when everything has already been said. However, the theories of intertextuality, based on Mikhail Bakhtin's insistence on the carnivalesque, and the power of laughter to destroy a hierarchical distance, which Julia Kristeva introduced to France in the mid-1960s, rapidly became common currency, even amongst writers hostile or indifferent to theory. Inescapably aware that texts exist only through some process of reading, and liberated rather than constrained by their acceptance of the fact that they themselves are necessarily always readers (before, after, and even during the act of writing), contemporary writers have begun to respond in new ways to the canon of 'the great works' of literature and to adapt creatively rather than purely defensively to life in the long shadows cast by their precursors or father-figures (with all the patriarchal authority this term implies).

In their desire to mark out their own personal creative space and to establish their own voice, writers are, as Harold Bloom puts it, subject to the 'anxiety of influence'. This anxiety, which is a form of melancholy, leads them to write against the work of their predecessors in an attempt to substitute their own authority for that of the 'strong' precursor and thereby to escape from the haunting feeling of living and writing when everything has already been said. One of the most celebrated examples of antagonistic rewriting is Michel Tournier's *Vendredi ou les limbes du Pacifique* (1967), which is a strategic rewriting of Daniel Defoe's *Robinson Crusoe*. Tournier recognizes that Defoe's text occupies a privileged place in the development of the novel, since it is one of the rare texts to have given birth to a modern myth—that of the castaway (and also, through Jean-Jacques Rousseau, who greatly admired Defoe's tale, that of the noble savage). However, as a twentieth-century person who had studied anthropology and ethnography at the Musée de l'homme, Tournier could not accept its apology for colonialism and capitalism and its Eurocentrism, and so set out to write a corrective version which would privilege the spontaneity, the spirituality, and, above all, the essential difference of Friday. While he retains the main elements of Defoe's plot, he adds considerations of sexuality, changes the ending to ensure that Robinson and his island are abandoned by Vendredi, and grafts onto the story both extraordinary poetic flights of imagination and philosophical meditations on morality, the Absolute, and the nature of knowledge. Tournier also shifts the action forward by exactly one hundred years to 30 September 1759 in order to allow Robinson to think in Enlightenment terms and the narrator to present his views on Robinson's evolution in Spinozan terms: Robinson's three stages of consciousness (through the senses in the mud-wallow, through rationality in his administration of the island, and through intuition in his experience of union with the elements) correspond to the three types of knowledge posited by Spinoza in his *Ethics* (1678), which Tournier considers the most important book after the New Testament Gospels. Furthermore, he relocates the island in the Pacific Ocean off the Chilean coast rather than in the Caribbean where Defoe sets it. In this geographical displacement, however, Tournier is not so much betraying Defoe as being faithful to the true story of the shipwrecked sailor Alexander Selkirk on which Defoe based his novel and reminding his readers to question the truth of all fictions.

*Vendredi* was an immediate popular and critical success, winning the Grand Prix du roman de l'Académie française, but its author was dissatisfied with it, because he felt that it was too obviously a philosophical novel and, perhaps, because once his corrective version of the Robinson Crusoe myth had been written, the urge to challenge the authority of the father of the modern novel had been satisfied. So he decided to rewrite it—in a way that would make it accessible even to chidren. The result was *Vendredi ou la vie sauvage* (1971), which is annually studied in schools throughout France and which has sold more than two and a half million copies. This rewriting of his own novel omits both Robinson's explorations of his sexuality and all but one of his Logbook entries, translating the intricate philosophical musings which structure the first version into concrete, physical experiences recounted by an omniscient narrator. The first *Vendredi* was generated by Tournier's conviction that Defoe's ideology was misplaced and that Defoe did not recognize the mythic dimension of Robinson Crusoe's adventure; in the second

*Vendredi*, Tournier takes for granted the mythic dimension revealed and emphasized in his own first version, choosing now to alter the fabric of the text—by replacing first person meditation with third person exposition and an abstract vocabulary with a concrete one. In this sense, the second *Vendredi* can be seen as having a pedagogical motivation, but this rewriting of a rewriting does not so much simply tell a story in clearer terms as change our attitude towards what reading is: by drawing attention to the potentially plural nature of his own discourse, Tournier engages the reader in speculations not only about the differences between the various versions of the Robinson Crusoe myth but, more important, about difference itself as the essence of literary discourse.

Tournier frequently speaks of his almost obsessive need to read and to talk and write about reading. Another highly intertextual writer is Christiane Baroche, who has said that, for her, reading is ultimately even more important than writing. She transfers this belief to Jaime Clerg, the main character of her novel *Les Ports du silence* (1992), who states that, while he knows that his favourite fictional characters are only shadowy ghosts, they none the less shape his life and determine his actions. Considered by many to be a writer in the tradition of Maupassant and Zola, Baroche was awarded the Prix Drakkar for *Les Feux du large* (1975) and the Prix Goncourt de la nouvelle for *Chambres, avec vue sur le passé* (1978). These awards have served to identify her publicly as a traditional, realist writer, but Baroche also vigorously challenges the authority of her predecessors. For example, in *Triolet 3* (1989), her story 'Si j'étais l'homme que tu dis . . .' offers an affectionate complement and tribute to Guy de Maupassant's *La Maison Tellier*, but it is also a forceful corrective, presenting a female alternative to the patriarchal views on love, sex, and marriage expressed by Maupassant in his classic tale and, through its play with pastiche and parody, highlighting his complicity with the very nineteenth-century bourgeois hypocrisy that he was criticizing. The fact that Baroche's text is printed after *La Maison Tellier* in the same book, and that she refuses to allow it to be published in any other collection, indicates her desire to recognize publicly her debt to one of her most important precursors, but in this expression of gratitude there is also an equally public revelation of annoyance and even some bitterness at the way in which men have written about women.

## A Woman's Rewriting: Christiane Baroche

After seeing Roger Vadim and Roger Vaillant's film version of *Les Liaisons dangereuses* (1959), which she found both ridiculous and demeaning to women, Baroche decided immediately to read the celebrated eighteenth-century novel on which the film was based and which she had somehow omitted to read before, in the hope that Choderlos de Laclos's text would offer a more positive account of women than that given in the film. And . . . she discovered a novel which enraged her, notably because of Laclos's hurried punishment of the Marquise de Mertueil at the very end of his novel when the Marquise is bankrupted, catches smallpox, loses an eye, and flees to Holland all on the last page! In a lecture given in 1992, Baroche spoke of the enormous effect exerted on her by this reading: 'For twenty years I brooded over that final apocalyptic scenario with suppressed rage, and although my fury was not expressed overtly or explicitly, it in fact affected almost every decision I have since made in my personal life.' The result of these twenty years of angry meditation was the novel *L'Hiver de beauté* (1987), which both tells of the Marquise de Mertueil's life after she leaves Paris and fills in the blanks in her past (she is, for example, given a first name, Isabelle, rather than being defined only in terms of her dead husband's name and social rank). Her story is told in part by herself and in part by her twentieth-century descendant Queria. Although Baroche dislikes being described as a feminist, this novel is as much a profoundly political text as it is a dazzling example of historical and intertextual playfulness, for it fulminates against the fact that men judge women by their external beauty and demonstrates that women have the right to be ugly, arguing that women can—and perhaps should—live simultaneously in solidarity (in sisterhood) with other women and in difference (as complementarity) with men. Furthermore, by 'feminizing' her heroes and 'masculinizing' her heroines, she challenges the accepted stereotypes of gender roles and draws her reader into a constant inter-rogation—of society, of history, of language, and of literature. Baroche invents a family, adventures, a past, a present, and a future for Isabelle in order to liberate her from the prison-house of narrow male expectations in which Laclos had en-closed her. However, it is significant that Isabelle's story is not told only by herself or by a traditional, all-knowing narrator; instead, Isabelle's descendant Queria (rather like the novelist herself) begins by relating and interpreting historical docu-ments and then goes on to imagine how Isabelle would act and react. Her story then becomes Isabelle's, just as Isabelle's story becomes hers—and the reader is drawn into a complex series of identifications and seduced into a personal co-creation of the novel and its meanings by the absence of a fixed authorial position.

If *L'Hiver de beauté* is a rewriting of a previous text, it is also a novel about rewriting—and a novel which demonstrates that rewriting is always (a new form of) writing. However, while Baroche may fill in the narrative gaps left by Laclos, she also draws our attention to other, different gaps: gaps in language, the blanks which feminist thinkers often define as the place of the woman, because language continues to be made for and by men. Isabelle cannot say all she wants or feels, so she sings. In this foregrounding of the voice and especially of singing, Baroche is presenting in novelistic terms an idea which is at the heart of the theoretical thinking of such different influential modern feminists as Marie Cardinal, Hélène Cixous, Catherine Clément, Luce Irigaray, and Julia Kristeva: women need to create a language by and for themselves, a language of the body, which will be an echo of the primeval song once heard, the first maternal voice of love. As Cixous puts it in *La*, a text which is as much a theoretical meditation as it is a novel or a long lyric poem: 'O mur, mur, muroir sur le mur. On essaie de se r . . .

Les vieux mots ne marchent plus' (O wall, wall, wall-glass on the wall. We try to r . . . The old words no longer work any more) (p. 22).

Aware that women have historically been socially and politically marginalized and that they have no adequate words to speak their self, women writers have sought a discourse which says both less and more than the usual words. Musicality, rhythm, resonances and vibrations, song and silence are important elements in this *écriture féminine*, which can, however, never be fully defined, theorized, enclosed, or coded, since its nature is to express, and be, difference (amongst women as well as in relation to men and in relation to Woman or the 'eternal feminine').

### Filling in the blanks: Marguerite Duras

Although she has often spoken of her reservations about being classified as a producer of *écriture féminine*, just as she frequently distanced herself in the 1950s and 1960s from the *nouveaux romanciers* with whom she tended to be identified, Marguerite Duras has done much to change the modern novel by her exploration of silences and her blurring of literary categories: for example, on the title-page of *India Song* (1973), which is a rewriting of *Le Vice-consul* (1965), she describes it as 'texte théâtre film', with neither commas nor hyphens to separate or join the names of the three different genres in which it might be classified. Her early novels, such as *Un barrage contre le Pacifique* (1950), can be described as written in the style of psychological realism, in that details are given that 'flesh out' the characters and explain their behaviour. Above all, the language used is fairly transparent and the dominant tense is the past historic, which Barthes and Robbe-Grillet denounced as the manipulative means by which an all-powerful author constructs the illusion that the world has coherence. In later novels, such as *Moderato cantabile* (1958) and *Le Vice-consul*, Duras experiments with tenses, often preferring the present tense which merely states—and thereby leaves interpretation, the making of sense, to the reader, who often does not know who is speaking or why. Indeed, the reader can never know for certain, because Duras's novels decline to furnish the information which would fill in the blanks. One reason for this is that her works are to a great extent fictionalized autobiography, either because they speak of facts or events in her life, as in *Un barrage contre le Pacifique*, or because they speak of her inner emotional life, as in *Moderato cantabile* and *Le Vice-consul*, and so total explicitness was not appropriate, especially as she and her brothers had been trained from an early age not to speak of their poverty, unhappiness, and loneliness. As she explains in *L'Amant* (1984):

J'ai beaucoup écrit de ces gens de ma famille, mais tandis que je le faisais ils vivaient encore, la mère et les frères, et j'ai écrit autour d'eux, autour de ces choses sans aller jusqu'à elles. L'histoire de ma vie n'existe pas. Ça n'existe pas. Il n'y a jamais de centre. Pas de chemin, pas de ligne. Il y a de vastes endroits où l'on fait croire qu'il y avait quelqu'un, ce n'est pas vrai il n'y avait personne.

(I've written a great deal about the members of my family, but when I was doing so, my mother and brothers were still alive and so my writing skirted round them, skirted round these important issues without tackling them head on. The story of my life doesn't exist. Does not exist. There is never any centre to it. No path, no line. There are great spaces where you pretend there once was someone there, but it's not true, there was no one.) (p. 14)

*L'Amant* was an immediate critical success, winning the Prix Goncourt and also becoming an international best seller, even though it is neither really a novel nor really an autobiography: although Duras uses the narrative 'je' here for the first time, she alternates it with 'elle', as if uncertain as to whether she can talk about herself except as a character in a novel. The story it tells is simple and has already been told, albeit partially and in different ways, in several of Duras's previous works: a girl of 15½ meets a Chinese man in his late twenties and has an affair with him for eighteen months, then leaves for France and does not hear from him until many years later, when he comes to Paris with his wife and telephones to say that he still loves her and always will. The story, which ends there, is not dissimilar from that found in many works of popular romantic fiction, but the way in which it is told sets *L'Amant* apart, for it is full of 'blanks' or gaps in the narration and in the presentation of the psychology of the characters. These blanks have always been a characteristic feature of her work: she has described them as suppressions, as the effects of an emotional anaesthesia caused by her complex response to her mother's madness, her elder brother's violent aggression, and her younger brother's symbolic and then literal death. However, in *L'Amant*, the blanks are even more powerful—they are the visible signs of something that cannot be put into words but which is none the less very real and very powerful, something that the reader intuitively recognizes and will therefore 'write' for herself or himself as s/he reads.

If *L'Amant* is a condensed or distilled repetition of the obsessions that haunt and structure all Duras's work, it is also the text in which we see and experience most strongly the passion that links the writer/narrator with writing. Duras's two main subjects are human injustice (in all its forms, both social and individual) and writing. She is driven to write—and to rewrite her texts and, indeed, to rewrite herself—in order to capture a sense of her life as neither a mere chronological development nor an existence determined and defined by outside events, in order to invent a creative truth out of destructive experiences: 'My books are more truthful than I am myself. *L'Amant* is more faithful to the truth than my actual memory. In fact, it is literature, not authors, which is to be believed' (*Travailler avec Duras*, 195).

## Literature as Repetition and Commemoration

At the end of Samuel Beckett's ironically named *Impromptu d'Ohio* (1981), the Reader L (*Lecteur*) twice sighs, 'Il ne reste rien à dire' (Nothing is left to tell), and then closes the book from which he has been reading aloud to a silent listener E (*Entendeur*—which means one who understands, even though his only reactions are to punctuate the reading with knocks on the table which stop and restart the recital). However, as with all of Beckett's work, the external reader knows that the same elegiac ritual, the same lament for creation, will be repeated tomorrow —and tomorrow and tomorrow. This is not purely mechanical, though: there is a necessity to tell, a compulsion to narrate; this is part of the human condition.

In Beckett's world where entropy is the sole principle of existence, repetition is the only thing that keeps the characters going. They may hope like L that there is an end and that what they tell is 'la triste histoire une dernière fois redite' (the sad tale a last time told) (p. 66), but this desperate optimism is always misplaced, for they are like machines that are running down but will never seize up completely. Alone and unheard (or, at best, misunderstood), they are condemned to repeat eternally, yet, even in their desperation, they must retain the hope that someone will one day hear and understand: at the end of *Quoi où*, V, the invisible voice of Bam who knows that 'Nous ne sommes plus que cinq' (we are the last five) and that time passes, first without words, then with words, and finally simply passes (pp. 86, 87, 89), says, just before plunging the stage into darkness: 'Comprenne qui pourra. J'éteins' (Make sense who may. I switch off ) (p. 98). In other words, there must always be belief in the possibility that someone will make sense, even when there seems to be no one present to listen to us.

The question of how to make sense is one of the burning issues of our modern age, in which language is increasingly being revealed to be inadequate; full, direct, or 'transparent' communication is recognized to be an illusion. The turn towards the reader as an active participant in the creation of texts and, ultimately, of all meaning, coupled with a heightened awareness that we are always readers before we can be writers, has led many writers to incorporate and to inscribe the process of reading into their literary works.

Perhaps the most insistently intertextual of contemporary French novelists is Tournier, who includes in all of his fictional works and in most of his collections of essays a version of the legend of Creation that we find in the first two chapters of Genesis. The obsessive need to rewrite continually—and in different ways— this founding text of Western culture arises undoubtedly out of Tournier's anxious metaphysical and ontological concern with origins, but it is also, crucially, grounded in his conviction that reading in general (but especially the traditional hermeneutic readings of sacred texts) often fails to take account of the detail and the problematical specificity of a text. Two elements in the Genesis legend which particularly intrigue him, and inspire several of his rewritings because of their apparent illogicality, are how God creates Adam both 'in our image' and 'after our likeness' (Genesis 1: 26) and as androgynous or even plural—'male and female created he them' (Genesis 1: 27).

Aware of the many blindnesses and/or misreadings that structure orthodox Jewish and Christian thinking, Tournier also draws our attention to gaps in canonical texts, gaps that he will fill with his own fictions. The most powerful example of this supplementation of the canon is *Gaspard, Melchior & Balthazar* (1980), in which Tournier embroiders the story of the traditional three kings or 'wise men from the east' of whom St Matthew speaks in his Gospel (Matthew 2) and invents a fourth wise man, Taor, whose halting quest for the Christ Child starts off as a search for the recipe for pistachio Turkish delight, but who fails to reach the stable in Bethlehem in time. He then spends the thirty-three years of Christ's life as a convict in the salt-mines of Sodom and finally arrives (late yet again!) in Jerusalem just after the Last Supper. Famished and exhausted, he eats the few crumbs left on the table and drinks the few drops left in the cup, whereupon two angels carry him up to Heaven, for he has become the first person to take Holy Communion and to participate in the Eucharist—which is the commemoration of the Passion and Resurrection of Christ.

Like Abel Tiffauges, the strange Parisian garage-keeper of Tournier's *Le Roi des Aulnes* (1970) who deludedly identifies with a series of mythic heroes and misreads all the prophetic signs around him, indeed like all of Tournier's protagonists, Taor fails in his 'real' quest, the one he sets himself, because he is unable to read correctly the signs he encounters on his way, but he does ultimately succeed in his true quest (the quest for a purpose to, and a justification for, his life) when he himself becomes a sign which the reader, now alerted to the need to read beyond and into signs, can interpret into life and meaningfulness. The discourse that Tournier has come to use in his more recent work may perhaps best be defined as a parabolic discourse. In religious terms, a parable is a story that has a pedagogical function: it never has one single, obvious, and authoritative meaning, but it reveals abstract truths through concrete visual images. Above all, it is a performative act of story-telling, an enigma given to the reader who must solve it for him or herself through the acts of questioning and making new connections.

All stories or fables are meant to be told and retold. Children love to hear the same story over and over again, especially when they know it by heart and can either recite along with the story-teller or demand that certain parts be told just once more. We know from Freud that repetition is often a defence against anxiety, against the fearful knowledge that we do not and can never control the world. However, there can also be in repetition a sense of the primeval, a sense of belonging to a community, a sense that life has some point. In *Désert* (1980), which won the Grand Prix Paul Morand of the Académie française, J.-M. G. Le Clézio tells the simple but incandescent story of Lalla Hawa, a Tuareg girl who is initiated (innocently) into womanhood by a mute goatherd le Hartani who, though said to be deaf and dumb, 'entend mieux que personne . . . le Hartani ne veut pas entendre le langage des hommes, parce qu'il vient d'un pays où il n'y a pas d'hommes, seulement le sable des dunes et le ciel' (hears better than anyone . . . le Hartani does not want to hear the language of men, because he comes from a land where there are no men, but only the sand of the dunes and the sky) (p. 123). Like so many other North Africans, Lalla goes in search of work to Marseilles, where she becomes yet one more of the immigrant 'slaves', then suddenly finds an unwanted celebrity as a model, and finally returns to the desert where, alone and clinging to a fig tree like her mother before her, she gives birth to her child: 'Instinctivement, elle retrouve les gestes ancestraux, les gestes dont la signification va au-delà d'elle-même, sans que personne n'ait eu à les lui apprendre' (Instinctively, she moves her body in an ancient, ancestral way, using gestures which no one needed to teach her, gestures whose meaning transcends her individual situation) (p. 393). If certain archaic, archetypal gestures are undoubtedly inherited and repeated instinctively in the crucial moments of our lives, we also choose to make litanies or lullabies of certain words or songs: when Lalla needs courage, she sings loudly her favourite song 'Médi-ter-ra-né-é e', and, exhausted after the birth, she silently repeats one last time her maternal genealogical name, this time for the future, for her daughter: '"Hawa, fille de Hawa", pense Lalla, une seule fois, parce que cela est drôle, et lui fait du bien, comme un sourire, après tant de souffrance' ('Hawa, daughter of Hawa', Lalla thinks, just once, because it sounds funny and cheers her up, rather like a smile, after all her suffering) (p. 395).

While much contemporary writing foregrounds the importance of repetition as instinctive or unconscious echo, Tournier engages in a reconstruction of repetition as creative and reparative, as commemoration, in *Le Médianoche amoureux* (1989). Neither quite a novel nor quite a collection of short stories, this work opens with the tale of two 'taciturn lovers' who have decided to end their marriage and separate 'parce qu'ils ne s'entendent plus. Il leur arrive même d'avoir des mots. Puis un mauvais silence les entoure . . .' (because they don't get on any more. Sometimes they even have words. Then a disagreeable silence surrounds them . . .) (p. 45). Playing on and with the almost contradictory literal and figurative meanings of 's'entendre' and 'avoir des mots', Tournier has them decide to hold a feast for their friends at which everyone will tell stories. After listening to these tales, Oudalle and Nadège realize that what they had lacked was 'une maison de mots où habiter ensemble' (a house of words where they could live together) and that literature is a 'panacée pour les couples en perdition' (a panacea for couples in distress) (p. 49). However, they come to understand that there is a clear and sharp distinction between two modes of fiction:

Il leur semblait que les nouvelles, âprement réalistes, pessimistes, dissolvantes, contribuaient à les séparer et à ruiner leur couple, alors que les contes, savoureux, chaleureux, affables, travaillaient au contraire à les rapprocher. . . . Et c'était surtout le dernier conte, celui des deux banquets, qui sauvait, semblait-il, la vie conjugale quotidienne en élevant les gestes répétés chaque jour et chaque nuit à la hauteur d'une cérémonie fervente et intime.

(They had the feeling that the short stories—grimly realistic, pessimistic, and demoralizing—were tending to further their separation and the break-up of their marriage, whereas on the contrary the tales—delectable, warm-hearted, and tender—were working to bring them together. . . . And it was above all the last tale, the one about the two banquets, that rescued, so it seemed, daily conjugal life by elevating the actions repeated every day and every night to the level of a fervent, intimate ceremony.) (pp. 47–8)

A calling to remembrance of an important person or event, a commemoration is defined by the fact that it is both repeated and ritualistic. Furthermore, it implies a particular engagement with time, bringing the past into the present in order to celebrate the past, to explain the present, and to prepare the future. Above all, the commemoration of someone or something gives to the celebrators a sense of community, a sense of belonging to both the living and the dead. The *conte* 'Les Deux Banquets ou la commémoration' saves the couple's marriage by revealing to them and to the reader that repetition is not necessarily a defeat or a defence and that the daily repetition of even dull domestic chores can be celebratory. Each repetition will, of course, be slightly different, but none the less a sense of continuity and permanence will be maintained, and, above all, the banal will be not merely excused or justified, but transformed into the site of potential transcendence.

## Orientalism

While the compulsion to rewrite the work of predecessors or to repeat (to re-write) oneself arises out of an anxiety about identity which has always haunted writers, it may, as we have seen, be channelled into creatively commemorative ends, and we should especially remember that many modern women writers celebrate—and incorporate—the work of their literary mothers with little or no sense of Oedipal or Electral struggle, offering a consciously plural or fluid model of writing which is radically changing the expectations of both writers and readers.

In their quest for identity within writing, writers have increasingly turned to the Orient for inspiration. This Orient may be geographically the same as that of Chateaubriand, Nerval, and Flaubert (that is to say, the Near and Middle East and North Africa as well as the Far East), but it is no longer constructed, as it was in the nineteenth century, as the absolute Other of Western fantasy, as a place veiled in exoticism. Although the mystery, the unknowable nature, and the (both liter-ally and metaphorically) veiled quality of the East are essential elements in the fantasy the West has created for itself of the Orient, it should be remembered that the Orient is also an essential part of the economic reality of Europe. Through their many colonies, France and Britain dominated the Orient until the end of the Second World War, and they continue to determine orientalism to a great extent, although the United States exerts an increasingly powerful influence both on how the countries of the East function economically and culturally and on how the West sees them and talks about them.

Orientalism is an essentially European way of speaking about the East, but this discourse is intended to control the East rather than to describe it. In orientalism, the West constructs the East as an inverted mirror image of its own values, thereby setting up a West versus East opposition, which is in fact narcissistic, because the West does not open itself to the true otherness of the East, refusing to accept that the East is extremely varied and divided. And even when the East is praised for its wisdom, its patience, or its sensuality, this is a way of keeping the East in its place and transforming its very real difference into an image of otherness that conforms to the needs and panders to the fantasies of the West.

Duras, who was born in Indo-China and remained there until she was 17, when she left Saigon for Paris, chooses to set many of her works either there or in India. The exoticism of her locations is no doubt attractive to readers, as is her evocation of the luxury enjoyed by the European ruling class during the Indian Raj. However, Duras repeatedly prevents her readers from wallowing in nostalgia by insistently revealing how the poverty and exploitation of the 'natives' and the 'poor whites' are inextricably bound up with the wealth, privilege, and power of the colonial masters. And perhaps the most original feature of her critique of colonialism in such texts as *L'Amant* is the way in which she exposes the violence of the colonial system by writing both personally and objectively, by presenting a poor family (which is partly her own real family, partly a fictional example of an oppressed social unit, and partly a metaphor for vulnerability and fragility) which is torn apart and destroyed by the machine of empire. The undecidability of the narrating voice(s) and the ambiguity of the narration itself ensure that no single political position can be deduced from the text: even the post-colonial guilt that haunts many Europeans and much European political policy is not offered as an adequate response; rather, we are invited to see the Orient as simultaneously the same as and different from the West.

Despite the enormous changes in the ways we acquire knowledge (and, indeed, in the very nature of knowledge) effected by the explosion of the audio-visual media, many contemporary writers have chosen, like their nineteenth-century precursors, to visit the Orient rather than merely reading about it, in order to test their presuppositions against reality—although they know, of course, that brief trips are likely only to reinforce general Western stereotypes and to bolster their personal orientalist fantasies.

The quest for otherness, be it in the personal, the political, or the artistic domain, is bound up with the problem of identity, because the Other, that which is essentially radically different, is necessary to the process of the construction of a notion of the self. However, once we know the Orient (even badly, even only a little), it can no longer be the Other and so must be 'used' differently. In his study of Japan, *L'Empire des signes* (1970), Barthes makes no attempt at objectivity, presenting rather a Japan which is a partial and highly personal construct and analysing only those things that he finds valuable in Japanese culture. Barthes's selective approach and the subjects on which he focuses undoubtedly influenced Tournier, whose orientalism in his novels is similar to Barthes's in his essay on Japan: in *Les Météores* (1975) the Zen garden is seen as a form of writing, and in *La Goutte d'or* (1986) the art of oriental calligraphy is presented as a means of liberation from the prison-house of the Western obsession with the image. Like Le Clézio with Lalla in *Désert*, Tournier in *La Goutte d'or* uses the story of Idriss, a young Berber goatherd, as a vehicle to discuss urgent political issues like racism, immigration, post-colonialism, exploitation of the poor, the manipulation of the media, the need for cultural identity. In both these novels, we find a powerful assault on what an increasingly mechanized and mediatized Europe has become. They both articulate a certain nostalgia (for a simpler life, for a sense of truly belonging somewhere, for a world of greater human warmth). It is important to note, though, that their Orient is not simply a utopia where true mystic wisdom is to be found, since both novelists point up the tensions that exist within the cultures of Arab North Africa.

The major difference between the Orient of Flaubert, say, and that of today's French novelists is that it is now a 'place' where meaning is not so much to be found as created. In this context, the importance of the *conte* or oriental fable as a formal model cannot be over-emphasized. What French writers appreciate and emulate most in the most famous example, the *Arabian Nights*, is the performative nature of the tales: Scheherazade tells her stories for a purpose (to save her life), but they are also tales which have a pedagogic function, which teach by posing questions that the reader or listener must answer for her- or himself.

One of the most fascinating creations of this new orientalism is Baroche's album *Le Collier* (1992). Illustrated by the paintings and Arabic calligraphies of Frédéric Clément, Baroche's narrative tells the story of a French woman's encounter with Arabic culture and charts her slow move towards understanding that the apparently subservient place of women in it may be interpreted positively—but only once one has accepted that no single culture should be regarded as authoritative. As always with Baroche, the book is highly intertextual: one of the characters is called Zobeïda, after a recurring character in the *Arabian Nights* (and a framing character in Tournier's *La Goutte d'or*), and she explicitly quotes from Flaubert's *Salammbô*. Through the device of a tale within the tale (the story of the necklet of silver hands holding a golden droplet), Baroche both indicates how cultures are often almost invisibly embedded in each other and shows how moral and social codes need constantly to be fluid and open to modification. Even more interestingly, the book is quite clearly to be seen as an object, as an artefact, in which Clément's occidental idealizations of Eastern beauty comment on the two narratives and are themselves complemented by the authentic calligraphs. Furthermore, all of these visual elements of the book are also fragmented into details which are then used both as frames to the text and as interruptions of it. Because most Western readers presuppose (though do not know) that the calligraphs have a real but hidden meaning, the book thus functions as an example of the very orientalism that it is unmasking and criticizing in its main narrative.

## The Temptations of Autobiography

In the post-Freudian world, it is no longer possible to consider an autobiography simply to be a confession or a self-justification, as it seemed to be for St Augustine or Rousseau, for example. Modern autobiographers know that it is impossible for anyone to give an accurate account of their own past existence or the development of their personality, because memory is both selective and deforming. They know also that an autobiography is necessarily read in a different way from a novel, for the reader has different expectations, especially with regard to the truth value of what is written. However, even writers associated with the *nouveau roman* and with the attempt to create new objectivities have recently chosen to publish autobiographies: Nathalie Sarraute opens her *Enfance* (1983) with an explicit recognition that, despite everything, she is 'tempted' to evoke memories, and in *Le Miroir qui revient* (1984) Robbe-Grillet goes so far as to claim that 'Je n'ai jamais parlé d'autre chose que de moi' (I have never talked about anything except myself). Indeed, this autobiography has a sequel *Angélique, ou l'enchantement* (1987). Other perhaps surprising autobiographers include Barthes, whose *La Chambre claire* (1980) is as much a work of autobiography inspired by the death of his mother as it is a meditation on the nature of photography, and Tournier, whose *Le Vent Paraclet* (1977) reveals as much about his childhood as about his views on philosophy or how he wrote his novels.

As we have seen, Duras's work often hovers almost uncertainly between fiction and autobiography, but she makes one of her most fascinating 'fictional' appearances in a novel by someone else: in Hervé Guibert's *Mon valet et moi* (1991), where a dying millionaire has his manipulative servant drive him into the forest of Rambouillet where he has found a factory that pulps the novels of Marguerite Duras, who is dismissively described as 'an author of the 1980s'. He loves to listen to the 'bruit divin du papier écrabouillé dans des mâchoires d'acier, qui le ressortent en pâte pour refaire du bon papier vierge' (the heavenly sound of paper being crushed in steel jaws which later spit it out in the form of pulp that will serve to make lovely new virgin paper). This noise evokes for him the screams of Duras's vice-consul of Lahore on the banks of the Ganges, but the servant is horrified by his fascination with it, asking him icily what on earth he has against 'poor' Marguerite Duras (pp. 54–5). Although he was reluctant to use the term autobiography, Guibert himself is present in most of his works—as are members of his family, notably his parents and his great-aunts Suzanne and Louise, whom he also photographed many times. Furthermore, Guibert often included evocations of his friends in his works: there is, for example, a cruel portrait of Gina Lollobrigida in *Les Aventures singulières* (1982) and, most famously, a portrait of Foucault (only vaguely masked as 'Muzil') as the philosopher lay dying of AIDS in *A l'ami qui ne m'a pas sauvé la vie* (1990). Guibert's revelations of Foucault's innermost secrets surprised and shocked many people, especially since Foucault normally talked very little in public about his family, his childhood, or his sexual life, and had indeed argued for years against the imperative to tell the truth and the duty to confess—which he viewed as the most corrosively destructive elements of Christianity's legacy to modern society. Guibert is astonishingly narcissistic and his autobiographical fictions are often spiteful and threaded through with betrayals of those who have cared for him, but his obsession with bodily functions (notably his own) results in a brutally honest discourse: 'Mon corps est un laboratoire que j'offre en exposition, l'unique acteur, l'unique instrument de mes délires organiques' (My body is a laboratory which I offer up for scrutiny and inspection as the single agent, the single instrument of the organic ravings I undergo) (*La Mort propagande*, 171).

Guibert died in 1991 of complications resulting from an unsuccessful suicide attempt. He had been ill with AIDS for several years, and had charted the progress of the disease and his responses to it in *Le Protocole compassionnel* (1991) and *Cytomégalovirus: journal d'hospitalisation* (1992). In these journals, which juxtapose—and give equal value to—raw emotion, banal scraps of everyday life like having a cup of coffee, poetic images, and medical details recorded clinically and objectively, there is a constant preoccupation with writing. One of Guibert's main concerns was to change our notions of what are appropriate and, more urgently, permissible subjects for literature. He also wanted to blur the distinctions between genres, not only publishing mysteries, pornographic stories, and essays on photography as well as autobiographical fiction, but also using the same highly personal and imagistic discourse in all of these 'different' genres. *La Mort propagande* (1977), his first book, began as a notebook of his love letters, and he immediately followed this by writing '*Il*' (*un récit de la mesquinerie*) (1991), which is 'a series of texts in which the 'I' of the daily transcription of actions and thoughts is somewhat thinly disguised under the identity of a character in a novel' (*Mes parents* (1986), 108). Herein perhaps lies the essence of Guibert's work: he himself repeatedly insisted that it was when he was writing a journal that he felt most strongly that he was writing fiction. In this respect, his work is both characteristic and symptomatic of contemporary literature, for he constantly articulates the anguished sense that identity is lost as much as it is found (or at least created) by and in the act of writing. The move towards autobiography in literature testifies to a concern with the nature of truth, of honesty, and of fiction; it suggests that writers now believe that the Other to the self may also be (at least in part) an Other in the self; above all, it is a mark of the increasingly acute sense writers have of the diminution of their authority and of the concomitant need to rethink the functioning (and even the point) of authority.

## The Gamble of Poetry

Prose writers may have experienced an acute sense of self-fragmentation and, at the same time, seen their authority dwindle considerably in the post-1968 period. But for well over a hundred years poets have been aware that their social position can never again be that of Victor Hugo, who was almost universally regarded as an emblem for France: as great a national hero as Napoleon, a *pair de France*, entitled to legal immunity, constitutionally above the law.

In a lecture entitled 'La Poésie et l'université' (1983) the poet Yves Bonnefoy argued that, from the time of Homer until Romanticism, poets spoke 'directly' to the people and, crucially, were listened to and understood. He reminded his audience at the University of Fribourg that in 1066, for instance, just before the Battle of Hastings, a minstrel strode up and down in front of the Norman troops, declaiming poetry in order to spur them on to victory. In other words, in the Middle Ages poetry was not the exclusive preserve of any élite, be it an educated aristocracy or a band of enthusiasts: it could be understood by all and even be the main rallying point for an army. Bonnefoy's main contention is that cultural history shows unequivocally that, until the mid-nineteenth century, poetry was not perceived as 'another' language or a 'foreign' language; rather, it was ordinary language in its most intense form, a distillation of the inherent possibilities of language. For this reason, even when it was difficult, it was speaking for and to the people and had its source in the collective identity and the collective memory of the French. Modern urban and technological society has lost its sense of the sacred and also its sense of a shared language, hence the return to a concern with Nature and with place, with a vanishing world of the mystical which must not be allowed to disappear completely.

In *Les Voisinages de Van Gogh* (1985) and his posthumous volume *Éloge d'une soupçonnée* (1988), René Char evokes several 'hauts lieux' of Provence, reminding us that, while they are important to us today mainly because they figure in the work of such painters as Cézanne and Van Gogh, they have a much deeper history which binds the twentieth century to the Roman Empire—and beyond. These volumes were acclaimed for the incandescence of the language, but there were also complaints that the poems were difficult and, in their many allusions to cultural history, élitist. Such blind and patronizing philistinism marks much discussion about poetry today, but its inverted snobbery was marvellously countered by Char in an interview published in *Le Figaro littéraire*, when he spoke in terms which he was to reiterate in subsequent interviews and which were to become a rallying point for poets: 'I have my own personal critic. He's a poacher. When I've written something, I read it to him and I can't help but laugh when people say that I'm hermetic, because he immediately understands and says, "Yes, you've got that right" or "You should change that word, and this one"' (30 Oct. 1948, p. 5).

The crucial question today is perhaps not so much 'Who reads poetry?' but 'Who can read poetry—and why do they bother?' For Bonnefoy, the crisis of poetry which is much discussed in contemporary France is not caused by any weakening of poetic inspiration, as some critics and commentators argue. Rather, it has arisen because poets no longer communicate properly with their readers. Indeed, Bonnefoy argued in his Fribourg lecture that poets no longer speak the same language or discuss the same issues as their fellow men and women, even though they continue to feel close to them. The problem, the tragedy for poets today is that they know that their language will always be personal, individual, and thus ultimately opaque, even when they are struggling to speak of some universal truth. The lessons learned from linguistics, philosophy, and psycho-analysis teach us that language is never neutral or objective and that communication is always only partially successful. Consequently, poets, as the most committed of explorers of language, are ever more urgently confronted by the burning question originally formulated by Hölderlin and brilliantly analysed and supplemented by Heidegger in his 1946 lecture on Rilke: 'Wozu Dichter in dürftiger Zeit?' (What are poets for in a destitute time?). What can poets say or do in the modern secular and de-sacralized world that will actually make any difference?

In 1981, a chair was created for Bonnefoy at the Collège de France. His Chaire d'Études comparées de la fonction poétique (Chair of Comparative Poetics) was created to replace Barthes's Chaire de Sémiologie littéraire (Chair of Literary Semiotics) and held by him from 1976 until his tragic death in 1980, so that a poet replaced a theorist and cultural critic. Indeed, as Bonnefoy pointed out in his *Leçon inaugurale* (1982), Barthes's last book *La Chambre claire* (on photography, memory, and mourning) was almost a work of prose poetry, as if Barthes had finally come to accept the supremacy of poetry as the most polysemically challenging and emotionally rewarding of genres. For Bonnefoy, the exposure both of the inadequacy of language and of the fragmentary nature of the self should not be seen as a disaster, but welcomed as a creative potentiality: 'Un des grands apports de notre époque a été la mise en valeur de ce qu'on appelle le travail du signifiant, et corrélativement la dénonciation de certains aspects illusoires de notre conscience de nous-mêmes' (One of the major contributions made by our modern age has been the revelation of the importance of what is known as the work of the signifier, and correlatively the denunciation of certain illusory and delusory aspects of our self-awareness) (p. 9).

Poetry's role must now be a prospective one: to explore and to expand the possibilities of language. It must, however, also be a retrospective activity, reminding us of the original language whose echo we hear increasingly faintly. In this respect, the project of poets such as Bonnefoy, Char, and Philippe Jaccottet is analogous to that of many women writers for whom the echo is a vital reality and a trace of lost belonging and wholeness. The poet is the guardian of the memory of primal unity, and so poetry should be explicitly grounded in memory—and in nostalgia. However, this nostalgia is no sentimental longing for times past; it is an experience of intensely felt suffering at our separation from original harmony (the etymology of the word is telling: it derives from the Greek *nostos*: return (home) and *algos*: pain). The modern poet who lives and writes in 'a destitute time' must, if he or she is to write authentically, articulate this anguish, however painful this may be. Bonnefoy's term for this lost primal harmony is 'l'unité'. In his seminal essay 'La Poésie française et le principe d'identité' (1965), which remains perhaps the most important statement made by a poet about contemporary French poetry, Bonnefoy insists that poetic language must always have a spiritual dimension; what he calls a 'syntaxe impossible' must always be postulated, even if it can never be attained and even if the attempt to attain it will always be fraught with danger. This approach is clearly close to mysticism; although not a believer, Bonnefoy is aware that Christian beliefs and Christian iconography haunt all modern Western art and that we have yet to finish the process of mourning, if the gods are indeed now dead, as Nietzsche famously proclaimed.

A translator whose French versions of Shakespeare and Yeats are towering achievements of translinguistic and transcultural shifting, Bonnefoy has meditated long on the nature of French poetry and on its difference from English poetry. Clearly thinking of the seventeenth-century English metaphysical poet John Donne, he wrote memorably in 'La Poésie française et le principe de l'identité': 'On répète volontiers que la poésie anglaise "commence par une puce et finit en Dieu". Je dirais alors que la poésie française a son mouvement à l'inverse, et commence "en Dieu", quand elle peut, pour "finir" par l'amour de la chose la plus quelconque' (People are fond of saying that English poetry 'begins with a flea and ends in God'. I myself would suggest that French poetry works in exactly the opposite way, beginning 'in God', when this is possible, and 'ending' in love for the most ordinary things) (p. 269).

For Bonnefoy, French is 'une langue d'essences' (p. 268), and poets should try always to choose 'pure' or 'essential' words and should aim to effect a process of recognition whereby the reader both universalizes and internalizes as his or her own the acts described in the poem. The words chosen for a poem should thus express something essential and maintain—and articulate—what Bonnefoy calls their 'capacité d'absolu' (their potential universality and absoluteness) (pp. 255–7): after all, 'nommer l'arbre trop aisément, c'est risquer de rester captif d'une image pauvre de l'arbre' (if you name the tree too quickly, you run the risk of remaining the prisoner of an inadequate, an impoverished image of the tree) (p. 272).

The most powerful, as well as the most pleasing and most seductive, French poetry today both proclaims and revels in the propensity to abstraction which is an undeniable feature of the French language. This means that poets often prefer the generic term to the particular: the thing evoked, be it an animal, a plant, or an emotion, is indicated by a bare noun which in its very nudity calls the reader into an activity both of remembering and creating. Any scientific or narrowly explicit classification of experience will always, in Bonnefoy's view, be a denial of presence, since this can only convey aspectual information, rather than engaging the reader in an encounter with existence as an individual but also communal and eternal phenomenon. Modern poetic language must thus be spare or 'essential'; poetry is to be emptied of precise, contingent terms; language must strive to re-become more than 'la langue' or 'le langage', to recover its force as a form of 'le Verbe' or the Logos or Law, whereby it determines existence rather than merely describing it. Above all, language must both be and tell of experience.

In 'Là où creuse le vent', Bonnefoy reminds us that words do have meaning, even if we have forgotten or lost sight of this meaning, and, more prospectively, he suggests that they can, when properly used, generate new meanings:

Et a sens le mot joie
Malgré la mort
Là où creuse le vent
Ces braises claires.

(And the word joy has meaning | Although death exists | Where the wind burrows into
| These bright shining embers.) (*Ce qui fut sans lumière*, 63)

The emotion of joy is rare and to be treasured by every individual who experiences it. But the word to describe this highly personal emotion is shared by all
and thus is banal, inappropriate. However, it also always-already has the potential
to mean beyond the private, individual context—because of its general(izing) force.

We all talk and speak in the mists of language, we all believe we hear words
truly exchanged, and yet we all are condemned to have as our currency for exchange only what Mallarmé called 'les mots de la tribu' (the words of the common herd). Rhetoric or verbal fireworks can never furnish a sufficient response to
metaphysical and ontological questions about existence, but poetry is a form of
hope. Centred on enigma and the impossibility of ever saying anything fully and
directly, it posits the possibility of a world redeemed or reclaimed by attention to
language, by attentiveness to the lost rhythms of our communal life, by meditation on the mysteries that exist evidently but unnoticed in the visible, phenomenal
world. We need to learn to listen to (or listen for) the echoes of the primal song
of harmony that resonate on down through the centuries; we need to learn to fall
silent when the poets are singing; and we need to know how to make the singing
stop when urgent business is to be done.

Today's French poets know that their work will never be chanted like a hymn
or a battle-cry. But they also see that their work is a bulwark against the erosion
of meaning and the first line of defence against any attack on the specificity of
French culture. The most searing modern French poems speak with anguish and
with longing of the presence of an absence. Yet in—and, perhaps, out of—this
articulation of a sense of loss is born a sense of hope. One way or another,
virtually every poet today speaks of the trace—of the lost-but-not-gone-forever.
Hope underpins all poetry in a way it does not necessarily inform the novel. And
this is because it cannot but remain true to its origins. The oldest, indeed the
primal form of human expression, poetry continues to sing out (for) the *unité* we
have lost, because only by making language resonate again can we hope to extri-
cate experience from the domain of the inevitable and the ineluctable and bring
it (back) into that of the possible.

## The Vivacity of Literature

As France has increasingly become a society dominated by images and the mass
media, writers, intellectuals, and critics have tended to lament that the French
have lost the habit of reading. However, literature continues to play an important

role in cultural life, and although it is undoubtedly true that many of the books bought are not read, the Prix Goncourt winner, for example, is usually assured of sales of over 300,000 copies. Literary texts, especially novels, are reviewed widely on the radio and television as well as in the press, and, significantly, writers are asked for their opinions whenever there is an event of national importance, like impending elections, a radical change in the law, a natural disaster, and so on. The writer (as a concept) is thus still at the heart of French consciousness, but writers themselves feel that they have lost their authority—and that this is perhaps a good thing, since they can now exert influence, without wielding power.

Authority has for centuries been conceived—and idealized—as the effect of a single individual or institution, whereas, in reality, it is always the effect of an interplay between different, tactical positions (in which complicity often has a strategic role to play). In the post-1968 period, the writer's anxiety of influence is counterbalanced by the pleasure he or she takes in experimentation or, alternatively, in the conservation-through-modification of such traditional forms as realism. Precisely because the reader has become more important and has been invested with greater power (largely through the intervention of theory) and because the reader has new expectations and, with these, new sources of anxiety also, writers have had to re-examine not only their own position but also the nature—and the possibilities—of writing, of *écriture* itself. And this process of re-evaluation which drives writers on to new modes of writing has been inscribed in much literature as one of the main themes of literature, thereby becoming the domain of the reader as much as of the writer.

## References

Baroche, Christiane, *Chambres avec vue sur le passé* (Paris: Gallimard, 1978).
—— *Le Collier* (Paris: Albin Michel, 1992).
—— *Les Feux du large* (Paris: Gallimard, 1975).
—— *L'Hiver de beauté* (Paris: Gallimard, 1987).
—— *Les Ports du silence* (Paris: Grasset, 1992).
—— *Triolet 3* (Paris: Éditions Hugo Marsan, 1989).
Barthes, Roland, 'La Mort de l'auteur', in *Le Bruissement de la langue: Essais critiques IV* (Paris: Seuil, 1984).
Beckett, Samuel, 'Impromptu d'Ohio' and 'Quoi où', in *Catastrophe et autres dramaticules* (Paris: Minuit, 1986).
Bloom, Harold, *The Anxiety of Influence: A Theory of Poetry* (New York: Oxford University Press, 1973).
—— *A Map of Misreading* (New York: Oxford University Press, 1975).
Bonnefoy, Yves, *Ce qui fut sans lumière* (Paris: Mercure de France, 1987).
—— *Leçon inaugurale* (Paris: Collège de France, 1982).
—— *La Poésie et l'université* (Fribourg: Éditions universitaires, 1984).
—— 'La Poésie française et le principe de l'identité', in *L'Improbable et autres essais* (Paris: Gallimard, 1983).
Char, René, *Les Voisinages de Van Gogh* (Paris: Gallimard, 1985).
—— *Éloge d'une soupçonnée* (Paris: Gallimard, 1988).

Cixous, Hélène, *La* (Paris: Gallimard, 1976).

Duras, Marguerite, *L'Amant* (Paris: Minuit, 1984).

—— *Un barrage contre le Pacifique* (Paris: Gallimard, 1977).

—— *Moderato cantabile* (Paris: Minuit, 1980).

—— *India Song* (Paris: Gallimard, 1973).

—— *Le Vice-consul* (Paris: Gallimard, 1977).

Fernandes, Marie-Pierre, *Travailler avec Duras. 'La Musica Deuxième'* (Paris: Gallimard, 1986).

Foucault, Michel, 'Qu'est-ce qu'un auteur?', *Bulletin de la Société française de philosophie*, 64 (1970), 74–104.

Guibert, Hervé, *A l'ami qui ne m'a pas sauvé la vie* (Paris: Gallimard, 1990).

—— *Les Aventures singulières* (Paris: Minuit, 1982).

—— *Cytomégalovirus* (Paris: Seuil, 1992).

—— 'Il' in *La Mort propagande et autres textes de jeunesse* (1977) (Paris: Régine Desforges, 1991).

—— *Le Protocole compassionnel* (Paris: Gallimard, 1991).

Le Clézio, J.-M. G., *Désert* (Paris: Gallimard, 1980).

Robbe-Grillet, Alain, *Angélique, ou l'enchantement* (Paris: Minuit, 1987).

—— *Le Miroir qui revient* (Paris: Minuit, 1984).

Sarraute, Nathalie, *Enfance* (Paris: Gallimard, 1983).

Tournier, Michel, *Gaspard, Melchior & Balthazar* (Paris: Gallimard, 1982).

—— *La Goutte d'or* (Paris: Gallimard, 1985).

—— *Le Médianoche amoureux* (Paris: Gallimard, 1989).

—— *Les Météores* (Paris: Gallimard, 1975).

—— *Le Roi des Aulnes* (Paris: Gallimard, 1971).

—— *Vendredi ou la vie sauvage* (Paris: Flammarion, 1984).

—— *Vendredi ou les limbes du Pacifique* (Paris: Gallimard, 1967).

—— *Le Vent Paraclet* (Paris: Gallimard, 1977).

# 6

# The Self and Others

IF there is one theme that can be said to have dominated contemporary French thought, it is assuredly that of *otherness*. The Other is a term perhaps most readily associated with the work of the Freudian psychoanalyst Jacques Lacan; but in one form or another it haunts most of the major conceptual adventures that have taken place in France since 1968, and even well before. Contemporary keywords such as 'contradiction', 'difference', 'heterogeneity', 'subjectivity' all bear the trace of the notion of otherness—a notion whose roots go back a long way into French culture, as a reading of Rimbaud or Rousseau's *Confessions* may suggest, and whose dominance in the field of thought might be best understood by a brief consideration of Ferdinand de Saussure's *Cours de linguistique générale*, published posthumously (from Saussure's lecture notes) in 1915.

Saussure's linguistics is probably the dominant influence on what came to be known as structuralism. It rests upon the view that meaning in language is systemically and differentially constructed rather than inhering essentially in words and phrases. The linguistic sign, in other words, is arbitrary, so that 'in language there are only differences *without positive terms*'; 'tree' is understood as different from 'free' or from 'treat', and it is that difference, that otherness, that constitutes its meaning. The view of difference and otherness as fundamental to meaning was itself to be fundamental to structuralist and post-structuralist thought, and to dominate the way in which the thinkers we shall consider here conceptualized language, society, and the formation of the human psyche.

Otherness was not, however, a structuralist invention. It was also fundamental to the work of Jean-Paul Sartre, whose attempts to define the necessary conditions for human freedom had led him in the 1950s from existentialism towards a Marxism grounded in the belief that the bourgeoisie was the inevitable enemy of freedom and that only its overthrow by its Other—the working class—would make such freedom possible. The seeming contradiction in his work after 1968—on the one hand writing his monumental study of Flaubert, *L'Idiot de la famille* (1971), on the other proclaiming through his work with *gauchiste* groups that the intellectual's duty was 'qu'il se supprime en tant qu'intellectuel' (that he should do away with himself as an intellectual) (*Situations*, 467)—can be seen as a dramatization or acting-out of the contradiction of the left-wing intellectual's role in that period, a product of the society he or she sought to overthrow and thus irreducibly other to him- or herself. Ronald Aronson's account of Sartre post-1968, wherein 'an anti-intellectual, unquenchably optimistic *gauchiste* emerged as the alter ego of the student of Flaubert' (p. 321), emphasizes the complementarity as much as the contradictoriness of Sartre's duality. Good faith was possible only by recognizing one's otherness to oneself, not by disavowing it.

For Jacques Lacan, arguably the most enduringly influential of post-war French thinkers, such a recognition is a chimera, requiring as it would a presence of the linguistic subject to itself that its very constitution through the signifying chain of language makes impossible. The introduction to his *Écrits I* proclaims that 'il n'y a de maître que le signifiant' (the only master is the signifier) (p. 7), which in simplified form means that human subjects are, precisely, subject to the laws of language, and that it is in and through those laws that our identities are articulated. Lacan's use of the term *signifiant* (signifier) refers to Saussurean linguistics, for which any linguistic sign is composed of a signifier—the verbal or written expression (tree, *arbre, arbor*)—and a signified—the concept or sense-impression which it designates (the same for all three examples given). Any linguistic text, from a note for the milkman to Heidegger's *Being and Time*, is thus made up of what Saussure calls a 'signifying chain'—a series of signifiers along and across which meanings are produced and articulated. One of Lacan's great originalities lies in his mapping of this concept, and the openness and lability of meaning(s) that it connotes, onto what he defines as the linguistically constituted world of the unconscious—by definition his territory of exploration as a psychoanalyst. For Lacan, 'l'inconscient, c'est le discours de l'Autre' (the unconscious is the discourse of the Other) (*Écrits* I, 24), which is to say that any notion of a self always and fully present to itself is always and everywhere illusory. In this Lacanian psychoanalysis lays claim to the authentic inheritance of Freud, distinguishing itself sharply from American 'feel-good' ego-psychology which purports to fill and bring under control the gaps and contradictions in the subject's self-constitution rather than engaging with the meanings they produce.

The Other (whose capitalization emphasizes its constitutive role in the production of the self) most obviously takes the form of the psychoanalyst, and more particularly of Lacan himself, whose histrionic seminars and notoriously brief and costly analytic sessions were one of the founding myths of 1960s and 1970s Paris. That the great man said of himself 'Je père-sévère' (I persevere/I father-severe) suggests, however, a parental antecedent for the Other in question. The young human animal—the in-fant (which etymologically means 'non-speaking')—is at first caught up in what Lacan calls the 'imaginary' relationship with its mother, a relationship that is, as Sherry Turkle puts it, 'fusional, dual and immediate, dominated by the desire to lose self in other'. This originary bliss—as impossible to eradicate from memory as to regain—is troubled, in a linguistically-inflected but none the less classic Oedipal scenario, by the intervention of the father as third party, negating the (male) child's desire for the mother through what Lacan calls the 'non/nom du Père' (no/name of the Father). This intervention is closely linked with two other phenomena which between them mark the child's accession to the 'symbolic' domain—ability to recognize and respond to its own reflection in the mirror (the essay 'Le Stade du miroir' (the mirror stage), in *Écrits I*, deals with this), and the concomitant acquisition of language. Our construction as subjects, that is to say, entails the disruption of a primordial imaginary unity by the potentially destructive irruption of the Other; only at that price do we become 'ourselves.'

Whilst much of Lacan's most important work was written before 1968, there is no doubt that he rose to prominence after, and largely as a result of, the events of May when the linguistic dislocation and hyperactivity clearly continued to work at the level of the individual subjects involved even after the events' more obviously political ambitions had been thwarted. This manifested itself in an upsurge in psychoanalytic culture—courses of analysis for those who could afford it, Lacan-written or Lacan-influenced books for the rest—that ranks among the most striking intellectual phenomena of the period. Lacan's later work is characterized by two major shifts in emphasis—towards the geometrization of desire (the algorithms and diagrams become more complex, striving at times towards three-dimensionality), and towards an attempted articulation of the essentially non-articulable that is the 'Other' of woman. 'Une géométrie, c'est l'hétérogénéité du lieu, à savoir qu'il y a un lieu de l'Autre' (A geometry is the heterogeneity of the place, which is to say that there is a place of the Other) (*Encore*, 14). That Other is 'feminized' in the celebrated/notorious essay 'Dieu et la jouissance de // la femme' (God and woman's ecstasy), in which it is said that 'cet Autre . . . doit bien avoir quelque rapport avec ce qui apparaît de l'autre sexe' (that Other . . . must have some relationship with what appears of the other sex) (*Encore*, 65). The ecstasy (mystical and/because orgasmic) of St Teresa in a Bernini sculpture in Rome is evoked to suggest the otherness of Woman and, by audacious theological extension, the (necessary?) feminization of God: 'pourquoi ne pas interpréter une face de l'Autre, la face Dieu, comme supportée par la jouissance féminine?' (why not interpret one face of the Other, the God-face, as endured/upheld by feminine ecstasy) (*Encore*, 71).

Lacan's willingness to speak the necessary unsayability of the 'Other' that is woman was to earn him much criticism from feminist writers such as Luce Irigaray. What is significant here is the way in which the work of his last period (he died in 1981) broaches two areas of otherness that became increasingly important in French thought during our period—woman (Freud's 'dark continent') and the divine. Marxism, which had been in one form or another hegemonic among French intellectuals from the end of the Second World War through to the mid-1970s, had decreed the death of God and often all but installed itself in his place. The May events, which involved many radical Christians and had undoubted spiritual resonances for many participants, marked the beginnings of a turning-point in this respect, and the move away from Marxism characteristic of the past fifteen or twenty years, as disillusionment with the Soviet system was confirmed by its disappearance and social democracy became dominant on the Left, went to reinforce it. The *nouveaux philosophes*, figures such as the former Maoists André Glucksmann and Bernard-Henri Lévy, deeply influenced by Alexander Solzhenitsyn's revelations about the existence of concentration camps in the Soviet Union in *The Gulag Archipelago*, enjoyed a brief vogue in the mid-1970s with their denunciations of the necessary spiritual impoverishment of Marxism, which often read much like a diluted and reheated version of Camus's *L'Homme révolté*. Spirituality, ethics, transcendence were no longer dirty words. But they had never been dirty feelings, for the revolutionary romanticism so characteristic of the period around 1968 harnessed both in full measure, even though they were often hidden under a rhetoric of materialist scientificity (as in Maoism or the Marxism of Louis Althusser) and in the dismissal of ethical questions as subordinate to the class struggle. When the claims of such rhetoric came to seem historically unjustified, the transcendental energies that had often fed them (re)appeared in various guises—most egregiously in the *nouveaux philosophes'* media gold-digging, most importantly in the work of such figures as Emmanuel Lévinas and Jean-Luc Nancy.

Lévinas—commentator on Blanchot, Husserl, and Heidegger, and a major influence on the work of Jacques Derrida—had as early as *Totalité et infini* (1961) been exploring what might be called the phenomenology of the divine. The question for him, as for such earlier thinkers as Simone Weil or indeed Heidegger, is less 'is there (a) God?' than 'how can God/the divine be understood as the horizon of language?' *De Dieu qui vient à l'idée* (1982) describes itself as 'une recherche sur la possibilité . . . d'entendre le mot Dieu comme un mot signifiant' (an investigation into the possibility of understanding the word God as a signifying word) (p. 7), and articulates that (re)search around the inescapability of otherness. For Lévinas, 'la responsabilité pour Autrui est transcendance' (the responsibility for Others is transcendence) (p. 32), which is to be understood not (solely) as an ultimate ethical imperative but as a phenomenological statement setting otherness at the core of identity. Lévinas goes on to define that responsibility as 'la relation exceptionnelle où le Même peut être concerné par l'Autre sans que l'Autre s'assimile au Même' (the exceptional relationship in which the Same can be concerned by the Other without the Other being assimilated to the Same) (p. 32). That insistence of otherness likewise pervades our perceptions of time (inhabited by infinity as its Other) and of God as semantic horizon rather than as immanent essence.

Nancy—like Lévinas a major commentator on Heidegger, and also one of the best exegetes of Lacan—has been spoken of as a 'thinker of limits, thresholds, and co-appearances', and such thinking would scarcely be possible without the insistence of the Other. In the article 'Des lieux divins' (1985) he explores the question of what the divine might mean without the metaphysics of presence that has been its traditional accompaniment in Western thought. God, for Nancy, is not the supreme being (which implies him as present as Lacanian 'big Other' or transcendental role-model), but 'the being we are not, but which is not a being at our disposal in the world around us either' ('Des lieux divins', 26) God resembles here more a 'signifying chain' of divinity, absolutely present nowhere, than the profound hidden essence of conventional religious discourse.

It is in the work of Jacques Derrida that the metaphysics of presence has been most stimulatingly and sophisticatedly challenged. Derrida's work before 1968, most notably *De la grammatologie* (1967) and *L'Écriture et la différence* (1967), has been influential through its deconstruction of the binary opposition between speech and writing on which Western literary and philosophical culture has based itself. 'Writing' (*écriture*) has traditionally been perceived as secondary to 'speech' (*parole*), as it were a 'writing down' of the immediacy and plenitude of the spoken word. Derrida's analyses show on the contrary that (*la*) *parole* is always/already inhabited by the processes of spacing, difference, deferral that we associate with the written word, that—in, precisely, a word—speech is not the prior origin of writing, but that each of those terms is rather the necessary Other of the other.

The 'opposition' of speech and writing is parallelled and re-enacted in that between literature and philosophy; the essays in *Marges de la philosophie* (1972) suggest in a multiplicity of ways how the literary and the philosophical inhabit each other. For readers of Nietzsche, Wittgenstein, Heidegger on the one hand and Joyce, Borges, Ponge on the other, this might come as confirmation rather than subversion. For those raised in a tradition of pragmatic philosophy and realist writing, however, it often acted as a red rag to a bull, and the attacks on Derrida by such figures as John Searle have bestowed on him a largely unwanted notoriety as the standard-bearer of supposed 'Continental' obscurantism. Deconstruction, properly understood as the unpicking of long-enshrined binary antitheses such as 'speech/writing' or 'literature/philosophy', came to be used as a catch-all term whose practical value was that it undermined transcendental notions of truth and thus allegedly enabled anybody to say or write anything whatever.

This is a travesty of Derrida's work, whose rigorous attention to the texts it discusses is unmistakable. It acquired, however, immense political and ethical relevance in the wake of the discovery that the Belgian *émigré* deconstructionist

Paul de Man (by then dead) had written a number of anti-Semitic articles in occupied Belgium during the war. Derrida's proclaimed political affiliations have always been of the Left, and his work (like that of Lévinas, like the Jewish mystical tradition of which both men bear the mark) has constantly emphasized respect for the Other's otherness as the *sine qua non* of any ethics whatever. The discovery that his colleague and friend had been complicit with the most ruthless and systematic of all enterprises of destruction of the Other was a profound personal and intellectual trauma, inscribed in the *Mémoires pour Paul de Man* (1988). The key themes in Derrida's later work recur with a particular intensity here, particularly in the final chapter 'La Guerre de Paul de Man' (Paul de Man's war), which was added in 1988: the inescapable aporia of mourning which when successful 'fait de l'autre une *partie* de nous, entre nous—et l'autre paraît alors n'être plus l'autre' (makes the other a *part* of us, among us—and the other then seems no longer to be the other) (p. 54); the no less inescapable theme of the promise to the other which forms the necessary, and thus unreachable and undeliverable, horizon of a deconstructive ethics and politics; the final recognition that texts invite their own reproduction and that in consequence 'il faut plus que jamais veiller à ne pas reproduire la logique qu'on prétend condamner' (we must more than ever be careful not to reproduce the logic we purport to condemn) (p. 221).

Derrida has subsequently foregrounded more prominently than before his own biography in 'Circonfession', his contribution to *Jacques Derrida* (1991), and his ethical and political commitment in *Spectres de Marx* (1993). The first text is an extraordinary poetic, philosophical, and autobiographical reflection on his circumcision and his relationship with his mother, in which phrases such as 'je posthume comme je respire' (I posthume as I breathe/I breathe as I approach death) (p. 28) evoke the centrality of death and mourning in Derrida's writing. Death, indeed, haunts the Derrida-text like a ghost—neither fully present (for then there could be no text) nor fully absent (for then there could be no text either), the figure of otherness at its most constitutive. *Spectres de Marx*, as the title suggests, is rooted in this image and in the 'hantologie' (a pun on 'hantise' (haunting) and 'ontologie' (ontology)) that accompanies it. Heidegger, again, is a major reference-point, along with Shakespeare's Hamlet for whom 'the time is out of joint'; but these immemorial alterities are here inscribed in the context of the work of Marx for which the time has indeed seemed out of joint in contemporary France.

## Marxism and Post-Marxism

Sartrean existentialism, the significance and credibility of the French communist party (largely thanks to its work in the Resistance), the May 1968 events, the election of Mitterrand in 1981 on a programme of collaboration with the communists were among the major reasons why Marxism was so politically and ideologically influential in France from the end of the Second World War through to the early 1980s. The impact of Reagano-Thatcherite capitalism, the socialist party's break with the communists and espousal of social democracy, the collapse of the Stalinist Eastern European regimes and then of the Soviet Union, all combined to undermine that influence dramatically (as, indeed, the *nouveaux philosophes* had predicted). Marx has thus of late been widely regarded as, if not dead, at least a ghost, and it is with the figure of the ghost or spectre—invoked at the beginning of Marx's *Communist Manifesto* as that of communism haunting Europe—that Derrida makes great play, perceiving it as necessary to any kind of constructed human identity: 'Partout où il y a Moi, *es spukt*, "ça hante"' (Wherever there is 'I', *es spukt*, 'there is haunting') (*Spectres de Marx*, 212). The Other here haunts us again, and the spectres of Marxism—for Derrida is insistent that there is more than one Marx, more than one Marxism, more than one Marxian legacy—are conjured up in a text that is as vehemently *engagé* as it is subtly philosophical. Marx's messianic horizon is seen as more than ever necessary to counter the 'end-of-history' thesis of Francis Fukuyama and his followers, and the chapter 'Usures' contains a ten-point indictment of the 'plaies du "nouvel ordre mondial"' (wounds of the 'new world order') (p. 134) which suggests that the death of Marxism has been all too prematurely celebrated.

The name that most ghoulishly evokes the connection between Marx(ism) and spectrality is that of Louis Althusser, whose work on Marxism and ideology exercised an immense influence in the 1970s and who, after he strangled his wife in 1980, was treated as one of the 'undead' until he himself died in 1991. Already in the essay 'Freud et Lacan' of 1964, he had demonstrated an interest in the contradictory constitution of human subjectivity and the importance of the Other's discourse. 'Idéologie et appareils idéologiques d'État' represents an (unacknowledged) communist party response to the events of 1968, which had taken the communist Left by surprise, largely because those events originated in the university world and emphasized the importance of cultural as much as more narrowly economic or political change. The education system, religion, publishing, political parties, the media are here seen as 'ideological state apparatuses' helping to maintain the domination of the bourgeois state just as surely as, if somewhat less obviously than, the 'repressive state apparatuses' of government, courts, police, and army. This approach was widely criticized for a narrow functionalism, for if all these systems of organization served merely to maintain the bourgeois stranglehold, what possibilities of meaningful social change were there? Yet its insistence upon the importance of the superstructural, and its awareness that relations of power in modern technological societies necessarily take on more complex and less apparent forms than in earlier periods, have retained their relevance despite the virtual evaporation of the communist party and the dwindling of Marxism's intellectual influence.

Althusser's killing of his wife, 'la tragédie' for which he was never found fit to stand trial, combined with the factors mentioned above to plunge his work and his life alike into obscurity until both dramatically resurfaced with the publication of *L'Avenir dure longtemps* in 1992. This is an autobiography, or at least that is what it purports to be, which tragically bears the traces of the delirium to which this most cerebral of manic-depressives was periodically subject. An assertion such as '. . . je n'ai jamais pu pénétrer . . . dans aucun texte de Freud! ni dans aucun de ses commentateurs!' (. . . I have never been able to get into . . . any of Freud's texts! nor into any of his commentators!) (p. 160), with its hyperactive neo-Célinian punctuation and its manifest absurdity for one who had helped to bring Lacan to wide public attention, shows the importance of according *L'Avenir dure longtemps* the same kind of symptomatic reading, the same attention to the gaps, silences, contradictions within the text, that Lacan practises on Freud or that Althusser himself gave to Marx in *Pour Marx* (1965) and *Lire 'Le Capital'* (1965). Althusser's continuing belief in 'l'absence de rapports marchands' (the absence of market relationships) shows that his sense of the need for social and political change had remained acute, though his reference to '[des] interstices de communisme' (the interstices of communism) (in *L'Avenir dure longtemps*, 217–18) suggests a less Leninist organizational perspective than that he had earlier adopted.

Althusser, like Derrida in 'Circonfession', writes movingly of his relationship with his mother and of the sense of otherness that haunted the earliest stirrings of his sense of identity. For Althusser, these came about because his mother had loved his father's brother (killed in action at Verdun, and after whom the young Louis was named) before marrying his father; Derrida speaks of the elder brother (Paul) who died before his birth, so that he felt himself to be 'un mortel de trop' (a mortal too many) (*Jacques Derrida*, 52). The decline of Freudian-Marxist Grand Theory had as one of its consequences the revalorization of individualities in their constitutive differences, and thus too of the autobiographical mode. It is a striking and moving illustration of this chapter's central thesis that these two writers, for twenty years colleagues at the École normale supérieure, should each articulate the importance of otherness and of mutilation, Althusser in his early sexual anguish and the strangling of his wife, Derrida in his lifelong haunting by his circumcision.

The decline of Grand Theory is closely associated with the movement, or movements, known as postmodernism. This term (most widely known in its architectural context) refers to the 'crise des récits' (crisis of narratives) character-istic of Western culture since the late nineteenth century, and accelerated by the development of new forms of technology. The 'récits' in question are, for Jean-François Lyotard in *La Condition postmoderne* (1979), those narratives that legiti-mize claims to (at least in principle) total or totalizable knowledge. The most significant of these are the narratives of scientific knowledge and of human eman-cipation—'the truth shall make you free'—and their Freudian and Marxist correlatives, with their claims to be sciences respectively of the unconscious and of society. These are implicitly called into question by postmodernism's appeal to a heterogeneous plurality of overlapping discourses.

Postmodernist thought is too often reduced to a 'rainbow coalition' of attitudes and vocabularies in and for which anything goes. In *Dérive à partir de Marx et de Freud* (1973) Lyotard engages rigorously in a critical interrogation of Marxist and Freudian concepts rather than sweeping them away in some lavish anarcho-technological flourish. *Économie libidinale* (1974), in which the term 'libido' is used in a sense far wider than the merely sexual, is critical of psychoanalysis for its systemic tendency to reduce the spiralling diversity of desire to a unitary narrative which the patient, so to speak, 'buys'. The simultaneous onslaught and reliance on Freudian and Marxist concepts in fact hinges on their interpenetration, for the economy that is socially determinant for Marxism is in its very constitution saturated with desire, whilst that desire itself (itselves?) can only exist within a framework of relations, intra- and extra-discursive, that partakes of the economic.

Frequently yoked together with the name of Lyotard is that of Jean Baudrillard, whose work after *Le Système des objets* (1968) adopted a much more nihilistic and even illusionistic perspective, suggested by a title such as *A l'ombre des majorités silencieuses ou la fin du social* (1982). The trouble with Baudrillard's work of this period is that it was all too often overtaken by the very reality whose provable existence it sought to undermine. There might seem little point writing books about the increasing virtualization of 'reality' when so derealized a reality had become the technological norm, to the point of calling the very future of the book into question.

Latterly, however, Baudrillard's work has acquired a harder edge. *La Guerre du Golfe n'a pas eu lieu* (1991) was widely, and surely misleadingly, represented as a denial that war(s) mattered, or even existed, any more than anything else. Baudrillard's account of the Gulf War as a high-tech 'lieu d'effondrement'—'preuve vivante de la débilité politique occidentale' (a place of collapse—a living proof of Western political debility) (pp. 76–7) is an accurate condemnation of it and his remarks on the atmosphere of the declining *années Mitterrand*, in which a resurgent and fast-spreading Islam displays more ideological verve than virtually any other system of political or religious belief, merit quotation:

Nous ne pratiquons pas l'intégrisme fondamentaliste dur, nous pratiquons l'intégrisme démocratique mou, subtil et honteux, celui du consensus. Cependant, l'intégrisme consensuel (celui des Lumières, des Droits de l'homme, de la gauche au pouvoir, de l'intellectuel repenti, de l'humanisme sentimental) est tout aussi féroce que celui de n'importe quelle religion tribale ou société primitive. Il dénonce l'autre exactement de la même façon, comme le Mal absolu.

(We don't practise hard-line fundamentalism, we practise soft, democratic fundamentalism, which is subtle and shameful—the fundamentalism of consensus. However, consensual fundamentalism (that of the Enlightenment, of human rights, of the left in power, of the penitent intellectual, of sentimental humanism) is quite as fierce as that of any tribal religion or primitive society. It denounces the other in just the same way, as absolute Evil.) (p. 90)

The blandness of 'post-socialist' consensus is here revealed to be a wolf in sheep's clothing, advocating *le droit à la différence* (the right to be different) as much to police and limit difference as to foster it. In *L'Illusion de la fin* Baudrillard excoriates (in a very different manner from Derrida) the Fukuyama view of the 'end of history', which for him is as illusory in its self-conferred triumph as the ideologies it has sought to supplant. History, for Baudrillard, has not so much ended as become trapped in an unending recycling and derealizing of itself, of which the pomp and circumstance of the Revolutionary bicentennial celebrations in 1989 were a striking example. The downfall of historical communism was not really an 'end' at all but a selling-off: 'Le communisme n'aura pas eu de fin historique, il aura été soldé, liquidé comme un stock inutile' (Communism has not come to an end historically, it has been sold off, liquidated, like superfluous items of stock) (p. 165), downgrading the supposedly momentous events in Eastern Europe from Hegelian apotheosis to bargain basement, locating them not in the domain of the unfolding of History but in that of the recessional market economy under whose sign the tawdry beginning of the end of the twentieth century is playing itself out.

## The Future of Literary Criticism

Endings, deaths, mournings seem to dominate the period under discussion. That of Roland Barthes had particular ironic poignancy because, as we have seen, one of Barthes's key themes was the 'death of the author', the upstaging of the omniscient holder and unfolder of meaning by the reader's joyously polymorphous opening-up of the text and fissuring of the edifice of sense. Again, as with the related areas of deconstruction and postmodernism, this has all too easily been taken, by hostile critics and mediocre practitioners alike, to mean open season on/ for coherence and rigour. Such a misrepresentation is nowhere better countered than in Barthes's *S/Z* (1970), the product of work in his seminar at the École pratique des hautes études. A hitherto little-known Balzac short story, 'Sarrasine', is analysed, in a convergence of the linguistic and the Freudian senses, through the medium of five codes: the hermeneutic ('riddles' posed by the text and their answers), the semantic (clusters of signifieds or 'themes'), the symbolic (the antithetical 'macro-themes' that structure the text), the proairetic (actions in their unfolding), and the cultural or referential (which relates to shared assumptions about or bodies of knowledge). The result, which breaks the source-text down into 561 lexical units, might at first seem to evoke the view of the structuralist as mad scientist rather than that of the post-structuralist as jester to a non-existent court. Reading it, however, is more like listening to music—the *Diabelli Variations* or *The Art of Fugue*—than such an account might suggest. The text is contrapuntal, working through the tissue it weaves from the interplay of its five codes rather than from the individual force of any or all of them. Its influence has been seminal in two respects: it inscribed Lacanian psychoanalysis into the domain of literary theory (the 'S/Z' of the title figures Sarrasine's emasculation by his passion for the *castrato* La Zambinella, and beyond that the encoding of sexuality and difference along the signifying chain), and it asserted the perverse ecstasy—the *jouissance*—of active and open reading(s) over against the more sage, more academically respectable, 'pleasure' to be derived from canonical consumption.

'Literary criticism', as an autonomous domain, has come to seem an increasingly untenable notion as linguistics, psychoanalysis, Marxism, and philosophy, separately or jointly, have called the independence of the literary text into question. Julia Kristeva's notion of 'intertextuality', denying as it does that any text can function without alluding to a host of other texts, has at once been perhaps the most significant theoretical axis of 'literary criticism' during the latter half of our period and made the term practically unusable in its more traditional senses. This simultaneous undermining and celebration of the textual is exhilaratingly bodied forth in Barthes's *Le Plaisir du texte* (1973), in which the 'pleasure' of a classic reading is opposed to the *jouissance*—ecstatic and/because menacing—of a perverse or subversive one. Sade, Nietzsche, Georges Bataille are major pre-texts here, but it is important to emphasize that textual pleasure and ecstasy are not primarily destructive: 'la destruction ne l'intéresse pas; ce qu'il [sc. le plaisir] veut, c'est le lieu d'une perte, c'est la faille, la coupure, la déflation, le *fading* qui saisit le sujet au cœur de la jouissance' (destruction is of no interest to it; what it (sc. pleasure) wants is the place of a loss, a gap, a break, the deflation and fade-out that seizes the subject at the heart of ecstasy) (*Le Plaisir du texte*, 15). The subject, that is to say, becomes other to itself in and through *jouissance*.

This otherness is marked throughout Barthes's work of this period. *L'Empire des signes* (1970) prefigures more recent Western fascination with Japan; *Fragments d'un discours amoureux* (1977) is a montage of aphorisms arranged by alphabetical keyword, to suggest that the lover's discourse, organized and structured as it here is (by quotations from Goethe's *Werther* and Japanese Buddhism as well as from Lacan), is at the same time and necessarily fragmentary, incapable of attaining the imaginary omnipotent plenitude to which it yearningly aspires. The tantalizing hints of autobiography in this text find a belated counterpart in *La Chambre claire* (1980), an essay on photography, and more particularly on a photograph—not reproduced in the book—of his mother, and *Incidents* (1987), containing two texts, set in Morocco and Paris respectively, which hinge on Barthes's various homosexual encounters. He had considered publishing these in his lifetime—his homosexuality was no secret—so that suggestions that the more recent text ('Soirées de Paris') in particular, with its often depressing evocations of ageing desire, might have been better left unpublished seem misplaced. The 'warts-and-all' element in his autobiographical writing is surely fundamental to it (as it is to that of Rousseau and Leiris or, as we have seen, of Guibert), because the narcissism of the human subject, that process by which it is at the same time other and not-other to itself, necessarily bears within it a negative side. To this Barthes's later work bears eloquent (and elegant) testimony.

## Foucault: From Document to Monument

Posthumous biographical revelations about Michel Foucault, by Hervé Guibert and others, have sensationalized his (homo)sexual activities to the point where the work he produced, especially the three volumes of his *Histoire de la sexualité* (1976–84), has sometimes seemed to act merely as pre-text for what, had he not been a philosopher, would doubtless have appeared a merely averagely scandalous life. Foucault's work in the period traces an evolution from the 'archaeological'—the delving into epistemological layers of the past—to the 'genealogical'—the emphasis on how the discourses in and through which that delving takes place themselves stem from, and depend on, that which has preceded them.

*L'Archéologie du savoir* (1969) is the best example of Foucault's earlier period. He had earlier traced the development of and changes in discourses on madness in *Histoire de la folie* (1961) and representation in *Les Mots et les choses* (1966); *L'Archéologie du savoir* makes plain his project of treating these and other discourses not as 'documents' but as 'monuments', viewing them not in their (frequently marginal) reference to what we now perceive as truth, but in their relationship to one another and the discursive formations and extra-discursive contexts that are thereby engendered. Foucault's concern here is the search for the conditions in which new concepts in their discursive articulation could appear. The shift from an archaeological to a genealogical method entailed a different, less detached approach to the discourses studied, and one in which the interlinked concepts of power and the body assume an ever-greater importance. *Surveiller et punir* (1975) traces the genealogy of the contemporary prison back to the Enlightenment, whose invention and proclamation of human liberties depended for its very existence on the 'disciplinary society' evoked by Foucault. Punishment (which has always existed) is less central here than the idea of 'bio-power' and the techniques of surveillance and control to which it gave rise, techniques embodied, for example, in Jeremy Bentham's 'Panopticon', a prison so laid out that all inmates can always be seen by a guard in the central tower without being able to see him or tell whether he has them in view or not. Electronic tagging—to say nothing of the language laboratory—here finds an obvious if in some ways unexpected ancestor. More generally, Foucault here shows how the human subject has depended for its very existence upon the carceral networks of bio-power he might appear to denounce: 'le réseau carcéral constitue une des armatures de ce pouvoir-savoir qui a rendu historiquement possible les sciences humaines' (the prison network is one of the structural supports of that power-in-knowledge which has made the human sciences historically possible) (*Surveiller et punir*, 312). Such power, whether or not it is punitive, is for Foucault perhaps more than any other major modern thinker omnipresent and inescapable.

To think power over the body is inevitably, at any rate in a France of Catholic traditions, to think sexuality. The first volume of *Histoire de la sexualité, La Volonté de savoir* (1976), tells us that sexuality, far from being a taboo or forbidden domain, is for Western Christianity on the contrary the domain of knowledge par excellence—a knowledge, and thus a power, at work alike in the confessional and on the psychoanalyst's couch. Foucault moved back from and beyond this position in the succeeding volumes, feeling that the human desiring subject could not simply be taken as given and that its genealogy needed to be retraced to classical antiquity. This he did in the second and third volumes, *L'Usage des plaisirs* (1984), and *Le Souci de soi* (1984), retracing what he calls 'la généalogie de l'homme de désir' (the genealogy of the man of desire) in the Greek culture of the aesthetic management of pleasure and the Roman concern with the culture of the self respectively. Foucault's erudition in these two volumes is all the more remarkable for being made so thoroughly relevant to the present day and, given the foregrounding of homosexuality in both volumes, to his own life.

## Régis Debray and the 'Communications Revolution'

The sensationalized promotion of that life, which we have already referred to, can be seen in our context as the mediatized—and trivialized—counterpart of the return to the (auto)biographical traced in Althusser, Derrida, and Barthes. A major strand in contemporary French thought has been the investigation, and often denunciation, of the role and effects of the media. Baudrillard, for whom life and television often seem to form one non-existent whole, is the most obvious example of this, but one of the conceptually richest and most systematic studies of the changing role of the media in modern Western societies is that of Régis Debray.

Debray's name still evokes his early period as theoretician of Third World revolution in *Révolution dans la révolution* (1967), and his imprisonment in Bolivia for having taken part in the liberation struggle alongside Che Guevara. For the last fifteen years, however, his work has focused primarily on cultural developments within France. *Modeste Contribution aux discours et cérémonies officielles du dixième anniversaire* (1978) saw the May events as harbinger not of post-Stalinist revolutionary change, but of the technological and cultural modernization (which is to say Americanization) of France. In *Le Pouvoir intellectuel en France* (1979) Debray denounces what he sees as one of the most pernicious effects of that modernization—the displacement of what Pierre Bourdieu calls 'symbolic power' from the universities and publishing houses towards the worlds of journalism and television. This needs to be seen in a specifically French context in which Paris, and particularly its fifth and sixth *arrondissements*, overwhelmingly dominates intellectual and cultural life, as well as concentrating within itself virtually all political and administrative power. Debray, right from his Latin-American period, has always been an unabashed apologist for the nation-state, whose legitimacy and accountability he sees as under threat from the brave new world in which images count for far more than ideas. His early enthusiasm for François Mitterrand, as a man of culture but also the best possibility for radical social change in post-

1968 France, became seriously tarnished by the political neutering and media cultivation of the 1988 re-election and the bicentennial celebrations, and *A demain de Gaulle* (1990) is, at least in part, a symbolic divorce from the Mitterrand regime. Recently, in *Cours de médiologie générale* (1991) and *Vie et mort de l'image* (1992), perhaps in response to the political void characteristic of the period, his work has moved from the polemical towards the theoretical and the analytic. The earlier text traces a movement from 'logosphere' through 'graphosphere' to 'videosphere' which *Vie et mort de l'image* recasts by showing how 'les trois césures médiologiques de l'humanité—écriture, imprimerie, audiovisuel—découpent dans le temps des images trois continents distincts: l'idole, l'art, le visuel' (the three mediological caesuras of human history—writing, printing, and the audio-visual—mark out in the history of images three distinct continents, the idol, art, and the visual) (p. 220). Debray here attempts to understand and systematize the communications revolution by treating it at once as a contemporary and as a historical phenomenon, in other words, as something that is at once part of us and *other* to us.

## The Feminist Critique

The upsurge of feminist theoretical writing is among the most striking intellectual phenomena of the period under discussion. Simone de Beauvoir became symbolic 'mother' to a generation with *Le Deuxième Sexe* (1949), for all that she was later criticized for over-dependence on Sartrean terminology and a refusal (until 1971) to identify herself as a 'feminist'. However, she joined the Mouvement de libération des femmes (MLF) in that year because, she said, she had come to realize that women must fight for an improvement in women's actual situation before achieving the socialism they hope for. The importance of the women's movements—it would be an over-simplification to use the term in the singular—is not difficult to account for. Women had very little control over their own fertility until the sale of contraceptives was legalized in 1967; abortion did not become legal until 1975 (and was not available free of charge until 1982); political organizations and parties of the Left often demonstrated sexist attitudes towards women, traditionally seen as good for little besides typing, coffee-making, and sex. The upheaval of 1968, in which women participated massively, began to change this, and inspired the foundation of the MLF two years later figuring the shift away from a centralized, even monolithic, drive for social change, epitomized by Leninist organization and the communist party, towards the greater pluralism and the wider range of voices that is one of the leitmotifs of this chapter.

Developments in the conceptual and theoretical field likewise foregrounded the importance of gender. Lacanian psychoanalysis, with its stress on the paramount importance of the phallus in the process of symbolization, could hardly do otherwise, and one of the most influential woman writers of our period, Luce Irigaray, was at one time a member of his École freudienne de Paris. She, in common with a great many others of both genders, quarrelled with Lacan, in Irigaray's case over his refusal to allow her to run a course at the University of Vincennes, and her theoretical rejection of patriarchy itself met rejection, as though in confirmation of the threat it posed. Irigaray's *Speculum de l'autre femme* (1974) interrogates the manner in which woman has been the 'dark continent', not only of psychoanalysis but also of the Western philosophical tradition since Plato. Its most influential chapter, 'La Mystérique' (mystic-hysteric), is a rejoinder to Lacan's observations about Bernini's statue of St Teresa in *Encore*. Hysteria—etymologically derived, we should remember, from 'uterus'—is seen as all that patriarchy leaves woman by way of expression for her 'pulsions' (the Freudian *Triebe*, rendered in English as 'drives'), and the *jouissance* of the 'mystérique' quite literally bodies forth that whereby '"Dieu" excède toute représentation' ('God' exceeds any representation) (*Speculum*, 246), so that it represents a threat for the 'phallogocentrism' (Derrida) of that new theology that is psychoanalysis as well as for theology itself.

The specific relationship between woman and language—explored by Irigaray in *Ce sexe qui n'en est pas un* (The sex that is not one) (1977), with its title's punning reference to the exclusion of women's sexuality from patriarchal discourse and to its non-penile plurality—forms a major area for feminist writers within our period. Annie Leclerc in *Parole de femme* (1974) and Benoîte Groult in *Ainsi soit-elle* (1975) pay particular attention to it, but more influential than either has been the work of Hélène Cixous, who sees the binary oppositions constitutive of Western thought, and which Derrida challenged as we have seen, as related to if not actually grounded in the founding binary opposition/couple of man and woman. Within this discourse, philosophy (both Irigaray and Cixous treat psychoanalysis as a branch of philosophy) downgrades the associative/receptive values characteristic of 'woman', subordinating them passively to the phallogocentric imposition of (a) unitary sense. Thus, in *La Jeune Née* (1975) and elsewhere, Cixous's work as novelist, essayist, autobiographer, and 'thinker'—it is impossible to disentangle these strands across her work—can be understood as a sustained reinscription of *écriture féminine*, a textual strategy designed to combat the sexist hierarchization at the heart of Western thought.

The most accessible of her non-fictional works is probably *Three Steps on the Ladder of Writing*, a series of lectures given in California in 1990 (and at the time of writing still available only in English). The 'three steps' in question involve death, dreams, and 'roots'—the 'nether realms' of the taboo. Mourning, the crossing of frontiers, the Freudian *unheimliche* or 'uncanny' are key themes here, the Brazilian writer Clarice Lispector, Genet, Kafka, Dostoevsky major reference-texts, as though to confirm that writing that poses a challenge to phallogocentric modes of representation need not be the sole province of women.

More representative of developments on the broader intellectual scene than any of the woman writers we have so far considered is Julia Kristeva, who came from Bulgaria to Paris to study linguistics and was for many years associated with the group around the journal *Tel Quel* (renamed *L'Infini* in 1982) edited by Kristeva's husband Philippe Sollers. *Tel Quel* adopted a conceptually rigorous textual strategy that articulated Marxism with structural linguistics, the influence of which is to be seen in Kristeva's earlier work such as *Semeiotike: recherches pour une sémanalyse* (1968).

Kristeva's shift towards a more gender-based approach can be said to date from *Des Chinoises* (1974), an essay on Chinese women written after the *Tel Quel* group visited China in 1972, though it would be inaccurate, in Kristeva's own terms, to describe this or any of her other work as a feminist text. For Kristeva, 'feminism' is a 'piège grossier mais combien efficace' (crude but all too effective trap), elevating as it does Woman to 'La Vérité de l'ordre temporel, pour nous empêcher de fonctionner comme sa "vérité" inconsciente, irreprésentable, hors du vrai et du faux, du présent-passé-avenir' (The Truth of the temporal order, to prevent us from functioning as its unconscious, unrepresentable 'truth', as outside truth and falsehood, or past-present-future) (*Des Chinoises*, 47). Woman, that is to say, functions as the troubling and unlocalizable Other of the symbolic order—and Chinese women, coming as they do from a matrilinear tradition that (Confucius notwithstanding) had remained influential right through to the communist era, clearly for Kristeva fulfilled that function more than almost any others. *Des Chinoises's* references to 'sexual liberation' under the Revolution strike a distinctly ironic note after recent revelations about Mao's sexual exploitativeness and voracity, and the text's sinophilia now appears somewhat incongruous. But the work remains of great interest for its mapping of gender, ethnic, and more narrowly 'political' questions onto and across one another, some of which were further explored in *Étrangers à nous-mêmes* (1988), as for its foreshadowing of the major turn in the Kristevan *œuvre* towards psychoanalysis.

This is most manifest in *Histoires d'amour* (1983), a work of immense depth and richness. Kristeva's textual sweep here encompasses Greek philosophy (Plato), the 'classics' of French literature (Stendhal), the founding Western myths of love (Don Juan, Narcissus, Romeo and Juliet), and—perhaps most significantly—references on the one hand to the Bible, on the other to the lives and experiences of her own analysands. The move from revolutionary politics towards a revolution of the self that is at once psychoanalytic and spiritual finds its profoundest and most moving articulation here, and one that—in its opening of space to non-canonical figures such as the analysands—is not without its political dimension or its echoes of the verbal liberation of 1968. Kristeva's major theoretical advance here, building on her work on pre-Oedipal relationships between children and parents of both sexes, lies in her stress on the importance of the 'père de la préhistoire individuelle' (father of individual prehistory)—that figure (pre-Oedipal, thus unthreatening) that, once the child has 'abjected' the mother (has acquired a sense of its own identity by separating itself from her), comes into play to fill the identificatory gap that abjection has produced. Without such a figure who, being pre-Oedipal, thereby partakes of both genders, the infant's capacity for love is dramatically stunted, as the testimonies of the analysands show. This 'père de la préhistoire individuelle' has clear affinities with (a version of) God the Father less forbidding by far than Lacan's 'père-sévère'.

The other key originality of *Histoires d'amour* lies in its stress on the metaphorical axis of love rather than the metonymic one of desire favoured by Lacan(ians) in particular. Metaphor is to be understood as a relationship of equivalence—the whole for the whole ('the dark night of the soul'); metonymy, conversely, as a relationship of part to whole ('a hundred head of cattle'), and one which is always verifiable in the 'real' world. (Anybody who has seen a cow knows that it has a head; not everybody who possesses—or believes themselves to possess—a soul knows that it can sometimes 'be' a dark night.) Metaphor, like the terms 'parole', 'ideology,' 'imaginary', has on the whole tended to be dethroned, in a more-or-less deconstructive move, in favour of metonymy, or *mutatis mutandis* 'écriture', 'science', 'the symbolic'. The latter, and latterly privileged, set of terms have in common that they break apart an imagined 'vertical' unity or metaphysics of presence, reinstating against it that which is deferred (*écriture*), constructed (science), or elusive (the symbolic) along the horizontal axis of the signifying chain. Kristeva, throughout *Histoires d'amour*, takes as her focus of attention the metaphoric—hence, in the real world, impossible—wish for fusion with the Other that is love. In poetry, in analysis, in love, we are in a 'lieu de production de métaphores' (place where metaphors are produced) (p. 342), so that 'l'amour, ça se parle, et ce n'est que ça: les poètes l'ont toujours su' (love speaks itself, and that is all it is: the poets have always known it) (p. 343). So one could speak of love, as one could speak of morality, once more (as perhaps one had always been doing).

## Other Voices: Voices of Others

In the wake of the demise of Grand Theory new and rigorous conceptual developments were also taking place, and the work of the sociologist Pierre Bourdieu perhaps offers the most eloquent example of this. Bourdieu enables us to hear another voice, and this happens in a less 'academic' and more shockingly polemical context in *La Misère du monde* (1993). This tackles the problems and incidence of poverty, in all its varying definitions, in present-day France. On one level it represents a scathing indictment of the shortfall of a decade of (interrupted) socialist rule. On another, it shows clearly how 'poverty' is no more an absolute abstract than any of the other concepts Bourdieu deploys. One can be poor through 'misère de position' (positional impoverishment), feeling oneself relegated to a position of powerlessness within society or one of its organizations. One can become poor through a sense of having lost one's centrality and empowerment within a social formation that has changed around one and shattered one's social imaginary in so doing (the example of some of the farmers Bourdieu and his team interview, overwhelmed symbolically even when not destituted materially, is a particularly powerful one in the context of France's rapid switch from an agrarian to an industrial society). What *La Misère du monde* does, through the host of interviews it reproduces along with analytical essays on them, is to return a voice— thus, a possibility of symbolic re-empowerment—to that host of Others deprived of, or simply never endowed with, their own. Those who had thought the era of the committed intellectual was past would do well to ponder Bourdieu's assertion that 'toute politique qui ne tire pas pleinement parti des possibilités, si réduites soient-elles, qui sont offertes à l'action, et que la science peut aider à dècouvrir, peut être considérée comme coupable de non-assistance à personne en danger' (any politics which does not fully exploit the potential for action, however re-duced, that knowledge can help to reveal, may be considered guilty of the crime of 'failing to come to the assistance of a person in danger') (p. 944). The lot of the Others, in contemporary France, is not invariably one of *jouissance*.

## References

Althusser, Louis, *L'Avenir dure longtemps* (Paris: Stock/IMEC, 1992).
—— 'Freud et Lacan' (1964), in *Positions* (Paris: Éditions sociales, 1976), 11–40.
—— 'Idéologie et appareils idéologiques d'État' (1970), in *Positions* (Paris: Éditions sociales, 1976), 79–138.
—— *Lire 'Le Capital'* (Paris: Maspéro, 1965).
—— *Pour Marx* (Paris: Maspéro, 1965).
Aronson, Ronald, *Jean-Paul Sartre: Philosophy in the World* (London: Verso, 1980).
Barthes, Roland, *La Chambre claire* (Paris: Cahiers du cinéma/Gallimard/Seuil, 1980).
—— *L'Empire des signes* (Geneva: Skira, 1970).
—— *Fragments d'un discours amoureux* (Paris: Seuil, 1977).
—— *Incidents* (Paris: Seuil, 1987).
—— *Mythologies* (Paris: Seuil, 1957).
—— *Le Plaisir du texte* (Paris: Seuil, 1973).
—— *S/Z* (Paris: Seuil, 1970).
Baudrillard, Jean, *A l'ombre des majorités silencieuses ou la fin du social* (Paris: Denoël, 1982).
—— *La Guerre du Golfe n'a pas eu lieu* (Paris: Galilée, 1991).
—— *L'Illusion de la fin* (Paris: Galilée, 1992).
—— *Le Système des objets* (Paris: Gallimard, 1978).
Bennington, Geoffrey, *Jacques Derrida* (Paris: Seuil, 1991).
Bourdieu, Pierre, *La Misère du monde* (Paris: Seuil, 1993).
Camus, Albert, *L'Homme révolté* (Paris: Gallimard, 1951).
Cixous, Hélène, *La* (Paris: Gallimard, 1976).
—— *La Jeune Née* (Paris: Gallimard, 1975).
—— *Three Steps on the Ladder of Writing* (New York: Columbia University Press, 1993).
Debray, Régis, *A demain de Gaulle* (Paris: Gallimard, 1990).
—— *Modeste Contribution aux discours et cérémonies du dixième anniversaire* (Paris: Maspéro, 1978).
—— *Le Pouvoir intellectuel en France* (Paris: Gallimard, 1979).
—— *Révolution dans la revolution* (Paris: Maspéro, 1967).
—— *Vie et mort de l'image* (Paris: Gallimard, 1992).
Derrida, Jacques, *De la grammatologie* (Paris: Minuit, 1967).
—— *L'Écriture et la différence* (Paris: Seuil, 1967).
—— *Marges de la philosophie* (Paris: Minuit, 1972).

Derrida, Jacques, *Mémoires pour Paul de Man* (Paris: Galilée, 1988).

—— *Spectres de Marx* (Paris: Galilée, 1993).

Foucault, Michel, *L'Archéologie du savoir* (Paris: Gallimard, 1969).

—— *Histoire de la folie à l'âge classique* (Paris: Gallimard, 1961).

—— *Histoire de la sexualité*, 3 vols. (Paris: Gallimard, 1976–84).

—— *Les Mots et les choses* (Paris: Gallimard, 1966).

—— *Surveiller et punir* (Paris: Gallimard, 1975).

Irigaray, Luce, *Ce sexe qui n'en est pas un* (Paris: Minuit, 1977).

—— *Speculum de l'autre femme* (Paris: Minuit, 1974).

Kristeva, Julia, *Des Chinoises* (Paris: Des Femmes, 1974).

—— *Étrangers à nous-mêmes* (Paris, Fayard, 1988).

—— *Histoires d'amour* (Paris: Denoël, 1983).

—— *Semeiotike: recherches pour une sémanalyse* (Paris: Seuil, 1968).

Lacan, Jacques, *Écrits I* (Paris: Seuil, 1966).

—— *Le Séminaire XX: Encore* (Paris: Seuil, 1975).

Lévinas, Emmanuel, *De Dieu qui vient à l'idée* (Paris: Vrin, 1982).

—— *Totalité et infini* (The Hague: Nijhoff, 1961).

Lyotard, Jean-François, *La Condition postmoderne: rapport sur le savoir* (Paris: Minuit, 1979).

—— *Dérive à partir de Marx et de Freud* (Paris: Minuit, 1973).

—— *Économie libidinale* (Paris: 1974).

Nancy, Jean-Luc, 'Des lieux divins', *Paragraph*, 72 (1985), 1–52.

Sartre, Jean-Paul, *L'Idiot de la famille*, 2 vols. (Paris: Gallimard, 1971).

—— *Situations VIII* (Paris: Gallimard, 1967).

Saussure, Ferdinand de, *A Course in General Linguistics*, trans. Baskin (London: Fontana/Collins, 1974).

Turkle, Sherry, *Psychoanalytic Politics* (London: Burnett Books, 1979).

# Popular Culture and Cultural Politics

## The Rise of Audio-visual Culture

ONE of the most important cultural characteristics of post-1968 France is the change in the focus of leisure activities. The average working week is now under forty hours; the average home has increased in size and has become a much pleasanter environment than that available to most French people before the 1960s; and a host of new technologies such as compact discs, video recorders and cameras, personal computers, electronic games, and telephone services have made leisure increasingly domestic. The result is, as one writer put it, that 'the home has become the main centre of entertainment'. Indeed, the most telling illustration of this trend is the sharp decline, over the past decades, in the number of people going to the cinema, and the equally sharp rise in the number of hours spent watching television, which has become the most important home entertainment of all.

Television did not begin to have a significant presence in French cultural life until the late 1960s, by which time virtually all French households had acquired a television set. For the first two decades of its existence in France television was seen as a 'window on the world' and a means of popular acculturation. Its single channel initially adopted a 'one genre a night' formula; it opened up hitherto unknown perspectives to its viewers and, like the press which, during the 1950s, replaced its regional focus with a much more national perspective, it attempted to create a 'national' cultural community. Television screened documentaries on far-flung places and public events (the example often given is the coronation of the Queen of England) and devoted its fiction slots to dramatizations of the classics of French and world literature. Jean Prat's production of Aeschylus's *Les Perses* (1961) and Marcel Bluwal's production of Molière's *Dom Juan* (1965) are frequently cited as high points of television culture. Its benign influence is affectionately celebrated in Georges Rouquier's film *Biquefarre* (1983), which looks at a village in the Aveyron which Rouquier had filmed in 1946 as *Farrebique* and comments approvingly on the differences. Of all the many changes that have occurred since *Farrebique* was made, television is seen to be one of the most beneficial because it has allowed the country-dwellers and farm workers to become integral to the national community. In this way, by broadening mental horizons and offering new perspectives on the world, French television accompanied the 'désenclavement' (opening up) of the country which was accomplished by improved physical communications.

Television was also seen by politicians, and especially de Gaulle, as a useful means of talking directly to the people, a way of conducting the 'plebiscite de tous les jours' (daily plebiscite) required by a directly elected president, as 'la voix de la France' (the voice of France), unitary, one and indivisible like the Republic. This was not just because until 1963 there was only one television channel but also because the government maintained censorship over television, the press, and the cinema, through its Ministry of Information, justifying the mechanisms of control it had inherited from the Vichy regime by the war in Indo-China and subsequently by the state of emergency in Algeria. But the growth in television ownership exposed the partisan nature of television reporting, particularly during the 'first television elections', the presidential elections of 1965 when the opposition candidates (among whom was François Mitterrand) had equal access to air time and surprised many viewers by how personable they were. The events of May 1968, which occurred at just the time when total coverage of TV ownership was achieved, revealed the full extent of government control and, in so doing, created doubts about the veracity of news reporting on television, challenged the need for television to speak with a single voice, and precipitated theoretical examination of questions of realism and verisimilitude in the audio-visual media.

Since 1968 French television has been torn apart by the difficulty of reconciling technological innovation and financial viability, and by debates about the role of a public service in maintaining national cultural integrity. In 1974 President Giscard d'Estaing destroyed the monolithic and vertically integrated ORTF, creating in its place an 'internal market' in which seven newly created and separate companies were to 'sell' their services to one another. This measure created an engineering company Télévision de France (TDF), which could pursue technological development untrammelled by financial or political arguments and which later formed a powerful nationalized electronics company by collaboration with Thomson CSF; it obliged the broadcasters to compete for advertising and audiences without any qualitative guarantees, making audience share the arbiter of success; and it limited the fictional output of the broadcasting companies (TF1, Antenne 2, and FR3) by requiring that television films and series should be produced by the Société française de production (SFP). In separating the artists from the engineers, the producers of programmes from those who deliver them, Giscard's measures ensured that the electronics industry was protected but they did little to support programme-making. The predictable result was that throughout the 1970s and even more throughout the 1980s French television companies could not produce enough indigenous material to fill their screens and were forced to import material, much of it inexpensive American series, and although in 1979 TV stations were finally allowed to produce their own fictional programmes and rapidly became important financial backers for cinema film production, this did not mean that they invested in programmes produced specially for television.

The 1980s was another decade of radical changes in television broadcasting. The socialist government of 1981 removed television from direct government control by setting up a tutelary body known as the Haute autorité (later called the Commission nationale de la communication et les libertés, and subsequently the Comité supérieur de l'audiovisuel). Four new terrestrial television stations were launched, the pay-per-view channel Canal plus, the private stations La Cinq and M6 of which only the latter has survived, and the public service arts channel La Sept which subsequently became the Franco-German arts channel Arte. In addition, the 1986 Chirac government sold off the first television channel TF1, whose principal private sector shareholder became Hachette. The expansion of private television was partly motivated by the desire to foster competition with private video, and with satellite broadcasting which was about to commence in surrounding countries like Luxembourg, as well as to offer slots for more American-style French production. Canal plus, launched in 1984 with leisure conglomerates such as L'Oréal and Perrier as its major shareholders, was created to specialize in news, sport, and feature films, rather than the whole range of TV genres, and it has subsequently become a major producer of cinema films. Similarly, M6 was originally intended as a young people's music station, an outlet for French-produced video clips and music programmes, and it has, more recently, developed serials such as *Hélène et les garçons* directed at teenagers and young people. Although these new stations are outside the public sector they are still theoretically obliged to screen a fixed proportion of French and EU-generated material, a rule which was designed to protect French production. But it has proved difficult, and in the case of the bankrupt La Cinq impossible, for them to remain both financially viable and culturally legal. In this way, far from stimulating French production, the 1974 reforms and the privatizations of the 1980s actually hastened and expanded imports of foreign material, much of it from the USA, which was the principal source of programmes that were cheap enough for the new stations to afford. The domestic experience of the 1980s undoubtedly lies behind the French government's unswerving promotion of European film production and inspired its successful demand that audio-visual products should not be included in the GATT free trade agreements concluded in 1993.

While it is true that in its early years television (together with other forms of entertainment) drained audiences from the cinemas, for the last fifteen years or so it has become financially essential to the survival of the French film industry, which is now by far the largest and most successful in Europe and one of the largest in the world. The relationship between television and cinema, compared by Jean-Luc Godard in *Sauve qui peut (la vie)* (1979) to that of the warring brothers Cain and Abel, reached an enforced truce which was not altogether well accepted by the film industry. There have been periods when the creative possibilities of television have been encouraged and explored, particularly at the Institut national de l'audiovisuel in the latter part of the 1970s, and film-makers like Jacques Doillon, Jean Eustache, and especially Jean-Luc Godard with *Sur et sous la communication* (1976) and *France/Tour/Détour/Deux Enfants* (1978), have all made remarkable television films or series. But television is still viewed very much as a poor relation, a medium whose principal function is news and current affairs together with the retransmission of material made elsewhere. Television has never recaptured that sense of cultural mission with which it was imbued in the 1950s and 1960s. French television is therefore an object of love and hatred: it is indubitably the saviour of France's audio-visual industry, but at the same time it is seen as the agent cynically and deliberately used by America and, increasingly, by Japan to destroy French culture. The question of television, therefore, crystallizes much of the discourse about cultural integrity and national identity, the dialectic France entertains with its cultural 'Others' America and Japan, and adds to the confusion of thinking about mass and popular culture.

### The politics of the image

The events of May 1968 also raised questions not just about media censorship but about the veracity of media images. It was common to distinguish two historical traditions in French film-making, the fictional/fantastic deriving from Méliès and the documentary/verisimilitudinous deriving from Lumière. However, in the 1950s, at the height of the Cold War, the critic André Bazin had politicized this distinction by associating the former with the montage felt to be typical of Russian film-makers like Sergei Eisenstein and the latter with the deep focus and sequence editing of American film-makers like Orson Welles and William Wyler. Bazin linked the latter with individualism, freedom, and democracy because, he claimed, it 'manipulated' the image as little as possible and therefore left the viewer free to decide and interpret what was taking place on the screen.

The way the events of May 1968 were reported discredited any residual belief that the 'camera cannot lie', that it offers an unmediated recording of the real. Critics and film-makers began to show that even those documents such as non-fiction films or news photographs which purport to show or record reality have a 'rhetoric'. In other words, the elements of which they are composed are put together in such a way as to create a particular effect. In a series of fascinating articles relating to photographic images Roland Barthes developed the view that the photographic image was not a record of reality invested with 'ontological plenitude', as Bazin had thought, not a 'message without a code' but a rhetorical form, and that photographic images and documentary films, whether what is represented is true or false, fictional or real, attempt to persuade to a point of view, and enter into an economy of desire. This perception was shared by many of the most influential critics of film and television, particularly those writing for *Cahiers du cinéma*, and it changed the way in which media images of all kinds were interpreted.

The cinema saw a profusion of new interpretations after 1968. One way this occurred was through attention to the cinematic apparatus. What was now emphasized was the obvious, but nevertheless frequently neglected, fact that the camera is not 'innocent': its position, as well as the kind of lens, film, and lighting used, are all important in creating a particular illusion of reality, or 'effet de réel', based, in its essentials, on perspectival laws deriving from the Renaissance, and someone or some group of people has to take decisions and make choices about all these dispositions. Indeed, certain writers like Jean-Louis Baudry in *L'Effet cinéma* (1978) claimed that the technological development of the cinematic 'apparatus' since the nineteenth century was itself ideologically determined. Other approaches looked at the way films are edited after the initial footage is shot. All film-makers shoot more than they need, although the superfluous amount varies from individual to individual and from period to period. Films are then edited according to a series of narrative conventions which permit much material to be excised. Under the influence of structuralist linguistics with its emphasis on differential rather than inherent signification, film-makers discovered, or rather rediscovered, montage as practised by Eisenstein and other Russian film-makers who had demonstrated that the meaning of an image is profoundly modified by the contiguous images in a sequence of film. In other words, they emphasized that it is difficult to detect a given or inherent meaning in images when meaning can be shown to depend on context and situation. Thus the point of view from which a film is shot, the kind of technology used to shoot it, and the way it is edited are all factors contributing to signification, all are invested with values, and all can be changed without a change in the material in front of the camera, the so-called 'pro-filmic event'.

Once it is accepted that ALL film is the product of manipulation the nature of the 'truth' purveyed by the image is called in question. It is no longer possible to treat any visual medium as a 'window on the world'; all media, however informative their purpose, have a particular subjectivity, a particular point of view. The lens may be called an 'objectif' in French but what it allows us to record is not, and cannot be, 'objective'.

In the period between 1968 and 1972 the journal *Cahiers du cinéma* devoted much of its space to the exploration of the relationship between technology and ideology in the cinema and some of the most interesting essays were written by the theorist and film-maker Jean-Louis Comolli. He noted a fascinating paradox in documentary films when viewing the May 1968 Cinétract *La Rentrée des usines Wonder* which depicts the return to work by strikers at the electric battery factory. Comolli observed in this film that, by a process no doubt akin to hyper-realism in painting, the more 'unmediated' the film, the less authorial interference there appears to have been, the more it takes on a fictional quality. Of course, Comolli's choice of film is not accidental because *La Rentrée des usines Wonder* recalls one of the most famous films of the early French cinema, Lumière's *La Sortie des usines Lumière* (1895). But in reversing the movement of Lumière's film it not only provides an elegy for the events of May 1968 but also recalls, in nostalgic manner, the playful reverse movements in experimental films of the silent period like René Clair's *Paris qui dort* (1923) and Dziga Vertov's *Man with a Movie Camera* (1929) when the film is run through the camera backwards. Such intertextual references inevitably call attention to the process of film-making, to the 'materiality' of the image to use the terminology of the time, and therefore to the fact that a film is an artefact, that whether or not it is a documentary it takes its place within an aesthetic and technological economy.

Another area of interest was advertising, whose spread in France during the 1950s and 1960s was accompanied, as it was elsewhere, by a concern about its effects, particularly its hidden or unconscious effects. In the minds of some early commentators there was little to differentiate advertising from brainwashing, little to distinguish Stalin's 'engineers of the soul' from Vance Packard's 'hidden persuaders'. This concern is acutely reflected in some of Godard's early films such as *Une Femme mariée* (1964), *Masculin-féminin* (1966), and *Deux ou trois choses que je sais d'elle* (1966). Here, the techniques of marketing and public opinion sampling are treated with a combination of fascination and repulsion, as the heroines of the films are led to compare their life-style expectations with what is offered them in the press and on street hoardings (but not yet television). Godard takes issue with a particular form of modernity promoted and represented in articles and advertising in the 'new press', in such consciously modernist publications as *L'Express* and *Elle* (which is thinly disguised as *Mademoiselle 19 ans* in *Masculin-féminin*). He disturbingly shows in *Une Femme mariée*, for example, how the protagonist cannot constitute her image as a unity but is constantly encouraged by the advertisements she sees to perceive it as fragmentary and atomized. Many of the essays Barthes published under the collective title *Mythologies* (1957) were first published in *L'Express* and dealt with material from this new press, especially *Elle* and *Paris-Match*. One such essay, entitled 'La Cuisine ornementale' (decorative cookery), might serve as emblematic since it gives voice to many of the contemporary concerns about cultural transformation. It discusses the function of food in French life and suggests that the kind of recipes *Elle* publishes, in its famous *fiches cuisine*,

**Jean-Luc Godard** *Deux ou trois choses que je sais d'elle* (1966)

Subtitled 'Dix-huit leçons sur la société industrielle' (Eighteen lessons on industrial society) in reference to Raymond Aron's study of that name published in 1963, this film offers a mordant criticism of urban modernization and the consumer society. The physical transformation of the city of Paris, the 'elle' of the title', into a landscape of expressways and tower blocks is seen as linked to the profound physchological disorientation of the central character Juliette, played by Marina Vlady (seen here), who satisfies the contemporary need to be affluent through recourse to prostitution. Godard denounces cultural fragmentation, the breakup of communities, and the malignant influence of advertising as characteristic of capitalism. This leads to crises of identity especially among women, who are forced into a narcissistic concern for the image which imprisons them. The poster for Japan airlines, which gestures towards the orientalism that was to become such a feature of post-1968 French culture, sets up a comparison between Juliette and Japanese women in the way both are framed and defined by conventional images, objects of inspection for the sexual tourist.

are made to 'look like' advertisements because all the roughness is smoothed away and covered over (a favourite word in Barthes's *Mythologies* is 'napper', meaning 'to coat') with the result that food ceases to be the staff of life and becomes a prop of life-style, 'une cuisine du revêtement et de l'alibi' (cookery which is about covering up, which is a pretext), an elaborate metonymy.

But even while he was criticizing its ideology, Barthes did much to assist the serious study of advertising and to suggest how advertising, like any other source of texts and images, can usefully be regarded as a signifying practice and a source of cultural knowledge. His essay 'Le Message photographique' (1961) studies the visual economy of an advertisement for pasta, distinguishing what it 'denotes' and 'connotes', analysing the spatial disposition of the elements as well as the colours of the composition and the relation between the words and the image, and points to its source in classical and Renaissance images of the cornucopia, showing that advertisements, like any other visual form, can exploit the iconographical traditions of Western art. Similarly, throughout the essays in *Mythologies* and in the summarizing statement 'Le Mythe aujourd'hui', Barthes not only showed that the techniques of analysis initially developed in relation to 'high' culture could apply with equal pertinence to 'popular' culture, but also that when cultural forms are characterized by their common intertextuality, as he brilliantly demonstrated, the distinction between 'high' and 'popular' culture becomes difficult to sustain and justify.

A related, if more obviously 'academic' attempt to understand signifying practices has been carried out in a series of works by Pierre Bourdieu and his team. This is grounded in a picture of the interrelation of the social field with an individual habitus providing the context in which individual agents pursue the struggle for distinction and the accumulation of cultural capital by dint of symbolic violence. Early studies of the education system in Bourdieu and Jean-Claude Passeron's *Les Héritiers* (1965) and of the museum-going public in Bourdieu and A. Darbel's *L'Amour de l'art* (1966) were reinforced by two major volumes in the post-1968 period. In *La Distinction* (1980) and even more in *Les Règles de l'art* (1992) Bourdieu relates taste and aesthetic appreciation to social position and attempts to map criteria of judgement and value onto social class and social expectations rather than the origin of the cultural form. Concurrently, a series of studies by his pupils and collaborators have linked literary and cultural movements such as Naturalism or the *bande dessinée*, as well as the content of art, to 'strategies' for the acquisition of symbolic capital on the part of the artists themselves.

### The cinema of transformation

Political change and aesthetic transformation went hand in hand as film-makers after May 1968 began to 'film different things' and to 'film things differently'. One of the most exemplary works of the period is *Loin du Vietnam* (1967), a compilation film produced by Chris Marker and the SLON collective and directed by Agnès Varda, Jean-Luc Godard, Joris Ivens, William Klein, Claude Lelouch, and

Alain Resnais for which each film-maker provided a twenty-minute 'episode' embodying his or her view of the war in Vietnam. Adapting the popular episode formula of 'variations on a theme', the film juxtaposes a variety of points of view, offering six different 'essays' on the same topic and addressing the question of post-colonialism by suggesting that although the Algerian war has ended, France still has responsibilities for the situation in Indo-China (now called Vietnam) even though America has taken over as the imperial power.

*Loin du Vietnam* is radically different from the documentaries of the 1950s made by the 'Left Bank School' to which Varda, Resnais, and Marker all belonged. These typically combined a montage of images with a voice-over commentary providing the film-maker's poetic interpretation of the images, a technique which tended to distance the visual material and to increase its exoticism. Whatever their different treatments of the theme, all the contributors to *Loin du Vietnam* are critical of the American engagement in the war as well as of the French government's line of tacit support for the United States. But even more important, the war is not treated as some purely military engagement in a far-flung, exotic country, but as an event which has a profound impact on domestic politics and on the lives of ordinary people in France. *Loin du Vietnam* seeks to uncover the dialectical relationship between East and West and to question France's place politically, psychologically, and aesthetically within it. It therefore rejects the notional 'third way' for France, pursued by de Gaulle's foreign policy, by means of an aesthetic which implicates the West in the East, refusing the distance promulgated by earlier relationships between sound and image in which the film-maker is in some sense outside or above both.

Another seminal work of the period was *Le Chagrin et la pitié* (1971), which traces its origins to just before 1968 when the director Marcel Ophuls was working for the current affairs programme *Zoom* at the ORTF. It was conceived as part of a series intended to 'counter the wave of complacent and jingoistic self-satisfaction which . . . dominated and determined the content of most of the history programmes on French TV'. The film (which is over four hours long) consists of archive newsreels relating to events in Clermont-Ferrand at the time of the Occupation, intercalated with interviews with the survivors who feature in the events portrayed in the archive material. This has the political effect of making the actors of history reflect and comment upon their past actions and sometimes reveals that they were mistaken or that they lied. Aesthetically, the technique is highly innovative in disrupting the conventional or habitual relationship between sound and image in documentary and newsreel material where the sound-track traditionally carries authority and acts as the vehicle for the film-maker's interpretation of what is shown. Here, the images are given equal if not more significance, the 'correct' or unitary point of view is rejected, and the film proposes a multiplicity of points of view which enter into relationships of mutual modification. This said, it is clear that Ophuls exercised choices, although he claimed that they were aesthetic rather than political. For example, Pierre Mendès-France and the PSU position are granted overwhelming significance, at least in the first part of the film, while the testimony of women is virtually absent throughout. Nevertheless, *Le Chagrin et la pitié* stands as a work of revolutionary impact because it offered an aesthetic as well as a political fissure in the narrative of contemporary French history which had been imposed by the Gaullist-controlled media and demonstrated that there was more than one way of telling a story, that the 'truth' had multiple facets.

More, perhaps, than any other cultural form or signifying practice, the cinema of the 1970s was the place where the linked issues of narrative and history, public and private, fiction and documentary, and truth and lies were explored. The extraordinary fertility of theoretical and critical writing in these years is a measure of the profound intellectual transformation experienced in France as ideologies, particularly Marxism which had sustained many writers and thinkers since the 1940s, were now seen to have failed.

The challenge to the Gaullist version of history gathered momentum after de Gaulle's retirement in 1969. If Gaullism had been, as Michel Foucault suggested, 'the only way of writing . . . history in terms of an honourable nationalism', then it was hardly surprising that, with the passing of many of the generation who had been involved in either resistance to or collaboration with the Germans, the new historiography, adumbrated in *Le Chagrin et la pitié*, would be more sceptical towards claims that 'most French people had resisted'. A revaluation of the Occupation period now became possible and inevitable but it was closely followed by other revaluations in the early 1970s. With the publication of Alexander Solzhenitsyn's *The Gulag Archipelago* in French translation in 1974, the level of human rights violations and the totalitarian nature of the Soviet regime were cruelly exposed, and its claim to serve as a model society thoroughly discredited. The fall of Saigon and the ignominious American withdrawal from South Vietnam made possible a reassessment of Franco-American relations, while the end of the Cultural Revolution in China also occasioned concern about human rights there. These events did not merely strengthen the case for 'liberalism' and cause Western European socialists (though not the French communist party) to revise their views, but also reinforced the case for challenging previous representations of reality and earlier ways of writing history. Indeed, they called in question the very possibility of writing history.

Louis Malle's film *Lacombe Lucien* (1974) touched a profound chord with its not unsympathetic depiction of the erratic behaviour of a peasant lad during the Occupation as he tries to join the Resistance, finds himself rejected because he is too young (as well as too unreliable and not well-enough educated), and so begins working for the Gestapo, embarking at the same time, and with no apparent perception of the paradox, on an affair with the daughter of a Jewish refugee. Lucien's lack of political awareness, the way he is drawn towards the paraphernalia of militarism, his often mindless violence, and his combination of innocence and ignorance, all rendered him an appropriate anti-hero for the times. The director claimed that he had done no more than 'tell the truth' about French people working for the Gestapo. But the film is more significant for offering a new narrative of history which is profoundly anti-Brechtian in celebrating the merits of individualism against the collectivity and of the private rather than the public sphere. In the end, though he may work for the Gestapo, Lucien is indifferent to public events and prepared to tolerate any version of them he is offered while he pursues a private agenda. *Lacombe Lucien* offers in this way a contrast to historical narratives dating from the 1960s such as Alain Resnais's *Hiroshima mon amour* (1959) or *Muriel* (1963), both of which emphasize the complicit individual's incapacity to make a totalizing narrative from personal or private experience and the power of the collectivity in making sense of the private domain. In contrast with Resnais's protagonists, Lucien is politically inconsistent, even incoherent, but his actions have a perfect private logic.

Malle's refusal to subscribe to a left-wing orthodoxy about the Resistance is comparable to that of Ophuls, though its form of expression is different. Throughout the cinema of the 1970s, however, we find film-makers of all styles and persuasions tempted to offer alternative histories of different periods: Bertrand Tavernier's *Que la fête commence* (1975), *Le Juge et l'assassin* (1976), *La Passion Béatrice* (1987), and *La Vie et rien d'autre* (1989) ranged over the eighteenth-century Regency, the nineteenth-century anarchist movement, the medieval Hundred Years War, and the 1914–18 war; René Allio's *Les Camisards* (1972) and *Moi, Pierre Rivière* (1976) looked at episodes of religious and social history in the eighteenth and nineteenth centuries as did François Truffaut's *L'Enfant sauvage* (1969) and *L'Histoire d'Adèle H* (1975), while his *La Chambre verte* (1978) looked at the aftermath of the First World War and Frank Cassenti's *L'Affiche rouge* (1976) studied nineteenth-century political history. A striking number of these films and others like them, as though released from decades of enforced silence, deal with the persecution of minorities, with madness, and with death.

André Téchiné's *Souvenirs d'en France* (1975) offers a different, and perhaps more personal, approach to writing history in changed circumstances. The subject of his film is the memory of the past or childhood memories ('souvenirs d'enfance'). The history of France in the twentieth century is seen as the history of a small family business whose establishment, growth, and difficulties are narrated as a history of visual representations in painting, photography, and cinema. In treating the French nation metonymically as a family with its icons and relics, Téchiné is able to introduce a psychoanalytic perspective, positing a link between the 'family romance', the imaginary narrative of origins as described by Freud, and what he calls the 'petty-bourgeois consciousness', between the development of a particular kind of typically French capitalism, the small family business, and a particular way of showing or describing and conducting human relations. This is also why women characters gradually gain more and more control over the narrative as it progresses, for women are both the typical generators and consumers of romance, and the focus of the private or domestic sphere. In making his central character, Berthe, a 'hero' of the Resistance, Téchiné links her structural function in the narrative with the Gaullist version of history and so suggests that however emotionally satisfying it may be it is no different in structure and function from a bourgeois fiction.

Perhaps the most moving and at the same time most disturbing portrait of the 1970s is Jean Eustache's long film *La Maman et la putain* (1973), said by many critics at the time to speak for an entire generation. Alexandre, the rather unsavoury central character of *La Maman et la putain*, embodies the cultural malaise typical of post-1968. There are no grand ideological movements to inspire him and people like him. Instead, there exists a poignant contrast between the outward-looking *internationalism* of an earlier generation, preoccupied, in its commitment to universal values, with liberation struggles and alternative movements wherever they might be, and the inward-looking parochialism or 'médiocrité', as Alexandre calls it, of the present times, with horizons that do not extend beyond Saint-Germain-des-Prés (itself a pale copy of the international intellectual *carrefour* that it had been in the 1950s), and with preoccupations that are now almost exclusively sexual and private. Although *La Maman et la putain* struck a chord of recognition among its first viewers, on closer inspection what takes place in the film is profoundly improbable, resembling nothing so much as Alexandre's fantasies of seduction and sexual prowess, a representation of his point of view and, even more, his desire for sexual mastery. Indeed, in its refusal of narrative closure and its investment in endless repetition, Eustache's film closely resembles pornographic cinema even to the point of employing tropes, like a man in bed with two women and two women making love watched by a man, which are common in sex films.

Yet *La Maman et la putain* is a film which successfully masquerades as a record of reality, revealing the power of the visual and aesthetic codes it employs to make us believe it is true. It has all the elements of a documentary. It is shot in black and white and on 16 mm., which when blown up to 35 mm. for theatrical exhibition gives the image an added grainy quality; it is over three hours in length, giving the impression that very little editing has taken place; it is set in recognizable locations (the Café de Flore, the Jardin du Luxembourg) rather than in a studio; it uses natural light; it has a script that in its use of everyday colloquial and vulgar language is the obverse of 'literary'. In short, everything is done to make the film appear to be an authentic record of the lives of a small group of young people, in every way comparable to Eustache's various TV documentaries such as *La Rosière de Pessac* (1968), in which he had aimed for an unmediated realism, in order to 'present the viewer directly with events'. In their different ways, therefore, both Téchiné and Eustache show how truth is a function of representation. In *Souvenirs d'en France* Berthe and Regina see their lives as Hollywood melodrama; in *La Maman et la putain* Alexandre sees his as a documentary about Saint-Germain-des-Prés and as a sex film with compliant women acting out his fantasies.

Berthe's vision takes place in heightened Technicolor, Alexandre's in grainy black and white. Both are memories of events, fictions of history, in which the private increasingly dominates the public.

One of the most intriguing facets of these films is the way they depict relations between men and women. In *Souvenirs d'en France* the male members of the Pédret family are all christened with resoundingly heroic names—Victor, Hector, Prosper—but they are all conspicuously lacking in the masculine qualities their names imply, and while they are unable to make things happen, Berthe controls the narrative and becomes its 'hero'. Téchiné's sexual politics are typical of a thread running through French cinema in the wake of May 1968, which points to a crisis of masculinity. In a number of films the depiction of the youthful, energetic, heterosexual couple to be found in *nouvelle vague* works has given way to that of groups of men who are weak or in some way threatened. In Claude Sautet's *Vincent, François, Paul et les autres* (1974) the men have lost their potency and their creativity because of the demise of a sense of national community and the rise of affluence and rampant individualism. In Marco Ferreri's *La Grande Bouffe* (1973) and Bertrand Blier's *Calmos* (1976) the men are more misogynistic, getting together in exclusive buddy groups to blame women for their sense of impotence.

But while men find their masculinity challenged, women begin to speak. In Godard's *Tout va bien* (1972) we find the central female character criticizing the traditional association between the right to speech and the phallus and in his *Numéro deux* (1975) the female protagonist attempting to get beyond the sterile dialectic of sexual difference, his and hers, outside and inside. Suddenly film-makers were able to find backers for fictional portrayals of situations of particular concern to women like the rape and breast cancer in Yannick Bellon's films *L'Amour violé* (1978) and *L'Amour nu* (1981). In all these ways the cinema reflected the reappraisal of social and sexual relations which occurred after May 1968 and the increasing focus on the politics of private life through the growth of the women's movement.

But there were also much more radical works which attempted to change the way women are represented and how they speak and to represent women's voices as profoundly creative. The style of Agnès Varda's film-making, for example, was fundamentally changed by feminism. Two of her films are about how women voice their feelings. But in *Cléo de 5 à 7* (1962) the heroine is a singer who is about to be silenced because she is dying of cancer while in *L'une chante, l'autre pas* (1977) one of the two heroines is a woman who has left her husband, changed her name, and become a singer who composes and performs, with an extraordinary enthusiasm and gusto, songs about women's liberation. Both women represent a kind of eternal feminine, but the first woman, Cléo, is the creature of her image, existing in the representation of others, while the second woman, Pomme, has created her own image. Many of Varda's films explore the way women are looked at by men and how this creates a particular kind of visual regime in our culture. In *Lion's Love* (1970) and in *Jane B. par Agnès V.* (1987) Varda tells the life stories of two real women, Viva and Jane Birkin, who were icons of the 1960s, whose bodies, generously but not erotically displayed in the films, are androgynous in the style required by fashion (and in contrast to Pomme's rounded contours). In *Les Dites cariatides* (1984), in *Réponse de femmes* (1975), and again in *Jane B. par Agnès V.*, Varda considers the representation of women in painting, sculpture, and on television, showing how women are stripped naked for the pleasure of men but how the reverse, a live male nude in a Paris street for example, is seen as scandalous. And in what is perhaps her most accomplished film, *Sans Toit ni loi* (1985), Varda takes as her central character a woman who is an unkempt, unwashed, malodorous rough sleeper and turns her into an accidental Venus, an ironic comment on the conventional insistence that in order to be an object of contemplation a woman must be fragrant, thin, and clean.

Marguerite Duras's film-making is an even more radical recasting of the conventional cinema. Although in her novels she may have rejected the notion of *écriture féminine*, in her cinema she embraced it in full knowledge of the paradox that cinema is traditionally held to be a visual art. In many of her films, and most comprehensively in *Le Camion* (1977), Duras makes the woman writer's voice constitute the film, quite literally conjuring it up before our eyes. *Le Camion* can be considered a companion piece to Duras's earlier script for *Hiroshima mon amour*, in which a woman's voice, speaking a highly theatrical text, gives some meaning to the fragmented images we see on the screen. In *Le Camion* we in fact see little on the screen but an elderly and rather fragile woman who from time to time reads from a script and prompts a young man to speak words she has written. But as if to confirm that a feminine *prise de parole* can change our ways of seeing, this time all the heavily encoded images of masculinity (the large young man, the lorry) are created by a woman's voice.

In this way women film-makers after 1968 engage with the central questions of realism in the cinema which, as has frequently been shown, derives from an ideal 'somatography', that is, the imaginary conjunction of sound and image in the human body. Many post-war French film-makers, men as well as women, had begun to show this body as fragmented, either through images of dismemberment and partial representation or, increasingly, in an absence of synchronization of sound and image, offering a powerful response to the bland synthesization they perceived in public discourses (such as television) and public images (such as advertising). Both Varda in *Sans Toit ni loi* and Duras in *Le Camion* acknowledge the importance of the body in feminine writing. However, unlike Hélène Cixous who had seen the inscription of the body as the creation of the text, Varda and Duras are pessimistically unable to achieve the reconciliation of feminine body and feminine speech, so that in these films Varda's protagonist is not an autobiographical subject and Duras's is simply absent, spoken but not seen.

## The City as Signifying Practice

*The theatre from agonistic spectacle to postmodern space*

As we have seen, Brecht gained immense influence in France in the 1950s and 1960s: the Berliner Ensemble's tours in 1954, 1955, and again in 1960 dazzled Parisian audiences, while the theory and practice of Brecht's work was widely discussed in the pages of journals such as *Théâtre populaire*. By calling on themes and images from popular culture and by privileging non-heroic or anti-heroic protagonists like Mother Courage, one of Brecht's achievements was to have opened up new possibilities for popular theatre. These possibilities appeared to have been realized in May 1968 when the demonstrations, the slogans, the marches could all from one point of view be interpreted as a show performed by the people, a kind of street theatre based on the mockery of established authority and its representatives, and on the use of objects and spaces for different purposes from those for which they were intended: a gigantic carnival lasting for a month, a massive *détournement*. Following from these experiences, some of the most interesting productions in the period after 1968 were inspired by the desire to restore theatre to the central role in the life of the city that it had, for example, in classical Greece, and to do this in the spirit of satirical humour which had proved so successfully subversive.

The most famous of all the shows which attempted to recreate the spirit of the May events was *1789*, performed by Ariane Mnouchkine's company Théâtre du soleil. The company was originally a student group with a repertoire that included adaptations of the Russian novelist Maxim Gorky and of Théophile Gautier's *Le Capitaine Fracasse*, as well as works by Arnold Wesker and by Shakespeare. It tried to work collectively through communal living and performances based on group improvisation and to move away from notions of authorship and directorial control, inspired by the belief that the company could collectively write its own play in much the same way as the people themselves had become the actors of history. After experimenting with works whose subject is in some way theatricality and performance, like *A Midsummer Night's Dream*, the Théâtre du soleil hit upon the perfect public subject, 'the only heritage common to all French people', which is the Revolution of 1789. Around this they developed a play, or more properly a show or performance, based on the mythical high points of the Revolution, the moments commonly illustrated in children's books or popular histories: *la prise de la Bastille, la nuit du 4 août, les journées d'octobre, la nuit de Varennes*, enacted by famous characters from history such as Lafayette, Babeuf, Marat, Mirabeau, Louis XVI, and so on.

The production of *1789* was a 'promenade' performance. The actors walked the boards or trestles which were designed so that the company could perform in any town with an appropriate open space, rather as travelling players or fairground entertainers of earlier periods who used to take their shows from town to town. The actors did not respect a designated theatrical space and the audience, similarly, was not fixed in its banks of raked seats but could walk round the performers, eating, drinking, talking, participating, while the performers mingled with the audience so that it was impossible to tell where the next action would come from. With its comprehensive destruction of the proscenium arch, the unitary point of view and its implied realism, as well as of the specificity of the actor who was incorporated into the audience, 1789 allowed the audience to become the actor of its own spectacle.

The Théâtre du soleil obviously took much from the Shakespearean tradition of the 'play within a play' as we find it in Hamlet or A Midsummer Night's Dream as well as from the example of workers' theatre such as the Groupe Octobre, for which Jacques Prévert wrote La Bataille de Fontenoy in the 1930s. Like Brecht's plays, and indeed much agitprop, 1789 takes a well-known event or series of events and embroiders on them, focusing not so much on what happened—since this is held to be common knowledge—as on a reading of events. But the audience of a Brecht play is never in any doubt as to the moral scheme proposed. By contrast, 1789 is a play of discourses and genres, some of them popular, some of them erudite, some of them heroic, some of them farcical, some of them quotation, some of them improvisation. The acting style mixed the heroic and the farcical, juxtaposing slapstick and tirade, actors costumed as puppets and as ordinary people.

The performance of 1789 was one of the most brilliant reinterpretations of popular cultural forms to have been inspired by May 1968. It may be that the Théâtre du soleil was influenced by Bakhtin, whose study of Rabelais, as we have seen, was becoming known in France in the late 1960s, and it is certainly tempting to link the Renaud–Barrault company's comparable promenade production of Rabelais (1968), based on the life and works of the author of Gargantua, with Bakhtin's Rabelais and his World. But trends in historical scholarship, such as Mona Ozouf's La Fête révolutionnaire (1976) and Emmanuel Le Roy Ladurie's Le Carnaval de Romans (1979) also suggested the relevance of the interpretation of popular festivals and forms of entertainment to understanding the events of 1968. Historians were led to question the meaning of carnival and particularly to ask whether carnival is a radical transformation or a moment when the people let off steam in order for the status quo to be preserved. Was May 1968 a carnival in the historical sense and, if so, did this not mean it was catharsis rather than revolution?

Today what seems most significant in 1789 is its rejection of the asceticism often associated with revolution in favour of a degree of hedonism expressed in its epigraph from Gracchus Babeuf, 'la Révolution doit s'arrêter à la perfection du bonheur' (the Revolution will stop when perfect happiness is achieved), and the sheer exuberance of its games with codes of performance and registers of language. It is a gigantic Situationist détournement or 're-use of pre-existing artistic elements in a new unity', much more a microcosm of the 'city of play' imagined by the Situationists than a commemoration of a bloody revolution. The ludic dimension of May 1968 is sometimes ignored in considerations of its social and political importance, yet it is to be found elsewhere in the theatre, as well as in the cinema, the press, and in cartoon strips.

Side by side with ambitious, large-scale performances like those of the Théâtre du soleil, the Compagnie Renaud–Barrault, and Jérôme Savary's Grand Magic Circus, the *café-théâtre* flourished after May 1968 as a kind of sardonic running commentary on politics, current affairs, and social change. The Café de la gare, the Splendide, and the Vrai Chic parisien were all established by young performers with little money and no prospects of breaking into the 'official' theatre. The *café-théâtres* were not unlike the turn of the century cabarets which had flourished in Montmartre, small-scale venues without numbered seats, where the audience sometimes drew lots to see what price they would pay. The enforced intimacy created a bond of complicity between audience and performers. With limited space and props, the performers had to concentrate on their own physical resources, and their material consisted mainly of routines and sketches of a humorous or satirical kind whose target was typically the habits of the so-called 'new middle classes', white-collar workers with social ambitions. Just as the Grand Magic Circus had subverted or otherwise sent up classics of Western popular literature in shows like *Zartan, frère mal aimé de Tarzan*, *Les Derniers Jours de solitude de Robinson Crusoë*, and *Cendrillon ou la lutte des classes*, so performers in the *café-théâtre* like Josiane Balasko or Romain Bouteille attacked social norms in sketches such as *Les Hommes préfèrent les grosses* (1978) or leisure habits in the celebrated *Amours, coquillages et crustacés*, a satire on Club Méditerranée holidays first performed at the Splendide in 1977. The *café-théâtre* launched the careers of performers like Patrick Dewaere and Miou-Miou who were later successful in the cinema, and of Coluche whose one-man shows subsequently played to huge audiences on stage and on television. In fact, Coluche's clown persona, his monologues as the 'ordinary bloke', the 'mec' whose down-to-earth, no-nonsense common sense is strangely out of step with the ideas of French opinion formers, so endeared him to the public that his supreme act of *dérision*, announcing that he would be a candidate for the presidency in 1981, was taken extremely seriously. Although many *café-théâtre* shows were subsequently turned into films (Patrice Leconte's *Les Bronzés* (1978), for example, is the film version of *Amours, coquillages et crustacés*) and in this way reached a large audience, the essence of *café-théâtre*, particularly as performed by Coluche, is the audience's impression of eavesdropping on an individual's conversation with himself or herself. It is intimate not just because the performance space is restricted, but because it mimics a stream of consciousness in all its associative incoherence and offers, in the case of Coluche's 'mec', an unsanitized glimpse of an unattractive, chauvinist, racist, misogynist, mean-minded individual who is implicitly presented as typically French and therefore typical of Coluche's audience.

In spatial organization as well as in narrative construction the routines of *café-théâtre* often resembled the new *bandes dessinées* which flourished in the 1960s and 1970s. Alongside the children's comic industry, there emerged a growing adult

### Coluche at the Gymnase

Coluche (Michel Colucchi) began his performing career in the alternative theatre of the early 1970s, in venues such as Le Splendide, but he made his national reputation with one-man shows and television series built round neo-Poujadist monologues which became celebrated as expressions of the feelings of the ordinary French bloke, 'le mec', a man who was worried about his job and his wife, and who thought France was being overrun by foreigners. He is shown here on stage at the Gymnase in 1980 in his role as putative candidate in the presidential election to be held the following year, with the tricolour sash of office draped incongruously over his clown's dungarees. Opinion polls, which suggested that he might have hoped to garner a respectable percentage of the vote had he really stood for election, demonstrated the extent to which Coluche had become a national institution by the 1980s, and in 1985 he used his popularity to launch the *restaurants du cœur*, soup kitchens for the unemployed, whose numbers swelled alarmingly in that decade. He died in a motorcycle accident in 1986.

market for comic strips. Aimed at a mainly male readership in the 18–30 age group, that of the post-war baby-boom, *bande dessinée*, or BD for short, carved an anarchic niche between childish whimsy and eroticism, in which fantasy of whatever kind predominated. Appearing initially in small magazines, the more successful *bandes* were often taken up by large-circulation daily newspapers, and were usually collected and republished in the characteristic large-format *albums* which still occupy a prominent place in retail outlets from bookstores to *grandes surfaces*.

René Goscinny's *Pilote*, founded in 1959, paved the way with Astérix and a succession of engaging comic characters, such as the power-hungry Grand Vizier Iznogoud (is no good), and the pompous, well-meaning Achille Talon (Achilles heel). *V-Magazine*, founded in 1962, was more representative of the new mood, providing the most emblematic figure of the new BD, Barbarella, created by Jean-Claude Forest. Set in a science fiction world, its eponymous heroine was a mix of Flash Gordon and Brigitte Bardot, sumptuously drawn and scantily clad, who, like the heroines of silent film comedies, always emerged unscathed from her extraordinary adventures. Barbarella's success was international, and was in 1967 transposed into a film by Roger Vadim, with Jane Fonda in the title-role. The formula was adapted by others to different settings: the nineteenth-century melodrama of nubile but innocent *Blanche Épiphanie* (1967), the urban violence of mean streets in pop-art style with *Pravda la surviveuse* (1967), or the life and hard times of an heiress become working girl, *Paulette* (1970). The erotic appeal, though accompanied by social comment and humour, was apparently unaware of the questions beginning to be raised by the nascent women's movement.

An anarchistic sense of wilful transgression gradually assumed more importance in BD throughout the 1960s. The magazine *Hara-Kiri*, launched in 1960 by Fred and Cavanna, boasted the subtitle 'journal bête et méchant', advertising its desire to shock and provoke through childish unreasonableness, bad taste, vulgarity, pornography, and any other verbal or visual means. Protesting against the strait-laced conservatism prevalent in French society, it also provided a platform for some of the wittiest and most inventive cartoonists of the new generation, including Fred, Reiser, Gébé, Willem, Cabu, and Wolinski. Between them, they did much to articulate the spirit of May 1968. A companion monthly *Charlie*, founded in 1969, was modelled on the Italian magazine *Linus*, which offered more explicitly sexual adventures, but it also drew on the American 'underground press' comics. Perhaps the most representative member of this generation is Jean Giraud, who, under the pseudonym Gir, wrote for most of the magazines, and under the name Moebius co-founded the magazine *Métal hurlant* (1975–88) and the publishing house Les Humanoïdes associés. Specializing in fantasy and science fiction, he adapted a wide range of visual techniques from the cinema to produce striking graphics which were integral to the Surrealist imagination of his narrative.

A weekly spin-off from *Hara-Kiri*, entitled *Hebdo-Hara-Kiri*, was banned in November 1970 for having lampooned the death of Charles de Gaulle at his home in Colombey-les-Deux-Églises under the mocking headline 'Bal tragique à

Colombey. Un mort' (Tragic Ball at Colombey. One Dead). A week later, an almost identical magazine appeared under the title *Charlie-Hebdo*. With hindsight, this event marks a shift in the centre of gravity of BD, which gradually turned from an indiscriminate anarchism towards more focused social and political comment. A classic of the new direction was the '100% French Superhero', *Superdupont*, devised by Lob, Gotlib, and Alexis, complete with beret and carpet slippers. The incompetent superhero lurched through crusades against assorted foreign subversives, with suitably patriotic determination. Concomitant with this was the emergence of a more feminist awareness, and the arrival of a new generation of women writers and artists. The most influential of these is undoubtedly Claire Bretécher, who co-founded the magazine *L'Écho des savanes* in 1972 with Gotlib and Mandryka as a breakaway from *Pilote*. The following year she began her long-running weekly page in *Le Nouvel Observateur*, under the general title *Les Frustrés*. Aimed at, and depicting, the post-1968 educated middle classes, it dissects the hypocrisy and self-deception of intellectuals or would-be intellectuals on the slippery surface between overweening complacency and existential *Angst*.

Throughout the 1970s, BD established itself as a characteristic component of French culture, and gradually developed institutional structures which gave substance to its claim to be recognized as the 'Ninth Art'. With its gradual acceptance in some school and university syllabuses, studies began to emerge, both popular and academic, journals were founded to discuss it, exhibitions and conferences held, and in due course two national centres were established, at Angoulême and Grenoble, with sponsorship from the Ministry of Culture. Several critics have commented that the attainment of official recognition has coincided with a decline of BD, and certainly it is difficult to see how the early iconoclastic and transgressive impulse can survive the benevolent embrace of the legitimizing state.

### Performance and the politics of urban space

If the 1950s and the 1960s was the era of purpose-built theatres in Paris and the regions, when a policy of decentralization attempted to bring in the popular audience to educate it to an appreciation of the classical repertoire, the 1970s was the decade when the theatre stretched outside and beyond the proscenium arch in every possible way. Many companies took over spaces which had been designed for other uses and transformed them into theatres—the Théâtre du soleil performed *1789* in the Cartoucherie de Vincennes, the Compagnie Renaud–Barrault staged *Rabelais* in the Gare d'Orsay. Although this was a European phenomenon, in France the movement extended well beyond the theatre to affect the architecture of the city as a whole. The reallocation of space, initially based on popular participation and reappropriation of buildings and of the street, was viewed as a transformation of consciousness.

The students expelled from the amphitheatres of the Sorbonne in May 1968 took over the Théâtre de l'Odéon in an act of *détournement* and created a new forum for their general meetings. But in subsequent years such acts of reclamation lost their revolutionary edge. In and around Paris and in its inner suburbs, and to a lesser extent in the provinces, disused buildings were co-opted and recovered for use as spaces of art and leisure rather than as theatres of revolution. Thus after having been used as a theatre, the Gare d'Orsay became what it is today, a museum of nineteenth-century art, the cattle and meat market at La Villette became an exhibition centre and science museum, and, most symbolic of all because of its central location and its function as the lifeblood of the community, the fruit and vegetable market of Les Halles, called by Zola 'le ventre de Paris', was turned into Le Forum des Halles, a huge shopping mall rather than a centre for debate.

Of course the expansion of road and air transport meant that city centre locations for food and commodity markets had become unnecessary and impractical. But such transformations had a powerful symbolic dimension because they often changed what had been the lifelines of French capitalism and imperialism—railway stations, markets, warehouses—into temples of culture. Such architectural schemes are eloquent illustrations of the economic revolution of the last quarter of a century and of the artistic and cultural changes which have accompanied it. Nothing could better signify the shift from an economy based on production to one based on services than the hysterectomy performed on Les Halles and its reconstitution as a shopping mall and leisure centre. In fact the process itself became art when the Italian film director Marco Ferreri made *Touche pas à la femme blanche* (1974) in the location familiarly known to Parisians as the 'trou Pompidou'—because it was President Pompidou who had supported the destruction of the food market and had caused an enormous hole to be dug in the ground prior to building on the site. Ferreri's film is a spoof western, staged as a combat between cowboys and Indians in the adventitiously theatrical space provided by the crater, a veritable storm in a teacup, a teasingly Rabelaisian experiment with the comedy of size and spatial relations, and a microcosm of the battle over American influence in France.

Economic change has offered golden opportunities to combine urban renovation with the expression of *grandeur*. The city of Paris bears the imprint of successive monarchical and imperial rulers and, like Louis XIV and Napoleon III before them, the presidents of the Fifth Republic have all contributed to the transformation of the capital, turning it into perhaps the most postmodern of European cities. De Gaulle, through his Minister of Culture André Malraux, embarked on a programme of cleaning and restoring public buildings, the most recent and most ambitious of which, only nearing completion at the end of Mitterrand's second term of office, is that of the Louvre; Pompidou created the museum of modern art named after him; Giscard d'Estaing began the renovation of La Villette and the Musée d'Orsay, whilst also banning further construction of high-rise buildings; Jacques Chirac, having twice failed to be elected President, instead became the next best thing, mayor of Paris, which gave him oversight of all urban projects; finally, Mitterrand commissioned the Pyramide du Louvre, the Opéra de la Bastille, and the Très Grande Bibliothèque. Nor is it inappropriate to speak of the personal

## The 'Trou Pompidou'

After work had begun to demolish the market pavilions of Les Halles designed by Victor Baltard (1804–74) and erected between 1854 and 1857, a conservationist backlash condemned the destruction of one of the most important examples of ninteenth-century industrial architecture to be found in the Paris region. Thereafter the conservationist movement gained momentum: President Giscard d'Estaing (elected 1974) banned further high-rise construction in central Paris, and redundant buildings such as the Gare d'Orsay were adapted to new purposes instead of being bulldozed. However, this did not solve the problem of what to build in the space vacated by Les Halles since the original proposal, based on office developments, had become unacceptable. The result was that the crater seen here, with the last pavilion to be demolished in the background, remained unfilled for nearly a decade, and when it was eventually redeveloped into Le Forum des Halles the project was carried through piecemeal, with none of the ambition or grandeur which marked subsequent *grands travaux*.

involvement of the successive presidents in these *grands chantiers* as they are called, since each of these projects is to some degree 'le fait du prince', often in defiance of financial rationality, realistic timescales, or sensible planning.

Of course, this process is not new. From Roman times to the present day, Paris has undergone constant transformation as the purpose and function of city spaces has changed. Typically, these transformations took the form of an ever widening set of concentric circles as the city boundaries were enlarged to encompass first the old fortifications (the *enceinte Philippe Auguste*), then the customs barriers (*le mur des fermiers généraux*), and then the *périphérique* (ring road). It might have been expected that the separation between Paris and its outlying districts would have been blurred by the creation of the Réseau express régional (RER), the rapid transit system, which enables individuals to get to work in central Paris even if they live some distance outside the centre, and the more recent expansion of the TGV train network which brings within the suburban purview of Paris towns such as Orléans or Le Mans, or even Nantes. But in fact the distinction between Paris *intra muros* (the twenty *arrondissements* 'within the walls' created in 1859) and Paris without the walls (which needless to say are entirely symbolic) has been exacerbated, and the poor have, as they were in the time of Zola, been expelled further and further from the centre of the city to the outlying parts. The area of dangerous criminality known generically as *la Zone* has seen its confines and boundaries shifted outwards with the expansion of the city. Today it figures in films such as Bertrand Blier's *Les Valseuses* (1974) and Alain Corneau's *Série noire* (1979), which are set in the bleak *grands ensembles* (high-rise estates) constructed on the very edge of cities and which cause the characters in these films profound psychological and linguistic dislocation.

In some ways *la Zone* appears necessary for Paris to preserve a certain identity. The new configuration of city space suggests that the further people are from the centre the more likely they are to be concerned with work than with leisure, a configuration embodied in the design of the Centre Georges Pompidou, which reverses the traditional show-case concept of museum display by exposing the workings of the building on the outside and concealing the art objects within. The centre of Paris not only contains an increasing number of museums, but is itself becoming a museum of a way of life whose rationale is tourism and leisure as it was perceived to be at the *belle époque*. This is undoubtedly one reason why Giscard banned new high-rise buildings, why Jacques Chirac places art nouveau lamps and cobble-stones in city squares, and why there is a preference for transforming buildings, rather than pulling them down and starting afresh. In Paris it has not only become less and less possible to discern from the exterior appearance of a structure what its function is, but façades have in some sense become functions. It is as though Haussmann's concern with imposing uniformity in the height and design of façades had been translated to the entire city, turning it into one immense façade which, like its many modern buildings faced with reflecting glass, tells us nothing about what goes on inside.

Economic development no longer takes place in the centre of the city. Paris like Berlin or London has attempted to shift activity from west to east with the construction of the Très Grande Bibliothèque and the removal of the Ministry of Finances eastwards from the Louvre to the redeveloped Bercy site, or outwards beyond the city to greenfield sites like Roissy or Marne-la-Vallée's Euro-Disney. The spaces vacated in the city centre, like the Louvre and the Bibliothèque nationale, usually become museums, so enacting a pastiche of a previous function. What has happened to the Place des Innocents is a good illustration of this process. In the eighteenth century, the graveyard on this site ceased to be used for health reasons and the bones of those buried in it were transported to the catacombs. Until the 1960s, however, the beautiful Fontaine des Innocents sculpted by Goujon and erected in 1549 continued to stand in the middle of a little square on the edge of Les Halles. When the market pavilions designed by Victor Baltard were demolished and the shopping mall created, the fountain was incorporated into a large piazza where tourists watch street performers. But this is not the real fountain, any more than it is the real square; both are substitute reproductions: the fountain has been removed to a museum to protect it from pollution and the square has been redesigned to give tourists more space to disport themselves. The redevelopment of urban space, however economically rational and artistically prudent it may be, renders appearance more important than substance and makes the map of the contemporary city confusing to interpret because nothing is as it seems.

The transformation of the city also underlines the increasingly intimate link between culture, leisure, and economic growth, a link which is starkly revealed by the development of the Euro-Disney theme park at Marne-la-Vallée north-east of Paris. Despite the socialists' public statements defending the integrity of French culture, they fought hard to ensure that the Disney Corporation would choose France, rather than Spain, as its European site. They provided an unusual legal framework and numerous financial 'sweeteners' because Euro-Disney was conceived as a large job-creation scheme providing much needed economic stimulation to an area which had been designated as a new town. As well as a theme park, Euro-Disney is a huge infrastructure project with a branch of the RER extended to a purpose-built terminus and a station on the TGV Nord route, facilitating access from England, Belgium, Holland, and points north and east. The American cultural take-over which Euro-Disney seemed to confirm offended many intellectuals who viewed it, in Ariane Mnouchkine's words, as a 'cultural Chernobyl', even though the toxic effluent, on this occasion, flowed from the West not the East.

But Euro-Disney is in reality a confirmation of many of the cultural trends at work in Paris over more than two decades. First, it substitutes appearance for reality, the pastiche for the authentic. It does not just look like a film set, it is constructed like one, with the building materials 'imitating' the authentic wood and iron used to construct an American town in frontier days. The architecture of Main Street USA, the centre-piece of the park, is not American vernacular but a pastiche of American vernacular, where the 'reality' resides in the surface alone. In addition, by a strange detour, it exploits European cultural traditions filtered through American eyes. Alongside the standard fairground items like 'ghost train', 'dodgem cars', and 'runaway train' (the latter admittedly in a landscape which imitates the Spanish American desert), are 'rides' inspired by classics of European children's literature—Stevenson and Barrie, Grimm, Perrault, Andersen, and Lewis Carroll, all of which were cannibalized by Walt Disney for his Hollywood cartoons and which now return, much reworked and altered, to their 'European home'. Finally, and most fascinating of all, it offers in 'Discoveryland' a pastiche of the great nineteenth-century world fairs. Just as for the nineteenth-century *Expositions universelles* industrialists and engineers were invited to exhibit their new products and inventions, so here leading French corporations like Renault, Aérospatiale, and France Telecom (all still public sector companies at the time Euro-Disney was developed) have contributed to the design and execution of a film entertainment based, like George Méliès's films, on Jules Verne's *Le Tour du monde en quatre-vingts jours* (1873) and H. G. Wells's *The Time Machine* (1895), while leading actors like Gérard Depardieu, Michel Piccoli, and Philippe Noiret play small parts in it as though to confirm their role in 'industry' and the export drive. This is therefore a show-case for advanced technology and a demonstration that industry and entertainment are now thoroughly conflated. Leisure, which has itself become a major industry, parodies or mimics the 'real' industries of the nineteenth century. Never was Theodor Adorno's expression the 'culture industries' seen to be more apposite.

Urban space has become the privileged confluence of contemporary concerns not just because the conditions in outlying housing estates impinge with increasing regularity on the minds of politicians but because the city has become a dictionary of signs and spatial organization a crucial signifying practice. In *L'Empire des signes* (1970), a record of his visit to Japan, Roland Barthes offered a playful guide round this postmodern city—a covertly homosexual guide it has been suggested—using it to suggest pathways through French culture. The topological displacement allowed him to 'défaire notre "réel" sous l'effet d'autres découpages' (undo our reality by means of different scenarios). Thus in *Mythologies* it was the bourgeoisie who were denounced for transforming culture into nature but in *L'Empire des signes* it is the whole of Western culture 'qui nous fait pères et propriétaires d'une culture que précisément l'histoire transforme en nature' (which makes us fathers and owners of a culture which history indeed transforms into nature/renders natural).

The East, by contrast, permits and requires everything to be decentred, fragmented, disseminated, disrupting the smooth reality which our Western aesthetic and our Western modes of reading assume. The most powerful image of this decentring process is the city of Tokyo. Barthes observes: 'conformément au mouvement même de la métaphysique occidentale, pour laquelle tout centre est lieu de vérité, le centre de nos villes est toujours plein; lieu marqué, c'est en lui que se rassemblent et se condensent toutes les valeurs de la civilisation . . . aller dans le centre c'est recontrer la vérité sociale, c'est participer à la plénitude superbe de la réalité' (conforming to the very thrust of Western metaphysics, for which any centre is a locus of truth, the centre of our cities is always full; it is a place which is marked out, and in which all the values of civilization are gathered and condensed . . . to go into the centre is to encounter social truth, to participate in the superb fullness of reality). But the scenography of Tokyo is a graphic illustration of the decentred modern consciousness, with a vacuum where meaning used to be: 'Tokyo présente ce paradoxe précieux: elle possède bien un centre, mais ce centre est vide . . . une idée évaporée' (Tokyo offers a valuable paradox: it does indeed have a centre, but this centre is empty . . . an idea which has evaporated).

By the late 1980s this was no longer a paradox, nor a phenomenon confined to a far-off Orient. The art of the 1980s and 1990s celebrates a different city, one which belongs to the marginal and the underground as the perhaps paradoxical source of creativity and energy. The opening scenes of Bertrand Blier's film *Buffet froid* (1979) are set in a paranoia-inducing RER station, much of the action of Luc Besson's *Subway* (1985) takes place in the RER station Châtelet-les-Halles, parts of Blier's *Les Valseuses* and of Alain Corneau's *Série noire*, as we have seen, are set in *la Zone*. Indeed, even canonical texts like Flaubert's *L'Éducation sentimentale* have been reread as exercises in topographical displacement. By contrast, the hidden or obscure places under and around the city and their eccentric denizens are now taken as its defining locus, its source of meaning and *lieu de vérité*. More than this, the artist no longer observes from a fixed point. The ethnologists and film-makers of the 1960s typically proposed a cityscape viewed in panorama or from a high, all-encompassing shot, looking down over a crossroads, as in Truffaut's *Les 400 coups* (1959) or Eustache's *Les Mauvaises Fréquentations* (1963) and the certainty of their perspective is still evident in Georges Perec's *Espèces d'espaces* (1974). But their successors in the 1980s and 1990s are in transit or displacement across the city; their point of view is mobile and fragmented, not all-embracing. Thus Marc Augé in *Un Ethnologue dans le métro* (1986) sits in the carriage of a Métro train and notes the variety of social practices while Pascal Bruckner and Alain Finkielkraut speak, in *Au Coin de la rue l'aventure* (1979), of 'le chaos des villes' (the chaos of cities). Similarly, the writer François Maspéro devotes his summer holiday to riding the RER Ligne B accompanied by a photographer and publishes the record of this adventure as *Les Passagers du Roissy-Express* (1990), portraits of chance acquaintances encountered in these outer suburbs, snatches of conversation, and snapshots of the odd or eccentric characters inhabiting these outlying districts. A similar eccentric rumble makes itself heard when Agnès Varda records, in *Mur murs* (1982), the naif murals painted by the Chicano population of Los Angeles. As Lyotard put it in an interesting extension of the urban metaphor: 'De nouveaux langages viennent s'ajouter aux anciens, formant les faubourgs de la vieille ville' (new languages are being added to the old ones, and these form the suburbs of the old city) (*La Condition postmoderne*, 67).

## Cultural Politics and the Postmodern Condition

In the period after 1968 many artists, writers, and critics looked outside France, both to the East and the West, to get beyond their own cultural limitations. Sometimes, as we have seen with French novelists, this took the form of a new orientalism. The Chinese Cultural Revolution briefly seemed to offer a model for the West and, in a special number of the influential review *Tel Quel* entitled 'En Chine' (1974), Marcelin Pleynet explained that China, which he and other members of the editorial team visited in 1972, was a political and economic alternative to both the American and Soviet 'models'—a view shared by Julia Kristeva in *Des Chinoises*, by Philippe Sollers, as well as by other visitors who published their own accounts of China such as Maria-Antonietta Macciocchi in *De la Chine* (1971) and Claudie Broyelle in *La Moitié du ciel* (1973). A powerful sense of community was felt with the struggles of the Chinese people and particularly Chinese women because, as the title of the Bellocchio film put it in 1973, 'China is near' (*La Cina e' vicina*). This mood of political optimism did not last after China was revealed as quite as totalitarian and repressive as the Soviet Union, and *Tel Quel*, for example, executed a spectacular act of revisionism in the special number entitled 'États-Unis' (1977). After their 'Chinese period' the *Tel Quel* group, like Michel Butor in *Mobile* (1962), like Jean Baudrillard in *Amérique* (1986), and indeed like so many French writers before them from Simone de Beauvoir to Louis-Ferdinand Céline to Alexis de Tocqueville, were seduced by the exoticism of America and the possibilities for cultural transcendence which it appeared to offer, and now the United States was presented as 'une autre solution à l'impasse occidentale' (an alternative solution to the Western impasse) because of 'la multiplicité des groupes sociaux, ethniques, culturels, sexuels, des discours' (because of its variety of social, ethnic, cultural, and sexual groups and discourses).

Wherever their gaze was focused, the common concern of all these writers was to get outside or beyond what had come to be seen as the stifling constraints of Western culture. We have seen that Foucault, like many philosophers before him, placed himself in the position of the outsider, the dispassionate archaeologist, the better to criticize his own culture. But for all that he considers, in *Les Mots et les choses*, 'l'homme n'est qu'une invention récente . . . un simple pli dans notre savoir' (man is only a recent invention, just a wrinkle in our knowledge) (p. 15), he at least considered the archaeology of Western humanism would be revelatory. For Lyotard, writing in 1979, even this possibility has evaporated; there is no central epistemological core, even one delimited temporarily and spatially, that legitimizes knowledge. One of the characteristics of the postmodern condition as Lyotard describes it is the collapse of 'grand narratives'. With this goes a loss of the state's power and influence and the concomitant shift of decision-making away from politicians and elected representatives towards an amorphous group of 'chief executives, top civil servants, leaders of big professional organizations.' Lyotard attributes this shift to the 'computerization of society'. Privatization and decentralization in the broader sense extend from economics to culture, and the spread of information technology to all areas of life can amount to taking power away from 'the people'. In a democracy they can and do 'speak' but neither they nor the representatives they elect are any longer actors invested with power. By the same token, the rival or opponent has also been privatized. The adversary is no longer an economically hostile nation such as America or Japan, or even an identifiable corporation like IBM or SONY, but an unidentifiable quantity of microcentres of power. In this way Lyotard very neatly illustrates the cultural dilemma posed to modern states forced to implement their own criterion of 'maximum operational performance' which at the same time causes them to invest in the means rather than the ends and to lose their own centralizing power. Thus

les anciens pôles d'attraction formées par les États-nations, les partis, les professions, les institutions, les traditions historiques, perdent leur attrait . . . les identifications à des grands noms, à des Héros de l'Histoire présente se font plus difficiles . . . Dans la société et la culture contemporaines, société post-industrielle, culture postmoderne, la question de la légitimation du savoir se pose en d'autres termes. Le grand récit a perdu sa crédibilité, quel que soit le mode d'unification qui lui est assigné.

(The nation-states, parties, professions, institutions, historical traditions, all the old centres are losing their powers of attraction . . . identification with great names, with the Heroes of contemporary History, is becoming more difficult . . . In contemporary society and culture, post-industrial society and postmodern culture, the question of the legitimization of knowledge is being posed in different terms. The grand narrative has lost its credibility whatever the means of unification accredited to it.)

The socialist government elected in 1981 placed great faith in its cultural policies. The Minister of Culture Jack Lang, one of the 'hommes de 68' and a former director of the Nancy theatre festival, toured the world echoing his predecessor André Malraux by proclaiming every country's right to 'cultural self-determination' and to freedom from the sinister cultural influence of the United States. In the early years of the administration the President also made speeches in which he asserted that cultural and economic policies were two sides of the same coin to be pursued with equal vigour. Jack Lang secured a large increase in his budget which he devoted partly to the President's grands chantiers (the renovation of the Louvre, the Opéra de la Bastille, the Très Grande Bibliothèque), partly to the incorporation of new art-forms such as circus, chanson, and bande dessinée within the domain of 'official' culture, and partly to 'cultural development', that is, financial support for new cultural activities in the workplace, within trade unions, in the regions. Cultural policy also benefited from the legislation on decentralization enacted in 1982 which enabled many provincial cities and many regions outside the Île de France to restore and renovate their architectural and archaeological 'heritage', to refurbish old museums and to open new ones, and to subsidize the performing arts in the regions. As a result, the physical appearance of many provincial cities has radically altered since 1981 and the tourist and cultural activities they offer have been greatly extended.

Because culture, leisure, and tourism have become major sources of employment, few critics have found fault with the economic logic of Lang's cultural policies, and although the 'culture budget' was reduced when the government changed in 1986, and again in 1993, the thrust of the policies hardly altered. Their ideological foundation is another matter. On the one hand, there are those like Marc Fumaroli who in the name of the market economy are opposed to any state intervention in cultural practices; on the other, there is the obvious mismatch between a cultural policy which attempts to generate a form of national unity with its emphasis on the French 'heritage' and the often counter-cultural practices of artists throughout the post-1981 period.

The huge sums of money spent on culture, which the socialists made the centrepiece of their new approach to government, did not generate new definitions of culture but instead put a populist gloss on traditional budget items or consecrated as 'art' activities which had a traditional popular appeal. Thus the Opéra de la Bastille was supposed to be an opera-house 'for the people' (which was partly why it was located on the place de la Bastille), the Très Grande Bibliothèque (subsequently called the Bibliothèque nationale de France) was initially intended to make available the holdings of the French copyright library to all comers, while circus, *chanson*, and *bande dessinée* were all designated integral and typical parts of the French heritage and therefore worthy of conservation and financial support in the same way as painting and opera. The views expressed in Alain Finkielkraut's widely read pamphlet *La Défaite de la pensée* (1987), with its attack on multiculturalism and its plea for the reinforcement of the French 'identity' through culture, touched a chord not just because their publication coincided with a period of intense political debate about the integration of 'immigrants' into French society, but also, perhaps, because they corresponded to a strong statist and centralizing impetus outside government circles as well as within them. Finkielkraut's recommendations proved attractive because they would have amounted to a return to the cultural and educational policies of the early years of the Third Republic. In the same way, some of the most popular films of the late 1980s and early 1990s exploited the idea of the Third Republic as the quintessential French heritage, whether represented in an idyllic rural setting in Claude Berri's *Jean de Florette* (1985) and *Manon des sources* (1986), or an exploitative industrial environment in his adaptation of Émile Zola's *Germinal* (1993).

However, the audio-visual media have continued to provide the major cultural battlefield, the arena of open conflict between a certain idea of French culture and the financial and technological imperatives of the late twentieth century. The French government has tried to resist American domination of French media industries and Japanese inroads into French technology markets, particularly those related to the culture and leisure industries. France was a prime mover in the promotion of what is known as the 'European audio-visual space', in the creation of development funds for film production within the European Community, in insisting on the establishment of quotas for the screening of EC-generated material on television, and in ensuring that 'audio-visual products' were exempted from the GATT round of free-trade agreements in 1993. In the same way, the French manufacturers of the domestic leisure technologies have been protected from American and Japanese competition by such means as channelling all imports of video recorders through one, small, slow customs point, insisting that all instructions and specifications should be written in French, and developing technical standards which are not compatible with those used elsewhere in Europe and America.

But many media policy decisions can also be seen as last-ditch attempts to hang on to central state control in the name of the public service, before capitulation to the centrifugal *force majeure* of the multiplication of television stations and the diversification of the technologies for delivering television programmes. In the early 1980s the government resisted the creation of private TV stations, claiming that they were protecting French production, and then created the private stations La Cinq and M6. When private video recorders and pre-recorded tapes started to become widespread, they taxed blank tapes. But when satellite broadcasting from surrounding countries like Luxembourg threatened to offer an alternative, and largely American, diet of programmes, they licensed the pay-per-view channel Canal plus, whose programming schedules encouraged off-air recording. By the 1990s Canal plus had been floated on the stock exchange and had become a highly profitable company which had developed an adventurous cinema film production portfolio.

Throughout the 1980s and into the 1990s, therefore, the gap between official and unofficial culture, between intellectuals such as Alain Finkielkraut and Régis Debray, on the one hand, and film-makers and writers on the other, seemed to grow inexorably wider. Neither America nor Japan appeared to pose a threat to the cinema, which was arguably the most confident and lively cultural form of the late 1980s and early 1990s, typically celebrating cultural and ethnic diversity and the erosion of gender distinctions. While the debate over the number of immigrants in France, and the degree to which they were or were not integrated into the national community, occupied the political agenda, many popular films effected a comic reversal of received social values. Coline Serreau's *Romuald et Juliette* (1989) turned a black woman employed as a cleaning lady into the most desirable life partner for a wealthy businessman; Bertrand Blier's *Un deux trois soleil* (1993) celebrated the resourcefulness of the immigrant families on a rundown estate in Marseilles; Étienne Chatiliez's *La Vie est un long fleuve tranquille* (1988) showed how a changeling who is returned from his adoptive to his 'real' family rejects the bourgeois values which are his birthright and pines for the warmth and humour of the feckless welfare spongers who brought him up. These films are all fairy stories of one kind or another, fables which perhaps point to a deep yearning for a less conflictual, more harmonious social environment, but they are entirely without the imposition of the uniformity that cultural integration under the Third Republic implied and which writers like Finkielkraut proposed as a solution to the problems of the 1980s. Indeed, part of the fun of Chatiliez's film is provided by people refusing to conform to the social categories in which they are classified for marketing purposes by the advertising industry.

In general, despite what politicians say, film-makers have not betrayed any sign that they are artistically dominated by Hollywood influences. Instead, the reference to America has become positive for, as the director Jean-Jacques Beineix said, 'it is part of our cultural heritage'. The so-called *cinéma du look*, evident in the films of Beineix, Luc Besson, and Léos Carax, was often criticized, as indeed the *nouveau roman* had been at its inception, for its exclusive attention to surface appearances and its apparent lack of moral or psychological depth. This was particularly evident in Beineix's best-known and most successful film *Diva* (1981), whose locations encompass the architecture of reflecting glass and redesignated spaces that we think of as postmodern, and whose plot is a thoroughly eclectic web of intertextual borrowings from other films and other periods whose juxtaposition undermines any linear narrative.

The *cinéma du look* directors certainly incorporate into their films many techniques which have become familiar from television, and particularly from the television commercials which they have all directed. The visual syntax of their films, with its emphasis on rhythmic montage and ellipsis, non-naturalistic lighting and distorting lenses, and their insistent use of loud music to articulate the images, comes from the world of advertising and pop videos. The opening sequence of Besson's *Subway* (1985), a spoof car chase filmed in wide-angle to the accompaniment of rock music, is typical of this cartoon style. On the other hand, there are positive values of a social and artistic kind in all the films of the *cinéma du look*. *Diva* is a vindication of the mass media, a demonstration that the dissemination and democratization of art can be achieved by what Walter Benjamin called 'mechanical reproduction', in this case, the tape recording of an opera singer's voice. The film contrasts the physically frail and socially modest youth who is an emblematic French 'Jules' (bloke), with the fleshly splendour and the glorious voice of a beautiful black American diva. We cannot fail to sympathize with Jules in his quest for a recording any more than we can fail to be dazzled by the diva. There is a positive value in this film—but it is offered by a black American woman.

In Besson's *Subway* the non-metropolitan and the marginal, represented by the denizens of the underground, are the sources of invention and creative energy, while the *gendarmes* who uphold the law are seen as dull-witted and plodding. And in Carax's *Les Amants du Pont Neuf* (1991) the traumatic opening sequence shows a drunken driver brutally injuring a lame tramp who lies across his route and failing to stop after the accident. But it goes on to show how the tramp, whom Chaplin first rendered emblematic of the people, can fall in love, and how he and his partner celebrate their romance by waterskiing on the Seine whilst the official Republic celebrates its bicentenary with fireworks in the background.

Indeed, one of the most moving works in this vein was made by the director who also promoted Third Republic culture in his 'heritage' films. Claude Berri's *Tchao Pantin* (1983) concerns the relationship between a small-time drug-dealer of North African extraction and a renegade policeman turned night petrol pump attendant, a lonely drunk brilliantly acted by Coluche, the master of petty-bourgeois misanthropy. The film deploys all the visual clichés of low-life Paris symbolized by the district round Barbès. Yet in showing how the former cop, against his will and better judgement, goes after the murderers of the drug-dealer and is himself accidentally killed for his pains, *Tchao Pantin* is a subtle presentation of common humanity and shared purpose, of the difficulties and necessity of a social harmony which cuts across class and race, and it is rendered all the more convincing because of the *garagiste*'s initial reluctance to intervene.

## References

**Augé, Marc**, *Un Ethnologue dans le métro* (Paris: Hachette, 1986).

**Bakhtin, Mikhail**, *Rabelais and his World* (Cambridge, Mass.: MIT Press, 1968).

**Barthes, Roland**, *L'Empire des signes* (Geneva: Skira, 1970).

—— 'Le Message photographique', *Communications*, 1 (1961) and 'Rhétorique de l'image', *Communications*, 4 (1964), both repr. and trans. in Stephen Heath (ed.), *Roland Barthes Image Music Text* (London: Fontana, 1977).

—— *Mythologies* (Paris: Seuil, 1957).

**Baudry, Jean-Louis**, *L'Effet cinéma* (Paris: Albatros, 1978).

**Bazin, André**, *Qu'est-ce que le cinéma?* (Paris: Éditions du cerf, 1975).

**Bourdieu, Pierre**, *La Distinction* (Paris: Minuit, 1980).

—— *Les Règles de l'art* (Paris: Seuil, 1992).

—— and **Darbel, André**, *L'Amour de l'art* (Paris: Minuit, 1966).

—— and **Passeron, Jean-Claude**, *Les Héritiers* (Paris: Minuit, 1966).

—— *La Reproduction* (Paris: Minuit, 1970).

**Broyelle, Claudie**, *et al.*, *Deuxième Retour de Chine* (Paris: Seuil, 1977).

—— *La Moitié du ciel* (Paris: Denoël, 1973).

**Bruckner, Pascal**, and **Finkielkraut, Alain**, *Au Coin de la rue l'aventure* (Paris: Seuil, 1979).

**Butor, Michel**, *Mobile* (Paris: Gallimard, 1962).

**Finkielkraut, Alain**, *La Défaite de la pensée* (Paris: Gallimard, 1987).

**Foucault, Michel**, *Les Mots et les choses* (Paris: Gallimard, 1966).

**Fumaroli, Marc**, *L'État culturel* (Paris: Éditions de Fallois, 1991).

**Kristeva, Julia**, *Des Chinoises* (Paris: Des Femmes, 1974).

**Le Roy Ladurie, Emmanuel**, *Le Carnaval de Romans* (Paris: Gallimard, 1979).

**Lyotard, Jean-François**, *La Condition postmoderne: rapport sur le savoir* (Paris: Minuit, 1979).

**Macciocchi, Maria Antonietta**, *De la Chine* (Paris: Seuil, 1971).

**Maspéro, François**, *Les Passagers du Roissy-Express* (Paris: Seuil, 1990).

**Ozouf, Mona**, *La Fête révolutionnaire* (Paris: Gallimard, 1976).

**Perec, Georges**, *Espèces d'espaces* (Paris: Galilée, 1974).

# French in the World: From Imperialism to Diversity

## Preservationists vs. Innovators and the Contemporary French Language

The common thread linking African, Canadian, and mainland French cultures is, of course, the language and language-related matters are given great prominence not simply in metropolitan France but, as we have seen, throughout francophone culture. Many national and provincial dailies carry regular columns in which correct usage is discussed, or offer their readers quizzes and other entertainments on points of grammar. Any 'librairie-papeterie' will offer the linguistically insecure a selection of publications with titles like *Améliorez votre français, Les 1000 Difficultés du français, Je connais mieux le français*, or *Le Français correct*. Government commissions devise—and publish in the *Journal officiel de la République française*—appropriate new French terminology for fields as varied as tourism, architecture, and aviation. By virtue of the *loi Bas-Auriol*, passed in 1975, and recently updated, the use of non-French terms instead of the official coinages became an offence in those sectors of the economy that supply goods and services, and businesses have on occasion been successfully prosecuted as a result. In Quebec, the 1977 *Charte de la langue française* makes still more stringent provision along these lines—even requiring private firms to supply evidence to a team of government inspectors that they use French, not English, as their working language. And, every Thursday in Paris, the state-funded Académie française (a forty-member committee of distinguished men of letters together with a few journalists, historians, and scientists and, nowadays, even one or two women members) meets to compile the latest edition of the official dictionary of the French language. Progress on this is leisurely: work on the current edition began in the 1930s and, despite the assistance of a team of lexicographers, is not expected to be completed before the next century! Meanwhile those in search of information are more than adequately served by private sector products like the Larousse, Robert, Bordas and other dictionaries.

This particular edition of the *Dictionnaire de l'Académie* is in fact the ninth to appear since that institution was founded in 1634 by Cardinal Richelieu. The seventeenth century, and notably the reign of Louis XIV, was a period in which much political and cultural importance was attached to order, regularity, and centralization, whether in government, administration, architecture, the theatre, the layout of the gardens at Versailles—or language. It is to this age of classicism that we owe the ideal of a standardized, official French language with a rigorously codified vocabulary and rules of grammar that are supposedly fixed for all time. The following characterization of the Academy's aims by one of its seventeenth-century members is revealing of the élitism which, then as now, inspired the purist enterprise: 'nettoyer la langue des ordures qu'elle avait contractées, ou dans la bouche du peuple, ou dans la foule de Paris . . . ou par les mauvais usages des courtisans ignorants' (to cleanse the language of the filth it had acquired, either in the mouths of the people, or among the Paris crowd . . . or from the improper usage of ignorant courtiers). In fact, before the late eighteenth century there was no attempt to impose the use of 'Academy French' outside aristocratic circles, though the bourgeoisie found it difficult to refrain from aping the aristocracy in language as in so much else. But from the Revolution onward, the erstwhile dialect of the Versailles courtiers achieved the status of 'national language'. During the nineteenth century, much of the work of the elementary schoolmaster involved teaching this language to the children of artisans and peasants who, although French citizens and 'francophones' in a broad sense, had as their native speech a working-class dialect or a rural patois.

For a contrast had arisen between, on the one hand, the official, highly regimented variety of speech and (more especially) writing and, on the other, various kinds of colloquial speech which continued to develop in their own way in spite of the Academy and its grammarians. Now this contrast is still very much with us today—to the extent that many native speakers of French have problems in learning how to express themselves 'correctly' in writing (or in formal speech) or indeed in learning how to spell. Paradoxical though it may sound, some will even admit to 'speaking French badly'. As the well-known linguist André Martinet put it in *Le Français sans fard* (1969): 'Les Français n'osent plus parler leur langue parce que des générations de grammairiens, professionnels et amateurs, en ont fait un domaine parsemé d'embûches et d'interdits' (French people no longer dare to speak their language because generations of professional and amateur grammarians have transformed it into a field littered with pitfalls and taboos) (p. 29). Hence the ready market for pocket guides to French grammar, and, no doubt, the fascination exerted by the annual, televised, spelling competition the Championnats d'orthographe.

A related aspect of this official/unofficial language dichotomy is of course that the official variety, being the product of three centuries of constant refinement, is felt by many to need preserving from 'contamination'. This may come from within, taking the form of 'sloppy usage', 'bad grammar', or 'misuse of words' (i.e. any deviation from the standard, however natural or widely encountered). Alternatively contamination may have an external origin, the main threat at the present time being the proliferation of English terminology. The French language, moreover, can be perceived as embodying French/francophone cultural identity and values (there is, for example, a long-established mythology that French is clearer, more logical, and better suited to abstract thought than other languages). Consequently there lurks in the background the conviction that any threat to the language is also a cultural threat in a more general sense. It can hardly be a coincidence that René Étiemble's celebrated attack on the influence of English on French, *Parlez-vous franglais?* was published in 1964, when Gaullist anti-Americanism was at its height. So preservation of the language can be seen as fundamental to the preservation of national or ethnic identity—be it the identity of the French nation against encroaching Anglo-Saxon values, that of the Québécois against the anglophone Canadians, the Walloons of southern Belgium against their Dutch-speaking compatriots in Flanders, or the centralized power of the élite of many 'francophone' African states against tribal fragmentation. As a result, *la défense de la langue française* is a serious issue in francophone society, and some of its manifestations have been referred to earlier.

However, it is important to note that the efforts of the 'preservationists' often go unheeded—fortunately or unfortunately according to one's point of view. There are for instance many examples of 'bad French' that were vigorously attacked in popular grammar-books in the late eighteenth century, and have survived to be condemned no less vigorously at the end of the twentieth (cases include the use of *conséquent* to mean 'important', or the use of *je m'en rappelle* instead of *je me le rappelle* for 'I remember it'). The natural evolution of the language is hard to resist, and so too is the appeal of modernity and internationalism. In particular, the last couple of decades have seen some striking developments in a culture which has long been regarded by outsiders as inflexible and conservative in linguistic matters. Inflexibility and conservatism are undoubtedly features of 'classical French': the point is that other varieties—as inventive and as receptive to outside influence as language anywhere else—have begun to encroach on its territory. Particularly noticeable is the way in which both the traditional colloquialisms and the trendy new coinages of informal French are increasingly finding their way into writing—notably novels and journalism—and into spoken contexts (political discourse, television interviews, etc.) that were once considered too elevated for this sort of usage. No doubt this reflects a growing desire for expression on the part of cultures other than the official one, and there are perhaps parallels in some francophone African writing. Furthermore, although many commentators deplore the influx of English words, there are at least as many users of the language (advertisers and journalists obviously, but plenty of others too) who find them chic and cosmopolitan—or else convenient in technical documents even though an approved French alternative may be available.

Such changing attitudes towards what is and what is not respectable in language are for some a sure sign of decadence—hence the need to 'defend the language'—but for others they are an intriguing spectacle in their own right. So in the last few years there has not only been much condemnation of these trends, but also a spate of books and newspaper or magazine articles simply chronicling the new developments, sometimes with ill-disguised delectation. And a whole new range of possibilities has opened up for the dictionary makers. It is as though the general public are discovering that their language possesses unsuspected and fascinating resources.

In anglophone cultures the language has not been subjected to anything like the same amount of interventionist regulation, and the dividing line between formal and informal usage has tended to be less sharply drawn. Consequently French has been more dramatically affected than English by the recent sudden explosion of media technology, and breaking down of communication barriers between social groups. Nor have speakers of English any reason to be linguistically on the defensive in the way that some speakers of French apparently are: protagonists of 'francophonie' (who tend to take a strongly preservationist stance) frequently claim that French is the world's second most important international language, a claim that suggests simultaneously a certain cultural assertiveness and an awareness of being overshadowed. In this respect, considerable symbolic value attaches to the fact that it was possible to hold the 1992 final of the Championnats d'orthographe in New York—with competitors from 123 different countries.

So the French language, or perhaps more specifically the outlook of its users, is currently subjected to two opposing forces: a desire to maintain the status quo on the part of some; a desire to welcome and encourage innovation on the part of others.

One reflection of the resulting tensions is the recent national debate in France over the spelling reform proposed by a government commission in 1989 in response to representations made by primary school teachers. It is, incidentally, revelatory of the French tradition of linguistic centralization that such a government-led initiative should be conceivable at all: the hierarchical path led from the Prime Minister to a special committee appointed by him (the Comité supérieur de la langue française); then to the French Academy for approval of the committee's proposals, which would eventually be incorporated in the dictionary (at this stage Belgian, Canadian, and Swiss approval was also sought); then to the Ministry of

Education for the appropriate circulars to be issued to head teachers. Once the reformed spelling was in place on the national school curriculum, then textbook writers, dictionary makers, printers, publishers, and so on would have no option but to come into line.

The proposed changes were actually quite minor, the most drastic being the abolition of the circumflex accent except in cases where ambiguity might result, like *tache* (spot)/*tâche* (task). Even so, the strength of preservationist opinion was such that the reform got no further than the first two or three of the above stages, and can now be considered a dead letter, as it were. However, the debate was extremely animated. Pamphlets, articles, and books poured from the presses, the traditionalists making emotional reference to the precious cultural heritage that was being placed at risk, while the progressives claimed merely to be streamlining the orthography for the new millennium, and thereby improving the chances of French in the ongoing struggle with English. This particular attempt at spelling reform was the third to be made this century (both the others were equally unsuccessful), and no doubt more will follow in the next.

It is characteristic of the intensity of the polemic that, hardly had the spelling controversy died down, than a new argument began, this time over the reinforcement of the 1975 language legislation. A bill (the *projet de loi relatif à l'emploi de la langue française*) brought before the French parliament by the then Minister of Culture, Jacques Toubon, was passed by both chambers in the spring of 1994. Like the earlier *loi Bas-Auriol*, the Toubon law seeks to ban the use of 'foreign' terms when approved French equivalents are available (a special Minitel line was set up to provide information about the latter), and generally to safeguard the position of French in such domains as advertising, work contracts, or instructions for the use of appliances. Sanctions include fines of up to 10,000 francs and withdrawal or refusal of government subsidies. More controversially, the 1975 provisions were extended to the internal notices and memoranda of firms operating on French territory and employing French staff, as well as to conferences and congresses held in France by French organizations (programmes must be in French, and translations or résumés of the proceedings supplied). In all cases, the guiding principle is—ostensibly at least—the right of French citizens to conduct their business in their native language.

As with the spelling reform, the reaction was as polarized as it was passionate. Some—by and large those who had favoured the new-style orthography—felt that the legislation was intolerably repressive, would alienate young people, ossify the language, and damage France's business and scientific standing. (The Académie des sciences was particularly eloquent on the latter point, given that the international scientific community operates increasingly in English.) Others found that the law did not go nearly far enough in preserving what Toubon referred to as the 'language of liberty and democracy', particularly as regards the usage of the media. Interestingly, these reactions cut across the conventional political divisions: in the Senate, for instance, the communists joined the Gaullists of the RPR in voting for the bill, while certain UC (centre-right) members opposed it. (After the vote, however, senators from all parties proceeded to the dining-room where—ironically and illegally—'un mixed grill' was among the offerings on the menu!)

It took only a few years for the 1975 legislation to fall into disuse, and even disrepute. Many commentators—supporters of the *loi Toubon* among them—are of the opinion that the latest measures will encounter the same fate. This seems all the more likely since, just a few months after the bill became law, and following an appeal to the Conseil constitutionnel (France's highest constitutional body) by certain socialist deputies, some of the provisions relating to the use of 'foreign words' by private individuals were declared contrary to the right to free expression. But at least the Minister's efforts will have provided yet more fuel for the ongoing language debate.

## Beur Culture

One of the most vivacious examples of cultural diversity in contemporary France is provided by Beur culture, which has its origins among the population of North African origin that now constitutes France's largest ethnic minority. Immigrant workers from Algeria, and to a lesser extent Morocco and Tunisia, have been part of the French economy since the early twentieth century, but it is only since the 1960s that family settlement by North Africans has become a major part of French urban life. Until then, most immigrant workers had been temporary residents who eventually returned home to North Africa, where their families remained. Few first-generation immigrants engaged in any formal artistic activities. The explosion of cultural practices among their children, popularly known as *Beurs*, first came to the attention of the general public in the early 1980s. Today, there is hardly an area of cultural activity where they are not present. There are Beur actors, painters, writers, film-makers, musicians, and comedians.

Some of the key practitioners of Beur culture grew up only a stone's throw away from the Nanterre university campus where the May 1968 movement began, but in many respects they seemed to come almost literally from another world. Until well into the 1970s—and in some cases even later—Nanterre and similar areas in other French cities were the sites of sprawling *bidonvilles*, shanty towns housing poor families, principally of immigrant origin. Unlike France's expanding student population, which came primarily from the middle classes, the immigrant community was mainly working-class, and higher education was largely beyond its reach. North Africans were also ethnically different from the majority of the population. Immigrants from across the Mediterranean spoke Arabic or Berber and had been brought up as Muslims, rather than as Catholics, Protestants, or free-thinkers. Their children shared in this cultural heritage, while at the same time becoming deeply impregnated with French culture, notably at school.

In his autobiographical novel *La Menthe sauvage* (1984) Mohammed Kenzi recalls how, during the events of 1968, he woke up one morning to find that some of the students at Nanterre had broken down the wall separating the university from the *bidonville* in which he lived:

Pour une fois que [*sic*] des jeunes français essayaient de casser les barrières qui isolaient les uns des autres dans des réserves. Pour une fois qu'ils s'élévaient contre le parquage des différents groupes sociaux, divisés par ethnies, si bien élaboré dans la région parisienne, les immigrés restaient de marbre. Ils ne bougeaient pas d'un pouce, refusant jusqu'au discours séducteur des universitaires. Seuls leurs enfants avaient peut-être saisi le sens de cette démarche. C'était l'occasion pour eux de s'ouvrir à un autre monde.

(For once young French kids were trying to break down the barriers which divided us and confined us in reservations. Yet in spite of this assault on the calculated way in which, in the Paris region, social groups had been divided by ethnic differences and dumped in different areas, the immigrants didn't budge. They didn't lift a finger and even rejected the seductive appeals of the university teachers. Perhaps only their children understood the meaning of these actions. For them it opened up a new world.) (p. 59)

Kenzi's description captures both the social and ethnic gulf separating first-generation immigrants from the rest of the population and the greater openness of their children to French influences. While most of the *soixante-huitards* soon lost interest in the immigrant community, most young North Africans instinctively felt the need to find a place for themselves in French society. The creative works produced by Beur artists during the last twenty years are to a large extent an expression of their quest for acceptance into French society whilst retaining a deep attachment to the cultural heritage of their parents. Kenzi's own desire to make his future in France was made plain when he was expelled from the country in 1974 after serving a short prison sentence for assaulting a police officer. He longed to return to France and made clandestine visits to the Paris area, eventually resettling there legally in the late 1980s after obtaining a presidential pardon.

Kenzi's involuntary exile had prevented him from participating directly in the upsurge of what we now know as Beur culture, the earliest stirrings of which came during the mid-1970s, when youngsters of North African origin began forming amateur theatre groups. Typical of these was a troupe called Weekend à Nanterre. Like similar groups in other cities, it used a mixture of heavily colloquial French together with dashes of Arabic and Berber to dramatize the everyday lives of young North Africans confronted with poverty, racial discrimination, and the cultural contradictions commonly experienced by the children of immigrants.

During this same period, some of these youths began calling themselves *Beurs*. This was a *verlan* (backslang) expression formed by inverting and contracting the word *Arabe*. The term first entered public usage in 1981, with creation of a local radio station based in northern Paris called Radio Beur run by young men and women from North African immigrant families. A chain of similar stations, Beur FM, now broadcasts in France's major conurbations, alongside other ethnically based stations such as Radio Gazelle in Marseilles. As in the theatrical productions already mentioned, the dominant language used on air is French, but much of the music played on these stations is performed in Arabic or Berber. Programming of this kind has helped to popularize *raï*, a musical style pioneered in the Oran region of Algeria blending traditional Arab forms with rock instruments and rhythms.

A similar blend is heard in the music of Beur groups such as Carte de séjour, whose best-known recording is a brilliantly ambiguous rendering of a song originally made famous by Charles Trenet, the chorus of which celebrates 'Douce France, cher pays de mon enfance' (Sweet France, dear land of my childhood). In the eyes of many ordinary French people, the Beurs and their parents are an alien presence. Carte de séjour's rearrangement of Trenet's romantic song, bringing in a rock beat and Arabic instrumentation, may seem at one level to confirm this alien quality. At another level, however, it reveals the genuine attachment of the Beurs to the country in which they have grown up. Wrongly stereotyped as immigrants, most of the Beurs have been born in France. This truly is the land of their childhood, a place for which they often feel real tenderness. Yet their childhood has generally been one of acute social deprivation, and many native-born French people have proved anything but sweet or gentle in their attitude towards the Beurs. This hostility—which at its worst has taken the form of racist shootings—lends a further and deeply ironic dimension to Carte de séjour's version of 'Douce France'.

The world in which the Beurs have grown up is summed up in the title of a song written and performed by another Beur musician, Karim Kacel, who shot to stardom in 1983 with his first single, 'Banlieue'. Unlike its literal English translation, 'suburb', which often has middle-class connotations, 'banlieue' has become synonymous in France with urban deprivation. This is the world that Mehdi Charef explores in one of the best known of all Beur creations, the feature film *Le Thé au harem d'Archimède* (1985).

Charef was born in Maghnia, a small town in western Algeria, in 1952. During his early years, he seldom saw his father, who was working as a labourer on building sites in the Paris area. When Charef was 11 the family moved to France, settling initially in a Nanterre *bidonville*. Later, they transferred into a nearby *cité de transit*, a slightly less ramshackle but still deficient form of housing, before eventually securing an apartment in a low-grade housing block. A poor student, Charef was drummed out of school at the age of 17. His *CAP de mécanicien* qualified him for nothing more than a semi-skilled factory job. Bored with the dead-end world in which he found himself, Charef drifted into a life of petty crime which soon led to a short prison sentence. On his release, he went back into factory work and began writing film scenarios in his spare time. With no contacts in cinematic circles, it was not until ten years later that he eventually struck lucky, when novelist and script-writer Georges Conchon suggested that Charef transform one of his scenarios into a novel. Charef duly obliged, and Conchon was so impressed with the manuscript of *Le Thé au harem d'Archi Ahmed* that he arranged for it to be published by Mercure de France, one of the most prestigious imprints in France. When the novel came out in 1983, Charef was invited to appear on Bernard Pivot's *Apostrophes*, the most popular literary magazine programme on French television. In so doing, he became the first Beur artist to reach a genuinely national audience. Shortly afterwards, the producer Costa-Gavras asked him to turn the novel back into a scenario, and the film which Charef had always wanted to make was released two years later.

It is an uncompromisingly tough film, set in the grey and soulless suburbs of Charef's youth. Unemployment, petty crime, drugs, and prostitution are part of everyday life. The two main characters, Madjid (closely modelled on Charef himself) and his French friend Pat, enjoy a camaraderie that occasionally enables them to forget the dead-end world they inhabit. It also enables Charef subtly to signal that the real divisions in French society are not between foreign- and native-born people, but between the haves and the have-nots. Madjid and Pat have different ethnic origins, but they are united by a common experience of social disadvantage. The underlying logic of their condition leads remorselessly to the final scene in which they are arrested and driven off in a police van.

Because the Beurs have to a large extent assimilated French norms, ethnic clashes are apt to be more common inside the family home than beyond its walls, for immigrant parents generally remain much more wedded than their children to North African traditions. The most divisive issues often revolve around relations between the sexes, with the role and status of women particularly sensitive. In Islamic societies, women are traditionally assigned a subordinate role in relation to their menfolk, and are required to behave with great reserve in public places. The marriages of immigrant parents were often arranged by their families, and they expect to exercise a similar prerogative over their own children. These expectations cut across those of most French-born youngsters, for whom the choice of a sexual or marital partner is essentially a personal decision. Young women of North African origin who wish to exercise a similar degree of independence often find their way blocked by parental pressures. If women are so far in a minority among recognized Beur artists, this may perhaps be due in part to the more restricted opportunities which they have enjoyed, compared with their male counterparts. Those who have succeeded in making their voices heard have often stressed the particular difficulties experienced by female members of the immigrant community.

One of the best-known women performers from a North African immigrant family is Djura, lead singer with the musical group Djurdjura. The songs created and performed by this all-female ensemble highlight the plight of women who wish to throw off traditional constraints on their independence. Yet the group never adopts a directly anti-Islamic posture. On the contrary, its members have stressed their attachment to their North African roots by writing new songs in the Berber language which they have inherited from their parents. Djura's balancing trick has, however, proved to be anything but easy. In her autobiography, *Le Voile du silence* (1990), she recounts a long series of repressive and sometimes brutal acts by her family, particularly her father and brother, designed to block her career. These tactics culminated in an armed attack on Djura and her French partner when the singer was seven months pregnant. The couple and their unborn baby survived, but the incident amply demonstrates the fierce passions which can sometimes divide male and female and first- and second-generation members of the immigrant community. Similar tensions are explored by women writers such as Sakinna Boukhedenna in her autobiographical *Journal: 'nationalité: immigré(e)'* (1987) and by Ferrudja Kessas in her novel *Beur's Story* (1990).

It would nevertheless be a mistake to imagine that most immigrant families are torn apart by irreconcilable conflicts. Most succeed in finding compromises despite the differences which often exist within them. In a light-hearted vein, these disagreements and the solutions which are found to them are the subject of one of the most successful Beur productions to date, a forty-part television situation comedy entitled *La Famille Ramdam* broadcast on M6 in 1990–1. The show was conceived by Aïssa Djabri and Farid Lahouassa, who grew up together in Nanterre. It presents a far less grim picture of the immigrant condition than many other Beur creations. Whatever problems they encounter, the Ramdams always find help and support within the family unit. In this respect, *La Famille Ramdam* replicates the classic values of French situation comedies, which in turn are based on long-established American models. The effectiveness with which Djabri and Lahouassa have internalized and inflected this model so as to reflect their own experiences bears witness to the richness of the cultural alloy which Beur artists are engaged in creating.

### References

**Boukhedenna, Sakinna,** *Journal: 'nationalité: immigré(e)'* (Paris: L'Harmattan, 1987).
**Charef, Mehdi,** *Le Thé au harem d'Archi Ahmed* (Paris: Mercure de France, 1983).
—— *Le Thé au harem d'Archimède* (film) (1985).
**Djura,** *Le Voile du silence* (Paris: Michel Lafon, 1990).
**Kenzi, Mohammed,** *La Menthe sauvage* (Lutry: Jean-Marie, Bouchain, 1984).
**Kessas, Ferrudja,** *Beur's Story* (Paris: L'Harmattan, 1990).
**Laronde, Michel,** *Autour du roman beur: immigration et identité* (Paris: L'Harmattan, 1993).

## National Allegory in Francophone Canada

The British conquest of New France in 1759 and especially the suppression of the Patriots' democratic rebellion in 1837, the influx of British capital and Anglo-Celtic immigration which for a few decades in the nineteenth century turned Montreal into a majority anglophone city, led to the emergence of an official nationalist ideology in Quebec. After Confederation in 1867, the protection of 'French Canadians' was seen as lying in a defensive posture in which the Catholic clergy and (largely rural) *notables* retained power in the province to preserve (the myth of) an agrarian, religious culture against the ravages of Anglo-Saxon Protestant-led materialism, French Canada having in addition been 'saved' from the French Republic by the events of 1759. The social contradictions of this posture led eventually to its defeat in 1960 and the beginning of what is referred to as *la révolution tranquille* (the quiet revolution), when a new Liberal government in Quebec ushered in a programme of modernization and state-led accumulation and investment which dethroned the clergy to foster and produce a new Québécois economic and technocratic élite whose variously dosed nationalist ideology is more interventionist and aggressive *vis-à-vis* the Canadian federal government in Ottawa, and is concerned to play a more locally empowered role in the North American and world economy. This process continued with the governments of the Parti québécois (1976–85), although their option for independence from, or rather 'sovereignty-association' with, the rest of Canada was roundly defeated in a referendum in 1980. The 1960s also saw the emergence of more radical nationalisms, in which Quebec (as opposed to *le Canada français*) was seen as suffering from the evils of colonialism, on the model of experiences in the Third World.

The film *Nelligan*, shot in six weeks in November and December 1990 in time for the fiftieth anniversary of the poet's death, came at a moment of resurgent Québécois nationalism after the collapse of the 1987 Meech Lake accord on a new Canadian constitution, a collapse read by the Québécois as a rejection by English Canada of Quebec and of its 'distinct society' status central to the agreement, and it is thus a useful introduction to the way the Quebec nation and all the contradictions of that concept are constructed in the narratives of its cinema. Here we shall consider ways in which connections between the film and the social and political context can be explored through its conditions of production, the question of allegory, genre, sexuality, and the family.

*Nelligan* is a biographical costume drama, premiered in September 1991, about the life of Émile Nelligan (1879–1941), Quebec's national poet, who produced his major literary output as a teenager before being interned in 1899 in a psychiatric hospital, where he was to spend the rest of his life. In the film, the young Nelligan (Marc St-Pierre), in his all-exclusive passion for his poetic vocation, comes into conflict with his Irish anglophone father, a postal official; is protected and indulged by his francophone mother, who introduces him to the priest Eugène Seers who was to edit his works; is misunderstood by his peers at the École littéraire; and is an object of desire for both the bohemian Arthur de Bussières and the bourgeois childhood friend Idola St-Jean. Eventually, Nelligan is thrown out of the parental home and leads a miserable existence until, just before he and Arthur are to set off for France, he is carted off to the psychiatric hospital at the instigation of his parents. Nelligan's status as national poet, the anglophone/francophone confrontation in the family drama, and the portrait of the unjust *past* society clearly invite a connection with social and political questions which in Quebec inevitably mean narratives and representations of the nation.

Although we should not underestimate the input of the director Robert Favreau, his career and his film would not exist were it not for the extensive support of state agencies in Quebec and Canadian cinema. For while the 6.8 million Québécois often express the fear of cultural assimilation by anglophone North America, the cultural identity of the 20 million English Canadians is rendered equally fragile by the immense output and immense home market represented by the USA with its 250 million people, and an audio-visual industry that treats Canada as part of that home market and beams its television networks into every Canadian home. Hence the policy, weakened financially but continued by the Mulroney Conservative government after 1984, of subsidizing Canadian production. Rarely do or can Canadian and Québécois productions recoup their production costs at the box-office, and this was certainly not the case for *Nelligan*. The film's budget was around $2.75 million, a figure made possible only by being a co-production with the National Film Board (in French, ONF-Office national du film), the state-owned production house and training and research centre, with some financial participation from Telefilm Canada, which administers an aid programme ($60 million over five years from 1988 for feature films), and from the francophone pay-TV channel Super Écran. Intriguingly, the biopic of Quebec's national poet owed its existence to federal institutions, since the Quebec agency SOGIC (Société générale des industries culturelles) refused its participation, a decision variously attributed to a dismissal of literary topics as box-office poison, or to disagreement with director Favreau's revisionist approach to *Nelligan*, in which the poet is supposedly *not* seen as a national monument. The budget made the film possible but was still low by international standards for a costume drama, which explains for example why one of the first of the genre in Quebec in an urban as opposed to rural setting has so few exteriors.

A familiar critical approach to the relation between text and context is of course that of allegory. Thus Ian Lockerbie, in his overview of Quebec cinema of the 1980s, discerns manifestations of the *québécois* collective unconscious, or what he calls 'l'imaginaire québécois' (the Québécois imaginary), at work in many films of the period: narratives of 'private' life are seen to be over-determined, individual destinies experience a lack (of the 'completely reassuring social experience' that 'full' nationhood might be), or else are figured in terms of generational conflict in the family (read the quest for group formation represented by nationhood). The three ages of man represented in individuals thus come to stand for 'the historical stage of conservation, the stage when Quebec, with some difficulty caught up with the modern world, and the present stage when new vistas are opening up to Quebec'. In this view, *Nelligan* represents the oppressive nature both of British colonialism (the tyrannical anglophone father, the attempted rape by anglophone sailors) and of the clerical, hypocritical Quebec society of the 1890s, a view illustrated in the film by the poet's insistence on the French pronunciation of his name, and by his mocking of the clergy when in middle age the hospital authorities ask him to recite his works for them. Nelligan is not permitted to enter adulthood, that is 'modernity'.

The problems with this approach lie in its assumption that there *is* one Québécois or indeed any 'culture' (any individual even) that is an accomplished and complete fact rather than being constantly in process or produced. Instead of this 'oneness', an alternative approach might stress the points of difference (gender, sexuality, class, race—witness the expansion of different ethnic groups in Quebec through immigration, or the fact that most Québécois have some Amerindian ancestry) rather than similarity that constitute 'us, the nation'. This would stress, rather than identity, plural identities which Stuart Hall describes as 'the names we give to the different ways we are positioned by, and position ourselves within, the narratives of the past'. Thus it is possible, like Fredric Jameson who argues that 'third-world texts' (in which, because of its peculiar history, we might include those of Quebec) invariably present themselves as national allegories, to conserve that critical notion, but, rather than seeking one-to-one homologies between text and social, historical, and political context, to stress the gaps, fissures, discontinuities, and untotalizing heterogeneities in the text. For the conventional view of allegory also assumes that the *text* itself is a site of complete, totalized meaning, of closure.

This point is illustrated in *Nelligan's* generic status as historical costume drama, for it is invariably riven with a textual instability, crucial in this national context, that is the gap between the *énonciation* of the moment in time of the narration (the relationship between narrator and implied reader/viewer) and the *énoncé* of the events being narrated. This national text is both an authenticating narrative of origins and an elaboration of national truths and values. The relationship of past to present is problematized: the post-Quiet Revolution spectator is invited to read the past as the same ('our' national poet) and as other (its oppressive society). Homi Bhabha has suggested this gap embraces a fundamental split, in 'the writing of the nation', between the 'pedagogical' and the 'performative'. The poet Nelligan thus bears the authority of the pregiven, of the already constituted *object*, of the 'authentic'; but on the other hand 'we' as *subjects* are interpellated by and *constructed in* the narrative performance to continue, repeat, and live 'the life of the nation'.

The family drama portrayed in the film, coupled with the investment in Nelligan as embodiment of the nation, raises questions concerning the eroticized nature of nationalism ('love of country'), and of the national/sexual body as an erotically troubled theatre of national anxieties. It could be argued that the fantasy of the nation is the most powerful form of family romance subsisting, when the feelings of early childhood towards seemingly omnipotent and ideal parents are nostalgically transferred to the nation in later life. In the case of Nelligan and the film *Nelligan*, the erection of the poet as idealized national genius is however counteracted by his failure and confinement. It is Nelligan as exemplum of 'nos fissures et nos fêlures collectives' (our collective cracks and breaks) that Jean Larose analyses in *Le Mythe de Nelligan* (1981), one of the major works of literary criticism in Quebec in the 1980s. For Nelligan 'fails', or is made to fail, because of the social context, in the classic Freudian Oedipal scenario, when the male child relinquishes the desire for the mother under the threat of castration and identifies with the father and the phallus. Instead, this adolescent, who in the film has no sexual liaison except for a hint of incest with the mother, while being a passive object of desire for others, is surrounded by bad fathers with whom identification is impossible, and is thus 'feminized': the attribute 'cissy' is given to him by the father. For Larose, this is determined by his status as a colonized subject, in which the poet/ nation is characterized by a Lack subsequently filled with a false plenitude associated with the Mother and with France (as site of the literature of Baudelaire, Verlaine, and Rimbaud to which Nelligan aspires—his quasi-Parnassian and Symbolist poems rarely feature Québécois references or landscapes—but also the lost origin, the abandoning parent of 1759). Quebec is caught in a dialectic (colonizer, then colonized, then . . .) which it seems unable to surpass into true independence. Instead of engaging in a progressive process of libidinal maturity, Nelligan indulges a fantasm, incorporating the lost object, exiling himself as a *poète maudit* (doomed poet) rather than facing his status as a colonized subject. For Larose, the dissimulation practised by the nineteenth-century clerical élites, and their investment in religion and agriculture, corresponds to Nelligan's flight into 'poetry', a position which allows him to appropriate the maternal phallus: 'le procédé par lequel l'objet le plus intime au sujet (on pourrait dire: le sexe maternel—c'est si simple . . .), se trouve tenu à (bonne) distance, puis aperçu et approprié depuis la position d'un "exil", et, à travers de fascinants voiles et d'impalpables voilures érectiles . . . poétisé, c'est-à-dire investi, muni, doté' (a process whereby the subject's most intimate object (let us say straight out the mother's genitals) is kept at an (acceptable) distance; then perceived and appropriated from the position of an 'exile', through veils so fascinating as to suggest intangible erectile shapes, it is granted a full flush of meaning, yet one which is limited to the poetic).

Whereas Larose's aversion to the inversions proposed by these phallic, falsely feminine structures, sabotaging with the notion of 'la présence pleine' (complete presence) the maturely Symbolic idea of a Quebec nation characterized by difference, leads him to some homophobic conclusions concerning the complicity therein of gay images, the film *Nelligan* invests homo-erotically in the young poet's physicality. This is the reverse of classic Hollywood scopophilic regimes, in which the woman is the object of the desiring male heterosexual gaze but also a castration threat that must be brought under control. The fact that this 'feminized' failure is simultaneously an object of desire in the enunciatory present of the film's projection and consumption further complicates the problematic relationship with the past. Instead of regarding the past as different and distant, the plausible reading emerges that Nelligan's victimization could be applied more generally to those marginalized, in particular, by Montreal's current deep economic recession a reading, among others, offered by Robert Favreau: 'I believe that among certain outcast social groups there are Émile Nelligans whose voices we shall never hear.' The past/present relationship might therefore be one of similarity rather than difference, an alternative or perhaps simultaneous reading to the one offered above.

## References

**Bhabha, Homi,** 'DissemiNation: Time, Narrative and the Margins of the Modern Nation', in Homi Bhabha (ed.), *Nation and Narration* (London: Routledge, 1990), 291–322.
**Hall, Stuart,** 'Cultural Identity and Cinematic Representation', *Framework*, 36 (1989), 68–81.
**Jameson, Fredric,** 'Third World Literature in the Era of Multinational Capitalism', *Social Text*, 15 (Fall 1986), 65–88.
**Larose, Jean,** *Le Mythe de Nelligan* (Montreal: Les Quinze, 1981).
**Lockerbie, Ian,** 'Le Cinéma québécois: une allégorie de la conscience collective', in Claude Chabot *et al.* (eds.), *Le Cinéma québécois des années 80* (Montreal: Cinémathèque québécoise/Musée du cinéma, 1989), 8–21.
**Petrowski, N.,** 'Robert Favreau: pour en finir avec Nelligan', *Le Devoir*, 28 (Sept. 1991), C1–2.
**Schwartzwald, Robert,** '(Homo)sexualité et problématique identitaire', in S. Simon *et al.* (eds.), *Fictions de l'identitaire au Québec* (Montréal: XYZ, 1991), 115–50.

## African Literature and Cinema in French after 1968

Much has been said about the disillusionments of the independence era. Every African country has been faced with increasing problems as the relationship between north and south has become ever more unfavourable to Africa. Life for ordinary people has become harder at the same time as the independence era has seen the consolidation of local bourgeoisies, generally based on import trade rather than production and thus closely linked to the political and economic power centres of the former colonizers. The wave of democratization movements since 1990 has emphasized the extent to which Africa has been run by undemocratic rulers, generally supported by the West. The drift from the countryside to the towns has accelerated, due to poverty in the countryside (frequently resulting from misconceived official agricultural policies) and the tendency of new rulers and their Western backers to privilege urban over rural development. However, this drift has not produced an urban working class of any proportions; indeed, the previously developing working class has tended to wither as industrial production has atrophied. It has, however, produced a new and very large sector of society: the under-employed or unemployed urban poor. While retaining many rural traditions and forms of identity, this sector has also been a powerful force in creating a supra-ethnic, semi-national identity with new linguistic forms (in Senegal the urban language has become a form of 'urban' Wolof mixed with French) and a common culture often very different from that dreamed of during the struggle for independence. The cultural expressions of this include such forms as football and popular music, both of which are rapidly becoming vehicles of identity at a number of levels: in many cases, the identity of youth set against a more traditional older generation; regional and national identity; democratic aspirations set against a caste-dominated society; and importantly, with the World Cup on the one hand and the recent Western commercial interest in African music on the other, football and music are coming to express identity on a continental scale.

### The language situation

The linguistic situation of most African countries is complex and politically delicate. Almost invariably, the frontiers laid down by the colonial authorities in the nineteenth century cut through ethnic boundaries, dividing peoples into different nationalities and grouping together peoples who may be culturally very different. In this situation, it is generally impossible to identify one African language which can become the official language of the nation. In Ivory Coast, for instance, thirteen main African languages are spoken. One (Baule) is the first language of 24 per cent of the population, and none of the others is spoken as a first language by more than 11 per cent; the smallest (Abe and Ebrie) are each spoken by 1 per cent of the population. Eighteen per cent of the population are identified as speaking 'other' languages. French, the only official language, is the mother tongue of less than 1 per cent of the people. In Cameroon there are six main African languages, but 73 per cent of the population speak 'other' languages.

However desirable it would be to replace the language of the colonizers by an African official language, the difficulties are immense: to privilege one language above others would have unacceptable political implications. Even in Senegal, where Wolof, the first language of 36 per cent of the population, is spoken as a second language by a further 45 per cent and is thus virtually a *lingua franca*, there still exist a further thirty-four languages apart from French. Six 'national languages' are recognized, but only French is the official language. In this situation, most post-independence governments have opted for the retention of the colonial language(s) as the official means of communication. The advantages are even-handedness in regard to all linguistic groups within the country, and access to the international community. The disadvantage is that, as the official language is also the language of education, cultural alienation is perpetuated and increased, and the gap between the educated and uneducated population widens. African languages are the losers in this. The battle for their use continues, as does work done to develop their written forms and to demonstrate their capability to express contemporary realities; but there is clearly a tension between the aims of national unity, international communication, and full cultural expression, and in the Western-oriented world of official African politics, considerations of international and national power tend to dominate.

The adoption of the colonial languages further unbalances the centre–periphery relationship between the ex-colonies and their ex-colonizers which exists on both a material and a cultural level. All African societies have a rich fund of oral culture and history which is largely unrecognized in written literature in European languages. The debate as to what is the proper language of African literature has sharpened over the past decade, but has generally been less fierce in 'francophone' than in 'anglophone' Africa, francophone writers tending towards a more pragmatic acceptance that, given the realities of contemporary Africa, access to publishers and to a wide readership lies through the medium of French. The French colonial policy of monolingualism of course also exerts an influence. On the other side are those who argue that a culture can only be fully expressed through its own language, and that no literature written in a European language can ever be considered fully African. This position has been adopted for instance by the Kenyan novelist Ngugi wa Thiongò, who now writes exclusively in Kikuyu, subsequently translating into English. Others such as the Nigerian Chinua Achebe have opted for developing in written form a distinctively African English. Similar approaches have been adopted in French: for instance by Ahmadou Kourouma (Ivory Coast), whose work is discussed below, but also by Henri Lopès (Congo), who in *Le Pleurer-rire* (Paris: Présence africaine, 1982) developed a style reflecting the patterns of demotic, township French, and Sony Labou Tansi (Congo), who uses a mixture of vocabulary and syntax to stretch the bounds of French.

Despite, or perhaps even because of, this debate, literature in French continues to flourish and develop new forms. However, the immense difficulty of getting published means that African literature is a largely unpublished literature, and it must be the case that large numbers of excellent manuscripts are unknown to the public. We have picked out two authors who exemplify different developments in African fiction.

*Literature*

Ousmane Sembène (Senegal), whose early work was discussed in the previous chapter, has continued to produce fiction although turning increasingly to the cinema. He has made a considerable contribution to the technique of the African novel, and it is no denigration of this to say that the overriding preoccupation of his fiction has been to express the class realities of modern-day Senegal.

Sembène's two main works of fiction since 1968 are *Xala* (Paris: Présence africaine, 1973) and *Le Dernier de l'empire* (Paris: L'Harmattan, 1981). In both of them, Sembène dissects the behaviour of the new bourgeoisie and the means by which it gains and retains power. *Xala* is better known in its film version (Sembène has several times produced a novel or story and a film at about the same time, neither being strictly speaking an adaptation of the other). *Xala* revolves around the problems of El Hadji Abdou Kader Beye, a former teacher and trade unionist under colonialism, now a wealthy importer/retailer. When he takes a third wife the same age as his daughter, his wealth and status seem assured; but he is cursed with impotence, and both the book and the film revolve largely around his search for a cure. While the film version of *Xala* is more richly symbolic, the novel version is more explicit in its examination of the central character's rootlessness— with his materialistic Westernized aspirations and his betrayal of African culture and solidarity and his lack of any real home, since he moves constantly between the houses of his wives. It also enters into more areas of Senegalese life. El Hadji's daughter Rama, for instance, is more fully delineated in the book, and through her fiancé Pathé, the psychologist, the scientific approach to impotence is valorized. Sembène thus indicates that it is possible to be fully African and at the same time modern and scientific. In order to be 'African' it is not necessary to *hold* all traditional beliefs; but it is important to recognize their existence. The alienation and hypocrisy of the bourgeois characters arise in part from their repression of their own traditional beliefs; at the same time, they have highly selective recourse to traditions such as polygamy, which shore up their artificial authority.

*Le Dernier de l'empire* deals with an imaginary *coup d'état* in which the President disappears, leaving his Cabinet to decide how to deal with the crisis. The majority of the action takes place within the Cabinet, covering, over a period of five days, the power struggle between contenders for the succession. There is a minute dissection of the corruption and alienation of the ruling group, and Sembène casts a particularly cold eye on the way in which the real decisions are made in the Élysée, often on information not yet available in Dakar. *Le Dernier de l'empire* is widely regarded as a *roman à clef*; it is certainly a courageous attack on neocolonial government, not only in Senegal, and has great interest for any student of the political novel.

In this period Sembène has also published two novellas in a joint volume: *Niiwam* and *Taaw* (Paris: Présence africaine, 1987), of which *Taaw* appeared as a film in 1970). Both deal with the everyday reality of life for the poor of Dakar. In *Niiwam* a man from the country travels across Dakar by bus to take the corpse of his baby to the cemetery: the work is remarkable for its use of psychological and geographical space. *Taaw* centres on a young unemployed man, his search for work, and his attempts to defend his mother against the brutality of his father.

Ahmadou Kourouma's two novels, *Les Soleils des indépendances* (Paris: Seuil, 1970) and *Monnè, outrages et défis* (Paris: Seuil, 1990), have both contributed to the development of a non-metropolitan French. Both novels are in large part an exploration of the difficult coexistence of Malinke culture with colonialism and post-independence society. *Les Soleils des indépendances* centres on Fama (Prince) Doumbouya, an unemployed inhabitant of Abidjan. Profoundly conscious of his position as the heir to a once-glorious empire, Fama deeply resents his loss of social prestige and power. His frustrations are centred in resentment of a society he regards as bastardized, and of his hard-working wife Salimata, whom he believes to be sterile. Symbolically, as it turns out, it is Fama himself who is sterile. His return to his village reveals the extent of the fall from glory: the seat of his kingdom now consists of a few decrepit huts inhabited by his elderly and infirm subjects. At the same time, Fama displays great courage (or is it obstinacy?) in defence of his values. He is thrown into prison for a more or less accidental political crime and, after his release, dies defending his right to sovereignty.

At every point, this work is ambiguous and elusive: is Fama's courage merely an obstinate nostalgia for what is dead and gone, an impotence to create anything for the future? Some critics have found the book reactionary rather than merely confusing. However, Kourouma's undoubted contribution lies in the fact that, in trying to get inside his character's head, he has produced a form of *style indirect libre* of great originality and complexity which constitutes a very distinctive contribution to the technique of the novel, and enables him both to express and to ironize about Fama's point of view. Along with this he has developed a new and distinctive form of French, embracing images, proverbs, vocabulary, and grammatical structures drawn from Malinke and from African French ('marcher un voyage' (walk a journey), 'marier une épouse (marry a wife), etc.). This of course helps Kourouma in his stated aim of expressing Fama from the inside, but it does much more, and it distinguishes the African novel in French, stylistically, from the French novel as no previous work had managed to do. The cultural universe conveyed by Kourouma may in theory be the same as that conveyed by other Malinke authors such as Camara Laye and Cheikh Hamidou Kane: but the richness with which it is evoked is quite new.

In *Monnè, outrages et défis* the central character is again a Malinke ruler: Djigui, who lives to be well over 100, and whose reign covers the period from the arrival of the French as colonizers to the coming of independence. The richness of tone which Kourouma had already found in *Les Soleils* is increased here by the use of multiple voices. *Monnè* traces the relationship between Djigui's kingdom and the colonial power. Djigui allows himself, step by step, to be ensnared in collaboration with the French, only realizing much later how dearly his people have paid in starvation, forced labour, and military conscription for their king's retention of power. The novel ends with an uncompromising denunciation of neo-colonial power and the rhetoric with which it is propped up, but also with an appreciation of the complexities of African identity and of the ethical choices involved in that history on which so many modern dictators call to legitimize their power.

*Les Soleils* had already condemned neo-colonial power, and *Monnè* does so even more clearly. Kourouma's weakness is perhaps in not offering any vision for the future. However, through his thematic and linguistic innovations, he joins with those African writers and cinematographers who are now going beyond the condemnation of colonialism and the disillusions of independence to a re-examination of pre-colonial African society. Like Ousmane Sembène and Ibrahima Ly, one of Kourouma's achievements is to bring to the surface some of the fault-lines of caste and ethnicity which, while they may have given pre-colonial societies an internal cohesion, made it difficult for Africa to resist colonial incursion, and contribute to the difficulties of building a united and forward-looking society today.

*Cinema*

Since 1968 African cinema in French has continued to be beset by problems of finance, marketing, and distribution: in other words, the Western monopoly of the market. Since independence a few countries have managed, with great difficulty, to achieve a degree of independence for their cinemas, but in general the networks still tend to be dominated by cheap European and American products. The result is that it is often easier to see African films in Paris than in Africa, and to an extent African directors have to cater for European critical reactions as well as African audiences.

African film-directors face enormous obstacles. Lack of finance forces them into international co-productions; film has to be imported and subsequently processed abroad; and they have great difficulty in getting their films shown at home.

Film production in francophone Africa has nevertheless been a notable success story. A great spur to this success has been FESPACO: the biennial film festival in Ouagadougou, capital of Burkina Faso, set up in 1969 and alternating with the Carthage Festival in Tunisia. FESPACO has become a gathering-point for film-makers from 'francophone' Africa, and the enthusiasm of Burkinabè audiences is a testimony to the potential of African cinema.

At first glance, film would seem to be an ideal cultural medium for Africa: it is immensely popular, it is accessible to a non-literate audience, it is capable of translating oral forms of culture, and the language problem can be overcome by dubbing or subtitling. In fact things are not so easy: there are few cinemas outside the big cities, subtitling is no help to the non-literate, and both it and dubbing are expensive, particularly when a number of different languages are needed. The very popularity of the cinema makes it a potentially subversive medium, and African film-makers have frequently suffered from cuts (for instance in the case of Ousmane Sembène's *Xala*) and outright censorship. This latter seems to be relatively rare, though there is little information on it: a famous case is that of Sembène's *Ceddo* (1977), which depicts the often violent spread of Islam in Senegal in the eighteenth and nineteenth centuries. The subject was clearly delicate in a mainly Muslim country, but the film was banned in Senegal ostensibly because of a dispute about the spelling of the title. Most effectively, simple lack of support and finance pushes directors towards self-censorship. Disapproval can also emanate from non-African governments: Med Hondo's *Sarraounia* (see below) and Ousmane Sembène's *Camp de Thiaroye* have had great difficulty in obtaining showings in France.

In film as in literature, Ousmane Sembène remains a dominant figure. He has always been viewed with unease by the authorities, and has been a fearless critic of all forms of exploitation, as his themes indicate. *Le Mandat* (1968) deals with poverty in Dakar (as does *Taaw*, 1970) and with bureaucracy and corruption;

*Emitaï* (1971) recounts a village's struggle against colonial domination; *Xala* (1974) deals with the corruption and impotence of the African capitalist class; *Ceddo* (1977) with the violent imposition of Islam; *Camp de Thiaroye* (1988) with the French massacre of African troops returning to Dakar in 1944; and *Guelwaar* (1992) with the indignity of dependence on foreign aid.

In a number of his films, Sembène has been concerned to rescue episodes overlooked or distorted by the 'official', Eurocentric version of African history. His contribution also extends to a rescuing and revalorizing of African culture. In *Ceddo*, for instance, he throws into relief a culture which existed before the arrival of Islam. He is frequently concerned not only to revalorize African culture but also to interrogate the weaknesses which made it unable to resist external domination, seeking to establish an African identity capable of strengthening the people in contrast to the factitious identity portrayed in *Xala*. This involves developing a distinctively African, or Senegalese, film style, using movement, clothing, diction, shot (often long shot rather than close-up, and generally avoiding shot/reverse shot close-up), speed (often slower than in Western films), and sound (Sembène like some other African directors tends to eschew background music, preferring 'the cinema of silence' to the excessive musical accompaniment of Western films). He also generally does not use professional actors, preferring the naturalness and spontaneity of amateurs, and particularly avoiding the star system. As far as verbal language is concerned, he has moved from the non-synchronized French interior monologue accompanying *Borom Sarret* (1963) and *La Noire de . . .* (1966) to a more naturalistic mixture of languages with subtitles. A notable use of French occurs in *Camp de Thiaroye*, in which soldiers from different parts of West Africa communicate with each other in pidgin French: as Mantha Diawara has said, Sembène here 'takes the French language away from the élite and gives it to the people'.

Other directors have explored and extended this range. Med Hondo (Mauritania) has produced a number of films: the latest, *Sarraounia* (1986), the first African film in Cinemascope, is the story of a nineteenth-century queen leading her army against the French invasion. Drawing together different languages and cultures, Hondo achieves an epic film which not only illuminates African resistance to brutal conquest, but also rescues the history of African women. Souleymane Cissé (Mali), after a number of directly political and social films (*Cinq jours d'une vie*, 1972; *Den Muso*, 1975; *Finyé*, 1982; etc.), broke new ground in *Yeelen* (light) (1987), an exploration of pre-colonial Bambara culture and religion which at the same time examines generation conflicts, since it concerns the attempts of a father to prevent his son from gaining access to mystic knowledge. Visually exceptionally beautiful, the film is also accepting of the supernatural without in any way detracting from the importance of human beings. Courage and wisdom are needed in order to defeat the father's possessiveness and offer the possibility of progress to later generations.

Idrissa Ouedraogo (Burkina Faso), in his films about village life, avoids overtly political themes, while still delivering powerful social messages. The central plot of *Yaaba* (the grandmother) (1989) concerns the friendship between two children and an outcast old woman regarded as a witch. Again, this is an exceptionally beautiful film, every frame carefully composed. *Yaaba* has been criticized for being too bland and apolitical. While it is true that Ouedraogo does not address the problems of neo-colonialism, his film does attack the cruel ostracism of those labelled 'witches', and shows how the closeness of village life depends on a claustrophobic intolerance of difference. Similarly *Yam Daabo* (the choice) (1986) has been criticized for constructing the city and modernization as evil, while nature is benevolent. Nevertheless, its story of two families moving away from the Sahel to farm in a more fertile area contains a strong critique of those still waiting, with their arms crossed, for the aid lorry to arrive. These are perhaps 'civic' rather than directly political messages, but they address specifically African problems. *Tilaï* (the law) (1990) deals starkly with the story of a young man returning after two years away from the village (implicity, in the city) to find that his fiancée is now his aged father's second wife. The film opens up the contradictions between the social cohesion achieved by traditional values (involving much suffering, especially for women), and the younger generation's disruptive claim to fulfilment; the tragic ending implies no moral judgement, certainly not a condemnation of the younger man.

# Suggestions for Further Reading

### The social and historical background

Several recent works in English offer useful overviews of the social and political history of France since 1968, including Christopher Flockton and Eleanore Kofman, *France* (London: Paul Chapman, 1989), Jill Forbes and Nick Hewlett, *Contemporary France: Essays and Texts on Politics, Economics and Society* (London: Longman, 1994), J. Hollifield and G. Ross (eds.), *Searching for the New France* (London: Routledge, 1991), and George Ross (ed.), *The Mitterrand Experiment: Continuity and Change in Modern France* (London: Polity Press, 1987). The latter two devote space to cultural policy and the role of intellectuals in public life as does Sonia Mazey and Michael Newman, (eds.), *Mitterrand's France* (Brighton: Croom Helm, 1987). For May 1968 the best analysis in English is Keith Reader, *The May 1968 Events in France* (London: Macmillan, 1993) and in French Hervé Hamon and Patrick Rotman, *Génération*, 2 vols. (Paris: Seuil, 1987–8) provides fascinating interviews with many of the protagonists. The most accessible short introduction to contemporary France in French is Dominique Borne, *Histoire de la société française depuis 1945* (Paris: Armand Colin, 1990) while the successive editions of *L'État de la France* (Paris: La Découverte) contain many short essays relevant to cultural studies.

### Literature in French after 1968

One of the best ways to gain ideas about which new authors to read or which new types of writing to explore is to consult one of the major surveys of contemporary French literature. The following are highly recommended: Claude Bonnefoy, *Panorama de la littérature moderne* (Paris: Belfond, 1980), Jacques Brenner, *Histoire de la littérature française de 1940 à nos jours* (Paris: Fayard, 1978), *Tableau de la vie littéraire en France d'avant-guerre à nos jours* (Paris: Luneau Ascot éditeurs, 1982), and *Mon histoire de la littérature française contemporaine* (Paris: Grasset, 1987). All these 'histories' are eminently readable and often contain individualistic views and trenchant opinions. A more obviously pedagogical guide is Bruno Vercier and Jacques Lecarme, *La Littérature en France depuis 1968* (Paris: Bordas, 1982), while Denis Hollier (ed.), *A New History of French Literature* (Cambridge, Mass.: Harvard University Press, 1989) offers a survey in the form of punchy and idiosyncratic essays by a variety of critics each centred on a particular date. Of the many collections of interviews with writers the most useful are Jean-Louis Ézine, *Les Écrivains sur la sellette* (Paris: Seuil, 1981) and Elizabeth Fallaize, *French Women's Writing: Recent Fiction* (London: Macmillan, 1993). Priscilla Parkhurst Clark's *Literary France* (Berkeley and Los Angeles:

University of California Press, 1987) is a useful study of the continuing importance of literature in French culture.

For insights into the relationship between critical theory and writing practice see Michael Worton and Judith Still (eds.), *Intertextuality: Theories and Practices* (Manchester: Manchester University Press, 1993) and Maurice Biriotti and Nicola Miller (eds.), *What is an Author?* (Manchester: Manchester University Press, 1993). The starting-point for serious thinking on orientalism is the provocative work of Edward Said, especially *Orientalism: Western Conceptions of the Orient* (London: Penguin Books, 1978) and *Culture and Imperialism* (London: Chatto & Windus, 1993). For an understanding of the complex workings of autobiography see Philippe Lejeune's *Le Pacte autobiographique* (Paris: Seuil, 1975) and *Je est un autre: l'autobiographie, de la littérature aux médias* (Paris: Seuil, 1980) as well as Michael Sheringham's excellent *French Autobiography: Devices and Desires: From Rousseau to Perec* (London: Oxford University Press, 1993).

As far as 'francophone' literature is concerned D. Blair, *African Literature in French* (Cambridge: Cambridge University Press, 1976) and Hans M. Zell, Carol Bundy, and Virginia Coulon, *A New Reader's Guide to African Literature* (2nd edn.), (London: Heinemann, 1983), Belinda Jack, *Francophone Literatures: An Introduction* (London: Oxford University Press, 1995) can all be recommended as useful surveys, while more specialist studies are to be found in the two-volume special issue of *Yale French Studies*, 82 (1993) devoted to 'Post/Colonial Conditions'. The best introduction to problems of literature and identity in French-speaking Canada is S. Simon *et al.* (eds.), *Fictions de l'identité au Québec* (Montreal: XYZ, 1991) and to Beur literature Alec Hargreaves, *Voices from the North African Community in France: Immigration and Identity in Beur Fiction* (Oxford: Berg, 1991), while nationalism and literature is reconsidered in Homi Bhabha (ed.), *Nation and Narration* (London: Routledge, 1990).

## French thought since 1968

The specialist literature on post-1968 French thought is voluminous and much of it is extremely difficult to read without extensive knowledge of the subject. The following works in English can all, however, be recommended as useful and accessible introductions to what are often very complex and difficult subjects. Malcolm Bowie, *Lacan* (London: Fontana, 1991) and *Psychoanalysis and the Future of Theory* (Oxford, Blackwell, 1993), Jonathan Culler, *Barthes* (London: Fontana, 1983) and *On Deconstruction* (London: Routledge, 1983), Peter Dews, *Logics of Disintegration* (London: Verso, 1987), Claire Duchen, *Feminism in France: From May 68 to Mitterrand* (London: Routledge, 1986), Mike Gane, *Baudrillard's Bestiary: Baudrillard and Culture* (London: Routledge, 1991), Sean Hand (ed.), *The Lévinas Reader* (Oxford: Blackwell, 1989), Fredric Jameson, *Postmodernism or, The Cultural Logic of Late Capitalism* (London: Verso, 1991), Michael Kelly, *Modern French Marxism* (Oxford: Blackwell, 1983), David Macey, *The Lives of Michel Foucault* (London: Hutchinson, 1993), Elaine Marks and Isabelle de Courtivron (eds.), *New French Feminisms* (Brighton: Harvester, 1983), Toril Moi, *French Feminist Thought* (Oxford, Blackwell, 1987) and *The Kristeva Reader* (Oxford, Blackwell, 1986), Christopher Norris, *Derrida* (London: Fontana, 1987), Keith Reader, *Intellectuals and the Left in France since 1968* (London: Macmillan, 1987), Morag Shiach, *Hélène Cixous: A Politics of Writing* (London: Routledge, 1991), Margaret Whitford (ed.), *The Irigaray Reader* (Oxford: Blackwell, 1991).

## Popular culture and cultural politics

The best overview of cultural policy in France is Pascal Ory, *L'Aventure culturelle française* (Paris: Flammarion, 1989) and the most critical of state intervention in cultural matters is Marc Fumaroli, *L'État culturel* (Paris: Éditions de Fallois, 1991). These can be complemented by the wealth of information and statistics in Augustin Girard, *Les Pratiques culturelles des Français* (Paris: La Documentation française, 1990) and by essays on specific aspects of culture and leisure habits in *L'État de la France*, various editions (Paris: La Découverte). Post-1968 French theatre is well discussed in David Bradby, *Modern French Drama 1945–1990* (2nd edn. Cambridge: Cambridge University Press, 1991), while a useful introduction to alternative theatre is Pierre Merle, *Le Café-théâtre* (Paris: Presses universitaires de France, 1985). There is no good overview of popular culture in France. However the recent history of television is discussed in John Flower (ed.), *France Today* (7th edn. London: Hodder 1993) and in Jill Forbes, 'Television in France', in Geoffrey Nowell-Smith (ed.), *Broadcasting in Europe* (London: BFI, 1989). Several recent books on cinema provide good introductions, the best of which is Susan Hayward, *French National Cinema* (London: Routledge, 1994). For post-1968 cinema Jill Forbes, *The Cinema in France after the New Wave* (London: Macmillan, 1992) is an overview of directors and genres while Susan Hayward and Ginette Vincendeau (eds.), *French Film: Texts and Contexts* (London: Routledge, 1990) has essays on individual films of the post-1968 period. In French, René Prédal, *Le Cinéma français depuis 1945* (Paris: Nathan, 1991) is highly recommended as an introduction, with useful filmographies and bibliographies. For francophone cinemas F. Pfaff, *The Cinema of Ousmane Sembène: A Pioneer of African Cinema* (London: Greenwood Press, 1984) and M. Diawara, *African Cinema: Politics and Culture* (Bloomington, Ind.: Indiana University Press, 1992) are both helpful, as is the guide published by the Museum of the Moving Image, *After Empire: The African Cinema* (London: MOMI, 1991), while French Canadian cinema is best discussed in C. Chabot *et al.* (eds.), *Le Cinéma québécois des années 80* (Montreal: Cinémathèque québécoise/Musée du cinéma, 1989).

## Language questions

Good general accounts of modern French which are intended for readers with some knowledge of the language but not necessarily specialist knowledge of French linguistics are: Denis Ager, *Sociolinguistics and Contemporary French* (Cambridge: Cambridge University Press, 1990), R. A. Lodge, *French: From Dialect to Standard* (London: Routledge, 1993), Malcolm Offord, *Varieties of French* (London: Macmillan, 1990), and Henriette Walter, *Le Français dans tous les sens* (Paris: Robert Laffont, 1988). On spelling, A. Goosse, *La Nouvelle Orthographe* (Paris: Duculot, 1991) is a detailed but readable account of the proposed reform while J. Leconte and P. Cibois, *Que vive l'orthografe!* (Paris: Seuil, 1989) is a highly polemical plea for change. Bernard Pivot, *Le Livre de l'orthographe* (Paris: Hatier, 1989), by the genial host of the Championnat national d'orthographe, includes an outline of various earlier spelling reform projects and a survey of pro- and anti- views, as well as the texts of Championship dictations. The results of the work of the terminology commissions are embodied in the *Dictionnaires des termes officiels* published from time to time by the *Journal officiel de la République française*. The latest edition appeared in 1991. *Guide des mots nouveaux* (Paris: Nathan, 1985) may also be consulted. As regards language legislation Philippe de Saint-Robert, *Lettre ouverte à ceux qui perdent leur français* (Paris: Albin Michel, 1986) is the personal testimony of an official involved in attempts to enforce the 1975 *loi Bas-Auriol*. For

Quebec, see J.-C. Corbeil, *L'Aménagement linguistique au Québec* (Montreal: Guérin, 1980) and Marc V. Levine, *The Reconquest of Montreal: Language Policy and Social Change in a Bilingual City* (Montreal: Temple University Press, 1990), while for French in Africa, J.-P. Lapierre, *Le Pouvoir politique des langues* (Paris: Presses universitaires de France, 1988) provides a stimulating discussion.

# Conclusion:
# French Cultural Studies
# in the Future

RUNNING through the narrative of this book is a perception that, over a century and a quarter, France has invested its national and social identities in its culture. Culture is the visible territory on which the struggle continues, to define and defend a certain idea of France. But that struggle is also about more than images and representations. At stake is the power to shape the development of the country and its people, and to assert their distinctive position in Europe and on the global stage.

The beginning of the Third Republic saw two intimately linked events of great significance, the introduction of universal male suffrage and of compulsory primary education. In response to the humiliating military defeat inflicted by Prussia in 1870, the new Republic which enacted these measures embarked on a project of moral and ideological reconstruction, making education and suffrage the centre-piece of its urgent attempt to forge the nation or to forge it anew. In the primary schools, the *instituteurs* and *institutrices* received a mission to inculcate adherence to the Republic among their charges by teaching them the language, the geography, and the history of their country. In the university, scholars undertook the gigantic task of describing and classifying the intellectual heritage of the nation, the fruit of which is to be found in works such as Gustave Lanson's *Histoire de la littérature française* (1895) and Ferdinand Brunot's *Histoire de la langue française*, the first of whose many volumes appeared in 1905.

Just as traditional instruction in the languages and literatures of ancient civilizations had been the foundation of Enlightenment universalism, and had inspired the revolutionaries of 1789, so the study of French, which superseded all the other languages, dialects, and *patois* which were still widely spoken in France in the latter part of the nineteenth century, underpinned Republicanism. Brunot was in no doubt of the link between language and politics when he described the dialects and *patois* as 'dissidents', and attributed the imposition of French to the will of the people, to a spontaneous and almost mystical desire 'that came from the guts of the revolutionary nation' and was designed to incorporate and integrate the people by giving them a sense of their common national identity.

In 1940 another invasion and defeat of France by Germany was again seen as an intellectual as well as a military débâcle, but it provoked a quite different response which attempted to discredit the republican idea of culture. The Vichy government sought moral regeneration in a different kind of populism and supposedly more authentic cultural tradition. Its conception of culture was not based on great works of literature but on objects, artefacts, and practices to be found among rural communities, on folk customs, festivals, and traditional occupations. Between 1940 and 1944 all these formed the basis for a new educational and cultural policy which derived its inspiration from popular ethnology and drew on a different archive in the Musée des arts et traditions populaires.

The Vichy government's view of culture was backward-looking, nostalgic, and thoroughly exclusive; it attempted to replace the social formations of democracy by a hierarchically ordered society which rejected as antipathetic what it defined as foreign. But its substitution of one cultural tradition for another is an interesting example of the relativism which was to gain ascendancy after the Second World War. In showing that the narrative of the nation is only one of many possible ways of classifying cultural objects and practices, and that different objects may be significant at different times and for different reasons, the Vichy experience is particularly fascinating for French cultural studies. It throws into sharp relief the interdisciplinary endeavour which seeks to understand and interpret signifying practices over a spectrum which might range from poetry at one extreme to agricultural implements at the other.

The Vichy episode is also interesting because its attempt to turn the clock back was an initial, and futile, response to the breakup of traditional culture that became a characteristic feature of all Western countries after 1945. For it is this common process of social and economic change that gave birth to the cultural studies which attempt to 'register', in Stuart Hall's words, 'the impact of new forms of affluence and consumer society'. The particular local variety to be found in France was contained in the challenge posed by the processes of modernization to the conception of national culture elaborated after 1870 and the ways in which modernization brought about reinterpretations and reorderings of the past. This is the agenda of French cultural studies outlined in this book. Modernization has taken many forms, but four processes have been of particular concern to us here. They concern technological advance, international realignments, shifting sociocultural patterns, and the emergence of globalization. Each of them has been a tangible pressure for change in French cultural development.

The first process is technological change. The growth of literacy and the spread of education in the nineteenth century were accompanied by a series of technological revolutions which made possible cheap editions of books and the launch of mass circulation newspapers. The changes in the methods of reproducing and distributing printed material, so powerfully evoked in Balzac's novel *Illusions perdues* (1837), accelerated as the century drew to a close and were joined by new techniques for reproducing and disseminating images and sounds, through photography, the gramophone, and the cinema. These were followed in the twentieth century by radio, television, the electronic reproduction of sounds, images, and texts, and the invention of ever more powerful means of manipulating and communicating them. All these new technologies changed not just the form of traditional arts like writing, painting, and composing music, but their content, meaning, and reception too. Realism and originality, the twin pillars of nineteenth-century aesthetics, were shaken by the rise of the electric media to such a degree that, as the German critic Walter Benjamin pointed out in his much-quoted essay 'The Work of Art in the Age of Mechanical Reproduction' (1936), the definition of an 'authentic' work of art and the value traditionally attached to it become problematical when it is no longer possible to identify a single 'original'. The electronic revolution of the last thirty years has compounded the change. Montage and sound engineering have altered the process of composition, while the repetition, borrowing, and recycling made possible by technology have become an aesthetic principle, not just in the electronic media but in printed texts as well, a fundamental element of postmodernism for which critics have coined the term 'intertextuality'. In this way, the cultural forms which were codified in the nineteenth century have themselves been transformed by the mass reading and viewing public that they were instrumental in creating, and by the technologies which enable this mass public to apprehend them.

The second process is the post-war realignment of France in the world. Like Britain, France was an imperial power at the start of the Second World War, able to impose its language and culture, its educational and administrative systems on large areas of the globe in the name of its 'mission civilisatrice'. The pretension to cultural universalism was predicated on a geopolitical reality, albeit one that was already in difficulties before 1940. After 1945, with a much reduced military capacity and an economy in ruins, France embarked on a period of rapid decolonization culminating in 1962 in the independence of Algeria. Led by Claude Lévi-Strauss, anthropologists, who as a profession had often been apologists for the 'mission civilisatrice', now began to emphasize the homologies between so-called developed and primitive societies, and to discover common foundations for human activity wherever it occurred. Over time, therefore, decolonization eroded a system of values which placed the culture of metropolitan France at the pinnacle of a hierarchy and, instead, forced a recognition of the plurality and diversity of varieties of French and of French-speaking cultures in those large areas of the world where French remains an important language. An association of francophone countries was substituted for the earlier colonial system but could not disguise the fact that the political borders of France and those of French-speaking parts of the world were no longer the almost perfect match that they had previously been. Linguistic and cultural unity could hardly be maintained in the face of such political divergence. Different varieties of French and different literatures in French became as potentially significant as the French of mainland France which itself ceased to be a 'universal' language and became, like English in England, just another dialect.

The third process of modernization is the social transformation of the post-war period. If decolonization posed the question 'what is France?', post-war social change posed the question 'who is French?' The democratic reforms of the early Third Republic were intended to metamorphose, in Eugen Weber's celebrated formula, 'peasants into Frenchmen', and, together with compulsory military service and an improved communications infrastructure, were held to have forged the national community. But the new anthropology opened up the possibility that French society itself might be studied as though from outside, using the tools and gaze of the ethnographer to satisfy curiosity about the social formation. This revealed a heterogeneity which was astonishing because ideologically inadmissible. In the analyses of Pierre Bourdieu and his school, society is perceived not as bound together by culture but as divided and separated by it. Educational achievement is described in terms of the acquisition of 'cultural capital', that is, the ability to master the language, concepts, opinions, and tastes of an educational élite, and the education system is seen neither as a benign agent of enlightenment, nor an instrument of equality, but as a battlefield on which 'agents' compete for domination by means of symbolic (that is, cultural) goods. The social debates of the 1980s about the problems of immigration and poverty turned on the issue of whether cultural knowledge (such as command of the language) is essential in defining whether an individual is French. In this way they underlined Bourdieu's conception of a society divided by culture, one in which the peasants and workers have undoubtedly been subsumed into the national community, but where they have been succeeded in their status as 'exclus' by other groups whose marginality is frequently based on race or ethnicity. The Beurs are now one of several groups of French nationals who define themselves by their cultural difference.

The final process is that of internationalization and more recently globalization. What are often referred to as the 'points of reference' or the 'norms' of French culture are felt to have slipped away in the period after 1945, to be replaced, essentially, by those inspired by or deriving from America. The American model, however defined, is never unambiguously condemned. The discovery of American painting, music, and architecture after the Second World War, and the example of the American cinema, proved an extraordinary stimulus to French artists, while powerful groups of individuals, particularly among the new managerial classes whose house journal was L'Express and whose bible Jean-Jacques Servan-Schreiber's Le Défi américain, consciously endeavoured to emulate American business methods. By contrast, a strong current of thinking among intellectuals perceived American values as inappropriate at best and illegitimate at worst. French scholars are often mystified and angry when French culture is recodified by their American counterparts, as it is in Denis Hollier's *A New History of French Literature*, to produce a hierarchy of values in conformity with 'modern [American] concerns', but which omits what Antoine Compagnon affirms is the 'quintessential France—provincial, petit bourgeois, Catholic, reactionary, anti-Semitic'.

American influence on social and artistic élites in France may be more or less well accepted, but when the people appear to have been won over to 'coca-cola culture' the process is described as one of dispossession or alienation. A powerful current of writing in cultural studies (of which Bourdieu's work is a version) sees education as a process which instead of empowering the people alienates the birthright of the working class, analogous to the way capitalism alienates their labour. This is the message of Richard Hoggart's *The Uses of Literacy* or Claude Duneton's *Je suis comme une truie qui doute*. But American influence is most acutely felt and acutely resented because, as Claude Hagège points out in *Le Français et les siècles*, it is felt to rob the people of their most precious possession which is their language. American culture is felt to infiltrate France by all kinds of underhand means: in the 1950s, American cinema was often referred to as a 'Trojan horse'. Euro-Disney, as we have seen, was labelled a 'cultural Chernobyl'. If, as Brunot suggests, language change and the will of the people traditionally go hand in hand, then the American-speaking media are considered to alienate in every sense the people from their natural and spontaneous inventiveness, rendering them the passive creatures of a foreign power.

An introduction to French cultural studies can do no more than begin to mark out what is a vast territory for new investigations. These will certainly be interdisciplinary, drawing on the strong traditions of language and literary studies and their methodological insights, but transgressing their traditional boundaries of genre and medium in order to make connections with other established cultural forms, and to take account of the new cultural technologies invented over the last hundred years and of the cultural forms they in turn have created. These studies will undoubtedly be historical too, for the identification of what has been called a 'usable past' is a matter of strong concern to all kinds of social groups who, in the modern world, recognize one another across national or linguistic boundaries, groups based on ethnicity and gender as well as or instead of class, but also on distinctions such as generation and sexuality. The identification, intellectual exploitation, and, perhaps, creation of new archives is thus central to the enterprise of French cultural studies. Discouraged by the fact that they may be commercially run and are often housed away from the major repositories of printed material, scholars have barely begun to scratch the surface of archives of sounds and images, still less to explore the possibilities of comparative analyses of material in different media held in alternative archives. And they will call on information technology, which increasingly opens up new possibilities for research through the organization of data in ways which do not necessarily conform to the taxonomies of author and subject familiar from the great national libraries and record offices. As the volume of material available in electronic form increases exponentially through CD-ROM, on-line databases, the Internet, and other media, the 'virtual archive' thus composed will undoubtedly invite practical and theoretical innovations in the ways it is studied.

The diversity of French culture makes any introduction to it a matter of choice and selection. The present study is of course informed by the tastes, preferences, and preoccupations of its authors, yet its contents are not arbitrary. The way French—or any other—culture is conceived and interpreted is conditioned to a great extent by previous attempts to classify and synthesize, particularly in schools and universities, and depends on the work of analysing and interpreting cultural objects in a way that makes them seem meaningful, that brings out their function as signifying practices. In this way cultural studies is not just the study of the constructed rather than the given world, but also of the ways in which, over time, cultural objects and the relations between them have come to seem significant, how they have reflected or responded to social and scientific change, and how they become ideologically eloquent. The version of French culture outlined here embodies what seems most pertinent and urgent today, but a vast territory remains to be explored so as to elucidate the aesthetic, social, and ethical concerns which are broached in the pages of this book.

## References

Benjamin, Walter, 'The Work of Art in the Age of Mechanical Reproduction', in *Illuminations* (London: Cape, 1970), 219–54.
Bourdieu, Pierre, *La Distinction* (Paris: Minuit, 1979).
—— *Les Héritiers* (Paris: Minuit, 1966).
—— *La Reproduction* (Paris: Minuit, 1970).
Brunot, Ferdinand, *Histoire de la langue française* (1905– ), 9 vols. (Paris: Armand Colin, 1966).
Compagnon, Antoine, 'The Diminishing Canon of French Literature', *Stanford Review*, 15/1–2 (1991), 103–15.
Duneton, Claude, *Je suis comme une truie qui doute* (Paris: Seuil, 1979).
Faure, Christian, *Le Projet culturel de Vichy* (Lyons: Presses universitaires de Lyon, 1989).
Hagège, Claude, *Le Français et les siècles* (Paris: Odile Jacob, 1987).
Hall, Stuart, 'The Emergence of Cultural Studies and the Crisis of the Humanities', *October*, 53 (Summer 1990), 11–23.
Hoggart, Richard, *The Uses of Literacy* (London: Chatto & Windus, 1957).
Hollier, Denis, 'On Writing Literary History', in *A New History of French Literature* (Cambridge, Mass.: Harvard University Press, 1989), pp. xxi–xxv.
Lanson, Gustave, *Histoire de la littérature française* (Paris: Hachette, 1895).
Servan-Schreiber, Jean-Jacques, *Le Défi américain* (Paris: Denoël, 1967).
Weber, Eugen, *Peasants into Frenchmen* (London: Chatto & Windus, 1979).
Worton, Michael, and Still, Judith, (eds.), *Intertextuality: Theories and Practices* (Manchester: Manchester University Press, 1990).

# Chronology 1870–1994

| Political and economic | Cultural and social |
|---|---|
| **1870** | |
| French defeated at Sedan | |
| Proclamation of the Third Republic | |
| Siege of Paris (19 Sept.–28 Jan.) | |
| **1871** | |
| Paris Commune (Feb.–May) | Arthur Rimbaud *Le Bateau ivre* |
| *La Semaine sanglante* (21–8 May)—end of Commune | Ernest Renan *La Réforme intellectuelle et morale* |
| **1872** | |
| École des sciences politiques founded | Jean Charcot *Leçons sur les maladies du système nerveux* |
| | Edgar Degas *Le Foyer de la danse* |
| **1873** | |
| Edme-Patrice de Mac Mahon elected President | Arthur Rimbaud *Une saison en enfer* |
| | Jules Verne *Le Tour du monde en quatre-vingts jours* |
| | Edme-Patrice de Mac Mahon *L'Ordre moral* |
| | Remington typewriter launched |
| | Start of *Concerts Colonne* |
| **1874** | |
| | First Impressionist exhibition, the *Salon des refusés*, in studio of Félix Tournachon called Nadar |
| | Claude Monet *Impression, soleil levant* |
| **1875** | |
| | Creation of Havas news agency |
| | Edmond Schuré *Le Drame musical* |
| | First issue of *La République des lettres* |
| | Opening of Paris Opera at the Palais Garnier |
| **1876** | |
| Phylloxera destroys French vineyards | Alexander Graham Bell invents the telephone |
| | Stéphane Mallarmé *L'Après-midi d'un faune* |
| | Auguste Renoir *Le Moulin de la galette* |

Opening of Richard Wagner's theatre in
Bayreuth
Launch of *Le Petit Parisien* newspaper

**1877**

Thomas Edison invents phonograph
Emil Berliner invents gramophone
Émile Zola *L'Assommoir*

**1878**
Franco-British condominium over Egypt
*Plan Freycinet* investment programme in
railways and canals
Electric street-lighting in Paris

Paris *Exposition universelle* at le Palais du
Trocadéro
Thomas Edison invents incandescent lamp
Théodore Duret *Les Peintres impressionistes*

**1879**
Mac Mahon resigns. Jules Grévy elected
President
Louis Pasteur discovers vaccination

'La Marseillaise' becomes French national
anthem
Thomas Edison invents light bulb

**1880**
*Loi Camille Sée* on girls' education
14 July becomes *la Fête nationale*

Émile Zola *Nana*
Auguste Rodin *Le Penseur*

**1881**
Creation of free primary education

**1882**
Primary education becomes compulsory and
secular

Edgar Degas *La Danseuse de 14 ans*
Ferdinand Buisson *Les Dictionnaires de
pédagogie et d'instruction primaire*
Racing-Club de France founded

**1883**

Death of Richard Wagner
Georges Seurat *Une Baignade à Asnières*
Paul Lafargue *Le Droit à la paresse*

**1884**
*Loi Waldeck-Rousseau* legalizes trade unions
Berlin Conference on colonization

Joris-Karl Huysmans *A Rebours*
First *Salon des indépendants*
Launch of *Le Matin*

**1885**
Boulangist movement begins
Karl Benz invents petrol engine

Émile Zola *Germinal*
Vincent Van Gogh *The Potato Eaters*
Édouard Dujardin launches *La Revue
wagnérienne*
Peugot's *Vélocipède*

**1886**
Decazeville: defenestration and strike
Army acquires repeating rifle

Georges Seurat *Un dimanche à l'Île de la
Grande Jatte*
Jean Moréas *Symbolist Manifesto*
Arthur Rimbaud *Les Illuminations*
Edouard Drumont *La France juive*
Auguste Rodin *Le Baiser*

**1887**
École des arts décoratifs founded

Antoine creates Le Théâtre libre
Gabriel Fauré *Requiem*
Athletes union founded

**1888**

Institut Pasteur founded
Hertz invents electromagnetic waves
Dunlop launches pneumatic tyre
Vincent Van Gogh *Café de minuit*

**1889**

Second International created at Congress of
Paris
Compulsory military service

Paris *Exposition universelle*
Completion of Eiffel Tower
Camille Claudel *Le Satountala*
Paul Bourget *Le Disciple*
Henri Bergson *Essai sur les données
immédiates de la conscience*

**1890**

Boulanger commits suicide
1 May celebrated as International Workers'
Day

Creation of Touring Club de France and
*Guides Michelin*
Gabriel Tarde *Les Lois de l'imitation*

**1891**

Armand Peugot's first car built

Eric Satie meets Debussy
Henri de Toulouse-Lautrec poster
advertising the Moulin Rouge
Jules Huret *Enquête sur l'évolution littéraire*

**1892**

Panama canal scandal
Pope Leo XIII encourages 'ralliement' of
French Catholics and royalists to the
Republic

Launch of *Le Journal*
Death of Hippolyte Taine
Joséphin Péladan founds the Salon de la
Rose+Croix
Étienne Marey invents chronophotography
Claude Monet, *La Cathédrale de Rouen*

**1893**

First Paris–Rouen automobile race
Vélodrome d'hiver set up in Champ de
Mars

Death of Ernest Renan
Max Nordau *Die Entartung/Dégénérescence*
Opening of Olympia Music-Hall

**1894**

Conviction of Dreyfus
Italian anarchist assassinates President Sadi
Carnot; *lois scélerates* against anarchists

Stéphane Mallarmé 'La Musique et les lettres'
Claude Debussy *Prélude à 'L'Après-midi d'un
faune'*

**1895**

CGT Trade Union Confederation founded
Foundation of Automobile Club de France

Louis Lumière demonstrates the
Cinématographe in Paris
Joséphin Péladan *Le Dernier Bourbon*
Siegfried Bing's first exhibition
Gustave Le Bon *La Psychologie des foules*

**1896**

Becquerel discovers radioactivity

Guglielmo Marconi invents radio-telegraphy
Georges Méliès builds film studio at
Montreuil and makes *Escamotage d'une
dame chez Robert Houdin*
Alfred Jarry's *Ubu Roi* premièred

**1897**

André Gide *Les Nourritures terrestres*
Edmond Rostand *Cyrano de Bergerac*
Maurice Barrès *Les Déracinés*

**1898**
Foundation of Action française
Ligue française des droits de l'homme
  founded
Marie and Pierre Curie discover radium

Émile Zola *J'accuse*
Giacomo Puccini's *La Bohème* staged in Paris
Death of Stéphane Mallarmé
First dirigible airship

**1899**
Paul Deroulède attempts *coup d'état*
Dreyfus pardoned

**1900**
International Congress on Women's Rights
Olympic Games in Paris
First section of Paris Métro opened
François Hennebique erects first concrete
  building in Paris

Gustave Charpentier *Louise*
Paris *Exposition universelle*
Charles Péguy launches *Les Cahiers de la
  quinzaine*
Invention of wireless telegraph

**1901**
Émile Combes becomes Prime Minister

Launch of *L'Assiette au beurre*
Charles-Louis Philippe *Bubu de Montparnasse*

**1902**
Foundation of Académie Goncourt

Claude Debussy *Pelléas et Mélisande*
Arthur Conan Doyle *Hound of the Baskervilles*
Georges Méliès *Voyage dans la lune*

**1903**

First Tour de France
Creation of Prix Goncourt
Wright brothers Orvill and Wilbur make
  first aeroplane flight
Ernest Lavisse *Histoire de France*
Claude Debussy *La Mer*

**1904**
Beginning of Franco-British *Entente Cordiale*
Closure of most Catholic schools

Launch of *L'Humanité* by Jean Jaurès
Romain Rolland *Jean Christophe*

**1905**
Georges Clemenceau becomes Prime
  Minister
First Russian Revolution
Creation of SFIO (Section française de
  l'Internationale ouvrière)
Law separating Church and State

Paul Claudel *Le Partage de midi*
Joseph Pinchon creates the Bécassine
  cartoon character in *La Semaine de Suzette*
Paul Cézanne *Les Grandes Baigneuses*
Invention of zip fastener

**1906**
Institution of six-day working week
Marie Curie first woman professor at
  Sorbonne
Dreyfus rehabilitated

**1907**
Triple Entente (France, Britain, Russia)
Married women gain control of their
  earnings

Pablo Picasso *Les Demoiselles d'Avignon*
Victor Margueritte *Prostituée*

**1908**
Creation of Comité national des sports

Banquet at the Bateau Lavoir
Maurice Leblanc *Arsène Lupin, gentleman
  cambrioleur*

**1909**

Louis Blériot flies across Channel
Launch of *La Nouvelle Revue française*
Ballets Russes perform in Paris

**1910**

Jaurès proposes creation of l'Armée nouvelle
Constitution of French Equatorial Africa

Igor Stravinsky *Firebird*

**1911**

Agadir incident

Frederick W. Taylor *Scientific Organisation of Labour*
Marie Curie wins Nobel Prize for chemistry

**1912**

Socialist Peace Congress in Basel

Paul Claudel *L'Annonce faite à Marie*

**1913**

Raymond Poincaré elected President
Military service extended to three years
Roland Garros flies across Mediterranean

Guillaume Apollinaire *Alcools*
Igor Stravinsky *Rite of Spring*
Alain-Fournier *Le Grand Meaulnes*
Marcel Proust *Du côté de chez Swann*
Gaston Leroux *Le Mystère de la chambre jaune*

**1914**

Jean Jaurès assassinated
Declaration of war; battles of the Marne, the Somme, and Ypres

Romain Rolland *Au-dessus de la mêlée*
Charles Péguy and Alain-Fournier die in battle
André Gide *Les Caves du Vatican*

**1916**

Battle of Verdun; first tank attacks

Louis Feuillade *Fantômas*
Henri Barbusse *Le Feu*
Dada introduced into France
Cave paintings discovered in the Ariège

**1917**

Second battle of the Marne
Russian Revolution: Bolsheviks seize power
United States enters war

*Parade* ballet by Eric Satie, words by Jean Cocteau, sets by Pablo Picasso

**1918**

Armistice: Alsace-Lorrraine restored to France
Food rationing
Airmail begins from Toulouse

Serious influenza epidemic
Groupe des six composers formed

**1919**

Treaty of Versailles
Lenin founds Third International in Moscow
Creation of League of Nations
Election of 'Chambre bleu horizon'
Citroën 10CV car

Abel Gance *J'accuse*
André Gide *La Symphonie pastorale*
Coin-operated phonograph ('autophone')

**1920**

Congrès de Tours: birth of French Communist Party (PCF)
Georges Clemenceau loses presidential election
Jeanne d'Arc canonized
First international air traffic agreement

**1921**
French occupy Rhineland
Rif War begins

Coco Chanel fashion collection

**1922**

Creation of Radio-Paris

**1923**
France occupies the Ruhr
First 24 heures du Mans
First *Salon des arts ménagers*

René Clair *Paris qui dort*
Raymond Radiguet *Le Diable au corps*

**1924**
*Cartel des gauches* wins parliamentary
elections
France recognizes USSR
First non-stop Paris–Tokyo flight

André Breton *Manifeste du surréalisme*
Radio stations in Lyons, Agen, and
Fécamp
Olympic Games held in Paris and
Chamonix

**1925**
Locarno Pact
Thérèse of Lisieux canonized
Suzanne Lenglen wins Wimbledon

Radio stations created in Bordeaux,
Toulouse, and Montpellier
First exhibition of Surrealist painting
*Exposition des arts décoratifs*
Maurice Chevalier 'Valentine'

**1926**
Action française condemned by Pope Pius
XI
Raymond Poincaré establishes strong franc
Abd-el-Krim defeated in Rif

Louis Aragon *Le Paysan de Paris*
André Gide *Les Faux-monnayeurs*
Paul Éluard *Capitale de la douleur*
Georges Bernanos *Sous le soleil de Satan*
Jean Renoir *Nana*
André Malraux *La Tentation de l'Occident*

**1927**
Croix de feu founded
France evacuates Sarre

François Mauriac *Thérèse Desqueyroux*
Marcel Proust *Le Temps retrouvé*
Julien Benda *La Trahison des clercs*
Al Jolson *The Jazz Singer*
Abel Gance *Napoléon*
René Clair *Un chapeau de paille d'Italie*
Charles-Édouard Jeanneret called Le
Corbusier, Villa Stein, Garches

**1928**
Briand–Kellogg Pact against war
Invention of talking pictures

Luis Buñuel/Salvador Dali *Un chien andalou*

**1929**
Wall Street Crash
Construction of Maginot Line begins
Youth hostels introduced

Second Surrealist Manifesto
Pierre Teilhard de Chardin discovers 'Peking
Man' fossils

**1930**
Transatlantic airmail begins
Hélène Boucher first woman air pilot

Launch of *Je suis partout*
Luis Buñuel/Salvador Dali *L'Âge d'or*
René Clair *Sous les toits de Paris*
Le Corbusier Pavillon suisse in Cité
universitaire
Jean Vigo *A propos de Nice*

**1931**
Paul Doumer elected President

Paul Nizan *Aden, Arabie*
*Exposition coloniale* in Paris at Vincennes
Antoine de Saint-Exupéry *Vol de nuit*
René Clair *Le Million*

**1932**
Failure of International Conference on
  Disarmament
Launch of liner *Le Normandie*
Assassination of President Doumer

First television broadcasts in Paris
Louis-Ferdinand Céline *Voyage au bout de la
  nuit*
Jacques Prévert *La Bataille de Fontenoy*
Jules Romains *Les Hommes de bonne volonté*

**1933**
Hitler elected Chancellor of the Reich
Amsterdam–Pleyel peace movement
  founded
Creation of National Lottery
Creation of Air France

André Malraux *La Condition humaine*
Henri Matisse *La Danse*
Jean Vigo *Zéro de conduite*

**1934**
Anti-parliamentary riots in Paris (6 Feb.)
Stavisky Affair
Irène and Frédéric Joliot-Curie discover
  artificial radioactivity

Jean Vigo *L'Atalante*
Charles de Gaulle *Vers une armée de métier*
Louis Aragon *Les Cloches de Bâle*

**1935**

Jean Giraudoux *La Guerre de Troie n'aura pas
  lieu*
Jacques Feyder *La Kermesse héroïque*

**1936**
Election of *Front populaire*
*Accords de Matignon*: creation of paid
  holidays and forty-hour week
School-leaving age raised to 14
Outbreak of Spanish Civil War
Hitler occupies Rhineland

Jean Renoir *Le Crime de Monsieur Lange*
Louis Aragon *Les Beaux Quartiers*
Henri Langlois founds the Cinémathèque
  française

**1937**
SNCF, French national railways created

*Exposition universelle*, Paris
Pablo Picasso *Guernica*
Jean Renoir *La Grande Illusion*
Julien Duvivier *Pépé le Moko*
Gabriel Marcel *Être et avoir*

**1938**
Édouard Daladier and Neville Chamberlain
  negotiate Munich agreement with Hitler
Tunisian uprising suppressed

Creation of L'IFOP (Institut français de
  l'opinion publique)
Jean-Paul Sartre *La Nausée*
Antonin Artaud *Le Théâtre et son double*
Paul Nizan *La Conspiration*
Musée de l'homme opens at Palais de Chaillot
Censorship established

**1939**
Germany invades Poland; general call up;
  war declared (3 Sept.)
German–Soviet Non-aggression Pact

Henri Lefebvre *Matérialisme dialectique*
Jean Renoir *La Règle du jeu*
Nathalie Sarraute *Tropismes*

## 1940

Philippe Pétain becomes Prime Minister
Government moves to Bordeaux
German troops invade France and enter
  Paris in June
De Gaulle in London becomes head of Free
  French: broadcasts *Appel du 18 juin*
Demise of Third Republic; government
  moves to Vichy
Britain sinks French fleet at Mers-el-Kebir
Pétain shakes hands with Hitler at Montoire
  (24 Oct.)
Launch of *Chantiers de jeunesse*
Government introduces first anti-Jewish laws

Lascaux cave paintings discovered
Louis Aragon *Les Yeux d'Elsa*

## 1941

First French hostages executed (Oct.)
USSR enters war (21 June)
Creation of Ligue des volontaires français

Olivier Messiaen *Quatuor pour la fin des temps*

## 1942

Large-scale arrests of Jews by French police
  (July)

Marcel Carné *Les Visiteurs du soir*
Albert Camus *L'Étranger; Le Mythe de Sisyphe*
Lucien Rebatet *Les Décombres*

## 1943

Free French HQ established in Algiers

Henri-Georges Clouzot *Le Corbeau*
Jean-Paul Sartre *L'Être et le néant; Les
  Mouches*

## 1944

Allies land in Normandy; liberation of Paris;
  provisional government under de Gaulle
Women obtain right to vote

Louis Aragon *La Diane française*
Jean-Paul Sartre *Huis clos*
Albert Camus edits *Combat*
Jean Anouilh *Antigone*
Newspaper *Le Monde* launched

## 1945

Germans surrender
Atom bomb dropped on Hiroshima: end of
  war in Far East
Trial and execution of Robert Brasillach

Press censorship ends
Hélène Lazareff and Françoise Giroud
  launch *Elle*
Radiodiffusion-télévision française (RTF)
  created
Marcel Carné *Les Enfants du paradis*
Jean-Paul Sartre *L'Âge de raison; Le Sursis*
Maurice Merleau-Ponty *Phénoménologie de la
  perception*
Albert Camus *Caligula* (1938)

## 1946

Churchill makes 'Iron Curtain' speech
De Gaulle resigns; referendum accepts
  constitution of Fourth Republic
Blum–Byrnes Agreements on Franco-
  American economic relations
*Loi Marthe Richard* closes brothels

Launch of Renault 4CV
*Annales (ESC)* edited by Lucien Febvre,
  Fernand Braudel, and Georges Friedmann
Launch of *Critique*
Orson Welles's *Citizen Kane* released in
  France
First Cannes Film Festival
Marcel Carné *Les Portes de la nuit*

Jacques Prévert *Paroles*
Jean-Paul Sartre *Réflexions sur la question juive*
Vernon Sullivan (Boris Vian) *J'irai cracher sur vos tombes*

## 1947

France accepts Marshall Aid
De Gaulle creates Rassemblement du peuple français (RPF)
Paul Ramadier removes communists from government

Georges Rouquier *Farrebique*
Marcel Duhamel launches *Série noire*
Alexandre Kojève *Introduction à la lecture de Hegel*
Jean Genet *Les Bonnes*
Jean-Paul Sartre *Les Jeux sont faits*
Nathalie Sarraute *Portrait d'un inconnu*
Henri Lefebvre *Critique de la vie quotidienne*
Emmanuel Mounier *Qu'est-ce que le personnalisme?*
Musée d'art moderne opens in Paris
Launch of ballpoint pens (Bic)
Bell Telephone Company discovers transistor effect

## 1948

Communists seize power in Czechoslovakia
Universal Declaration of Human Rights

Jean-Paul Sartre *Les Mains sales; Qu'est ce que la littérature?; L'Engrenage*
L. Sedar Senghor *Anthologie de la nouvelle poésie nègre et malgache de langue française*
Launch of journal *La Nouvelle Critique*
CBS invents long-playing records
Henri Lefebvre *Le Marxisme*
Simone de Beauvoir *L'Amérique au jour le jour*
André Malraux *Les Noyers de l'Altenburg*
Marcel Aymé *Uranus*

## 1949

Creation of North Atlantic Treaty Organization (NATO)
*Loi du 16 juillet 1949* regulates publications for children
Vatican condemns communism

Launch of journal *Socialisme ou barbarie*
Simone de Beauvoir *Le Deuxième sexe*
Jean-Paul Sartre *La Mort dans l'âme*
Albert Camus *Les Justes*
Claude Lévi-Strauss *Les Structures élémentaires de la parenté*
Juliette Gréco's début at L'Œil de bœuf
Launch of *Paris-Match*
Emmanuel Mounier *Le Personnalisme*

## 1950

Korean War
SMIG, national minimum wage introduced

Launch of weekly *France-Observateur*
Regular TV programmes begin broadcasting in Paris region
Eugène Ionesco *La Cantatrice chauve*
Marguerite Duras *Un barrage contre le Pacifique*
Roger Nimier *Le Hussard bleu*

## 1951

Creation of Communauté européenne du charbon et de l'acier (CECA) including France, Germany, Italy, and Benelux countries

Samuel Beckett *Molloy; Malone meurt*
Launch of journal *Cahiers du cinéma*
Jean-Paul Sartre *Le Diable et le bon dieu*
Albert Camus *L'Homme révolté*

Jean Vilar produces *Henry IV, Le Cid*, and
    *Prince of Hamburg* at Avignon Festival and
    becomes director of Théâtre national
    populaire (TNP)

**1952**

Protests against General Ridgway's visit

Launch of film journal *Positif*
Frantz Fanon *Peau noire, masques blancs*
Marcel Pagnol *Manon des sources*

**1953**

Workers' uprising in East Germany
Death of Stalin
Poujade launches his movement

Samuel Beckett *En attendant Godot;*
    *L'Innommable*
Jean Anouilh *L'Alouette*
Georges Brassens 'Le Gorille'
Alain Robbe-Grillet *Les Gommes*
Roland Barthes *Le Degré zéro de l'écriture*
Camara Laye *L'Enfant noir*
Jean-Jacques Servan-Schreiber launches
    *L'Express*
*Lectures pour tous* television programme
Relaunch of annual *Salon des arts ménagers*

**1954**

French forces defeated by Viet Minh at Dien
    Bien Phu and withdraw from Indo-China
Abbé Pierre launches campaign for homeless

First concert (Webern) of Pierre Boulez's
    Association culturelle du domaine musical
Simone de Beauvoir *Les Mandarins*
Nathalie Sarraute *Martereau*
François Truffaut 'Une certaine tendance du
    cinéma français'
Jacques Becker *Touchez pas au grisbi*
Bernard Borderie *La Môme vert-de-gris*
Françoise Sagan *Bonjour tristesse*

**1955**

Uprising in Algeria

Pierre Boulez *Le Marteau sans maître*
Claude Lévi-Strauss *Tristes Tropiques*
Roger Vailland *325 000 francs*
Raymond Aron *L'Opium des intellectuels*
Chris Marker *Dimanche à Pékin*
Raymond Borde and Étienne Chaumeton
    *Panorama du film noir américain*

**1956**

Soviet troops invade and occupy Hungary
Tunisia and Morocco gain independence
Franco-British Suez expedition

Renault launches the *Dauphine*
Lucien Goldmann *Le Dieu caché*
Nathalie Sarraute *L'Ère du soupçon*
Ferdinand Oyono *Une vie de boy; Le Vieux
    Nègre et la médaille*
Ousmane Sembène *Le Docker noir*
Alain Resnais/Jean Cayrol *Nuit et brouillard*
Albert Camus *La Chute*
Kateb Yacine *Nedjma*
Roger Vadim *Et Dieu créa la femme*
Launch of journal *Arguments*
Three weeks paid annual holiday
Alain Robbe-Grillet *Pour un nouveau roman*

## 1957

Soviet Union launches Sputnik

France, Germany, Belgium, Luxembourg, the Netherlands, and Italy sign Treaty of Rome creating European Economic Community

Battle of Algiers

Roland Barthes *Mythologies*

Françoise Giroud *La Nouvelle Vague: portraits de jeunesse*

Michel Butor *La Modification*

Alain Robbe-Grillet *La Jalousie*

Jean-Paul Sartre *Questions de méthode*

Samuel Beckett *Fin de partie*

Chris Marker *Lettre de Sibérie*

## 1958

Military *putsch* in Algeria: establishment of Fifth Republic

De Gaulle becomes President

André Malraux becomes Minister of Culture

Louis Malle *L'Ascenseur pour l'échafaud*

Marguerite Duras *Moderato cantabile*

Claude Lévi-Strauss *Anthropologie structurale*

Launch of *Internationale situationniste*

Simone de Beauvoir *Mémoires d'une jeune fille rangée*

Henri Alleg *La Question*

Agnès Varda *Opéra Mouffe*

## 1959

Common Market begins

Caravelle jet airliner enters service

Pierre Desgraupes launches TV current affairs programme *Cinq Colonnes à la une*

Francois Truffaut *Les 400 coups*

Alain Resnais *Hiroshima mon amour*

Jean Genet *Les Nègres*

René Goscinny launches *Pilote*

School-leaving age raised to 16 years

André Malraux launches *maisons de la culture*

Elsa Triolet *Roses à crédit*

Alain Robbe-Grillet *Dans le labyrinthe*

Claude Chabrol 'Grands Sujets, petits sujets'

## 1960

Creation of *nouveau franc*

Creation of Parti socialiste unifié (PSU)

Uprising in Algeria; 121 writers and artists sign 'déclaration sur le droit à l'insoumission en Algérie'

Independence of Central African Republic, Chad, Congo, Dahomey, Gabon, Ivory Coast, Mali, Niger, Upper Volta

France explodes atomic bomb

Launch of *Télé sept jours*

Launch of *Tel Quel*

François Truffaut *Tirez sur le pianiste*

Jean-Luc Godard *A Bout de souffle*

Claude Chabrol *Les Bonnes Femmes*

Jean-Paul Sartre *Critique de la raison dialectique*

Jean Genet *Le Balcon*

Claude Simon *La Route des Flandres*

Launch of *Hara-Kiri*

Jean Vilar produces Brecht's *Arturo Ui* at the TNP

## 1961

Construction of Berlin Wall

French generals attempt coup in Algeria

Michel Foucault *Histoire de la folie à l'âge classique*

Frantz Fanon *Les Damnés de la terre*

Launch of journal *Communications*

Emmanuel Lévinas *Transcendance et infini*

Jean Prat Aeschylus's *Les Perses* for TV

Christiane Rochefort *Les Petits Enfants du siècle*

Alain Resnais *L'Année dernière à Marienbad*

First *maison de la culture* opens in Le Havre

## 1962

Eight people killed during anti-OAS demonstration at Métro Charonne in Paris

*Accords d'Évian* for Algerian independence; more than one million *pieds noirs* leave Algeria for France

De Gaulle visits Germany: Franco-German treaty of co-operation

François Truffaut *Jules et Jim*
Agnès Varda *Cléo de 5 à 7*
Launch of TV satellite Telstar
Launch of *Salut les copains*
Pierre Boulez *Pli selon pli*
Jacques Dumazedier *Vers une civilisation du loisir?*
Claude Lévi-Strauss *La Pensée sauvage*
Francis Lacassin and Alain Resnais launch *Giff-Wiff*

## 1963

Assassination of President Kennedy
De Gaulle vetoes British EEC membership
Senghor becomes President of Sénégal
Opening of first French nuclear power station

Roland Barthes *Sur Racine*
Michel Foucault *Naissance de la clinique*
Launch of Éclair 16 mm. lightweight film camera
Alain Resnais *Muriel*
Jean Eustache *Les Mauvaises Fréquentations*
Opening of first Carrefour hypermarket
Roman Jakobson *Essais de linguistique générale*
Serge Mallet *La Nouvelle Classe ouvrière*
J.-M. G. Le Clézio *Le Procès verbal*

## 1964

France withdraws from NATO military command

Claude Lévi-Strauss *Le Cru et le cuit*
Pierre Boulez *Penser la musique aujourd'hui*
Launch of second television channel; creation of Office de radiodiffusion-télévision française (ORTF)
Jacques Lacan creates École Freudienne de Paris
Monique Wittig *L'Opoponax*
Launch of *Le Nouvel Observateur*
Roland Barthes publishes 'Éléments de sémiologie' in *Communications*
Jean-Luc Godard *Une femme mariée*
René Étiemble *Parlez-vous franglais?*

## 1965

Presidential elections; de Gaulle (55%) defeats François Mitterrand (45%) in second round

Mass no longer conducted in Latin
Pierre Bourdieu *et al. Les Héritiers*
France Gall wins Eurovision Song Contest with 'Poupée de cire, poupée de son'
Courrèges launches geometric 'spacewoman' look.
Beatles concert at Palais des Sports
Marcel Bluwal produces *Dom Juan* for TV
Louis Althusser *Pour Marx; Lire 'Le Capital'*
Raymond Picard *Nouvelle Critique ou nouvelle imposture?*
Opening of Drugstore Saint-Germain designed by Slavik
Georges Perec *Les Choses*
Four weeks annual paid holiday

Jacques Derrida publishes 'De la grammatologie' in *Critique*
Marguerite Duras *Le Vice-consul*
Yves Bonnefoy 'La Poésie française et le principe d'identité'
Jean-Luc Godard *Alphaville*

## 1966

Trial and conviction of writers Siniavsky and Daniel in Soviet Union
France leaves NATO and demands withdrawal of NATO forces and bases
Alain Krivine founds Trotskyist Jeunesse communiste révolutionnaire (JCR)
Launch of the *Plan Calcul* for development of electronics industry in France
Chinese Communist Party launches Cultural Revolution

J. Farran and I. Barrère launch *Face à face* TV programme
Jean-Luc Godard *Masculin-féminin; Deux ou trois choses que je sais d'elle*
Pierre Sabbagh launches *Au théâtre ce soir* TV programme
Launch of *La Quinzaine littéraire*
Jacques Lacan *Écrits*
Jacques Rivette *La Religieuse* (banned despite selection for Cannes Film Festival)
Philips launches pocket transistors
Michel Foucault *Les Mots et les choses*

## 1967

Gaullists win general election with small majority
Régis Debray imprisoned in Bolivia
De Gaulle makes 'Vive le Québec libre' speech in Montreal
*Loi Neuwirth* legalizes contraception
First French nuclear submarine launched

Mao's *Little Red Book* published in French
Régis Debray *Révolution dans la révolution*
Michel Tournier *Vendredi ou les limbes du Pacifique*
Exhibition *Bande dessinée et figuration narrative*
Jean-Luc Godard *La Chinoise*
Chris Market *et al. Loin du Vietnam*
Launch of Nouvelles Frontières travel agency
Jacques Derrida *L'Écriture et la différence; De la grammatologie; La Voix et le phénomène*
Jean-Jacques Servan-Schreiber launches *L'Expansion* and publishes *Le Défi américain*
Guy Debord *La Société du spectacle*
Launch of *Carte bleue* credit card
TV begins colour broadcasting
Claire Etcherelli *Élise ou la vraie vie*

## 1968

Red Army Fraction bombs two shops in Frankfurt
Martin Luther King assassinated
Student demonstrations at Nanterre university campus (February); strikes and demonstrations throughout May; students occupy Sorbonne; barricades appear in Paris streets
*Accords de Grenelle* raise wages and institute workers' rights
De Gaulle calls general election: large right-wing victory
*Loi Faure* reforms universities

Launch of Maoist newspaper *La Cause du peuple*, Trotskyist papers *Lutte ouvrière* and *Rouge*
Jean Baudrillard *Le Système des objets*
Oswald Ducrot *et al. Qu'est-ce que le structuralisme?*
Jean-Louis Barrault produces *Rabelais*
Roland Barthes 'La Mort de l'auteur'
Jean Eustache *La Rosière de Pessac*
Advertising allowed on TV

**1969**

De Gaulle resigns: Georges Pompidou
  elected President
Prime Minister Chaban-Delmas launches
  'nouvelle société' project
Creation of Parti socialiste (PS)

Launch of *Cinéthique*
François Truffaut *L'Enfant sauvage*
Michel Foucault 'Qu'est-ce qu'un auteur?';
  *L'Archéologie du savoir*
Léo Ferré *Ni dieu, ni maître; Les Anarchistes*
Woodstock pop festival in New York State
  attracts half a million visitors
Julia Kristeva *Semeiotike*
First section of RER opened

**1970**

Death of de Gaulle
Creation of Mouvement de libération des
  femmes (MLF)

Roland Barthes *S/Z; L'Empire des signes*
Sartre becomes director of *La Cause du
  peuple*
École polytechnique becomes coeducational
Jean Baudrillard *La Société de consommation*
Louis Althusser 'Idéologie et appareils
  idéologiques de l'État'
Michel Crozier *La Société bloquée*
Partisans *Libération des femmes année zéro*
Completion of A6 autoroute between Lille
  and Marseilles
Launch of *Charlie-Hebdo*
Michel Tournier *Le Roi des Aulnes*
Ariane Mnouchkine produces *1789*
Michel Foucault *L'Ordre du discours*
Agnès Varda *Lion's Love*
Ahmadou Kourouma *Les Soleils des
  indépendances*

**1971**

343 prominent women sign manifesto in
  favour of abortion
Creation of Front homosexuel d'action
  révolutionnaire (FHAR)
François Mitterrand elected First Secretary
  of socialist party at Congrès d'Épinay
First flight of supersonic aircraft Concorde

J.-P. Sartre *L'Idiot de la famille*
Maria-Antonietta Macciocchi *De la Chine*
Marcel Ophuls *Le Chagrin et la pitié*
Launch of feminist newspaper *Le Torchon
  brûle*
Jean-François Lyotard *Discours, figure*
Demolition of Les Halles
Michel Tournier *Vendredi ou la vie sauvage*

**1972**

Socialist party and communist party sign
  *Programme commun de gouvernement*
Execution of Buffet and Bontemps. Robert
  Badinter demands abolition of death
  penalty.
*Procès de Bobigny*—trial of mother who
  arranged an abortion for her 15-year-old
  daughter
Legislation on equal pay for men and
  women

Gallimard launches 'Folio' paperback series
René Allio *Les Camisards*
Marin Karmitz *Coup pour coup*
Jean-Luc Godard *Tout va bien*
Gilles Deleuze and Félix Guattari *L'Anti-
  Œdipe*
Jacques Derrida *Marges de la philosophie*
Ariane Mnouchkine *1793*
Patrice Chéreau produces Marlowe's *The
  Massacre at Paris*
Launch of *L'Écho des savanes* (BD)
Launch of weekly *Le Point*
Jean-Pierre Faye *Langages totalitaires*

Jean-Pierre Manchette *Nada*
Launch of third TV channel FR3
Opening of Musée des arts et traditions
populaires (ATP)

## 1973

First oil crisis: price of crude oil increases
70%
Creation of MLAC (Mouvement pour
l'avortement et la contraception)

Launch of *gauchiste* daily newspaper
*Libération* financed by readers'
subscriptions not advertising
Roland Barthes *Le Plaisir du texte*
Robert Paxton *La France de Vichy*
André Harris and Alain de Sédouy *Français
si vous saviez*
Jacques Doillon *L'An 01*
Marco Ferreri *La Grande Bouffe*
Jacques Lacan *Le Séminaire XI*
*Les Quatre concepts fondamentaux de la
psychanalyse*
Jean-François Lyotard *Dérive à partir de Marx
et de Freud*
Paris ring road (*la périphérique*) opened
Jean Eustache *La Maman et la putain*
Claire Bretécher joins *Le Nouvel Observateur*
Michel Foucault *et al. Moi, Pierre Rivière. . .*
Marguerite Duras *India Song*
Claudie Broyelle *La Moitié du ciel*
Ousmane Sembène *Xala* (book)

## 1974

Death of Georges Pompidou; Valéry Giscard
d'Estaing elected President with narrow
majority (50.8%)
Françoise Giroud becomes *Secrétaire d'État à
la condition féminine*
Reform of ORTF; creation of seven separate
companies
*Loi Veil* legalizes abortion
Age of majority lowered to 18 years
Immigration suspended

*Les Temps modernes* launches regular column
'le sexisme ordinaire'
First BD festival in Angoulême
Annie Leclerc *Parole de femme*
Yannick Bellon *La Femme de Jean*
Bertrand Blier *Les Valseuses*
Claude Sautet *Vincent, François, Paul et les
autres*
Marco Ferreri *Touche pas à la femme blanche*
Marguerite Duras and Xavière Gautier *Les
Parleuses*
Launch of Des Femmes publishers
Just Jaeckin *Emmanuelle*
*Les Temps modernes* 'Les Femmes s'entêtent'
Julia Kristeva *Des Chinoises*
Alexander Solzhenitsyn *L'Archipel du goulag*
Boulez organizes first IRCAM concerts
Luce Irigaray *Speculum de l'autre femme*
Jean-François Lyotard *Économie libidinale*
Louis Malle *Lacombe Lucien*

## 1975

Fall of Saigon; victory of pro-communist
forces
Trial of Baader–Meinhof gang
Helsinki Agreement on Human Rights

Bernard Pivot launches *Apostrophes* TV
programme
Roland Barthes *Barthes par lui-même*
Michel Foucault *Surveiller et punir*
Launch of *Métal hurlant* (BD)

Marie Cardinal *Les Mots pour le dire*
Benoîte Groult *Ainsi soit-elle*
Christiane Baroche *Les Feux du large*
Hélène Cixous and Catherine Clément *La Jeune Née*
Agnès Varda *Réponse de femmes*
Michel Tournier *Les Météores*
Jean-François Davy *Exhibition*
Just Jaeckin *Histoire d'O*
Bertrand Tavernier *Que la fête commence*
François Truffaut *L'Histoire d'Adèle H*
André Téchiné *Souvenirs d'en France*
Jean-Luc Godard *Numéro deux*
Robert Hersant buys *Le Figaro*
Launch of *Le Nouvel Économiste*

## 1976

PCF abandons notion of 'dictatorship of the proletariat'

Death of Mao; denunciation of Gang of Four

Giscard d'Estaing publishes *La Démocratie française* describing 'la société libérale avancée'

Launch of the journal *Hérodote*

*Plan télécommunication*: crash modernization of telephone system

'Les nouveaux philosophes' identified by *Les Nouvelles littéraires*

Hachette acquires *Paris-Match* and *Télé 7 jours*

Pierre Boulez and Patrice Chéreau produce Wagner's *Ring Cycle* at Bayreuth

Robert Hersant buys *France-soir*

*Libération* launches free small ads service

Bertrand Tavernier *Le Juge et l'assassin*

Frank Cassenti *L'Affiche rouge*

Bertrand Blier *Calmos*

*Les Temps modernes* special number 'Les États-Unis en question'

Michel Foucault *Histoire de la sexualité* vol. I

## 1977

Giscard d'Estaing appears on TV programme *Les Dossiers de l'écran*

Jacques Chirac elected mayor of Paris

Televised debate between Prime Minister Raymond Barre and François Mitterrand

PCF withdraws from *Union de la gauche*

Creation of *aide au retour* for immigrants

Quebec adopts *Charte de la langue française*

Opening of Centre Georges Pompidou designed by Rogers and Piano

Launch of socialist newspaper *Le Matin de Paris*

Agnès Varda *L'Une chante, l'autre pas*

Luce Irigaray *Ce sexe qui n'en est pas un*

Marguerite Duras *Le Camion*

Roland Barthes *Fragments d'un discours amoureux*

Michel Tournier *Le Vent Paraclet*

Hervé Guibert *La Mort propagande*

J. and C. Broyelle and E. Tschirhart *Deuxième Retour de Chine*

Ousmane Sembène *Ceddo*

## 1978

General election: defeat of the Left

Launch of *F-magazine*

Launch of *Des femmes en mouvement*

Simon Nora and Alain Minc *L'Informatisation de la société*

Régis Debray *Modeste Contribution...*
Renaud *Laisse béton*
Pierre Boulez opens Institut de recherche et
  de coordination acoustique/musique
  (IRCAM) at Pompidon Centre
Robert Hossein produces *Notre-dame de Paris*
  at the Palais des Sports
François Truffaut *La Chambre verte*
Yannick Bellon *L'Amour violé*
Patrice Leconte *Les Bronzés*

## 1979

Creation of European Monetary System
Second oil crisis
Affaire Bokassa: Giscard d'Estaing accused of
  corruption

Patrice Chéreau and Pierre Boulez produce
  Berg's *Lulu*
Emmanuel Le Roy Ladurie *Le Carnaval de
  Romans*
Jean Fourastié *Les Trente glorieuses*
Régis Debray *Le Pouvoir intellectuel en France*
Serge Gainsbourg's reggae version of 'La
  Marseillaise'
Launch of Sony Walkman
Opening of Forum des Halles
Antoine Vitez produces Molière's *Dom Juan,
  Le Misanthrope, Le Tartuffe*, and *L'École des
  femmes*
Pierre Bourdieu *La Distinction*
Jean-François Lyotard *La Condition
  postmoderne*
Jean-Luc Godard *Sauve qui peut (la vie)*
Alain Corneau *Série noire*
Bertrand Blier *Buffet froid*

## 1980

Brandt Report on north–south development
Creation of Solidarność in Poland
Rehabilitation of La Villette begins

Marguerite Yourcenar first woman elected
  to Académie française
Roland Barthes *La Chambre claire*; death of
  Barthes
Josiane Balasko *et al.* perform *Le Père Noël est
  une ordure* at the Splendide
Renaud Camus *Tricks*
Creation of first *radios locales*
Launch of *Le Débat*
François Truffaut *Le Dernier Métro*
Gilles Deleuze and Félix Guattari *Mille
  plateaux: capitalisme et schizophrénie*
Élisabeth Badinter *L'Amour en plus*
Michel Tournier *Gaspard, Melchior &
  Balthazar*
J.-M. G. Le Clézio *Le Désert*
Death of Jean-Paul Sartre

## 1981

François Mitterrand elected President with
  narrow majority (51.7%), defeating
  Giscard; socialists' overall majority in

Pierre Boulez *Répons*
*Dallas* broadcast on French TV
Jean-Jacques Beineix *Diva*

general election; new government includes four communist ministers
Abolition of death penalty
Nationalization of five conglomerates
Status of 130,000 illegal immigrants regularized

Yannick Bellon *L'Amour nu*
Relaunch of *Libération*
Death of Jacques Lacan
Opening of TGV Paris–Lyons service
Antoine Vitez becomes director of TNP
Independent local radio stations legalized
Samuel Beckett *Impromptu d'Ohio*
Ousmane Sembène *Le Dernier de l'empire*

## 1982

*Loi Defferre* on decentralization gives greater power to local and regional councils
Thirty-nine-hour week, five weeks paid annual holiday; retirement age lowered to 60 years

*Rapport Moinot* on broadcasting creates independent regulatory *Haute Autorité*
Hervé Guibert *Les Aventures singulières*
Emmanuel Lévinas *De Dieu qui vient à l'idée*
Jean Baudrillard *A l'ombre des majorités silencieuses*
*Tel quel* becomes *L'Infini*
Agnès Varda *Mur murs*

## 1983

First flight of Airbus
Nathalie Sarraute *Enfance*
Yves Bonnefoy 'La Poésie et l'université'
Georges Rouquier *Biquefarre*
Claude Berri *Tchao Pantin*
Mehdi Charef *Le Thé au harem d'Archi Ahmed*

## 1984

Launch of Canal plus pay-TV channel
Alain Robbe-Grillet *Le Miroir qui revient*
Marguerite Duras *L'Amant*
Agnès Varda *Les Dites cariatides*
Mohammed Kenzi *La Menthe sauvage*

## 1985

Creation of private TV channels La Cinq and M6
René Char *Les Voisinages de Van Gogh*
Jean-Luc Nancy 'Des lieux divins'
Agnès Varda *Sans toit ni loi*
Luc Besson *Subway*
Claude Berri *Jean de Florette*

## 1986

Right-wing parties win general election; Jacques Chirac is Prime Minister: start of *la cohabitation*
*Loi Pasqua* reinforces controls on immigrants and immigration

Commission nationale de la communication et des libertés (CNCL) replaces *Haute Autorité*
Michel Tournier *La Goutte d'or*
Jean Baudrillard *Amérique*
Claude Berri *Manon des sources*
Med Hondo *Sarraounia*
Opening of Cité des sciences et de l'industrie at La Villette
Death of Simone de Beauvoir

**1987**

Privatization of TF1
Creation of Institut du monde arabe
Christiane Baroche *L'Hiver de beauté*
Alain Robbe-Grillet *Angélique, ou l'enchantement*
Roland Barthes *Incidents*
Bertrand Tavernier *La Passion Béatrice*
Agnès Varda *Jane B. par Agnès V.*
Alain Finkielkraut *La Défaite de la pensée*
Sakinna Boukhedenna *Journal: 'nationalité: immigré(e)'*
Souleymane Cissé *Yeelen*

**1988**

François Mitterrand re-elected President
(54%) beating Jacques Chirac (46%); PS
wins general election without overall
majority

René Char *Éloge d'une soupçonnée*
Julia Kristeva *Étrangers à nous-mêmes*
Étienne Chatiliez *La Vie est un long fleuve tranquille*

**1989**

Bicentenary of French Revolution
*Affaire des foulards islamiques*; creation of
Haut Conseil de l'intégration
Destruction of Berlin Wall

Conseil supérieur de l'audiovisuel (CSA)
replaces CNCL
Christiane Baroche *Triolet 3*
Julia Kristeva *Histoires d'amour*
Bertrand Tavernier *La Vie et rien d'autre*
Coline Serreau *Romuald et Juliette*
Idrissa Ouedraogo *Yaaba*
Luc Moullet *Les Sièges de l'Alcazar*

**1990**

Reunification of Germany

Opening of Opéra de la Bastille
Hervé Guibert *A l'ami qui ne m'a pas sauvé la vie*
Hélène Cixous *Three Steps on the Ladder of Writing*
François Maspéro *Les Passagers du Roissy-Express*
Régis Debray *A demain de Gaulle*
Djura *Le Voile du silence*
M6 broadcasts Aïssa Djabri and Farid
Lahouassa's *La Famille Ramdam* series
Ferrudja Kessas *Beur's Story*
Robert Favreau *Nelligan*
Ahmadou Kourouma *Monnè, outrages et défis*

**1991**

Édith Cresson first woman Prime Minister

Hervé Guibert *Mon valet et moi; Le Protocol compassionnel; 'Il': un récit de la mesquinerie*
Jacques Derrida 'Circonfession'
Jean Baudrillard *La Guerre du Golfe n'a pas eu lieu*
Régis Debray *Cours de médiologie générale*
Léos Carax *Les Amants du Pont Neuf*

**1992**

Referendum on Treaty of Maastricht:
narrow victory (51%) for 'Yes'

Opening of Euro-Disneyland
La Cinq closes; Arte replaces La Sept

Christiane Baroche *Les Ports du silence; Le Collier*
Hervé Guibert *Cytomégalovirus: journal d'hospitalisation*
Louis Althusser *L'Avenir dure longtemps*
Régis Debray *Vie et mort de l'image*
Pierre Bourdieu *Les Règles de l'art*

**1993**
General election: right-wing parties win large majority

Jacques Derrida *Spectres de Marx*
Pierre Bourdieu *et al. La Misère du monde*
Claude Berri *Germinal*

**1994**
*Loi Toubon relatif à la langue française*

# Index

democracy 40, 43, 87, 109, 124,
131, 278, 291
Dempsey, Jack 66
Déon, Michel 126
Depardieu, Gérard 256
Derain, André 64
Derrida, Jacques 169, 216–20,
222, 225, 227
*De la grammatologie* (1967)
169, 217
*L'Écriture et la différence* (1967)
169, 217
*Jacques Derrida* (1991) 218
*Marges de la philosophie* (1972)
217
*Mémoires pour Paul de Man*
(1988) 218
*Spectres de Marx* (1993) 218,
219
Descartes, René 112
Deschamps, Bernard 66
detective fiction 166
Deux magots, les 118
Dewaere, Patrick 248
Diaghilev, Sergei 65
Diamant-Berger, Maurice,
pseudonym of André
Gillois 66
Diawara, Mantha 284
*Dictionnaire de l'Académie* 264
Dien Bien Phu 131
Dior, Christian 141
Disney, Walt 74, 256
Disneyland 47
divine 216, 217
divorce 186
Djabri, Aïssa 273
Djura, Djurdjura 272, 273
*Le Voile du silence* (1990) 273
documentaries 147, 175, 233
Doillon, Jacques 186, 235
*L'An 01* (1973) 186
Dominici, Gaston 143, 148
Donne, John 209
Dorgelès, Roland 56
*Les Croix de bois* (1919) 56
Doriot, Jacques 69, 81, 82
Dostoevsky, Fyodor 227
Doubrovski, Serge 168
Doucet, Jacques 36
Dreyfus Affair 76, 83
Drieu la Rochelle, Pierre 58, 69,
84, 126
*Les Chiens de Paille* (1943) 84
*La Comédie de Charleroi* (1934)
58
drôle de guerre 78
Duchamp, Marcel 64
Duhamel, Georges 56
*La Vie des martyrs* (1917) 56

Duhamel, Marcel 64, 173
Dullin, Charles 161
Dumas, Roland 133
Dumont, Ernest 65
'Du Gris' (1920) 65
'Nuits de Chine' (1922) 65
Duneton, Claude 294
*Je suis comme une truie qui
doute* (1979) 294
Dunkirk 72, 78
Dupuy, Jean 60
Durand, Yves 85
*Vichy 1940–4* (1972) 85
Durand-Ruel, Paul 17, 33
Duras, Marguerite 128, 133, 165,
167, 197, 198, 203, 205, 245
*L'Amant* (1984) 197, 198, 203
*Le Camion* (1977) 245
*Hiroshima, mon amour* (1959)
90, 245
*India Song* (1973) 197
*Moderato cantabile* (1958) 167,
197
*Travailler avec Duras* (1986)
198
*Un Barrage contre le Pacifique*
(1950) 197
*Le Vice-consul* (1965) 197
Duret, Théodore 20
*Les peintres impressionistes*
(1878) 20

Ebrie language 279
EC, European Communities 261
*Écho de Paris* 60
*Écho des Savannes, l'* 251
École des beaux arts 28, 187
École freudienne de Paris 226
École normale supérieure 130,
220
École pratique des hautes études
222
ecologists 185
economy, economics 105, 142,
150, 221, 252, 255, 259, 292
écriture 169, 193, 211, 217, 229
écriture féminine 197, 227, 245
Edison, Thomas Alva 48
education 11, 38–41, 82, 112,
119, 135, 136, 138, 144, 153,
188, 189, 219, 265, 269, 279,
290–4
Education, Ministry of 150, 151
EEC, European Economic
Community 144
Egejuru, Phanuel 136
Egypt 18, 74
Eiffel Tower 46, 65, 146
Eiffel, Gustave 46
Eisenstein, Sergei 235, 236

elections 234
Eliot, George, pseudonym of
Mary Ann Evans 124
*The Mill on the Floss* (1860)
124
élite 42, 110, 264, 294
Elizabeth II, Queen 233
*Elle* 147, 148, 237
Éluard, Paul 59, 68, 82, 102,
112, 113
Emmanuel, Pierre 82, 114
Empire 124, 130, 142, 252
enceinte Philippe-Auguste 254
Engels, Friedrich 120
England, *see* Britain
English language 6, 265–8, 280,
293
Enlightenment 40, 112, 290, 293
Épuration 100–3
Ernst, Max 64
*Esprit* 72, 82, 113, 114, 117, 118,
126
Esslin, Martin 157
*The Theatre of the Absurd*
(1962) 157
Etcherelli, Claire 150
*Élise ou la vraie vie* (1967) 150
ethics 216
ethnology, *see* anthropology
Étiemble, René 266
*Parlez-vous franglais?* (1964)
266
EU, European Union 187
Eurocentrism 194, 284
Eurodisney 255, 256, 294
*Europe* 112
Europe 2, 84, 111, 131, 144, 164,
187, 191, 204, 290
*Europe no 1* 146
European Audiovisual Space 260
Eustache, Jean 235, 243, 257
*La Maman et la putain* (1973)
243
*Les Mauvaises fréquentations*
(1963) 257
*La Rosière de Pessac* (1968) 243
everyday life 49, 72, 105, 112,
164, 185
Évian agreements 132
exclusion, les exclus 189, 293
exhibitions 15–18, 22, 28–30,
33, 47, 64, 73, 82, 143, 151,
256
Exposition Arno Brecker
(1942) 82
Exposition coloniale (1931) 73
Exposition des arts dècoratifs
(1925) 64
Exposition internationale
(1937) 73